D0426813

Console-ing Passions: *Television and Cultural Power*   *Edited by Lynn Spigel*

KIDS' MEDIA CULTURE   Edited by Marsha Kinder

DUKE UNIVERSITY PRESS   Durham and London 1999

© 1999 by Duke University Press
All rights reserved
Printed in the United States of America on acid-free paper ∞
Typeset in Quadraat by Keystone Typesetting, Inc.
Library of Congress Cataloging-in-Publication Data appear
on the last printed page of this book.

To my children, Victor and Gabriela,
and my grandsons, Nicolas and Jacob Fimbres

Contents

Acknowledgments

I want to thank my colleague, Lynn Spigel, who suggested I do this anthology for the Console-ing Passions book series, and all of the authors who contributed essays. At Duke University Press, I am grateful to my editors, Ken Wissoker and Richard Morrison, and to my copyeditor, Cindy Milstein, and to Paula Dragosh and Jean Brady who oversaw the editing process. I also want to thank Laurel Almerinda, Osa Hidalgo, and Monique Yamaguchi, who helped with the illustrations.

Kids' Media Culture: An Introduction   *Marsha Kinder*

Innocent Victims or Active Players

This volume explores children's mass media culture—that is, media software such as television programs, electronic games, movies, comic strips, books, and ancillary toys—produced for and consumed by youngsters in the United States. It addresses not only what that media culture is now, what it has been in past decades, and what it might potentially be in the future, but also the debates that have circulated around this form of cultural production—debates involving parents, teachers, children's advocates, policymakers, media producers, broadcasters, journalists, social critics, cultural theorists, researchers, and to a lesser extent, children themselves.

In the growing field of writings on children and media, those cultural debates include the widely covered confrontations between children's advocates and researchers, on the one side, calling for more responsible programming and policies from media producers, broadcasters, advertisers, and government agencies on the other. There is also a less publicized conflict within the former camp between those who see children primarily as passive victims being contaminated by an increasingly corrupt culture and those who perceive them as active players grappling with the inevitable processes of social and historical change. Given that many participants in this latter debate move fluidly from one position to the other (or somewhere in between, depending on the specific age of the child, the issue under discussion, or the particular opponent one is arguing with), there is usually a willingness to acknowledge the "good intentions" of those on the opposite side—particularly since they are frequently allies in the larger struggle for better programs, products, and policies.

Yet, at its most extreme, this conflict can be painted in much broader strokes. On one hand, there are the alarmists who demonize children's media culture as a terrible contemporary aberration that is somehow transforming our kids into a mass of dumbed-down zombies and killers, in contrast to "the good old days" when children were vibrantly active, creative, and innocent. One thinks of Marie Winn (The Plug-in Drug, 1977, and Unplugging the Plug-in Drug, 1987), or more recently, Barry Sanders (A Is for Ox: Violence, Electronic Media, and the Silencing of the Written Word, 1994) and Dr. Michael Brody, the child psychiatrist who has testified on television ratings and the V-chip (a mechanism that enables parents to block "harmful" programs from their children) before Congress and the Federal Communications Commission and helped write the American Medical Association's publication, A Physician's Guide to Violence in the Media. At a recent conference on these issues, after describing a nostalgic memory of how he once visited the set of the Howdy Doody show as a child, Brody proclaimed that today's children need protection. He pointed out the harmful effects of identifying with computers and the so-called "smart toys" run on computer chips, warning, "Children are being robbed of their souls!"[1] Then there are the optimists. They see kids as resilient players who (like youngsters from earlier eras) feel empowered when they appropriate popular images for their own goals—whether to express their own individuality, taste, or resistance, or to demonstrate their ability (and that of their generation) to navigate knowingly through the current social terrain, producing alternative images and meanings. In this camp, one finds both cultural theorists like Lawrence Grossberg (We Gotta Get Out of This Place: Popular Conservatism and Postmodern Culture, 1992), Angela McRobbie (Feminism and Youth Culture: From "Jackie" to "Just Seventeen," 1991), and Henry Jenkins (Textual Poachers: Television Fans and Participatory Culture, 1992), and clinical psychologist Sherry Turkle, who argues in Life on the Screen: Identity in the Age of the Internet (1995) that the Web provides a safe place for youngsters to experiment with multiple aspects of their postmodernist identity.

Given that neither side assumes that kids have all the power needed to totally govern their own choices, the key issue is what kinds of guidance are most effective. While the former position focuses primarily on designing protective interventions or censorship measures that would preserve kids' innocence by denying them access to offensive material, the latter is more concerned with providing equal and equitable access to all children (regardless of class, race, or gender), and studying how kids actually learn to cope with their culture and negotiate its meanings, not as passive subjects but as active historical agents. While the former frequently uses "children's innocence" as a symbolic rallying point for a broader crusade against what they perceive to be a disturbing moral decline in our society (for example, a sharp increase in and wide acceptance of consumerism, urban violence, political corruption, broken families, pornography, tabloid journalism, homosexuality, abortion, and so on), the latter tends to see the cultivation of free choice among all youngsters as a crucial tactic for preserving those civil liberties guaranteed by the Constitution.

One may be tempted to dub those in the former camp as censors with a "V-chip" mentality. Yet it is important to remember that this position has a long and vital history, traceable back to Plato, that has been applied not merely to current mass media—like pop music, movies, television, video games, and the Internet—but to virtually all of their popular precursors—including poetry, theater, novels, radio, comic strips, and comic books. The historicizing of this critical position, however, can sometimes undermine its most vehement arguments. For some of those very same media and texts once vilified as harmful to youth can, with a shift in discursive context, subsequently be converted into laudable "children's classics." This dramatic metamorphosis has been experienced by ancient Homeric epics like The Iliad and The Odyssey (once banned from Plato's Republic), satiric works like Gulliver's Travels and Alice in Wonderland, and also, as Heather Hendershot demonstrates in this volume, by recent popular television series such as Sesame Street.

It would be misleading to assume that only one of these "sides" is concerned with historical change or the relationship between children's media culture and its larger social context. Neither side can ignore the disturbing escalation of violent acts committed by youngsters, the increasingly early entry of kids into consumerism, the complex mix of new opportunities and risks provided to youth by the Internet, and the ongoing need for assessing and changing government policies concerning children and the media. Still, there are crucial differences in the way this relationship is perceived.

Those who see kids primarily as passive victims tend to focus on a single element of media culture (such as violence or pornography), which can readily be isolated for study or censorship, and whose representations and dangers are presumed to affect all children in the same way. Thus, it is hardly surprising that this camp tends to rely on monolithic depictions not only of the texts, but also of the children they affect, the media through which they are transmitted, and the eras in which they are produced and consumed. This is particularly so for the depiction of the past, since it serves both as a backdrop for nostalgic memories of the censor's own idyllic childhood and a foil for current aberrations. Such writers frequently rely on statistical rating surveys of violent representations, which are rarely attentive to nuances of context even when that is one of the announced goals of a study.[2] To validate their arguments and support their commonsense judgments, they also turn to empirical "effects" studies in the social sciences, sometimes exaggerating the findings to make the causal links appear more conclusive than they actually are. Here is how noted cognitive psychologists Rodney R. Cocking and Patricia M. Greenfield acknowledge the paucity of reliable empirical studies and this form of exaggeration (as well as their own appreciation of children's media culture) in the introduction to the section on "Violence, Gender, and Video" in their 1996 collection of essays, *Interacting with Video*:

> Violence in the media has taken on special significance in recent years for social scientists who are interested in prevention and intervention. Graphic violence in the media was initially a concern of television researchers who wanted to know more about the effects of watching the behaviors of others, but the issue of video violence has now become a broader concern of media researchers with the arrival of highly graphic video games, such as Mortal Kombat. The questions remain comparable to those asked about television violence, and the answers appear to be the same, too, according to latter-day philosophers, Calvin & Hobbes, by Bill Watterson:
>
> Does it glamorize violence? Sure.
> Does it desensitize us to violence? Of course.
> Does it help us tolerate more violence? You bet.
> Does it stunt empathy toward others? Heck yes.
> Does graphic violence in the media *cause* violence? Well, that's hard to prove.[3]

A similar point was made in a more serious vein by British researcher James D. Halloran, back in 1970, when he called for a broadening of the research agenda on media violence beyond the narrow American studies of "effects":

> It is not that the violence portrayed in these programs is more likely to be copied, or that it will stimulate aggressive drives. It is the reflections, the associations, the ambiguities, the definitions, the stereotypes, the emphases, the approvals, the tolerances, the familiarizations, the behavioural possibilities and solutions, and the pictures of the world, that these programmes provide that may make television an influential force with regard to violence in society.[4]

While none of these researchers endorse or condone violent representations, they caution against the kinds of simplistic, causal connections that are often derived from "effects studies." Instead, they advocate a research agenda that pays more attention to the broader social context of how these images are actually read.

Those who see children primarily as active agents perceive them as moving tactically through a diversified field of play that is part of a larger social history, which inevitably involves change. They are more interested in studying the connections between various factors—for example, how a violent act is represented visually and acoustically; how it is narrativized, gendered, and raced with cultural and historical specificity; how it is linked to other discourses, such as sexuality, power, and class; and how it is read differently by different groups. Hence, they tend to seek and construct a more pluralistic and over-determined account that emphasizes tensions and contradictions, and that generates "thick descriptions" both of the specific works and their meanings and of the diverse social contexts in which they are produced, consumed, and transformed through negotiated and resistant readings. They sometimes build on the work of scholars like David Morley, who has done in-depth studies of how television is actually watched within the domestic space of specific homes and how it is influenced by the power dynamics of the family, and Barrie Thorne, who has studied the complex gendering of play within the public space of schools.[5] Rejecting the presumption that childhood is a "natural" category unaffected by historical or cultural contexts, they draw on detailed accounts of the "construction" of childhood in earlier eras[6] and assume that a similarly intricate set of forces is also operative at present.

Although most of the contributors to this volume identify with the camp that sees children as active players, the discursive wars around children's media cannot be reduced to a simple binary opposition, for the issues are entangled in many other broader cultural debates. In fact, most of these contributors have arrived at their position by looking not just at media texts and kids, but also at the discourses about them, many of which have been derived from the theories of Antonio Gramsci and Michel Foucault, and the way their ideas have been mobilized within British and American cultural studies. Moving away from the passive models of spectatorship that drove leftist media theories (derived from the Frankfurt School and French theorist Louis Althusser), Stuart Hall and other members of the Birmingham school introduced a theory of active readership rooted in Gramsci, which explained how the meanings of popular culture could be actively negotiated by its fans. This reception theory quickly proved productive in the political contexts of British and American feminism in the 1970s, and subsequently queer theory, where "reading against the grain" became an active form of cultural resistance. When applied to the specific areas of teen and children's culture by theorists such as Dick Hebdige, Lawrence Grossberg, Angela McRobbie, and Valerie Walkerdine (who emphasize class and gender), as well as by some of the contributors to this volume (Lynn Spigel on Barbie and Batman; Henry Jenkins on Batman, Star Trek, and Pee-wee Herman; Ellen Seiter on Strawberry Shortcake and My Little Pony; and my own work on Teenage Mutant Ninja Turtles, Power Rangers, and Nickelodeon), these modes of negotiated or resistant readings were perceived as a means of empowering kids—to display personal knowledge and preferences as cultural capital, and to differentiate themselves from other niche groups and generations.[7]

In the 1980s, this discourse was also extended to media research on the representation of violence. This process, succinctly described by John and Marian Tulloch,

> emphasized "what the audience does with the media, rather than what the media does with the audience"—though with a new "cultural studies" thrust in terms of ideological focus and ethnographic method. At the end of the decade, [Graham] Murdock (1989) noted that the initial Frankfurt School emphasis in critical theory on media culture and social control had long given way to a dominant interpretative tradition that celebrated the resistive readings and strategies of audiences. In this context the issue of the effects of TV violence more or less fell off the agenda.[8]

Like their key influences, Halloran and Murdock, and several of the contributors to this volume, the Tullochs were arguing for what they call "a realist epistemology," an approach that is "both qualitative and quantitative," and goes beyond "the abstracted empiricism of much mainstream work" as well as "the 'thick description' characteristic of many interpretative studies."[9] In other words, they were advocating an approach that moves between the two positions I have been describing, and perhaps most important (to the Tullochs, their sources, and many contributors to this volume), emphasizes the historically specific activities of those who actually produce and consume these media:

> While being centrally concerned with "the underlying structures that provide the contexts and resources for audience activity," we view these structures not as an external determinant of action but as reproduced through daily activity. Social structures are historically made and remade. They are subject to the process of agentive restructuring; and this is as important to remember at the production end of the text/audience relationship as at the consumption end.[10]

As this emphasis on daily activity, social contextualization, and active readership moved from one discursive realm to another and was applied to various mass media, it was easy to see how the same kind of power struggles were being restaged (with evolving cultural and historical specificity) within each new medium that appeared. Thus, despite claims by utopian visionaries like Marshall McLuhan that "the medium is the message,"[11] and latter-day de-

monizations of television and other electronic media by conservative techno-
phobes such as Marie Winn and Barry Sanders, it has become difficult to accept
any notion of technological determinism, whereby the medium itself (whether
print, cinema, radio, television, video games, or the Internet) could prescribe
the content of its texts or the power dynamics of its production, distribution,
and consumption. This argument was made with considerable power by Raymond Williams within the emerging discourse on television; while still being
attentive to the technical and formal specificity of the medium, he showed
how this new form of cultural production was already being controlled by
old power struggles that had been remapped onto this new form.[12] More
recently, this contention has been greatly enriched and expanded by cultural
theorists—such as Carolyn Marvin on the telegraph, telephone, and incandes-
cent lamp; Lynn Spigel on television; and Sherry Turkle and Sandy Stone on the
Internet—who all stress issues of gender within their studies of the power
struggles and cultural debates that helped shape the early development of these
popular media.

The impact of feminism on the discursive debates around children's media
culture cannot be overemphasized. It has helped drive virtually all sides: from
the call for censorship and boycotting of sexist products to the celebration of
transgender impersonations in cyberspace; from the clamor for more products
and programs targeted specifically to girls to the condemnation of those (like
Barbies and My Little Pony) whose gendering is exaggerated; from the campaign for protecting the innocent to the cultivation of more opportunities for
"playing against the grain." The assumption that "the personal is political," a
key premise in the early waves of feminism, is still being used to justify the
serious attention now being devoted to kids' daily interactions with the most
banal forms of pop culture (from Pokémons to Furbies) and the methodological validation of autobiographical evidence (whether firsthand "ethnographic"
observations of one's own children or nostalgic memories and anecdotes from
one's own childhood). The corporate research used to rationalize the design
and marketing of "games for girls," as well as the empirical studies in this
volume by Heather Gilmour and Yasmin Kafai who critique these games, are
both based on the assumption that gender identification is at least partly constructed by toys, advertising, and media; yet there is sharp disagreement as to
whether such explicitly gendered products reinforce or eradicate the rigid
boundaries and inequities that currently exist between girls and boys in our
culture, particularly within the clearly divided pink-and-blue aisles of retail
stores like Toys "R" Us.[13]

Many of these issues were already being addressed in the eighteenth century
by pioneering feminist Mary Wollstonecraft in *A Vindication of the Rights of*

Woman (1792). She emphasized the connection between child's play and radical political change, advocating a plan that was "diametrically opposite" to the one proposed by Jean-Jacques Rousseau, the radical philosopher whose writings had profoundly influenced her, but whom she found obtuse on questions of gender. Instead of his "overprotective course" of not leaving a child (particularly a young female) "a moment to its own direction," and thus rendering that child forever "dependent" (a condition he erroneously called "natural"), she favored giving children *of both genders* as much freedom as possible. Wollstonecraft claimed that this was essential to children's "self-preservation"—an assumption shared by many of the contributors to this volume:

> I have, probably, had an opportunity of observing more girls in their infancy than J.-J. Rousseau—I can recollect my own feelings, and I have looked steadily around me. . . . I will venture to affirm, that a girl, whose spirits have not been damped by inactivity, or innocence tainted by false shame, will always be a romp, and the doll will never excite attention unless confinement allows her no alternative. Girls and boys, in short, would play harmlessly together, if the distinction of sex was not inculcated long before nature makes any difference. I will go further, and affirm, as an indisputable fact, that most of the women, in the circle of my observation, who have acted like rational creatures, or shown any vigour of intellect, have accidentally been allowed to run wild.[14]

Though referring primarily to outdoor play rather than interaction with media, her basic argument for cultivating active play instead of overprotectiveness is still relevant to the current debates I have been describing and several specific essays in this volume (by Spigel, Jenkins, Griffin, and Seiter) where the value of "running wild" is very much at stake.

Wollstonecraft's insistence on the connection between child's play and political change should remind us that if we restrict ourselves to a purely theoretical level, we risk succumbing to another form of "false purity." If we dismiss children's advocates or the kind of activism they propose, we risk losing some of our most valuable allies: figures such as Peggy Charren, founder of Action for Children's Television and one of the driving forces behind the Children's Television Act of 1990, whose primary concern has been the creation of more alternatives for children's programming rather than the reduction of options through censorship; and others like Kathryn Montgomery and Shelley Pasnik of the Center for Media Education (CME), whose recent campaign against the deceptive targeting of children by commercial interests on the Internet helped get Congress to pass the first federal privacy law for cyberspace, which prohibits commercial websites from gathering information from children thirteen and younger without their parents' verifiable permission.[15]

Nor should we reject those who put theory into practice by designing alternative programs and products for kids. This course has been followed by several veterans of Seymour Papert's constructionist group at the MIT Media Lab—including Justine Cassell (whose Junior Summit '98 project brought 1,000 children from 139 countries together on-line to communicate with each other in several languages on topics of international concern), Amy Bruckman (the designer of MOOSE Crossing, a MUD [multiple user domain] designed as a constructionist learning environment for kids), Idit Harel (founder of MaMa Media, Inc., a top-rated children's site on the Internet), and Alan Shaw (founder of Linking Up Villages, an organization that trains local teenagers in technical skills to run neighborhood microenterprises)—as well as by Brenda Laurel, who left the Interval Research Group to found Purple Moon, a commercial company that produced software for girls. Such combining of theory and practice is also being pursued by some of the contributors to this volume. For example, Yasmin Kafai, another former member of Papert's MIT group, now heads Kids' Interactive Design Studios at the University of California, Los Angeles, a research group dedicated to exploring interactive, multimedia design environments for young children. Ellen Seiter, for another, has produced an experimental CD-ROM game called "Hero TV," which leads young children to explore how heroes are created, and the implications of their traits and actions; and with documentary filmmaker Mark Jonathan Harris and a creative team of students, I coauthored a CD-ROM game titled "Runaways," which enables teens to explore their own sexual, gender, and ethnic identities as they search for teenage runaways.[16] Such crossovers further complicate the simplistic binary in this debate, obscuring the lines between researchers and producers, cultural theorists and activists.

Moving the Debate to Washington

On October 22, 1998, the same day that President Clinton signed two new congressional measures into law designed to protect children from pornography as well as privacy violations on the Internet, Kathryn Montgomery of CME and Ellen Wartella, dean of the College of Communication at the University of Texas, Austin, cohosted a two-day conference in Washington, D.C. on "Ensuring a Quality Digital Media Culture for Children." The strategic timing of the conference highlighted the political success of CME's recent campaign for Internet privacy, just as its location underscored the link between these cultural debates and congressional action. Bringing together a select group of children's advocates, media producers (both from industry and the public sector), and researchers from a variety of disciplines, this conference revealed how fast the field has been moving in designing innovative media products for kids. At the same time, it showed the lack of progress in generating reliable long-range studies on the impact of new digital media on children and of their socialization within a broader cultural field. But most pertinent to my argument here, the conference represented (at the time of this writing in October 1998) the latest reconfiguration of the debate on children's media culture, with a new realignment of sides.

Given that Montgomery is currently one of our nation's most influential children's advocates, and her cohost Wartella one of the most highly respected "effects" researchers in the field (as well as one of the principal investigators on the *National Television Violence Study*, whose findings are frequently cited by advocacy groups and censors), one might expect them to be in the camp that sees children primarily as victims in need of protection. Yet along with most of the other participants at the conference, they both opposed Congress's recent narrow focus on the porn issue (the new antiporn law that requires commercial websites containing sexually explicit and "patently offensive" material to block access to anyone seventeen or younger, a measure that was struck down by the Supreme Court as unconstitutional just like last year's Communications Decency Act). Instead, they advocated a new agenda built around four key assumptions, all of which are shared by the contributors to this volume.

First, we must move beyond the narrow "fear-driven" agenda that concentrates on violent representations in electronic games and pornography on the Internet, and begin considering constructive steps for using these new digital media to address the actual needs of children as they confront social and cultural changes in their daily lives. Such a shift in focus requires public policies that would encourage the development of positive alternatives, along with experimental programs in both the private and public sectors. This was precisely the conference's agenda and the reason for devoting so much time to showing new works in progress.

Second, some of our highest priorities should continue to be universal access and equity to these new technologies across existing lines of class, race, ethnicity, and gender, and on reserving part of the digital broadcast spectrum for the public sector—needs that are often denied by those advocating censorship. Apparently the primary focus of a new CME campaign, this is how the center describes the problem:

> In recent months, a number of conservative groups and pundits have launched assaults on the nation's longstanding Universal Service Program. The Cato Institute, for example, recently released a report, "Universal Service: The New Entitlement and Taxes," which called for the elimination of Universal Service for rural residents, low-income consumers,

schools and libraries. Others have quickly followed suit. The groups have argued that . . . the federal government should completely eliminate industry's Universal Service obligations and place blind trust in the forces of competition to bring affordable service to all Americans. . . . Many of the recent attacks center on the newest Universal Service program—the E-Rate, which provides discounted telecommunications services to school and libraries.[17]

According to Leslie A. Harris (Washington lobbyist, and founder of the Civic Media Project for the protection of free expression and public access to the Internet), before anyone got a penny from the Telecommunications Act of 1996, one billion dollars was already cut from the program under pressure from Congress and right-wing think tanks (like the Cato Foundation). She claims that in virtually every session of Congress, conservatives try to get rid of this measure and attack the principle of universal access by derisively dismissing it as "the right to porn." Thus, she explicitly links the campaign for censorship to the attack on universal access.

Next, it is essential to position children as active producers of media images rather than merely passive receivers, both by teaching media literacy in the schools and by designing media products with this capability. Papert's constructionist group at the MIT Media Lab was pioneering in fostering the latter, as was demonstrated in many of the experimental works on display at the conference by his former students and colleagues.[18]

Finally, there is a dire need for more long-term studies that are broader in scope, and that address the complex relations between these new media and their predecessors, as well as with other social formations with which students are daily involved at home, at school, and in the public sphere. Wartella and Kafai, two of the most prominent experimental researchers at the conference, were most emphatic about the lack of reliable long-range research that adequately assesses the educational value of the new technologies. According to Kafai, there have been only thirty studies over the past twenty-five years, and though we may know what makes electronic games fun, we still do not know what makes them good for learning. Like Cocking and Greenfield, several participants argued that because of this lack, there is a tendency (particularly by media) to jump to false conclusions or make exaggerated claims that go far beyond the scope of the research, as was recently the case with the Carnegie Tech study on the effects of computers on certain types of learning in schools. It was also widely acknowledged at the conference that most of the research in this area has been done by industry, which withholds findings to protect proprietary interests. As if echoing similar calls by Halloran and the Tullochs (quoted earlier), Bill Tally of the Center for Children and Technology contended that we must shift the research paradigm away from "black box studies" (which address narrowly defined questions of inputs and outputs, while bracketing out more complex relations with school, family, and daily life, therefore yielding little information of interest) to a program of "interactive research" (which looks at how technology actually functions in specific social contexts, focuses on process rather than effects, and is explicitly oriented toward change)—an approach that is consistent with this volume.

On this last point, however, there was some dissent. When several participants observed that this broader, long-term research was more difficult to fund and risked being rendered obsolete by the rapidity of technological change, a strategic alternative for a two-part research agenda was proposed, one that could recuperate the so-called narrower studies purely for their political effectiveness. It would include, on the one hand, the short-term, high-impact studies that help to set policy agendas (such as CME's publication on the Internet privacy issue, *Web of Deception: Threats to Children from Online Marketing*, and its more recent study, *Deepening the Digital Divide: The War on Universal Service*); and on the other hand, the more complex, longitudinal research that politicians usually ignore. Unlike Tally's approach, this tactic clearly privileges the former over the latter.

What was most interesting and disturbing about this proposal was the way it plainly acknowledged (without a trace of irony or condemnation) that research was and should continue to be evaluated (both by the academics who conduct it and the policymakers who fund or cite it) primarily on the basis of its usefulness in serving specific political agendas. The same thing could be said about the broader discourse on children's media, which has been mobilized and manipulated in the popular press as well as in Washington circles of power by a wide spectrum of politicians from both major parties over the past several decades, but perhaps most blatantly during the Clinton era, when this volume was conceived, written, and published.

Kids' Culture in the Clinton Era

Call it the Cult of the Child. From day care to children's health to keeping schools open all afternoon, the White House will be churning out new kid-focused proposals as fast as Gerber can make jars of mashed bananas. . . . "New programs for kids are a great way to unite the party," says a White House aide. . . . "The fastest growing segment of the electorate is the one concerned about protecting children and helping parents be good parents," says Clinton pollster Mark Penn.—*Time Magazine*, 25 August 1997

Although other recent American politicians—such as Jimmy Carter, Ronald Reagan, George Bush, and Dan Quayle—have used "family values" and "children and media" as campaign issues, and have introduced programs that specifically benefited youngsters, children's advocacy became much more central during the Clinton era. An "education president" who came into office only two years after the passage of the 1990 Children's Television Act, Clinton's campaign rhetoric both in 1992 and 1996 was strategically structured around kids' culture. Not only did Clinton appropriate the rhetoric of Reagan and Quayle on these topics to appease conservative Democrats and reposition his party more toward the center, but at the same time, he claimed to represent an entirely new generation that could identify more closely with kids. The 1992 campaign highlighted the generational contrast between the young Clinton and running mate Al Gore (both baby boomers) and the sixty-eight-year-old war veteran Bush, who was proverbially placed as being "over the hill." As if to oedipalize this conflict, Clinton repeatedly confessed that he was a fatherless son who had stood up against his alcoholic stepfather whenever he tried to abuse his mother or younger brother. In his television ads, he used phrases like "fiscal child abuse" and warned viewers, "Unless we change, our children can become the first generation of Americans to do worse than their parents." In his first inaugural address, he claimed: "We must do what no generation has done before . . . we must provide for our nation the way a family provides for its children." In this first presidential campaign, the child became symbolic of the whole culture—an embodiment of both our victimization and culpability, and a projection of both our past and future.

The inaugural ceremonies featured celebrities who were favorites with kids, as if inviting youngsters to participate in celebrating the Democratic victory and to make this national media event a multigenerational family affair. Preschoolers' beloved Barney joined other PBS stars in Clinton's inaugural parade. At the inauguration-eve party (broadcast on CBS), young *Home Alone* star Macaulay Culkin quipped, "This is the first inauguration party I ever attended and, I've been told, the first such Democratic event to occur in my lifetime!" at which point the camera quickly cut to a close-up of the youthful Clinton and Gore laughing at his remark, as if this child star were somehow emblematic of their own meteoric rise to power. At another inauguration party, superstar Michael Jackson (who was then still the world's most popular children's advocate) performed a medley of songs dedicated to younger kids (some of whom joined him on stage). The traditional notion of "looking up to elders" was being reversed before our eyes, for each generation was now being asked to turn their admiring gaze to their younger fans, just as Clinton had done during the campaign with appearances on MTV and the late-night Arsenio Hall show to woo the youth vote. Now, at the MTV inaugural ball, he could acknowledge the truth of what the station president had been widely quoted as saying: "MTV had a lot to do with the Clinton-Gore victory!"

In the 1996 campaign and its ceremonies of victory, daughter Chelsea Clinton was prominently featured as "the good child," the awkward adolescent duckling of the former campaign now transformed into a graceful swan gliding toward Stanford—a metamorphosis that could be mobilized to help whitewash her parents' moral murkiness due to the Whitewater investigation and subsequent sex scandals. Chelsea also provided a welcome relief from that dynamic duo, Culkin and Jackson, who had shared the role of "good child" at the 1992 inaugural balls, but who had since fallen from grace like the president and his first lady. Soon after the 1992 election when the tabloids featured stories about a brutal, exploitative father that cast Culkin as a bullied and abused child (a role with which both Jackson and Clinton could identify), his comic role as valiant, violent vanquisher of adult criminals in those domestic *Home Alone* comedies of the 1980s no longer seemed so funny.

The comic image of a child inflicting violence was even more disturbing when juxtaposed with the harrowing news stories of juvenile violence that increasingly obsessed the media: like that of the five-year-old African American boy who was dropped out a high-rise window by his eleven-year-old companions because he would not shoplift from a local store; or the teenage drive-by paintballers in Los Angeles who laughed as they shot their victims in the face at close range while documenting their crime spree on video, as if intending to submit their antics to *America's Funniest Home Videos.* In fact, the footage was actually broadcast on one of the more violent "reality television" spinoffs, accompanied by a hypocritical, moralizing voice-over.

Such scandals, crimes, and frenzied representations made it easier for politicians and journalists alike to turn toward media as the prime source both of the problem and its quick fix. They could demonize television as the main reason why American kids drop out of school, get pregnant, join violent gangs, and lag far behind students of less powerful nations in crucial subjects like math and science. Meanwhile, Clinton could take pride in the new 1996 FCC guidelines that strengthened the Children's Television Act by requiring all stations to broadcast at least three hours per week of educational programming for children under the age of sixteen. With the aid of journalists, and industry and bipartisan support from Congress, Clinton and Gore could also help fetishize computers and the Internet as the new miraculous media that would somehow enable our children to not merely catch-up with the educational achievements of other nations, but leapfrog ahead on what Gore dubbed the world's "information superhighway." In his acceptance speech at the 1996 Democratic Convention, Clinton promised to hardwire every school in the nation so that *all* kids (regardless of class, race, or gender) could have access to the Web. This plan would presumably raise academic achievement levels while simultaneously helping to eliminate socioeconomic inequities—a visionary agenda that had earlier been pursued by the Children's Television Workshop with educational shows like *Sesame Street*. Yet Clinton also promised his more conservative constituents that he would develop legislation to protect young Web browsers from pornography and sexual predators, legislation that his administration would succeed in passing, but which later would be struck down by the Supreme Court as unconstitutional. Despite Clinton's well-publicized programs, and Gore's continued proselytizing to make this information superhighway a safe haven and progressive force for all American children, the Democrats were far from "ruling" the Web, for this powerful medium (like all its predecessors) continued to function as a site of intense struggle for a wide spectrum of political agendas and conflicting interests from all over the world.

Still, no one could have foreseen that the Internet would soon be utilized as a weapon for Clinton's undoing. For in fall 1998, when Kenneth Starr's 445-page report to Congress on Clinton's "inappropriate" sexual relationship with young White House intern Monica Lewinsky was posted on this miraculous new medium, it compounded not only the presidential crisis concerning Clinton's possible impeachment, but also the media crisis for parents over whether they should let their children have access to this historic document with all its juicy sexual details. As if inspired by their own excesses, the moralizing forces on the Right previously leading the crusade against sexual content on the Internet and airwaves were now among those gleefully orchestrating and applauding the release of the Starr report on the mass media, turning to the broader social, legal, and historical contexts to justify this blatant inconsistency. In fact, at the very same time that the Republican-led House Judiciary Committee was voting to release the full report on the Internet, as well as the videotape of Clinton's Grand Jury testimony and 2,000 pages of supporting written material to broadcasters and print publications throughout the world, another congressional committee was deliberating on how to protect children from sexual material on the information superhighway (deliberations that eventually led to the bill that was signed into law on October 22, 1998). Meanwhile, as news journalists were righteously pointing out these moral and political ironies, their own stations and publications were proudly announcing their intention to transmit all of this information as soon as it was released, apparently feeling compelled to fiercely compete not only with each other but also with the immediacy of the Internet. For what appeared to be purposes of

exciting new ideas for reconceptualizing our understanding of consciousness. Most newsworthy were the implications for children's cognitive development and Clinton's educational reforms. Thus, it was not just the Internet and new media that were being mobilized in these discursive debates about kids' culture, but also hard science and its new take on the hardwiring of young brains.

For example, the Los Angeles Times ran an ongoing series called "The Brain: A Work in Progress," whose episodes were frequently positioned on the front page alongside articles about the dismal scores of American students on tests in math and science in contrast to those from other nations, as if this novel brain research might help our children regain the lead.[20] The new research indicated that the majority of those trillions of synapses that build pathways in the brain were actually determined by early experience rather than by genes or hardwiring. Moreover, these connections, when repeated and linked with emotion, proved surprisingly permanent. While this line of reasoning opened wonderful possibilities for cognitive growth and understanding the infinite differences among children, it also implied that the damage done by child abuse and neglect may be far more devastating and irreversible than formerly suspected. This research, then, provided another set of reasons for supporting Clinton's agenda—that is, for focusing our resources and attention on the nurture and protection of innocent and malleable young children who still have extraordinary potential. It could also be used to justify the primary emphasis on education that young children are exposed to—in those hardwired schools across the nation, and at home in early interactions with parents and television.

In summer of 1997, while Time Magazine was attacking the political opportunism of Clinton's Children's Crusade (as demonstrated in the passage already quoted), its chief print rival Newsweek published a single-topic issue that explicitly linked this new mapping of the brain (and its implications for learning) with the recent Educational Television Act (and its implications for presidential politics), as if mobilizing this juxtaposition for a reassessment of both Clinton's role in history and print journalism's role in the electronic age of the 1990s.[21] Newsweek's special edition opens with an article by Barbara Kantrowitz, reporting: "According to the Newsweek Poll, more than half of the parents surveyed said they did not believe that the policies of government and business were supportive of families with very young children" (p. 9); it ends with an article by Hillary Rodham Clinton called "Doing the Best for Our Kids," which proves just the opposite. Suggesting that she and her husband have served the nation as model parents (a theme stressed in the 1996 campaign), Hillary mobilizes the new brain research to personally reexamine the job she and her husband have done in raising Chelsea (who was soon leaving home for college): "Although Bill and I didn't realize it at the time, the countless hours we spent cuddling with Chelsea and reading her favorite stories not only strengthened our relationship with her but literally helped her brain grow." A few paragraphs later, she announces:

> This month, the president and I are convening a first-ever White House Conference on Early Childhood Development and Learning. Our aim is to bring together parents, scientists, policymakers, educators, business leaders and child-care providers to discuss the new research on the brain and early childhood development and explore how we can deliver this information to more homes. (pp. 94–95)

In between these two framing political articles are several others on the new brain research that lie at the core of this special issue and prove *Newsweek* is already doing its part to fulfill the Clinton agenda: it is making this cognitive research available to parents so that they can perceive the tremendous practical social value not only of an academic subject like science, but also of a responsible weekly magazine like *Newsweek*, particularly in contrast to its rival medium of television. For instance, we learn from John Leland in "The Magnetic Tube" that although "by the age of two, American kids spend an average of twenty-seven hours per week in front of the set,. . . . the Academy of Pediatrics advises that parents should limit TV time to one to two hours a day" (pp. 89–90). We might wonder whether television viewing would not provide some of those crucial cognitive synapses—especially since one of *Newsweek*'s contributors informs us that "the vast majority of 1,000 trillion connections (synapses) . . . [are] determined by early experience" (p. 30). As if to prevent such a conclusion, we are informed by Sharon Begley in "How to Build a Baby's Brain" that "only 'live' language, not television" (p. 31), can produce these cognitive advances in such skills as vocabulary and syntax boosting; Hillary Clinton's article clearly specifies that the best form of "live" language is reading aloud to your child. As if to strengthen the arguments for this exclusion of television, Begley tells us that researcher Janellen Huttenlocher of the University of Chicago "suspects" that "language has to be used in relation to ongoing events, or it's just noise" (p. 31), and "information embedded in an emotional context seems to stimulate neural circuitry more powerfully than information alone" (p. 31). Apparently, Begley assumes that children have no emotional response to television—an assumption that is certainly not shared by most children, nor by the president and his critics who were deeply concerned with how the Clinton scandals would affect American youngsters, nor by the contributors to this anthology, who believe that kids' interactions with media culture are far more complex than most cognitive scientists, politicians, or journalists are prepared to accept.

A Preview of Things to Come

The primary emphasis in this collection is on television and earlier media designed for children (such as comics and literature), rather than on the new digital media that were the focus of the Washington conference I described. Yet this volume contains several productive examples of how studies can be done "across media" within larger cultural and historical contexts, thereby broadening the scope of the debate and, in some ways, addressing Tally's call for "interactive research."

The essays that follow share five sets of key assumptions, crucial within the cultural debates I have been describing. First, they focus explicitly on the discursive controversies that have developed around children's media, while attempting (in varying degrees) to historicize these debates against broader social and political fields. They place particular emphasis on two specific historical moments—the 1950s and 1990s (following the Second World War and cold war, respectively)—when the nation was undergoing dramatic social transformations in the wake of global political and economic reconfigurations, and a new mass medium (television and the Internet, respectively) was emerging as a major cultural force.

Second, these essays explore the relationship between children's media culture and adult needs. More specifically, they examine the ways in which adult anxieties and fantasies about their own social realities, political agendas, and personal memories are sometimes projected onto these texts. They assume that adult assessments of these media texts frequently disagree with those of children, a conflict that can itself become a means of socialization for children or a potential object of commodification for media producers with transgenerational marketing goals. The authors, then, question what is at stake in the differences between these two sets of assessments by children and adults.

Third, these essays claim that children's reactions to media culture tend to be more active, variable, and negotiated than is usually realized; for such reception is often embedded in the context of play and other leisure activities, as well as in a complex network of social relations found at home within the family, at school among friends and teachers, and in the broader public sphere of the neighborhood, region, and nation. They assume that popular texts and the conflicting discourses around them contribute to children's growing understanding of themselves as gendered, raced, socially connected members of a network of linked communities, and to their emerging perception of their own position and potential empowerment within a changing global public sphere. Thus, these essays are suspicious of simplistic, monolithic readings by adults that ignore social context and assume all children respond in the same way.

Fourth, they share a concern with many children's advocates that kids' media culture has commodified youth and growth to such a degree that children are increasingly willing (and sometimes even eager) to see themselves as products. Although addressed by the Children's Television Act of 1990, this problem is sometimes eclipsed by the media's almost exclusive focus on what is widely perceived as the more compelling issues of violence and pornography in the debates around children and the media.[22]

Finally, building on John Hartley's idea that American commercial television tends to address its viewers as children—thereby undermining controversial divisions of class, ethnicity, race, and gender[23]—these essays assume that in a global market increasingly dominated by American media exports, American-produced programs for children become the advance guard for colonizing all popular media. According to this imperialist logic, if America is presented in the guise of an "innocent child abroad," then it is less likely to be seen as a threat to other national and cultural identities. For what is good and safe for American kids, must be presumed to be good for a safer world. Thus, these essays encourage an international perspective on children's media culture, a goal that was endorsed by many of the participants at the Washington conference.

This volume is divided into three sections. The first, "Children's Media Culture in the Postwar Era," contains four essays that explore how representations of children and child-raising practices are connected to larger issues of national identity and global politics. They describe with historical specificity how childhood was constructed at a crucial moment in American history—when the United States emerged as a triumphant, major world power after World War II. This moment was seminal for the rise of postmodernist culture, for it was in this period that mass media (especially television) became a major force in the domestic space of the home and American popular culture became a powerful colonizing force in the global sphere. These essays focus on three media—kid strips, books, and television (and the lucrative spin-offs they generated)—showing how they helped redefine American national identity in the postwar era both at home and abroad, and how they used the child as a trope to sell a distinctively American brand of ingenious innocence worldwide. In attending to the debates around earlier media in earlier periods, they urge us to avoid repeating the same mistakes.

The first section opens with Lynn Spigel's essay, "Innocence Abroad: The Geopolitics of Childhood in Postwar Kid Strips," which considers the relations among three key issues that underlie the current discourse around children's media: the commodification and politicizing of childhood against a broader cultural history, the use of children's media as a vehicle for colonizing the rest of the world, and the nostalgia for a period of childhood innocence that never really existed. Specifically, her essay studies the U.S. tendency to use its most innocent and universal products, children and cartoons, to conquer foreign markets. Spigel traces the rise to popularity of a new kind of comic strip kid after World War II, examining both *Dennis the Menace* and *Peanuts*. She shows how kids in these two strips came to represent the American nation during the cold war era, and how their conquest narratives played out the relationship between children and national supremacy by addressing issues of freedom, discipline, and authority. Though her primary emphasis is on the 1950s and 1960s, Spigel follows the fates of *Dennis* and *Peanuts* up to the 1990s, exploring their shifting meanings in other periods as well as the implications of their nostalgic revival in recent movies and merchandise.

Picking up on the issue of nostalgia where Spigel leaves off, Henry Jenkins's essay, " 'Her Suffering Aristocratic Majesty': The Sentimental Value of *Lassie*," investigates how many of these same dynamics worked through a single text and its transcultural and transmedia adaptations. Starting with Eric Knight's popular children's novel, *Lassie Come Home* (1940), Jenkins examines the ongoing process of adapting this story for television, from its debut in the 1954 pilot to its treatment of Lassie's transfer to a new owner in 1964. He connects the changes to the broader social history during that period, especially concerning issues of gender and the family. While exploring the sentimental and symbolic value of Lassie as a "popular hero" who succeeded in three media—literature, film, and television—the essay centers primarily on the historical contexts that shaped the popular circulation and consumption of *Lassie* as, in Jenkins's words, the "longest running children's series on American television," one that is "central both to our cultural understanding of the dog and to the postwar construction of American boyhood."

The topic shifts to the debates over the Davy "Crockett Craze" in the mid-1950s, in Sean Griffin's article, "Kings of the Wild Backyard: Davy Crockett and Children's Space." Griffin looks at the struggle between children and adults over which uses of the Crockett persona were appropriate. After examining postwar suburban America's conception of children's space, he shows how this was problematized by the Crockett myth of the wild frontier. His essay also considers the conflicting explanations for the "Crockett Craze"—such as Davy's appeal to children as a rebellious trickster who strongly preferred fun over work; or the myth's appeal to parents as a text (like the kid strips discussed by Spigel) that enabled their children to play out aggressive fantasies of conquest and westward expansion (which could be seen as nonelectronic, interactive simulations) in the safety of their own postwar suburban backyards; or the economic appeal to manufacturers and storekeepers of cashing in on the coonskin cap and other exploitable ancillary products. In highlighting reception issues, particularly the ongoing power struggle between adults and children over the meanings and effects of popular texts, Griffin reveals how such conflicts can become a vehicle for children's socialization.

Jyotsna Kapur's piece, "Out of Control: Television and the Transformation of Childhood in Late Capitalism," serves as a bridge between the first group of essays focused on the 1950s and those in section 2 that emphasize American television in the 1990s. Though she shares many common assumptions with the authors of both sections, she brings an additional cross-cultural dimension: growing up in India during the 1960s and 1970s. Her own children were born in the United States and are now being raised on American popular culture. Challenging the notion that the word *children* represents a natural category, she describes a fundamental transformation in the cultural conception of childhood, one that began in the postwar period of the 1950s with the mass-scale improvement in domestic standards of living and modern technologies, as well as the expansion of capitalism and market research, and that resulted in the construction of children as a niche market increasingly targeted by multinational advertisers in the 1990s. Children, she claims, are no longer seen as "untainted receivers of gifts" purchased by adults, but as "sovereign, playful, thinking consumers" who tell their parents what to buy. Instead of blaming television or permissive parenting for these developments, like Spigel, Jenkins, and Griffin, she links them to larger patterns of social and historical change. And rather than urging parents to regain protective authoritarian control over their kids, she offers alternative strategies for enabling children and adults to function as allied critical consumers within a market economy—both when watching television at home and when shopping in the public sphere. In this way, she challenges the opposition between parents and children, which has been intensified and commodified by both the commercial and critical discourses circulating around kids' media culture.

Section 2, "Reception and Cultural Identity," which contains four essays, focuses on reception issues surrounding popular television series in the contemporary period. Ranging from supposedly "good" educational shows like *Sesame Street* and *Where on Earth Is Carmen Sandiego?* to more controversial fare like *Xuxa* and *My So-Called Life*, to action series notorious for their violence like *X-Men* and *Mighty Morphin Power Rangers*, these essays highlight the differences in the reactions of children and adults, and center on the controversies generated by these series. Addressing issues of production and policymaking as well as reception, they interrogate the idea of "educational television," showing how the politics of adults is frequently projected onto these shows and the debates that surround them, not only by media producers and children's advocates, but also by the authors of these essays.

The second section opens with Heather Hendershot's "*Sesame Street:* Cognition and Communications Imperialism," which serves as an effective transition from section 1. Despite the show's sterling reputation as an ideal model for educational television, Hendershot traces the history of the cultural criticism vented against *Sesame Street* from the late 1960s to the present, revealing how each set of concerns was linked to the larger political issues of the times (including the fear of drugs, the counterculture, and the cold war anxieties of the 1960s and 1970s). The essay ends by offering new grounds for criticism of the show in the 1990s that pertain to its utopian faith in, as Hendershot writes, the "emancipatory effects of cognitive development." Although Hendershot focuses exclusively on a single television series, her essay is comprehensive in its approach, emphasizing production, government policy, and international distribution, while raising virtually all of the issues that are addressed by other works within this section.

My own essay, "Ranging with Power on the Fox Kids Network: Or, Where on Earth Is Children's Educational Television?" picks up where Hendershot ends: how so-called "good" and "bad" shows define themselves in relation to each other. It enters the debate over how television can better serve the "educational needs of children" by examining what kind of media literacy is already being taught to young viewers on Saturday morning television—not only in a highly praised educational show like *Where on Earth Is Carmen Sandiego?* but also in violent action series like *Power Rangers*, *X-Men*, *Batman and Robin*, and *MegaMan* as well as parodic comedies like *Animaniacs*, *Dog City*, *The Tick*, and *Eek!stravaganza*. Based on the morning block of children's programming on one Saturday in fall 1994, the analysis concentrates on four cognitive operations that are found systemically in every show—operations that are explicitly discussed in the dialogue, illustrated in the images, dramatized in the narrative, and sometimes even presented as "the moral" of the episode. I argue that these operations function as a system of how to read specific images, words, and sounds against the broader cultural field. In some ways, this system could be described as what Turkle calls "readership skills for a culture of simulation,"[24] skills that are not part of a media literacy curriculum taught within the schools, but rather a series of reflexive design components built into the programs. What is being taught is not merely (in Hendershot's terms) "the emancipatory effects of cognitive development," but a process that enables television to mediate children's understanding of all forms of cultural production, and to establish cognitive categories for organizing children's perceptions of and empowerment within the world.

Elissa Rashkin's article, "Xuxa S.A.: The Queen of Rede Globo in the Age of Transnational Capitalism," follows the production and reception history of a hugely popular and successful Latin American show that was "customized" in

1993 for its new location on American broadcast television. By considering the reverse of the situation described by Hendershot (the customization of *Sesame Street* for foreign markets), Rashkin's essay explores the political implications in this process of transcultural reinscription. In this case, it involved the de-eroticizing of its Brazilian hostess, Xuxa, and the flaunting of her commodification in a North American "mainstream" market that was becoming increasingly aware of the buying power of its Latino audience. Rashkin reads the show as an allegory of what it means to be a Latin American superstar in the era of transnational capitalism. The juxtaposition of this case study with those of *Sesame Street* and *Power Rangers* (an adaptation of a Japanese series) enables us to see more clearly that the political implications of these customized adaptations are determined more by the global power of the respective players than by their respective positions as an original source of conception or ultimate point of consumption.

Susan Murray's essay, "Saving Our So-Called Lives: Girl Fandom, Adolescent Subjectivity, and *My So-Called Life*," deals with a popular ABC series whose cancellation was strongly protested by its young female fans, who found it to be one of the few shows on television that realistically spoke to the concerns of teenage girls. They also found its protagonist, fifteen-year-old Angela Chase, to be a powerful site of identification for their ambivalent feelings about their own struggle toward womanhood. Though Murray does not address the connection, it might be possible to see this fandom as prefiguring the popularity and surprising commercial success of subsequent 1998 series like the WB network's *Felicity* and *Dawson's Creek*. Focusing on an Internet bulletin board in 1994–1995 that was devoted to *My So-Called Life*, Murray's piece makes a strong case for the kind of active reading processes and participatory spectatorship that are frequently disavowed by adults. She considers the political implications of this kind of girl-culture activism, particularly the way these "Lifers" took over the broadcasters' billboard and adapted it to their own agenda. Moreover, she demonstrates how they used it as an extension of the narrative, and as a play space for constructing and experimenting with their own sense of female identity. In giving greater voice to young female viewers in the cultural debates that surround popular texts, and in moving toward cyberspace and the new electronic technologies, this essay serves as an apt transition to section 3.

Titled "Pedagogy and Power," section 3 contains three essays that deal more directly with children's interaction with media within educational settings, while also focusing more specifically on issues of gender and socialization. Utilizing a wider range of empirical methodologies that combine quantitative and qualitative analysis—including in-depth interviews, ethnographic observations, questionnaires, assigned tasks, and statistical analysis—these essays attend more closely to children's actual responses and behavior, reading them not merely as an index of previous imprinting, but also as potentialities for designing future alternatives. In Tally's terms, these essays move beyond the "test-score tyranny" of "black box studies" that ignore the complex realities of the real-life educational context, including the subjectivity of teachers. They also address the introduction of new technologies into the schoolroom—whether television sets, VCRs, computers, or electronic games.

In "Power Rangers at Preschool: Negotiating Media in Child Care Settings," Ellen Seiter studies the use of videotapes and television viewing in group care settings for preschool children, analyzing the complex negotiations that exist between teachers, parents, and children over these issues. She claims that issues of class and status are extremely important in these negotiations, for the occupation of day-care provider is interpreted differently in different socio-economic communities. In this study, Seiter conducted in-depth interviews with teachers and child care givers concerning not only their attitudes about media effects on children, but also their own leisure time media preferences and childhood experiences with television. Although her research is based on many such interviews, this particular essay examines only the two most extreme cases from her sample: an exclusive, mostly white, upper-middle-class suburban Montessori school where popular videos are totally banned, and talk about television and popular media characters strictly forbidden, versus a low-income, racially integrated, downtown day-care center where kids watch commercial television programs, play Power Ranger games, and dress as their favorite media stars. Seiter uses these fascinating case studies to argue that rules about television and toys (which sometimes are applied differently to girls than to boys) come from a combination of the material circumstances of the setting and the beliefs and experiences of the teachers.

Heather Gilmour's essay, "What Girls Want: The Intersections of Leisure and Power in Female Computer Game Play," explores issues of socialization and gender within computer culture. While acknowledging there are differences in the way boys and girls play electronic games, she links these to historical patterns of gendering leisure rather than to essentializing binary oppositions that have come to dominate the electronic game market. Grounding her analysis in Karla Henderson's study of the historical discourse on leisure (which claims that while men's leisure activities have flourished in the public sphere, those of females have been restricted to domestic space, where they are linked to women's training as feminine subjects), Gilmour finds a similar pattern at play in the contemporary discourse on girls' taste in software—one skewed toward educational games or the use of computers for homework assignments. In an attempt to see whether these patterns were operative in the daily school setting, Gilmour conducted a study in three Los Angeles private schools with different demographics. She combined three methodologies: ethnographic observation of students' use of computers in the classroom; follow-up interviews with selected teachers, students, and parents; and a broader survey of 180 students who filled out a questionnaire. Finding more variety among girls in their use of computers than is ordinarily assumed, she concludes that it is necessary to resist those discourses that restrict female behavior, pleasure, and self-definition, and encourage those that challenge any monolithic notion of the feminine.

Addressing similar issues but with a very different methodology and perspective, Yasmin B. Kafai's chapter, "Video Game Designs by Girls and Boys: Variability and Consistency of Gender Differences," builds on her earlier innovative studies on children's game making, which have helped generate the new emphasis on positioning kids as creative designers and producers of multimedia, rather than merely passive push-button, mouse-clicking users and consumers. In this particular project, two coed groups of fourth graders were asked to design educational games for third graders. One group was assigned the task of teaching scientific concepts about the solar system and the other group the mathematical concept of fractions. Like Gilmour and Seiter's work, Kafai's research explains the existing gender differences in children's use of electronic media in educational settings as more dependent on context than on any fixed set of essentializing oppositions. Or as she put it at the Washington conference, "there are gender differences in style but not in performance." Although her research may be more empirical and distant from a cultural studies approach than the other essays in this collection, it also calls for greater attention to broader environmental forces and a stronger acknowledgment of children's active, imaginative engagement with their culture.

In all of the essays in this volume, then, the kids are not portrayed as timeless, innocent victims who desperately need to be protected from popular culture. Rather, they are seen as historically situated participants who actively collaborate in the production and negotiation of cultural meanings.

Notes

1 Brody made this statement on October 22, 1998, at a two-day conference in Washington, D.C., titled "Ensuring a Quality Digital Media Culture for Children."

2 For two recent, prominent examples, see *The UCLA Television Violence Monitoring Report* (Los Angeles: University of California, Los Angeles, Center for Communication, 1995); and *National Television Violence Study* (Studio City, Calif.: Mediascope, 1994–95).

3 Rodney R. Cocking and Patricia M. Greenfield, "Effects of Interactive Entertainment Technologies on Children's Development," in *Interacting with Video: Advances in Applied*

Developmental Psychology, ed. Patricia M. Greenfield and Rodney R. Cocking (Norwood, N.J.: Ablex Publishing, 1996), 4.

4 James D. Halloran, "The Social Effects of Television," in *The Effects of Television*, ed. James D. Halloran (London: Panther, 1970), 64.

5 See David Morley, *Family Television: Cultural Power and Domestic Leisure* (London: Comedia Publishing Group, 1986); and Barrie Thorne, *Gender Play: Girls and Boys in School* (New Brunswick, N.J.: Rutgers University Press, 1993).

6 See, for example, James R. Kincaid, *Child-Loving: The Erotic Child and Victorian Culture* (New York: Routledge, 1992); Carolyn Steedman, *Childhood, Culture, and Class in Britain: Margaret McMillan, 1860–1931* (New Brunswick, N.J.: Rutgers University Press, 1990); and Viviana A. Zelizer, *Pricing the Priceless Child: The Changing Social Value of Children* (New York: Basic Books, 1985). See also anthologies like Elliot West and Paula Petrik, eds., *Small Worlds: Children and Adolescents in America, 1850–1950* (Lawrence: University of Kansas Press, 1992); and Mary Heininger, et al., *A Century of Childhood, 1820–1920* (Rochester, New York: Margaret Woodbury Strong Museum, 1984).

7 See Dick Hebdige, *Subculture: The Meaning of Style* (London: Methuen, 1979); Lawrence Grossberg, *We Gotta Get out of This Place: Popular Conservatism and Postmodern Culture* (New York: Routledge, 1992) and *Dancing in Spite of Myself: Essays on Popular Culture* (Durham: Duke University Press, 1997); Angela McRobbie, *Feminism and Youth Culture: From "Jackie" to "Just Seventeen"* (Boston: Unwin Hyman, 1991); Valerie Walkerdine, *Daddy's Girl: Young Girls and Popular Culture* (Cambridge: Harvard University Press, 1997); Lynn Spigel and Henry Jenkins, "Same Bat Channel, Different Bat Times: Mass Culture and Popular Memory," in *The Many Faces of the Batman: Critical Approaches to a Superhero and His Media*, ed. William Urrichio and Roberta Pearson (New York: Routledge, 1991); Henry Jenkins, "Going Bonkers! Children, Play, and Pee-wee," *Camera Obscura*, no. 17 (May 1988): 169–95; Ellen Seiter, *Sold Separately: Parents and Children in Consumer Culture* (Brunswick, N.J.: Rutgers University Press, 1995); and Marsha Kinder, *Playing with Power in Movies, Television, and Video Games: From Muppet Babies to Teenage Mutant Ninja Turtles* (Berkeley: University of California Press, 1991) and "Home Alone in the '90s: Generational War and Transgenerational Address in American Movies, Television, and Presidential Politics," in *In Front of the Children: Screen Entertainment and Young Audiences*, ed. Cary Bazalgette and David Buckingham (London: British Film Institute, 1995), 75–91.

8 John Tulloch and Marian Tulloch, "Discourses about Violence: Critical Theory and the 'TV Violence' Debate," *Text* 12, no. 2 (1992): 184–85. See also Graham Murdock, "Critical Inquiry and Audience Activity," in *Rethinking Communication*, vol. 2 of *Paradigm Exemplars*, ed. Brenda Dervin, Lawrence Grossberg, Barbara J. O'Keefe, and Ellen Wartella (London: Sage, 1989), 226–48.

9 Ibid., 185.

10 Ibid.

11 Marshall McLuhan, *Understanding Media: The Extensions of Man* (New York: McGraw-Hill, 1964).

12 See Raymond Williams, *Television: Technology and Cultural Form* (New York: Schocken Books, 1975); Carolyn Marvin, *When Old Technologies Were New: Thinking about Electric Communication in the Late Nineteenth Century* (New York: Oxford University Press, 1988); Lynn Spigel, *Make Room for Television: Television and the Family Ideal in Postwar America* (Chicago: University of Chicago Press, 1992); Sherry Turkle, *The Second Self: Computers and the Human Spirit* (New York: Simon and Schuster, 1984) and *Life on the Screen: Identity in the Age of the*

Internet (New York: Simon and Schuster, 1995); and Allucquère Rosanne Stone, *The War of Desire and Technology at the Close of the Mechanical Age* (Cambridge, Mass.: MIT Press, 1995).

13 For an elaboration of this issue, see Justine Cassell and Henry Jenkins, eds., *From Barbie to Mortal Kombat: Gender and Computer Games* (Cambridge, Mass.: MIT Press, 1998).

14 Mary Wollstonecraft, *A Vindication of the Rights of Woman with Strictures on Political and Moral Subjects* (New York: W. W. Norton, 1967), 79, 81.

15 Kathryn Montgomery and Shelley Pasnik, *Web of Deception: Threats to Children from Online Marketing* (Washington, D.C.: Center for Media Education, 1996).

16 "Hero TV" and "Runaways" were both featured at the White House Internet Summit: Digital Media Content for Children and Teens, cosponsored by the Annenberg Center for Communication at the University of Southern California and EC² (Egg Company 2, the Annenberg Incubator Project at USC, which functions as a liaison between academic research and business applications and helps to develop innovative start-up companies in new communications media), Santa Monica, Calif., 11–12 June 1996. See Brenda Laurel, *Computers as Theatre* (Reading, Pa.: Addison-Wesley, 1993).

17 Center for Media Study, *Deepening the Digital Divide: The War on Universal Service* (Washington, D.C.: Center for Media Education, 1998), 5.

18 In addition to the projects by veterans of Papert's constructionist group already described, others from the public sector featuring a creative role for kids included Holly Brooks's "Girl Site 1998," which is available in inner-city, after-school clubs in the Los Angeles area; Tom Tate's National 4-H Youth Tech Corps, which involves 5.5 million kids from eight different states (88 percent of whom are from the inner city); Tony Streit's "Street Level Youth Media" program in Chicago, which uses media technology to empower "at-risk" urban youth to make their own films and videos as alternatives to broadcast television; and Gary Schwartz's "I Choose Me" CD-ROM on children's rights, sponsored by UNICEF.

19 Bettijane Levine, "Child Psychologists Urge Straight Talk on Scandal," *Los Angeles Times*, 12 September 1998, A23.

20 The front page of the 16 October 1997 *Los Angeles Times* featured the final episode of "The Brain: A Work in Progress" on its left-hand column, while the right-hand column carried a story titled "Study Faults U.S. Science, Math Courses" (by *Times* education writer Elaine Woo), describing a new international study of "why U.S. students lag behind their counterparts in many other countries," which concluded that American instruction in those fields is "a mile wide and an inch deep."

21 "Your Child," special issue of *Newsweek*, spring/summer 1997.

22 As already mentioned, a notable exception is Kathryn Montgomery and Shelley Pasnik, *Web of Deception: Threats to Children from Online Marketing*. This issue also arose recently within the European Union when Sweden advocated a ban on all television advertising aimed at children, a position rejected by other European nations.

23 John Hartley, "Invisible Fictions: Television, Audiences, Paedocracy, Pleasure," in *Television Studies: Textual Analysis*, ed. Gary Burns and Robert J. Thompson (New York: Praeger, 1989), 223–43.

24 From a speech made by Sherry Turkle at the Washington, D.C., conference, "Ensuring a Quality Digital Media Culture for Children," on October 22, 1998.

I CHILDREN'S MEDIA CULTURE IN THE POSTWAR ERA

Innocence Abroad: The Geopolitics of Childhood
in Postwar Kid Strips   *Lynn Spigel*

And suddenly I knew for sure what it is that for me, at least, makes parenthood so deeply worthwhile. It gives one the magic passport without which one can never re-enter the lost country of one's own youth—that nationless land from which one emigrated, willy-nilly, so many years ago.—*Parents*, August 1952

America's children are at once our most precious national resource and our most weighty responsibility. They represent our future hopes and aspirations. . . . We must interact in the future with any number of new and emerging nations. In order to do this successfully, we will need the talent, dedication, and best efforts of all our youth. . . . So I ask all Americans to reaffirm this nation's commitment to its children.—President William J. Clinton, National Children's Day proclamation, 1993

In fall 1993, President Clinton proclaimed the third Sunday in November as National Children's Day. Reminiscent of the 1913 act that created Mother's Day and the 1924 inauguration of Father's Day, Children's Day honors American youth as a cornerstone not only of the family's sentimental life, but also of the nation's public purpose.[1] Now an official part of our national culture, the child was immediately addressed with an appropriate display of multinational consumer capital as Disneyland opened its gates to honor underprivileged children across the globe. In a television special covering the event, Disney beamed in children from its theme parks in California, Florida, Tokyo, and Paris. With its multicultural medley of Mickey Mouse, Gloria Estefan, and teen rap group Kris Kross, this New World Disney jamboree was a complex embodiment of America's will to conquer foreign markets with its most "innocent" and "universal" of products—children and cartoons.

Disney's colonial quests have, of course, been the subject of previous studies about cultural imperialism—most notably Ariel Dorfman and Armand Mattelart's 1971 *How to Read Donald Duck*.[2] Here, I want to take a somewhat different tack by looking at the rise of a new type of comic strip "kid" that appeared shortly after World War II. It was during this postwar period that comics (and cartoons more generally) discovered a new "geography" of childhood in which kids (both real and imagined) wandered through the fantasy spaces of consumer culture epitomized by the mass-produced suburb and its fantastic corollary, the theme park. It was here, in these new prefabricated spaces, that two postwar kid strips, *Dennis the Menace* and *Peanuts*, would become part of America's national popular culture. Less studied than their Disney competitors, these kid strips (and their various "spin-off" incarnations) have important links to the postwar multinational culture in which childhood innocence has served as a green card for America's will abroad and at home. Like their Disney cousins, these two strips traveled across the globe to numerous markets, spreading a message of American family values everywhere they went. But, even more significant for my purposes, these strips were fundamentally "conquest narratives" in which children explored the new geographies of postwar life—especially the suburbs—and in the process, like any good explorer, defined who belonged there and who did not. The cast of characters in these strips—the white, middle-class family—is perhaps less surprising than their relationship to the way American postwar culture more generally defined the boundaries of the nation (and its ideal citizen) by invoking the figure of the innocent child.

The appearance of Charles M. Schulz's *Peanuts* and Hank Ketcham's *Dennis the Menace* after World War II was less a revolution in comic strip style than a reworking of a century-long fascination with the kid strip in American culture. These strips were the postwar answer to what historians typically agree is the first modern comic strip, Richard Outcault's *The Yellow Kid* (a naughty boy who first graced the pages of the *Sunday World* in 1895). In the years to follow, a spate of kid strips from Rudolf Dirks's *The Katzenjammer Kids* (1897) to Outcault's *Buster Browne* (1902) to Harold Gray's *Little Orphan Annie* (1924) would become part of America's visual culture, and they would also serve as mascots for a host of product and media tie-ins from children's shoes to Broadway plays.[3] By the time *Dennis the Menace* and *Peanuts* appeared, the nationwide audience for kid strips was a well-established American phenomenon.

Like their predecessors, both Ketcham and Schulz masterfully built media icons out of their child heroes. Schulz began drawing *Li'l Folks* (his original title for the strip) in 1947 as a weekly feature for the *St. Paul Pioneer Press*. By 1950, it was picked up for national distribution by United Features Syndicate and (despite Schulz's objections) renamed *Peanuts*.[4] One year later, in 1951, Ketcham and the Post-Hall Syndicate unveiled *Dennis the Menace* in sixteen newspapers, and by the end of the year, it was in a hundred of the country's largest papers. The strip soared to national fame, so quickly that by 1953, *Newsweek* already called Dennis a "national personage."[5] Over the course of their first two decades, both strips were also syndicated around the world (by 1961, *Dennis* appeared in forty-three foreign countries and *Peanuts* in thirty-five).[6] Following on the merchandising successes of their kid strip cousins, these media magnates included worldwide "tie-in" deals for *Dennis* objects and *Peanuts* paraphernalia, the latter becoming a major player on the international toy market as the strip grew to phenomenal popularity in the 1960s. Moreover, unlike their kid strip predecessors, both *Dennis* and *Peanuts* came of age in the same years that television established itself as the nation's primary means of communication, and both strips were apt fodder for a medium that, at least in the 1950s and 1960s, saw itself as the quintessential backbone of family fun. In the late 1950s, Screen Gems bought the television rights to Ketcham's strip and produced the live-action *Dennis the Menace*, which ran on CBS between October 1959 and September 1963 (and was subsequently rerun on Saturday mornings).[7] In 1965, Schulz joined hands with producer Lee Mendelson and animator Bill Melendez to make his first in a long line of award-winning television specials, "A Charlie Brown Christmas."[8] Both *Dennis* and *Peanuts* also diversified across a range of other media, including books, motion pictures, theme parks, records, home videos, and most recently, video games. These strips, in short, have become international media empires.

The status of *Dennis* and *Peanuts* as media empires was not lost on the U.S. government, which at different points in history, saw these sweet family strips as vehicles for international cold warfare. In 1959, in the midst of President Dwight Eisenhower's "People to People Campaign" (Ike's populist attempt to create goodwill between peoples of different nations through cultural exchanges), Ketcham decided to take a trip to Russia in hopes of establishing a "humor exchange." According to Ketcham, his plan "got a lot of attention in Washington" and the Eisenhower administration was "delighted." He was soon contacted by the CIA, whisked to San Francisco and Washington, and briefed on espionage techniques. Ketcham claims he was asked to "look out for certain shapes and things that I saw from the air" while in flight to the Soviet Union. Although the government equipped him with an 8 mm spy camera, Ketcham decided to use his preferred medium, drawing suspicious objects on his pad. "When the stewardess started coming down to find out what I was drawing," Ketcham recalls, "I'd quickly put an eye and a nose on it and a great big grin and hair, and make a series of cartoons."[9] The humor exchange was thus turned into an international spy mission as the father of Dennis battled the Red Menace in this heroic cold war flight. Six years later, airplane attacks on "Reds" of another kind became a long-standing gag in numerous *Peanuts* panels featuring Snoopy and the Red Baron.

Given their interests in international surveillance and aerial combat, it is no surprise that both Ketcham and Schulz lent their characters to the goals of the space project. In the early 1960s, Dennis became the mascot for the U.S. Junior Astronaut Program, which exploited Dennis's image to encourage children to buy savings bonds in support of the space program. Later in the decade, at the height of the space race, the National Aeronautics and Space Administration (NASA) enlisted Charlie Brown and Snoopy as its company mascots for the Apollo Ten lunar orbit mission. In a *New York Times* article titled "Lenin vs. Snoopy," the moon mission served as the occasion for a thorough examination of "the very different spirit in which Moscow and Washington approach the cosmos. The Kremlin," the article continued, "used its Venus rockets to further the cult of Lenin. . . . Apollo 10's astronauts chose to call their two vehicles 'Charlie Brown' and 'Snoopy,' after two comic strip characters who represent no ideology or political party but do exemplify the human condition in a frustrating world."[10] Obviously, the fact that the *New York Times* saw it appropriate to compare Snoopy to a Russian leader underscores the very thing that the author so completely denies. Comic strip characters do suggest ideologies and political choices; they do represent nations.

In their economic and political roles in international competition, both *Dennis* and *Peanuts* seem hardly as "innocent" as their childish heroes. It is this status of children as national mascots, with the kid strip as a case in point, that I want to explore in the following pages. Looking specifically at the rise of these strips in the 1950s and 1960s, I ask a series of related questions: How did the figure of the "kid" come to represent the postwar nation during the height of the cold war? How did this icon of American innocence come to be the figure par excellence of our nation's will to power abroad? And how was the relationship between children and national supremacy played out in the strips themselves, as well as in their related media spin-offs?

Childhood and Nationalism

Prior to addressing these questions, I want first to consider the nature of nationalism itself and the historical trends that placed children at the center of nationalist discourse. Recent work on nationalism has stressed its symbolic dimensions, and in particular, the way language and texts work to provide what Benedict Anderson calls an "imagined community."[11] The nation, according to

Anderson, is a historical construct formed primarily in symbolic texts through which people, living in disparate places and under different conditions, imagine themselves joined together. The development of a "mother tongue," along with the variety of poetry, prose, and songs that perform this language, forge links between people who have no personal knowledge of one another, and they also work to create imaginary boundaries between these people and those of other nations. For this reason, Anderson prefers to see nationalism less as an ideology than as a social bond like kinship or religion. While Anderson doesn't concentrate on the funny pages per se, he does show that the newspaper has historically been a central means for creating these imaginary bonds between strangers. From this perspective, we might conclude that the comic strip also served to tie Americans together by forging a shared visual culture, a set of images that were commonly recognized by people in distant locations. Although not all Americans interpreted these images in the same way, the funnies did form bonds between readers; they did create a "reception" community in which the nation (and its others) could be imagined. In the case of the kid strip, the national image involved has, of course, been the child. We might, therefore, begin to account for the kid strip's popularity by considering how the "kid" allowed a diverse American public to imagine itself as a community tied together by common struggles and distinct from other nations.

If the kid character functioned as a vehicle for imagining the nation, this is because, as President Clinton put it, children "represents our future hopes and aspirations." This concept of the child as a symbolic future for the nation became central to the Progressive Era discourses on childhood that emerged in the late nineteenth century and flourished in the early decades of the 1900s. Tying Charles Darwin's theories of evolution to a sense of national purpose, the Progressive Era's middle-class "child-saving" movement saw children as the key to future generations. Reformers fought to secure the child's (and nation's) destiny by promoting legislation against child labor as well as the establishment of government agencies to oversee the social welfare of the young.[12] While the child-saving movement had humanitarian goals, it belied power struggles in the adult culture—struggles between classes, sexes, races, and ethnic and religious groups that did not all have the same ideals for their children.[13] Moreover, since many working-class families depended on their children's wages for basic needs, child labor laws threatened the family's very survival. Thus, as the federal and state governments became increasingly involved in child welfare, numerous Americans questioned the extent to which the government should intervene in family life. Children, consequently, came to represent the more general crisis of American liberalism: the relationship between the state and private sector.

With the national reinvestment in family life after World War II, the child once again was crucial in public debates. During the baby boom years (roughly 1946 to 1964), conceptions of childhood still very much revolved around the dynamic between the state and private life, although the problem was often framed in different ways. Now, it was typically articulated in terms of psychological discourses of personality development in relation to larger national questions about authoritarianism and freedom. In both intellectual and popular culture, critics worried that the overly disciplined child would grow into a sociopath unsuited for the basic goals of the free world. In scholarly literature—most notably Arnold Gesell and Frances Ilg's *Infant and Childcare in the Culture of Today* (1943) and Theodore Adorno et al.'s *The Authoritarian Personality* (1950)—the analysis was connected to the specter of fascism. For Gesell and Ilg, German *Kultur* was based on "autocratic parent-child relationships," while findings in the Adorno collection suggested that excessively submissive children in authoritarian (as opposed to nurturing, egalitarian) family structures would develop the kinds of personalities that were susceptible to prejudice and authoritarian regimes. In popular media, the problem of discipline was communicated in a more "horse sense" way as the media provided advice on how to avoid damaging the individual child's psyche. A prime example here is Dr. Benjamin Spock's best-selling *Common Sense Book of Baby and Child Care*, which was first published in 1946 and went through 167 printings in ten years. It warned against the pitfalls of too much discipline, paving the way for the popular embrace of a liberal, permissive, and presumably democratic approach to child rearing.[14] Although this permissive approach had its critics, it prevailed as the central axis around which debates about child rearing revolved.

In the cold war climate of postwar America, this discourse on children and authoritarianism was generally linked to discussions about America's supremacy in world affairs. Nowhere was this better demonstrated than in popular magazines, which continually endorsed the American way of life by comparing U.S. children to their foreign counterparts across the globe. While this crosscultural perspective on childhood was historically rooted in anthropological studies (especially Margaret Mead's 1928 *Coming of Age in Samoa* and her 1949 *Male and Female: A Study of the Sexes in a Changing World*), in the postwar popular literature, critics were less concerned with questions of nature versus nurture than they were with questions of "us" versus "them." According to the logic of the popular press, children of other countries suffered from an ill-conceived relation between the nation and private life, and this in turn robbed them of their childhood.

Most emphatically here, the Communist nation served as the measure of American superiority. Comparisons between American and Soviet children often stressed the ways in which the Soviets had lost their childhood to the disciplinary will of the state. In 1961, *Saturday Review* asked its readers to consider what happens "When the State Brings up the Child." A cartoon at the top of the page encapsulated the general theme by including a split screen rendering of an American versus a Soviet family. The American family and their adoring dog were gathered together in their yard, with a church spire set in the distance. The Russian family, however, was metaphorically divided by the state as the parents posed like spies at a barbed wire fence, secretly gazing at their youngsters who were huddled in a school yard that looked ominously like a prison. To demonstrate its graphic point, the article detailed Chairman Nikita Khrushchev's plan to place all children in boarding schools, which "in essence . . . means complete domination of the home by the state and the breakup of the family as the basic unit of the new society."[15] Other articles suggested that not only family life but childhood itself was being sacrificed to the state. The grueling amount of schoolwork and the austerity of everyday life resulted in a world without childhood pleasures, which accounted for "the precociously adult-like behavior of Soviet children."[16]

This trope of lost childhood also ran through articles about children from other nations. In the war-torn, Communist-occupied countries of Eastern Europe and Korea, in the poverty-stricken regions of Western Europe, and in nonindustrialized countries, the hardships of life created such strict demands on youngsters that, as one article put it, they became "children without childishness."[17] Despite their value in creating obedient youth, it was argued, the Old World disciplinary techniques of Western Europe stifled children and impaired their ability to mature into free-spirited individuals prepared for the modern world. The British, with their overly protective nannies turned their boys into "fops"; the disciplinarian Germans transformed "Hans and Gretal" into "sneaks"; the upper-class Parisians created solemn "elderly gentleman"; or even worse, the lower-class Frenchmen, with their untamed passions, abused their young in the most violent of ways.[18] A 1956 article in *Look* titled "Lost Childhood" detailed the "new crisis in France" that put youngsters at peril. It described the miserable fate of one Jean-Pierre "who never knew the shining joy of childhood" due to the fact that his "indulgent" mother and his equally irresponsible father were feeding him a steady diet of wine. In between the swigs, as the photo layout demonstrated, his parents delivered him a "stinging wallop." Moreover, the wine and wallops dulled Jean-Pierre's brain, making him vulnerable to the low pleasures of mass culture—specifically comic books. One photo showed his "heavy-handed" mother who "lashes out suddenly at Jean-Pierre when he persists in looking at [a] comic book instead of finishing lessons."[19] Thus, according to popular wisdom, and in a variety of ways, the social customs and political conditions in foreign nations had robbed children of their right to be children. In the process, childhood became synonymous with America—the only place where it still existed.

In the context of this discourse on childhood, freedom, and national supremacy, the postwar kid strip contributed its own folksy wisdom. The figure of the "kid" became a conduit for larger social concerns, not just about family life, but also about the free world itself. As postwar social critics such as John Keats pondered over the massive conformity of "Mr. and Mrs. Drone" in the new suburban middle class, as sociologists such as William H. Whyte worried about the effects of bureaucracy on the "organization man," and as critics such as Betty Friedan became increasingly critical about the middle-class housewife's confinement in the doldrums of suburbia, the "kid" served as a perfect vehicle for thinking through the authoritarian structures of the postwar world.[20] It is in these contexts that the first two decades of *Dennis* and *Peanuts* might best be explored.

Menace or Egghead? Defining the American Kid

If foreign children suffered from an overdose of discipline, the reigning ethos in *Dennis the Menace* and *Peanuts* was the child's unbridled freedom. In line with the ideals of permissive child rearing, both strips shared a fascination with childhood as a time of exploration, a time when children played without fear of retaliation from their parents or any other social institution.

In *Dennis*, parents functioned like the "helper" characters of the folktale; they were there simply to aid in the adventures of the central hero. Mr. and Mrs. Mitchell practiced the "spare the rod" approach with a vengeance to the dismay of their more authoritarian neighbor, Mr. Wilson, who for all his bellowing, was completely unable to control the boy. Because the daily *Dennis* strips were single black-and-white panels rather than narrative sequences, Ketcham typically presented his hero in a kind of "caught-in-the-act" family snapshot that encapsulated Dennis's misadventures, drawn to scale from the child's point of view. The humor in the strips was initially directed at adults (although later in the series, when Ketcham realized that the strip had caught on with children, he directed it at both audiences). Ketcham often evoked humor by making adults and children alike laugh at the standards of middle-class adult decorum. In numerous panels, Dennis unveiled the secrets of parlor etiquette by telling guests exactly those things his parents would say only behind their backs. Dennis, for example, unwittingly insults what appears to be his father's business associate when he announces, "Aw, do I have to go to bed? I wanted to see Mr. Reid talk through his hat!"[21] In other panels, Dennis upsets authoritarian structures of adult life, misunderstanding traffic cops or misbehaving in church.

Many of the panels set in Dennis's home poked fun at the gender roles of family life, with Dennis serving as a foil for his father's work-a-day world. In one panel from the 1950s, Dennis's father returns home from a day at work, dressed in suit and hat and looking bedraggled. As opposed to his father, Dennis has been overindulged in the pursuit of leisure, and the remains of his fun-packed day—melting ice cream cones, toys, and baseball bats—lay scattered on the floor. The caption reads, "We had a Party this Afternoon! You missed all the fun."[22] Like the stereotypical fifties' dad, when Mr. Mitchell is not at the office, he is working in the garden, and Dennis consistently finds ways to subvert his work into play. In one panel, Dennis shoots his famous slingshot at a hornet's nest while his exhausted father mows the lawn; in numerous others, Dennis finds ways to wreak havoc as his father toils in the smoke and heat of the barbecue pit. Meanwhile, Mrs. Mitchell, the quintessential fifties' housewife, is similarly sabotaged by Dennis's interruption of her household chores. For instance, in one panel, Mr. and Mrs. Mitchell's complete submission to their child's "natural" need for boyish fun is humorously depicted as a complete inversion of the power dynamics between adult and child. As his parents busily wash the dinner dishes, Dennis runs out the kitchen door and cheerily remarks, "So long, slaves."[23]

Analyzing *Dennis* in the context of permissive child-rearing literature, Henry Jenkins argues that the strip constituted a particular version of permissive discourse that was linked to generic conventions of "bad boy" comedy. Jenkins shows how Dennis straddled the line between two postwar notions of "bad" boys. On the one hand, he claims, Dennis was a demonic child, symptomatic of postwar fears that permissiveness might lead to juvenile delinquency. On the other hand (and especially when the series made its way to television), as the quintessential bad boy, Dennis also embodied American ideals. His misbehavior and disrespect for adult authority was often championed as a sign of unbridled curiosity, a natural and normal part of growing up in the free world. From this perspective, Jenkins contends that Dennis exemplified what critic Leslie Fiedler calls the "good bad boy," a mischief-maker who nevertheless represents a healthy disregard for established order and, for that reason, is celebrated as a sign of American manhood.[24]

The world of *Peanuts* revealed yet another articulation of American childhood. While *Peanuts* still embraced an escape from authority, it did so by drawing on conventions of "gang" comedy rather than the bad boy tradition.[25] Famous for its elliptical treatment of adult characters, *Peanuts* literally evacuated them from the child's world, providing instead a picture of children free to roam the green hills of suburbia. Although the concerns of adult life lurked in the shadows of this pensive strip, the children in *Peanuts* played with these constraints and found ways to resist them outside their parents' domain.

While *Peanuts* still embraced an escape from authority, it did so by drawing on conventions of "gang" comedy rather than the bad boy tradition.

As opposed to *Dennis*, which placed the reader in the child's point of view, *Peanuts* typically evoked humor by having its childish heroes take up the roles of adults—at least insofar as those roles were seen from a child's perspective. In a world without grownups, the *Peanuts* clan reestablished various authoritarian relationships common to the postwar social world. Lucy acted as a domineering mother to her younger brother Linus, the exact kind of mother that Dr. Spock would advise against. In strip after strip, Lucy dominates Linus's activities, bossing her brother with a barrage of yelling and following him through the neighborhood in the most overprotective of ways. Perhaps not surprisingly, Lucy's misguided child-rearing techniques resulted in a classic "authoritarian personality" disorder—insecurity. And her attempts to cure Linus of his blanket dependency by continuously taking the object from him were also completely ill conceived. Just like the domineering mother in the advice literature of the day, the more Lucy attempted to discipline the child, the more maladjusted Linus became.

This aspect of the strip was not lost on critics, who during the 1960s, often read *Peanuts* as a parable for adult relationships. Analyzing the personality traits of Snoopy,[26] Lucy, Charlie, Linus, and the entire *Peanuts* gang became a genre of pop criticism onto itself. In interviews, Schulz even participated in this game, commenting on the way he put "adult fears and anxieties into the conversation of the children." Furthermore, Schulz said he liked to think about the "off-stage" adult characters and their relationships to the kids. These speculations turned into various interpretations of child rearing and the way discipline (or the lack thereof) led to neuroses. In a 1969 interview, Schulz suggested:

> Linus's mother seems to be the peculiar one. As Charlie Brown once re-marked, 'I am beginning to understand why you drag that blanket around.' She seems to be obsessed with his doing well in school, and tried to spur him on by sneaking notes into his lunch which read, 'Study hard today. Your father and I are very proud of you and want you to get a good education.'[27]

Schulz's interest in education was symptomatic of post-Sputnik America, where concerns about pedagogy were often linked to the fear that the United States had fallen behind the Soviets. After the successful launching of the Soviet satellite in 1957, the media presented a host of anxieties about America's scientific agenda and, with that, the agenda for education (both in the sciences and humanities). Arthur S. Trace Jr.'s *What Ivan Knows that Johnny Doesn't* (1961) further fueled these worries, and critics of liberal education took this as a moment for a thorough critique of the school system's privileging of emotional growth over hard facts.

Although, as we have seen, the popular press often criticized the Soviets for their overly austere educational system, as with most expressions of national supremacy, such comparisons were riddled with ambivalence. In 1961, for example, the *New York Times Magazine* argued that the extreme amount of discipline in the life of Soviet children could be interpreted from two angles. Admitting that some would see this disciplinary regime as the path to a conformist society (the authoritarian personality critique), the article nevertheless also concluded that

> in the realm of education the Communists are giving systematic attention and major emphasis to training in values and behavior consistent with their ideals. We can hardly claim we are doing as much or as well for our own value system. . . . Yet we are fond of saying that the American school is the bulwark of democracy. If this be, we had better look to our defenses.[28]

But the debates about childhood and education were even more complex than the "us" versus "them" logic that ran through this article. It wasn't only the Soviets that Americans defended themselves against, but also Europeans. Magazine articles comparing American to European children often indicated a "nature versus culture" logic in which too much of the latter resulted in "unnatural" habits—especially of the sexual kind. A 1953 *New York Times* article about two British boys who moved to America is a perfect example of the way European intellectualism was connected to homophobic fears about "sissies." "By American standards," the article claimed, British boys are "a little foppish," scrubbed and brushed "like apples (whereas to an American taste a little dirt and disorder would be signs of a real boy)." The accompanying "before and after" cartoon pictured the "demure little Londoners" complete with knee-length schoolboy suits and reading books by A. A. Milne. After eighteen months in America, the fops had been turned into "real boys"—here depicted as cowboys and spacemen, shooting each other in the back and reading space comics.[29] Thus, even if Americans needed to beef up their educational system to compete with Russia, there was always the nagging possibility that too much intellect would rob the good old American boy of his manhood and turn him into a European dandy.

In the contours of this debate, *Dennis the Menace* and *Peanuts* can be seen to work through a series of tensions and uncertainties about what it meant to be an American. While both strips presented popular visions of American children at play, they expressed different attitudes toward the child that belied fundamental ambivalences at the heart of the nationalist discourses described above.

Dennis was the more anti-intellectual version of American childhood. With his overalls, slingshot, and ruffled cowlick, he was decidedly not a "fop," a point hammered home in panels where he begrudgingly wore his Sunday best. In one such panel, he asks, "Why do I have to dress up. . . . Who am I tryin' to kid?"[30] In another, after having torn his suit in a fistfight, he tells his parents, "I was just sittin' there, keepin' clean, when this kid says, 'Hi, sissy.' "[31] As opposed to the squeaky clean sissy, Dennis was always ready to battle the elements. He went on camping trips, dug up flower beds, captured frogs, and soiled the civilized space of the family home with the dirty tracks of nature.

As the ultimate nature boy, Dennis clearly didn't care much for science or any other intellectual concerns. When he visited the library on a rainy day, his approach to scholarship was more outdoorsy than philosophical. At the checkout desk, he opens an oversized book, puts it on his head like a hat, and tells another boy, "Better get a BIG book! It's raining cats and dogs!"[32] His disregard for learning and disdain for adult authority carried over into his attitude toward school. Ketcham portrays school as one of a myriad of authoritarian institutions that restrain the child's liberties. In one strip, for instance, Dennis and a friend stand with noses pressed against the schoolyard gate. Obviously wishing to bust loose, they slip a note to a passerby on the other side. The caption reads, "Please take this message to the outside world."[33] Dennis, in short, views school as a kind of prison, an obstacle to his natural rights to freedom, and Ketcham usually asks the reader to sympathize with this child's point of view. In fact, when considering why Dennis never grew up in the strip, Ketcham said, "I don't want him to enter the educational system. . . . He's too old for the playpen and too young for jail."[34] Ketcham's distrust of the school system was reciprocated by the parent-teacher association (PTA) which criticized the television series on the grounds that the "devilish" Dennis set a bad example for children.[35]

In fact, on television, where the live-action Dennis did grow up, the character was presented as an average, even lazy, student. As one episode made clear, Dennis's averageness was a mark of pride for the family. After Dennis puts a piece of bubble gum on an IQ test at school, the computer mistakenly scores him as a genius. As a result of his new egghead status, Dennis loses his school chums and becomes increasingly despondent. The happy revelation that Dennis is, in fact, not a genius comes as comic relief, and Dennis immediately turns back to his menacing ways. In the context of Sputnik and the education race with Russia, this episode took a firm stand against those critics of American childhood who called for greater intellectual achievements. Intellectualism was the opposite of childhood in Dennis; the egghead was the ultimate threat to the pleasures and freedoms of American youth.

Despite the often anti-intellectual tone of both the strip and television version, Dennis the Menace was not simply a rejection of intelligence. While loathing the "egghead" and disciplinary education, the strip did appeal to the more populist (and racist) assumption that American boys (or at least white boys) had a natural curiosity, an innate capacity for supremacy in all endeavors and over all "others." For this reason, Dennis was considered by some to be an antidote to America's post-Sputnik fears about the state of Johnny's education in relation to Ivan's. As Jenkins notes, some critics of the day embraced Dennis for his natural curiosity and sense of exploration, seeing this as exemplary of "the very qualities we would prize in him twenty years from now in a laboratory."[36]

Like Dennis, Peanuts also glorified childhood play in pastoral settings—especially in its many panels depicting baseball games, football practice, and kite flying. But unlike Dennis, the Peanuts kids were more than just naturally curious; instead, they often openly welcomed school and intellectual pursuits. As opposed to Dennis, Charlie Brown and his friends read books. As Sally enthuses, "Happiness is having your own library card!"[37] And while Dennis made intellectuals the butt of a joke, Peanuts's humor frequently arose when intellectualism was put into the "mouths of babes." In 1961, when asked the basis of the strip's appeal, Schulz replied, "Well, it deals in intelligent things . . . the characters do talk like adults. . . . It makes their language hilarious."[38]

Despite the humor, Schulz's style of deliberately drawn lines gave his children an aura of seriousness. Charlie Brown's rotund body is weighted by the world, and his huge oval head begs the question, "What is he thinking and why?" Charlie is a literal egghead. Even Snoopy became (over the course of the fifties) a serious thinker with an active fantasy life. In the television series and motion pictures, the use of Vince Guaraldi's modern jazz piano on the sound track further suggested the "egghead" status of the strip. And of course, the *Peanuts* kids themselves took up an interest in adult intellect and high culture. Lucy set up shop as the neighborhood psychiatrist, Schroeder played Beethoven on his toy piano, Linus wanted to be an artist and read the classics, and over the years Snoopy donned a variety of erudite guises, from Sherlock Holmes to chess master. Moreover, while Schulz never showed the inside of Snoopy's doghouse, he did make it clear that Snoopy was an art connoisseur who lined his walls with a collection of modern masterpieces from van Goghs to Andrew Wyeths. Even though these examples could be read as parodies of professionalism and "highbrow" arts, they encouraged readers to think about childhood in relation to (and not simply as a rejection of) intellectual concerns.[39]

The different attitudes that *Dennis* and *Peanuts* took toward intellectualism were written into their cartoon styles. *Dennis* had an aura of commercial art, which Ketcham's early years at Disney might have encouraged. The strip's caricatures of family life fleshed out a detailed picture of the modern home filled with middle-class appointments. Ketcham was so concerned with producing an accurate and up-to-date portrayal of middle-class life that when he lived in Switzerland in the 1960s, he used the Sears catalog to follow trends in American domestic appliances and home furnishings.[40] *Dennis* was, in this sense, a genre piece that could be found in previous family comic strip portraits such as *Blondie* as well as in numerous magazine cartoons of the day. To execute his vision, Ketcham adopted a mass production attitude to the strip, hiring a team of commercial artists to illustrate his creation.

Meanwhile, his character Dennis often espoused a clear dislike for the intellectual circles of modern art of all kinds. In one panel, Dennis is pictured in a neighbor's home where modernist furniture and abstract paintings line the living room walls. Dennis exclaims, "Gee, if ya like THAT kind of pitchers, I can get ya whole kiddiegarter wall full!" In another, on a trip to an art museum, Dennis stares at modern paintings and complains, "SOME art place! Not even one picture of Santa Claus!"[41] Throughout the development of his comic strip oeuvre, Ketcham seems to have retained this disdain for modern art. Even in the 1980s, Dennis could still be found in a museum remarking, "I forgot, was Picasso in the second or the third grade?"[42] As opposed to Snoopy, who revels in the European modernist masters, Dennis delights in knocking them off their museum pedestals.

Although Ketcham never directly makes the link, it should be noted that his view of the modernist aesthetic also had nationalist implications during this period. Numerous critics saw modernism, with its roots in the European avant-garde, as patently subversive. The debate encompassed not only museum art, but also the more popular arts of home decor. In 1953, Elizabeth Gordon, the editor of *House Beautiful*, wrote an editorial titled "The Threat to the Next America" that argued modernism was an international conspiracy originating in Nazi Germany with the machine aesthetics of the Bauhaus school.[43] In his (albeit innocent) disdain for the high modernism of the European—and by now American—intelligentsia, Dennis thus espoused a view consistent with a populist notion of a distinctly American art that was skeptical of modernism's international roots.[44]

Schulz, on the other hand, represented an alternative strain in this nationalist rhetoric on the arts. As Serge Guilbaut demonstrates, while some critics mistrusted modern art, others embraced the burgeoning forms of modern American painting—especially abstract expressionism—as exemplary of the individual's freedom of self-expression in the "new liberalism" of postwar America.[45] From this standpoint, American artists like Jackson Pollock were hailed for their ability to use abstraction to express their own individuality. While Schulz did not travel in these fine art circles, his relation to his strip—and the responses he received—was very much in line with the idea that American art forms were exemplary of the artist's individual freedom, the right to make meanings that weren't necessarily in line with the goals of governments or corporations.

Indeed, unlike Ketcham, Schulz prided himself on the fact that he drew the strip alone, without the mass production techniques of a Disneyesque enterprise (a point that critics of the times also noted).[46] In 1961, Schulz (reportedly with some "grinning modesty") referred to his strip as a "work of art." Later, in 1969, he revised this slightly by suggesting that while comics are not "great art," they are among the "popular arts."[47] At the time that Schulz said this, the comic form was already being resurrected as "art" by intellectuals and collectors, and critics thought seriously about the philosophical things that comics had to say.

Certainly, Schulz's drawing style encouraged readers to think about his strip's meaning. Over the course of the 1950s, Schulz increasingly moved away from realistic rendering to more elliptical sketches. Unlike Ketcham's detailed mise-en-scène, Schulz's minimalist style (a line or two to connote emotion on the face, and sometimes as little as a horizon line to indicate a setting) asked the reader to imaginatively fill in the empty spaces. In fact, so minimal were his designs that his editors sometimes had to remind Schulz to draw the horizon line in the background.[48] One strip even presents a parable of the minimalist ethos when Linus draws a picture of Lucy that lacks her famous mouth. When Lucy demands that Linus draw her mouth, he tells her that it's "wrong to rush a work of art," but finally gives in and sketches an unflattering portrait of Lucy's big mouth. In return for his attempts to portray her in this more realistic fashion, Lucy socks Linus in the head.[49] Abstraction, then, has the advantage of discouraging instant recognition, and like other *Peanuts* stories, this one elicited critical reflection on the nature of the comic strip medium itself.

Still, it seems unlikely that Schulz intended these self-reflexive moments in the context of an avant-garde aesthetic. Instead, self-reflexivity in *Peanuts* appears connected to Schulz's deeply religious background. *Peanuts* reflects back on its own moral function as art, continually asking the reader to question the set of expectations one has when reading the funnies. The stories resolve less in "punch lines" than in fundamental queries about the nature of life.[50] Perhaps for this reason, numerous intellectuals, from psychiatrists to semioticians, found *Peanuts* an ideal metaphor for the human dilemma itself. In 1966, the strip even became fodder for Protestant Minister Robert L. Short, whose popular book, *The Gospel according to Peanuts*, envisioned *Peanuts* not through the terms of postwar permissive childrearing, but rather as a puritanical conception of childhood: he saw *Peanuts* as a parable for original sin.[51]

More generally, we might assume, both *Peanuts* and *Dennis* allowed a diverse reading public to think about the various tensions involved in defining the child and, with that, the nation. Were we a nation of eggheads or menaces? Or were we the last bastion of the free world—the only place on earth where children could escape authoritarian control? Like all artifacts of culture, these comics could certainly be read in a variety of ways, but the prospects that they proposed spoke to the larger social imagination where childhood was the ultimate measure of the nation.

It's a Small World: The Child Explorer

In both *Peanuts* and *Dennis*, the concern with freedom and discipline was often communicated through stories about children's abilities to master space in their suburban environs. If in social reality the mass-produced suburb was a place of insular domesticity where gates, cramped backyards, playpens, and cranky neighbors all served to constrict children's play, in the strips the burbs were places that children could control and dominate. In *Peanuts*, where adults exist only via elliptical allusion, children easily move from home to home. Without their parents' supervision, they open doors for one another, effectively controlling all entrances and exits in and out of the houses. By extension, these children propel the narrative progress of the strip itself, allowing the reader figuratively to move across the space of the story. Just as they control domestic space, the *Peanuts* kids move freely around the idyllic world of nature that constitutes their fictional neighborhood. The only character that seems to have any notion of property laws is Snoopy, who makes sure to keep his doghouse free of all human presence (including, of course, the reader, who is also denied access to the doghouse interior).

Ketcham's strip even more deliberately makes the child's domination over space the fodder for jokes about adult notions of property and propriety in the suburban town.[52] To the dismay of all grown-ups, Dennis constantly appears in places that he does not belong, turning adult property laws on their side. Despite the wishes of his cranky neighbor, he repeatedly appears in Mr. Wilson's home and garden, running amok through the flower beds and intruding on Mrs. Wilson's private parties. When he's bored with Mr. Wilson, he moves on to other neighbors, popping up in the most unexpected places. In one panel, he appears in the bathroom of his new neighbor, who is in the middle of taking a shower. Dennis pulls open the shower curtain and enthuses, "Hi! Remember me? I'm the little boy the real estate guy told you didn't live in this neighborhood."[53] Dennis also created mayhem in public spaces, losing his frog in a crowded elevator or breaking objects at a store. When his parents attempt to discipline his travels, he immediately finds escape clauses. One panel shows Mr. and Mrs. Mitchell trying to open the bathroom door, which Dennis has apparently locked himself behind. But Dennis outsmarts his parents, and entering the room from another door, boasts, "Hi! I'm not in there anymore. I got out the window."[54] More generally, when Dennis doesn't like the rules laid down by his parents, he grabs his things up in a bandanna, ties them to a stick in a hobo style, and runs away from home.

The child's ability to master space was, by the time of *Dennis* and *Peanuts*, a common convention in children's culture. The *Rollo Series*, one of the very first U.S. school primers, appearing in the 1830s, told adventure tales of boy travelers who explored exciting places. In the second *Rollo Series*, for example, young Rollo and his family members tour an array of European cities.[55] In the twentieth century, book series such as the *Hardy Boys*—as well as comics, movies, and radio and television programs—further popularized the figure of the child explorer. Sometimes in such tales, children journeyed to those locales (such as China or Africa) that were typically exoticized in the Western imagina-

Ready or not, here comes Dennis with a brand-new bagful of mirth, mayhem and monkeyshines

As the title of a 1961 edition put it, Dennis was the *Ambassador of Mischief*.

tion. In this regard, their exploits took on the colonialist tropes of more well-established "New World" narratives where white Europeans encroached on the "savage" and "primitive" cultures in other lands.

In the postwar kid strip, these conquest narratives took place in the suburban neighborhood itself. Schulz, in fact, admits that he originally wanted to draw an adventure strip like *Terry and the Pirates, Steve Canyon,* or *Prince Valiant*. While his kid strip was less fantastic, Snoopy opened up an imaginary space of endless conquest and foreign intrigue, a surrealistic space that existed somewhere in the "unconscious" of the suburban family dog. In his expansive imagination, Snoopy went to France, the Sahara, Mexico, Alaska, and a host of other places including, of course, the moon. Despite their humorous bent, Snoopy's journeys were imbricated in the more threatening side of travel—namely, military conquest. Inside Charlie Brown's bedroom community was a virtual war zone, embodied most graphically by Fort Zinderneuf, which as a member of the French foreign legion, Snoopy furtively patrolled. In October 1965, Snoopy donned his famous World War I flying ace helmet and set out in hot pursuit of the Red Baron. Schulz decided in the midst of Vietnam that war was no longer funny, and temporarily dropped the Red Baron theme in 1969.[56] But war scenarios continued in the following decades. In the 1980s, Schulz presented television specials such as *What Have We Learned, Charlie Brown?* (1983), which pays homage to the Allied invasion of Fortress Europe, as the *Peanuts* cast tours the Normandy battlefields.[57]

In *Dennis*, the little boy's freedom to roam was also communicated through foreign intrigue. Hall Syndicate and Fawcett Books published a series of junior travel books in the early 1960s featuring Dennis's adventures in various parts of the world, including Hollywood, Hawaii, and Mexico. In 1961, Holt, Reinhart and Winston released a book that detailed Dennis's trip to the Soviet Union, not so subtly titled *I Want to Go Home*. Meanwhile, in the book-length collections of strips that Fawcett produced in the early 1960s, Dennis's "bad boy" persona was linked explicitly to his status as a representation not just of childhood, but of nationhood as well. As the title of a 1961 edition put it, Dennis was the *Ambassador of Mischief*. And as the inside cover further announced, he was "zooming far above the range of guided missiles and diplomatic conferences . . . to a new summit of success. On his round-the-world mission of mischief he has disarmed entire nations via press and airwaves" with his "live frogs and devilry."[58]

More typically, Dennis's expeditions were connected to the Western genre as numerous panels depicted him in the role of cowboy. At a time when Disney's television portrayal of Davy Crockett turned the coonskin cap and cowboy suit into a popular fad, Dennis wreaked havoc on the suburban ranch house. Clad in his cowboy best, Dennis wakes his father by shooting arrows at his head. In another panel, Dennis plays the masked bandit, sneaking treats from the cookie jar.[59]

While the figure of the little cowboy out on the lonesome suburban prairie was certainly intended in jest, it wasn't necessarily so funny to all Americans, especially those who had been forced out of this new frontier. If in the old West the colonized groups were Native Americans, in the new suburban towns the subjects of exclusion comprised a wider range of ethnic and racial minorities as well as social outcasts that simply didn't fit into the family ideal. Government loans to builders and prospective buyers favored redlining (or zoning) practices that effectively kept people of color out of the neighborhood. Suburban architecture and community space was designed for nuclear families rather than lesbians, gays, or any other group that did not conform to community "standards." This design for living was, of course, inscribed in the strips themselves as the fictional neighborhoods (at least as they were originally conceived) were entirely homogeneous.

In their unbridled travels across the suburban frontier, kid characters, like all cowboys before them, defined who belonged on their turf and who did not. Dennis, for example, often found "indigents" living in the park and commented wryly on their unfamiliar ways. In one panel, when Dennis comes across a beatnik loafing on a park bench, he says to his pal Joey, "I must be growin'! Did you notice he kept callin' me 'man'?" The strangeness of the beatnik is further suggested by the fact that the park is filled with couples—parents and kids, husbands and wives, and even birds huddled together in family scenes. The beatnik is a loner, whose strange clothes and dark shades clearly don't belong in Dennis's world. Similarly, in another park scene, Dennis comes across a bum. "Boy are you lucky!" Dennis exclaims. "You mean nobody never tells you ya gotta get cleaned up?" In the background, a man in a business suit looks on with some surprise, although it's perhaps intentionally unclear whether this man is more shocked at the bum's presence in the park or Dennis's reverence for the tramp's unseemly lifestyle.⁶⁰ In these and other strips, Dennis implicitly demonstrates who doesn't fit in the suburbs; significantly, these misfits were dropouts (always single men) who served no purpose in the social maintenance of family life. If in the 1950s and 1960s the strip presented these tales of exclusion as innocent good clean fun, by the summer of 1993, the more sadistic elements of this joke were hard to miss. Indeed, the 1993 film takes this to a violent extreme, when the homeless man is posed not simply as a "moocher," but as a kidnapper who Dennis finally (and according to the film, justifiably) sets on fire.

Most important for our purposes, however, is the fact that these scenarios never once mention the more typical targets of suburban exclusion—people of color. Further, given the postwar suburb's actual ethnic and religious mix of second-generation European immigrants, it is even more surprising that these strips presented a world of Anglo-Americans with almost no representation of national heritage other than an imaginary idea of "Americanness." In this regard, it is especially worth noting those instances when national difference does become a central story element.

A 1962 television episode of Dennis the Menace is a perfect example. Here, the "good neighbor" policy is dramatically rendered as a young Chinese girl comes to visit the Wilson household. Dennis immediately develops a schoolboy crush, and the two set up a "date" in which they share their respective cultural heritage. The exchange comes in the form of a culinary lesson on the supremacy of American tastes—not only in food, but in child rearing. At the Wilson's home, Sen Yuen and Dennis share Chinese cuisine (a theme that also ran through various *Dennis* panels in which Dennis goes to Chinese restaurants and creates chaos because of his failure to understand their "mysterious" eating customs). After lunch, Dennis invites Sen Yuen to the malt shop, only to discover that this poor China girl has never eaten a banana split or, for that matter, any really good dessert. Dennis's shock at this revelation dramatically underscores the idea that foreign children simply have no childhood fun. This lesson is then narratively linked to another revelation—that Sen Yuen, like all Chinese girls of her age, is already promised in marriage. As this suggests, Sen Yuen has no freedom of choice in a culture based on marriage contracts. The episode then turns onto a thinly veiled lesson in miscegenation in which Dennis, through a series of narrative confusions, fears that he is her promised groom and runs for his life.

This innocent tale of national supremacy was, then, linked to a story about courtship and the little boy's fears of female sexuality. More often, the adventures of the child explorer were connected to conquests of another kind— romantic ones, which the girls in these strips most aggressively attempted. Lucy's endless struggles to win the affections of Schroeder, as well as Margaret's fierce efforts to get Dennis to the altar, were running gags over the years.[61] As Ketcham notes: "There is a Margaret Wade in every man's life. James Thurber knew her simply as Woman. Threatening, bossy, superior, always pursuing, the incipient castrator."[62] In the television episode described above, this fear of "woman" is directly related to a nationalist discourse that hinges on the competition between two female types: the American "loudmouth" and the exotic, mysterious "Oriental" girl. Dennis initially opts for the latter, which sets in motion a tale of female jealousy between East and West as Margaret desperately tries to win Dennis's affections.

This episode, and the figure of the loudmouth girl, are interesting in light of Nancy Armstrong's observation in "Occidental Alice."[63] In this reading of *Alice in Wonderland*, Armstrong shows how British imperialism depended on a representation of women as both out of control (possessed of consumer appetites) and self-regulated by taste. Armstrong argues that women with unruly appetites had historically been connected to prostitutes or native others, against which the proper British woman was defined. In a burgeoning consumer society, however, British women also became associated with the lust for things. The Victorian consumer, in this context, was marked as a good woman to the extent that she internalized taste as a means of self-control. Reading *Alice in Wonderland* as a parable of this "double-bodied" woman, she reveals how Alice's appetite for food was deemed improper (and potentially threatening to her figure). Rather than suffering distortions to her body, Alice must learn to regulate this appetite through adopting British tastes. Armstrong further shows how the story centers not simply around food, but around orality itself, and the little girl's mouth especially. In the episode of *Dennis the Menace*, we see a curious manifestation of this narrative logic. Now, the bad or unruly girl is Margaret, the Western loudmouth. Yet unlike Alice, who learns to control her appetite, Margaret is doomed to her brash, loudmouth ways. Taste is instead embodied in the Orient. But, as the episode suggests, the Orient is too rule governed, and it lacks the appropriate display of appetite and consumer pleasure. Faced with these two versions of femininity, Dennis finally rejects both, opting to return to the world of boys. In the process, however, the Occident and Orient are set in competition with each other through the figure of the girl.

Competition between female types from different nations is, in fact, something that Ketcham himself recognizes as an ongoing theme of his strip. When speaking about Gina Gillotti, an Italian American in Dennis's otherwise homogeneous suburb, Ketcham immediately compares her to her all-American counterpart, Margaret. He recalls, "We needed another ethnic group. And . . . I thought a cute little [Italian] gal would be fun to do and something to offset the rather brash feminist Margaret and her attempted conquest."[64]

Ketcham's recognition of the need for ethnic diversity was probably less a personal revelation than a response to wider demands and pressures on the comic strip industry generally. Since the early 1940s, African Americans had protested the racist stereotypes in strips such as *Joe Palooka*, *Happy Hooligan*, and *Barney Google*. But as *Ebony* noted in 1966, the comic industry responded to such protests mostly through omission, so that "Negroes—caricatures or otherwise—became noticeably absent from the comic pages."[65] By the mid-1960s, numerous black artists began to fill the void with a variety of comic strip genres. In 1965, Morrie Turner inaugurated *Wee Pals*, which *Ebony* dubbed, "the first truly integrated strip"; it included not just Caucasians and African Americans, but a multiracial cast who boasted of their "rainbow power."[66] Turner claims that he based his strip on the highly popular *Peanuts*, but his multiracial cast made it difficult to sell outside large urban areas. "They don't want to take a chance of offending some of their readers by having a feature with integrated children playing together," Turner told *Ebony* in 1966.[67] Still, Turner paved the way for a new representation of the American kid, and although in different ways, both Schulz and Ketcham responded to the demands of integration.

In 1968, Schulz introduced a black character, Franklin, who in an early strip, was invited to Charlie Brown's home. According to Schulz's biographer, "a worried syndicate executive didn't really object to Franklin's inclusion so much, but: did Charlie Brown have to invite him directly into his home?"[68] Schulz claims that he initially shied away from presenting a black character because he "didn't want to do it with a patronizing attitude."[69] It seems likely

In 1965, Morrie Turner inaugurated *Wee Pals*, which *Ebony* dubbed, "the first truly integrated strip."

that Turner's *Wee Pals* provided a model through which Schulz could imagine drawing a black child in less patronizing ways (like Turner, for example, Schulz used diagonal lines rather than the more stereotypical—and controversial—use of solid black to indicate skin color).[70] But Schulz never really developed Franklin's character, nor did he add more racial and ethnic diversity. Instead, race was displayed onto class difference when he included several white children like Marcie and Peppermint Patty who went to a tougher school on the other side of town. Despite these changes, Schulz still centered the strip around his middle-class white suburban town, and as might be expected, some critics were not pleased. In 1970, *Luther* artist Brumsic Brandon Jr. said, "*Peanuts* enjoys a universality among the white community. . . . But to the black community he's a little white boy."[71] One year later, Reverend Cecil Williams of San Francisco's Glide Memorial Church pointed out that "Schulz has stayed away from civil rights and social issues that relate to the Third World and especially black people."[72]

Like Schulz, in the late 1960s, Ketcham also added a black character named Jackson. In his autobiography, Ketcham claims he was "determined to join the parade led by Dr. Martin Luther King Jr., and introduce a black playmate to the Mitchell neighborhood." But unlike Schulz, Ketcham failed to consider the patronizing tone of his character. Ketcham recalls, "I designed him in the tradition of Little Black Sambo with huge lips, big white eyes, and just a suggestion of an Afro hairstyle." In the first panel, Ketcham made race the subject of a gag as Dennis tells his mother, "I have a race problem with Jackson. He can run faster than me!" While Ketcham still contends that this was a "harmless little play on words" and his "Stepin Fetchit" rendering was an "innocent cartoon," Jackson set off protests that began in Detroit and spread to cities across the nation.[73] As Ketcham remembers it, "the odds were against me pleasing everyone, so I just backed away."[74] More generally, Ketcham remains resolute that his characters should not be taken as role models for the real world, whether it be in terms of race, gender roles, or simple behaviors like Henry's pipe smoking. Rather, argues Ketcham, "these people behave and look the way they behave and look, and live where they live, because that's the way I want it. . . . This is my space, and I'm going to occupy it in my fashion."[75] Given Dennis's colonialist adventures, perhaps it is no coincidence that Ketcham's description of his comic strip production is itself a colonialist narrative about occupied territories and the rights of the artist literally to own space.

Colonizing the Market: The Meaning of Diversity

To be sure, neither Ketcham nor Schulz did much to diversify their neighborhoods, beyond their token gestures. Instead, they both pursued another kind of diversification that took place outside their fictional strips in the real world of market capitalism. Like their childish heroes, both artists assertively sought to place themselves in as many spaces as possible. Most literally here, in 1956, Ketcham opened the Dennis the Menace Playground in Monterey, California, and Schulz established a separate corporation in 1971 (called Snoopy Co.) to build a theme park on the outskirts of Disneyland. Although Schulz's plans never materialized, he did strike a deal with Knott's Berry Farm, which now includes Camp Snoopy as a separate attraction. Aside from their infiltration of the theme park tourist trade, both Ketcham and Schulz expanded their narrative spaces outside the strip into a host of related products, from Dennis toy rockets to Snoopy lamps.[76] In fact, as mentioned early on, Schulz was most agressive in this business; by 1971, *Newsweek* called his strip a "commercial empire" with thirty tie-in companies and a gross national income of $150 million.[77] Over the course of two decades, *Peanuts* had become the most popular strip in history.

Still, at least in the case of *Peanuts*, this forceful colonization of the market was not without its critics, who by the late 1960s, began to complain about the proliferation of product spin-offs. Perhaps it is no coincidence that such complaints circulated at a time when comics, and *Peanuts* in particular, were beginning to be conceptualized as "art." One critic for *Look* lambasted the spate of commercial tie-in books by comparing them to Picasso paintings and Nabokov novels. The very fact that this author found it appropriate to compare the *Peanuts* novelty book *Happiness Is a Warm Puppy* to Picasso's *Guernica* suggests that he, like other critics of his time, expected *Peanuts* to be art in the first place. Moreover, this diatribe against *Peanuts* was linked to fears about the commercialization of childhood itself. The critic lamented:

> Schulz first took a part of Charlie Brown away from me when he used his *Peanuts* characters in a series of ads for Falcon cars. I was hurt and puzzled to open a grown-up magazine and see my small friend touting a grown-up automobile. And why shouldn't I be? If there is one quality that particularly binds him to us as a character, it is his own hurt and puzzlement when innocence is betrayed.[78]

Look's adverse reaction to Charlie Brown's adventures on Madison Avenue can be understood in the context of the more widespread ambivalence about consumerism and children that circulated in both intellectual and popular culture. On the one hand, the ability to provide children with wondrous products became a hallmark not only of good parenting, but also of national pride. In the magazine literature that compared U.S. with foreign children, the opportunity to consume came to define the American way of life. In 1958, the vacation magazine *Holiday* reported on the misadventures of one American mother who tried to throw a birthday party for her son while on holiday in Moscow. With the inflated Russian economy, she could purchase only a pencil, some balloons, and a few other "cheap" items, and after searching the streets of Moscow, she discovered that Russians didn't have birthday cakes or gift wrap. The birthday party—the quintessential commodity display of affection between parent and child—became in Russia a shopping spree nightmare.[79]

On the other hand, even as the popular press championed American consumerism, it also presented parents with a stream of contradictory advice against "overindulgence" in the "synthetic pleasures" of consumer culture. Here, mass media aimed at children became key targets of attack. Dr. Fredric Wertham's *Seduction of the Innocent* (1953) lashed out at the comic's negative effects on youth, claiming that its violence and perverse sexuality could, among other things, lead to fascist tendencies. Although Wertham coupled his arguments on media effects with a critique of consumerism and American society, at the time, his theories became fodder for reactionary antimedia crusades launched both in popular venues (such as women's magazines) and Congress (Senator Estes Kefauver's 1954 hearings on juvenile delinquency featured Wertham as an expert witness).[80] Later in the decade, especially after the recession of 1957 and the Soviet launching of Sputnik, both intellectuals and the popular media became even more critical of the "affluent society," condemning American industry for putting its faith in consumer luxuries rather than the truly important goals of scientific progress and national security.

Not surprisingly, the postwar kid strip inherited the more general ambivalent attitudes toward children, consumer culture, and national supremacy that circulated at the period. At one level, *Peanuts* and *Dennis* glorified consumerism. These kid strip heroes had expensive toys, went on family vacations, and used their allowances to purchase objects of desire. Moreover, both strips depicted their kids as fervent fans of mass culture who bought baseball cards, watched television, and even read comics. Unlike their depression era cousin, Little Orphan Annie, Dennis and the *Peanuts* gang had no hardships to bear. Perhaps most revealingly here, when Little Orphan Annie took a job as a grocery clerk in 1947, venues such as the *Union Times* (a labor newspaper) cried out against the strip's endorsement of child labor: "Any suggestion they [children] be detoured into the bowels of industry or the business world is a menace to the very system and traditional progress that America represents."[81] In *Dennis* and *Peanuts*, the child was unquestionably divorced from the demands of capitalist production and associated with money only by way of consumer desire.

Still, as Jacqueline Rose has argued in her work on *Peter Pan*, in children's literature, money and childhood are always uncomfortably related.[82] From the adult's romantic and nostalgic vision, the child is ideally innocent of worldly woes. But money—even when used for consumption—reminds the reader that children are not immune to the problems that divide the adult world, including the divisions of a class-based society that money so fully organizes. Childhood, then, in popular imagery has often been connected to romantic notions of preindustrial, pastoral values separate from the world of market capitalism. Interestingly, however, in the popular imagination of the day, this return to innocence was not conducted through historical memories of America's own preindustrial, pastoral past, but instead through the geopolitical imagination of the "Third World." Indeed, rather than go back in time, Americans traveled across international space to imagine a world of childhood unsullied by modern life.

Here, popular magazine articles serve as a perfect example. As I mentioned early on, articles about nonindustrialized nations described in painstaking detail the social environments and personal poverty that had robbed children of their natural rights to childhood. Yet at the same time, they often presented romantic tales of the more simple pleasures available to the children of these lands. Holiday depicted the poverty-stricken life of a Cuban child named Juana, but in the most romantic way, it went on to describe the virtues of her simple island life, which according to the magazine, were encapsulated in a rhyme she loved to repeat: "Comer no comemos mucho / Pero rerire si no vemios mucho" ("We do not eat very well / but we can laugh, laugh like hell").[83] Similarly, in 1957, Parents claimed that Burmese children had more freedom because the "child's life space is not restricted [by] modern inventions to confine the energies of the young." The absence of modern commodities ranging from playpens to television sets helped make the Burmese "informal, spontaneous, optimistic, [and] tolerant," as opposed to the "busy, busy, busy" American.[84]

The connections between such images of international childhood and American national policy were especially pronounced in Edward Steichen's Family of Man exhibit, which appeared at the Caldren Gallery of Art in Washington, D.C. In a 1955 film made by the U.S. Information Service, Steichen takes the audience on a tour of the exhibit. He starts by admonishing the modern world filled with "hatred and fear," and then uses the image of a Third World child to appeal to us "as human beings." While offered as a humanitarian effort, the exhibit nevertheless was framed within the colonial gaze of the American photographer. Steichen continues, "We begin with a theme . . . a little Peruvian lad blowing the flute, blowing the little song, the song of life. In all his sweetness. The sweetness of a little dark man."[85] Even if Steichen used his image of this Third World child to evoke a kind of universal condition, his conflation of race with childhood innocence worked to infantilize people of color and assert the more sophisticated status of the First World. This becomes especially clear when Steichen compares the Peruvian boy to a tuba player in the French symphony or when he likens American children learning about Albert Einstein to a Middle Eastern child learning his "peculiar alphabet." Thus, even when Third World children were presented as "sweet" and untouched by the troubles of modern civilization, these images of childhood nevertheless reasserted the racist idea that in the end, the American child was in some way more knowledgeable, sophisticated, and evolved.

While such literal comparisons between American and Third World children did not appear explicitly in Dennis and Peanuts, the trope of the child native did manifest itself in significant ways. Here, Dennis and the Peanuts gang can be seen to be "modern primitives," children who lived in, but were as yet untouched by, the postwar industrial culture. The modern primitive, in this sense, is a figure who negotiates the competing ideals of modernity. On the one hand, as moderns, the kid strip children enjoyed the material goods of consumer capitalism, and in so doing, embodied the racist idea that modern capitalism was the product of a more evolved cultural, and even biological, form. On the other hand, as primitives, they also appreciated the simple life of nature and were able to find pleasure in "authentic" folk pastimes. Dennis always likes a good rock collection as much as a new toy rocket, while Charlie and the gang enjoy the "active" pastimes of arts and crafts or piano playing as much as they like to watch television (in fact, in numerous strips, they do both at once). In both the strips and television specials, Schulz often criticized the overcommercialization of Christmas and presented moralistic tales in which the *Peanuts* kids learn lessons about the more spiritual meanings of holidays like Thanksgiving or Valentine's Day. Sometimes, as in the case of Linus's furious Halloween search for the Great Pumpkin, Schulz even invented his own ritual traditions, so that in the most paradoxical of ways, his highly commercialized kid strip itself took on the status of an "authentic" children's folktale.

The Magic Passport: Childhood, Nation, and Nostalgia

In 1964, at the New York World's Fair, Walt Disney unveiled his popular theme park attraction, It's a Small World. A cruise around the globe, the ride whisks passengers across national cultures, each represented by a group of childlike dolls appropriately attired in native folk costume. Despite their sartorial difference, the children all sing the same "It's a Small World" song and all have the same message to share. And despite the humanist ethos, the small world cruise had the not-so-subtle overtones of Disney's more typical colonialist narrative. Dixieland jazz was the background theme for Africa (which the ride called the "mysterious dark continent"), and at the end of the cruise, the children of the world somehow all sang the English lyrics in a big-finish sing-along.[86]

I want to end this essay with a brief consideration of how these small world politics worked themselves out in the postwar kid strip, which like Disney, also depended on an international market for their phenomenal success. Given the nationalist rhetoric of *Dennis* and *Peanuts*, it is particularly interesting that these versions of Americana appealed to readers in distant lands. By 1990, *Peanuts* could be found in sixty-eight countries.[87] The international success of *Dennis* and the even more widespread popularity of *Peanuts* is certainly worthy of an essay of its own, but let me offer a few suggestions.

In the years after World War II, the comic strip industry had numerous problems with its image abroad. Since comics were widely read by American GIs stationed overseas, Europeans often associated them with American military occupation. In this regard, the comic conjured up the image of what one popular book called "the ugly American," the vulgar and uncultured brute who runs roughshod over foreign lands.[88] Insofar as wartime comics were themselves often blatantly racist, militaristic, and xenophobic, they further perpetuated the image of the ugly American in the minds of their readers. In Britain, Western and Eastern Europe, Japan, and the Soviet Union, American comics were variously called "psychological war preparation" and "ideological and moral poison," and several nations banned them.[89]

Despite the fact that American comics were frequently rejected in other nations, Schulz and Ketcham were convinced that their strips spoke a universal language, and U.S. media critics also indicated as much. To be sure, these kid strips were not the first visual media to be considered in terms of universal appeal. As opposed to the language-based texts that Benedict Anderson claims are integral to the "imagined community" of the nation, twentieth-century visual media (even dialogue-based media such as sound films, television, and comics) have often been conceptualized in terms of an *imagined global community* in which people in faraway spaces are joined together by a common lexicon of images. Of course, as is evident from the numerous protests in foreign countries, visual media are not interpreted the same way in all nations. Still, the utopian ideal of universality has been a central mode of understanding—and also legitimating—the spread of U.S. media abroad.[90]

The kid strip took this idea one step further by dealing exclusively with what was seen (at least in America and Western Europe) as a "universal" sign: the child, who according to popular wisdom, communicated the same message wherever it went. Paradoxically here, even while children were often used in discourses of national supremacy, childhood was nevertheless also considered the embodiment of "nature" outside culture. While child-rearing practices endemic to a nation could "ruin" the child, the child itself remained a blank slate. Both Ketcham and Schulz attributed their international popularity, as did many critics, to this "common language" of childhood and its immanent exportability. When asked about the reason for his international success, Ketcham claimed, "Any child, especially a male boy, a male child, preschool, is the same all over the world, regardless of what his culture is."[91] Ketcham's stress on "maleness" is particularly interesting in light of Donna Haraway's analysis of the anthropological sciences, where the "male" specimen is typically considered to be representative of the entire species.[92] Just as in the jungle, in the international image market, the male child seems to function precisely as a form of universal exchange currency—Dennis, Charlie Brown, and even male-coded animal characters like Snoopy are representatives of an essential humanity that exists prior to civilization (which in these strips, is generally associated with the girl characters Margaret and Lucy, who both want to domesticate the boys).

There were, of course, moments when these kid strips did not translate universally across cultures. When Ketcham went to Moscow in 1959, an editor at the humor magazine *Krokodil* asked, "What possible interest would avail readers in the Soviet Union to follow the adventures of a naughty child whose misbehavior is so self-evident due to the defects of a capitalistic society?"[93] And while Charlie Brown was immensely popular overseas, some countries initially failed to see its humor. The strip, for example, took two decades to spark the cultural imagination of France.[94]

By the 1970s, the kid strip became increasingly subject to international controversy. Worried about the amount of *Peanuts* (as well as *Donald Duck* and other American strips) in its nation's press, Brazil's National Executive Comic Strip Commission announced plans to establish a quota system. Despite the fact that U.S. newspapers have historically been entirely devoid of foreign comics, the *Wall Street Journal* found the quota system so offensive that it called for protectionist legislation, and mimicking the "innocent" wisdom of Charlie Brown, cried "Good Grief!" to the whole affair.[95] The *Journal* exclaimed "Good Grief!" a second time when Reverend Cecil Williams suggested that *Peanuts* should deal with Third World concerns.[96]

Despite the defensive logic of big business, the comic came to be a quintessential symbol of American cultural imperialism. In the same year that the *Journal* launched its attack on Brazilian quotas, Chilean scholars Ariel Dorfman and Armand Mattelart wrote their now-seminal marxist critique of Disney's imperialist ideology, *How to Read Donald Duck*. An immediate best-seller in Chile, and subsequently in other Latin American editions, this book forcefully demonstrated how companies such as Disney were using "innocence" as a guise for capitalist expansion overseas. Dorfman and Mattelart's harsh criticism of the Duck family made it clear that even the most childish of comics was not a universal language, but instead subject to oppositional interpretations by readers around the world.

Even on American soil, the kid character, as embodied by *Peanuts* and *Dennis*, began to lose ground. Although these two strips remain popular, at the present time, they are no longer the reigning symbols of contemporary childhood or, for that matter, the nation. Over the course of the 1960s and 1970s, as collectors, Pop artists, museums, and universities increasingly recognized comics as something more akin to "culture" than to "kitsch," critics increasingly expected funnies to deal with serious problems, from civil rights to the Vietnam War to women's liberation.[97] Meanwhile, the growth of underground comics created a new comic book avant-garde in which neither *Dennis* nor *Peanuts* belonged. Dennis is especially resistant to cultural transformation, and aside from some wardrobe and hairdo changes, the strip reads as a monument to its own historical place and time (as one critic said of the recent film, it applied "little imagination to an old-fashioned vision of America").[98] Perhaps it is because of their claims to universality (their attempt to speak outside history) that neither *Dennis* nor *Peanuts* did much to remain in step with the times. (And notably here, the new "yellow kid" on the block, Bart Simpson, still exhibits the bad boy charms of his kid strip cousins although he is the ultimate American parody, a comic inversion of postwar family ideals.)

Even in their present-day incarnations, *Dennis* and *Peanuts* seem more a part of a "residual" culture that harkens back to a prior time, but is not in sync with dominant contemporary social views. In this case, these comics can be seen as a residue of the cold war era's conceptions of childhood and national supremacy, conceptions that are no longer the dominant terms of social experience and cultural production. More Americana than American, these two strips of the baby boom generation represent a vision of childhood and suburban life so out of touch with real communities that they no longer provide the "imagined community" that constitutes a nation.

As numerous critics have argued, in a world of global culture and international information flows, nationalism may itself be becoming a residual sentiment, perhaps available primarily through nostalgia rather than any of the social realities that define the current world. The word *nostalgia* was originally intended to describe a soldier's longing for the homeland, but even in its more contemporary meanings of "a return to the past," it still engages nationalist sentiments. It is in this context that we might also understand the recent recycling of *Dennis* and *Peanuts* for the baby boom generation (and their children). The 1993 film release of *Dennis the Menace*, and the spate of Snoopy ties and boxer shorts that are now appearing in men's stores at the local mall, evoke their own romantic longing for a simpler, personal (and national) past where Snoopy fights the Red Baron and Dennis champions the American way. Such recycled objects link together a fragmented demographic group of Americans who imagine themselves as a generation. Still, for this baby boom generation, it seems likely that contemporary kid strip nostalgia is connected to nationalist sentiments, to the desire to return to a cold war past where nations still existed, and the boundaries between "us" and "them" were eminently clear. But, of course, the lines between nations, like the lines of kid strip heroes, are never as clear-cut as they first appear.

Notes

1   Mother's Day was first celebrated in 1908. Father's Day appeared in 1910; in 1916, President Woodrow Wilson endorsed its celebration, and in 1924, President Calvin Coolidge

recommended national observance of the holiday. U.S. Senate Joint Resolution 139 empowered President Clinton to proclaim Children's Day a holiday on November 18, 1993. (See President, Proclamation, "National Children's Day, Proclamation 6626," *Weekly Compilation of Presidential Documents* (19 November 1993).

2   Ariel Dorfman and Armand Mattelart, *How to Read Donald Duck: Imperialist Ideology in the Disney Comic*, trans. David Kunzle (New York: International General, 1971).

3   For a detailed description of the growth of comics and their relation to advertising and consumer product tie-ins, see Ian Gordon, *Comic Strips and Consumer Culture, 1890–1945* (Washington, D.C.: Smithsonian Institution Press, 1998).

4   Initially carried by seven newspapers, the strip took several years to secure its national popularity. In 1952, the first *Peanuts* book was published. See Rheta Grimsley Johnson, *Good Grief: The Story of Charles M. Schulz* (New York: Pharos Books, 1989), 28.

5   Hank Ketcham, *The Merchant of Dennis the Menace* (New York: Abbeville Press, 1990), 103, 106. For the national figures in 1953, see "Ketcham's Menace," *Newsweek*, 4 May 1953, 57. The same issue of *Newsweek* also reported that Ketcham won the "most coveted prize of comic-strip artists, Billy De Beck award for the outstanding cartoonist of the year." By 1961, *Publisher's Weekly* claimed that *Dennis* was in 700 daily and Sunday U.S. papers. See "From Cartoon to Big Business with *Dennis the Menace*," *Publisher's Weekly*, 9 January 1961, 34–35.

6   For the *Dennis* figure, see "From Cartoon to Big Business," 34; the *Peanuts* figure was reported in "Good Grief, Curly Hair," *Newsweek*, 6 March 1961, 68. *Peanuts* was reported to be in forty-one countries by 1969. See John Tebbel, "The Not-So Peanuts World of Charles M. Schulz," *Saturday Review*, 12 April 1969, 72.

7   For descriptions of Screen Gems's production of *Dennis*, see Screen Gems, Inc., Annual Report, 1 July 1961, Doheny Cinema Library clipping files, *Dennis the Menace* folder, University of Southern California; Jeb H. Perry, *Screen Gems: A History of Columbia Pictures Television from Cohn to Coke, 1948–1983* (Metuchen, N.J.: Scarecrow Press, 1991); and George W. Woolery, *Children's Television: The First Thirty-Five Years, 1946–1981*, Part II (Metuchen, N.J.: Scarecrow Press, 1985), 146–48. In later years, *Dennis* returned to television in a two-hour special for first-run syndication produced by DIC Enterprises and distributed by Coca-Cola. See Synopsis/Press Release, Doheny Cinema Library clipping files, University of Southern California. Currently, there is an animated *Dennis the Menace* in first-run syndication, which is also packaged for the home video market.

8   "A Charlie Brown Christmas" won a Peabody Award that year for "outstanding children and youths' program." For a retrospective of the many specials, see Museum of Broadcasting, *Charlie Brown, A Boy for All Seasons: Twenty Years on Television* (exhibition catalog, Museum of Broadcasting, New York, 15 November 1984 to 31 January 1985).

9   Hank Ketcham, telephone interview by Bill Forman, 4 August 1993, Los Angeles, Calif. Ketcham further recalls this incident in his autobiography, *The Merchant of Dennis the Menace*, 159.

10   "Lenin vs. Snoopy," *New York Times*, 24 May 1969, sec. 2, p. 34, col. 2.

11   Benedict Anderson, *Imagined Communities: Reflections on the Origin and Spread of Nationalism* (1983; reprint, London: Verso, 1992).

12   Viviana A. Zelizer, *Pricing the Priceless Child: The Changing Social Value of Children* (Princeton, N.J.: Princeton University Press, 1994).

13   For more on this point in relation to crusades against mass media, see Lynn Spigel, "Seducing the Innocent: Television and Childhood in Postwar America," in *Ruthless*

Criticism, ed. Robert McChesney and William Soloman (Minneapolis: University of Minnesota Press, 1993), 259–90.

14   On the sales of Spock's book, see Dewey W. Grantham, Recent America: The United States since 1945 (Arlington Heights, Ill.: Harlan Davidson, 1987), 201.

15   Abram Kardiner, "When the State Brings up the Child," Saturday Review, 26 August 1961, 9. For articles (explicitly or implicitly) comparing American children to those in the Soviet Union and other Communist countries, see "Cuba: And Now the Children?" Time, 6 October 1961, 41; Hugh Moffett, "The Moffetts Go A-Moseying," Life, 13 September 1963, 101–11; J. L., "The Russian Tragedy," Saturday Review, 3 March 1962, 42; and "Moscow," Life, 13 September 1963, 89–91.

16   Urie Bronfenbrenner, "Challenge of the 'New Soviet Man,' " New York Times Magazine, 27 August 1961, 78.

17   For examples, see George Kent, "Magic Carpet for Europe's Saddest Children," Reader's Digest, April 1956, 127–30; Roger Angell, "The Small One," Holiday, February 1956, 100–101; "The King's Man," Holiday, December 1955, 115–17; and Dr. Howard A. Rusk, "Voice from Korea: Won't You Please Help Us off Our Knees?" Life, 7 June 1954, 178–82.

18   Alastair Buchan, "Our Small Anglo-American Relations," New York Times Magazine, 12 April 1953, 17, 39; Alice Shabecoff, "Bringing up Hans and Gretal," New York Times Magazine, 13 November 1966, 180, 182–83; and Ruth McKenney, "Paris! City of Children," Holiday, April 1953, 62–66 (for the description of the abusive French parent, see n. 20).

19   Edward M. Korry, "Lost Childhood," Look, 20 March 1956, 65–73.

20   John Keats, The Crack in the Picture Window (1956; reprint, Boston: Houghton Mifflin Co., 1957); William H. Whyte Jr., The Organization Man (Garden City, N.Y.: Doubleday, 1956); and Betty Friedan, The Feminine Mystique (New York: W. W. Norton, 1963). It should be noted that many of these views were also expressed in a host of popular media.

21   Hank Ketcham, Dennis the Menace, A.M.: Ambassador of Mischief (New York: Fawcett World Library, 1961). This is an anthology of panels that appeared in daily newspapers. According to the copyright information, they were first published between 1959 and 1961, although they are not individually dated in this book. The book is not paginated, and therefore, all subsequent references will not include page numbers.

22   Ketcham, Merchant of Dennis, 154.

23   Hank Ketcham, In This Corner . . . Dennis the Menace (1959; reprint, Greenwich, Conn.: Fawcett Publications, 1971). The panels in this collection are copyrighted from 1957 to 1959. The book is not paginated, and therefore, all subsequent references will not include page numbers.

24   Henry Jenkins, "Dennis the Menace: 'The All American Handful,' " in The Revolution Wasn't Televised: Sixties Television and Social Conflict, ed. Lynn Spigel and Michael Curtin (New York: Routledge, 1997), 119–38.

25   As one of the readers for this essay suggested, Peanuts can be seen to inherit some of the characteristics of the Hal Roach series Our Gang, as children form the principal cast. Yet unlike Our Gang, which expressed class conflicts between rich and poor children, Peanuts presented a postwar consumerist ideology about children that placed them in a world where social mobility seemed possible for all.

26   Snoopy, like other animal characters before him, was presented through anthropomorphic logic. Often, he took on the role of an adult, so that the adult-child binary was displaced onto that of animal-human. As Richard deCordova argues in his work on

Disney, such displacements might be read in terms of the history of the regulation of childhood. He writes of early cinema: "Reformers were interested in conserving a set of distinctions between adult and child, which the cinema presumably blurred. One way of bringing those distinctions back into focus was to superimpose them on the more culturally stable distinction between animals and humans. That is what the association of animals and children worked to do." See Richard deCordova, "The Mickey in Macy's Window: Childhood, Consumerism, and Disney Animation," in *Disney Discourse: Producing the Magic Kingdom*, ed. Eric Smoodin (New York: Routledge, 1994), 211.

27   Charles M. Schulz, cited in Tebbel, "Not-So Peanuts World," 74.

28   Bronfenbrenner, "New Soviet Man," 79.

29   Buchan, "Our Small Anglo-American Relations," 39.

30   Hank Ketcham, *Dennis the Menace: His First 40 Years* (New York: Abbeville Press, 1991). This book is not paginated. All subsequent references will not include pagination.

31   Ketcham, *In This Corner*. Note that the strip often represented the "sissy" through Dennis's pal Joey. According to Henry Jenkins ("All American Handful," 129), Joey was constantly torn between Dennis's love of boyish games and Margaret's desire to play house. Jenkins offers this example as part of his larger thesis that Dennis portrayed American masculinity as a rejection of all things domestic, suburban, and feminine. Joey, then, illustrates the inability to choose between the man's world of rugged adventure and the domesticated world of women's suburban culture.

32   Ketcham, *His First 40 Years*.

33   Ketcham, *In This Corner*.

34   Hank Ketcham, telephone interview by Bill Forman, 2 August 1992, Los Angeles, Calif.

35   See review of televised version of *Dennis the Menace*, *National Parent Teacher*, April 1960, 25. According to George W. Woolery, "after the first season, the PTA asked the producers to tone down Dennis's shenanigans so he would not set a bad example for young children" (*Children's Television*, 147).

36   James L. Hymes cited in Jenkins, "All American Handful," 131.

37   Charles M. Schulz, *You Can Do It, Charlie Brown* (New York: Holt, Rinehart and Winston, 1965). The strips in this collection are copyrighted from 1962 to 1963. The book is not paginated, and therefore, all subsequent references will not include page numbers.

38   "Good Grief, Curly Hair," 68.

39   To be sure, some critics lashed out at Schulz's brainy, adultlike kids, and found his renderings unrealistic to the point of parody. Cartoonist Al Capp made his disapproval the subject of his strip *Li'l Abner*, which featured Schulz in the guise of "Good Old Bedly Damp," creator of "Pee-Wee." See Johnson, *Good Grief*, 76.

40   Ketcham, Forman interview, 4 August 1993.

41   Ketcham, *His First 40 Years*.

42   Ibid.

43   Elizabeth Gordon, "The Threat to the Next America," *House Beautiful*, April 1953, editorial. For a discussion of American modern art as it relates to postwar nationalism and cultural imperialism, see Emily S. Rosenberg's exploration of the State Department's 1946 international exhibit titled "Advancing American Art" in her book *Spreading the American Dream: American Economic and Cultural Expansion, 1890–1945* (New York: Hill and Wang, 1982), 216. See also Frank A. Ninkovich, "The Currents of Cultural Diplomacy: Art and the State Department, 1938–1947," *Diplomatic History* 1 (1977): 215–37.

44   Ketcham's various museum panels are the comic strip equivalent of Norman Rockwell's

The Connoisseur (1962) in which Rockwell juxtaposed his popular commercial art style to the intellectual art of abstract expressionism (the painting presented a Rockwellesque rendering of a museum where a patron gazes at a Jackson Pollock–type canvas).

45 See Serge Guilbaut, How New York Stole the Idea of Modern Art: Abstract Expressionism, Freedom, and the Cold War (Chicago: University of Chicago Press, 1983). While Guilbaut acknowledges that this "triumph of the avant garde was neither a total victory nor a popular one" and that it was "threatened by opposing tendencies in the work of art" (p. 3), he nevertheless argues that the avant-garde—particularly abstract expressionism—coincided with what was becoming the dominant ideology of the new liberalism.

46 Robert R. McElroy, "Good Grief, $150 Million!" Newsweek, 27 December 1971, 42.

47 "Good Grief, Curly Hair," 68; and Tebbel, "No-So Peanuts World," 74.

48 Johnson, Good Grief, 29.

49 Charles M. Schulz, Peanuts Treasury (New York: Holt, Rinehart and Winston, 1968), n.p.

50 While Peanuts often engaged profound questions, and while critics and Schulz himself liked to interpret the strip in this way, in his recent biography, Schulz denies that he is trying to send a "message," arguing that he's only "interested in being funny" (Johnson, Good Grief, 130).

51 Robert L. Short, The Gospel according to Peanuts (Richmond, Va.: John Knox Press, 1964). By 1969, this book had entered its twenty-first printing. Its popularity was met with some resistance by the church, which questioned the introduction of popular culture into Christian doctrine. See Edward B. Fiske, "Liturgies Embracing More Pop Art Forms," New York Times, 15 May 1967, 1: col. 1; 48: col. 4. Despite this, Short wrote a second volume titled The Parables of Peanuts (New York: Harper and Row, 1969), and went on to produce a theological reading of science fiction narratives about space, which also used comics (including Peanuts) as examples. See Robert L. Short, The Gospel from Outer Space (San Franciso: Harper and Row, 1983).

52 Note that in Dennis the Menace, the image of suburbia was more nostalgic than modern. It harkened back to the American small town suburb, even while it was in dialogue with the more contemporary mass-produced suburb of its time.

53 Ketcham, Dennis the Menace, A.M. Ketcham was particularly fond of these bathroom jokes, which became a running gag.

54 Ibid.

55 For a description of Rollo and other early children's series, see Faye Riter Kensinger, Children of the Series and How They Grew (Bowling Green, Ohio: Bowling Green State University Popular Press, 1987).

56 Johnson, Good Grief, 80.

57 In the television special Bon Voyage, Charlie Brown (1980), the Peanuts gang become exchange students in France and rescue a sad little French girl who has been tormented by her uncle. The program also deals with war-related themes.

58 Ketcham, Dennis the Menace, A.M., inside cover.

59 Ketcham, His First 40 Years; and Ketcham, In This Corner. Henry Jenkins ("All American Handful," 131) notes that in the television series, the Western frontier was often translated into the new frontier of outer space, as Dennis became a little astronaut ready to explore the universe.

60 Both of these are in Ketcham, Dennis the Menace, A.M.

61 While Charlie Brown pined after the Little Red-Headed Girl and Linus after his teacher Miss Othmar, unlike Lucy, they never badgered their beloved. Instead, they were the

victims of their inability to properly aggress the girls of their dreams. For boys, then, romance represented the failure of masculine prowess, while for the girls it became a weapon of the weak.

62 Ketcham, *Merchant of Dennis*, 136.

63 Nancy Armstrong, "Occidental Alice," *Differences* 2, no. 2 (1990): 4–41.

64 Ketcham, Forman interview, 4 August 1993. Just as in the television episode with the Chinese girl, Gina's nationality was often represented by her culinary difference. In numerous panels, Dennis becomes a big fan of Gina, rushing off to get a taste of her mother's Italian cuisine.

65 See Ponchitta Pierce, "What's Not So Funny about the Funnies," *Ebony*, November 1966, 50.

66 See Louie Robinson, "Cartoonist with a Conscience," *Ebony*, February 1973, 31–42. In 1968, *Luther*, a well-known kid strip that features an African American boy, also appeared. For more on this, see David A. Andelman, "Comics Find Negro Heroes," *New York Times*, 22 September 1970, 47.

67 Morrie Turner cited in Pierce, "What's Not So Funny," 53. Despite its slow start, *Wee Pals* went on to achieve national success. By 1973, it was picked up by King Syndicate and transformed into the ABC Saturday morning show, *Kid Power*.

68 Johnson, *Good Grief*, 66.

69 Andelman, "Comics Find Negro Heroes," 47.

70 *Ebony* listed the solid black face as one of a litany of racist stereotypes that had been the subject of black protest. See Pierce, "What's Not So Funny," 48.

71 Andelman, "Comics Find Negro Heroes," 47.

72 "Good Grief!" *Wall Street Journal*, 24 December 1971, p. 1, col. 4.

73 Ketcham, *Merchant of Dennis*, 210–11.

74 Ketcham, Forman interview, August 4, 1993.

75 Ibid.

76 In 1953, a comic magazine based on *Dennis* was published by Harry Slater of the Hall Syndicate, who was also in charge of merchandising Dennis products. By 1961, Holt, Rinehart and Winston had already published eight hardcover collections of the cartoons, which were reprinted in softcover by Fawcett. See "From Cartoon to Big Business," 35. In 1953, Rosemary Clooney and Jimmy Boyd made a *Dennis the Menace* record for Columbia. See "Ketcham's Menace," 57. In that same year, a line of *Dennis the Menace* children's clothing was in production. See "The Menace Gets Dressed," *Look*, 6 October 1953, 87–91. By 1961, a host of other products from paper plates to greeting cards were available. See "From Cartoon to Big Business."

With the exception of 1953, book collections of the *Peanuts* strip have appeared every year since 1952. Determined Productions has made novelty books of the *Peanuts* strip since 1962. The first was *Happiness Is a Warm Puppy*, which was a 1962–1963 best-seller for forty-five weeks. Holt, Rinehart and Winston and the John Fox Press (a religious publisher) went on to handle the higher-priced *Peanuts* books. By 1976, sixteen of the fifty-eight best-selling paperbacks were *Peanuts* books. See Paul Showers, "Snoopy in the Sky with Diamonds," *New York Times Book Review*, 12 February 1968, 28. In 1970, Schulz formed a company to build a Charlie Brown–theme amusement park. See *Wall Street Journal*, 12 October 1970, 5, col. 1. The Broadway musical "You're a Good Man, Charlie Brown" is one of the most frequently produced in history (see Johnson, *Good Grief*, xii); and the *Peanuts* characters have appeared in a host of other related media and products, from ice rink pageants to clothing, posters, and wristwatches.

77 McElroy, "Good Grief, $150 Million!" 40–42.

78 William K. Zinsser, "Enough Is a Warm Too Much," Look, 21 February 1967, 11.

79 Santha Rama Rau, "For a Russian Child—Everything," Holiday, June 1958, 68–69.

80 For a more thorough account of Wertham's intellectual history as well as a discussion of the congressional hearings, see James L. Gilbert, A Cycle of Outrage: America's Reaction to the Juvenile Delinquent in the 1950s (New York: Oxford University Press, 1986), esp. chapter 6. For the hearings themselves, see Senate Committee on the Judiciary, Hearings before the Subcommittee to Investigate Juvenile Delinquency, 83rd Cong., 2d sess., 5 June 1954, S. Res. 89. The committee reconvened on 19 and 20 October 1954, and also met on 6 and 7 April 1954 to continue the debates.

81 Bruce Smith, The History of Little Orphan Annie (New York: Ballantine, 1982), 64–65.

82 Jacqueline Rose, The Case of Peter Pan: Or the Impossibility of Children's Fiction (London: Macmillan Publishers Ltd., 1984), esp. chapter 4.

83 "The Girl on the Cay," Holiday, January 1956, 96.

84 Helen Trager, "The Burmese Way with Children," Parents, January 1957, 32, 44–45.

85 Edward Steichen, voice-over in The Family of Man, CBS TV and Robert Northshield Productions, 1956. In Museum of Modern Art Film Archives, N.Y., New York.

86 My description of this ride is based on an episode of Walt Disney's Wonderful World of Color, originally aired on NBC in 1964.

87 Johnson, Good Grief, xii. Peanuts may well be more popular in Italy, where it was translated into Latin, than it is in America. For instance, Italy's official 1993 entry for the Oscars's "Best Foreign Language Film" is called Grande Cocomero after Linus's search for the Great Pumpkin.

88 William J. Lederer, The Ugly American (New York: W. W. Norton, 1958).

89 Italian Communists called Mickey Mouse and Donald Duck "imperialist warmongers" (see "Italian Reds Bar a U.S. Comic," New York Times, 4 April 1952, 15, col. 1); Moscow radio said that Americans were "flooding Western Europe with ideological and moral poison" (see "Moscow Calls U.S. Comics Poison," New York Times, 25 November 1953, 10, col. 3); the Justice Ministry in West Germany banned comics portraying "primitive" and "barbarous acts" (see "Bonn Curbing 'Comic' Books," New York Times, 21 August 1955, 5, col. 3); East Germany called American comics "psychological war preparation," and Education Minister Fritz Lange said that distributors of American-style comics would be "punished severely and mercilessly" (see "German Reds Propose 'Punishment' for Comics," New York Times, 20 May 1955, 3, col. 2); a Tokyo newspaper dropped Pogo because of its rendering of a Khrushchev-like pig (see "Tokyo Newspaper Drops Pogo because of Khrushchev-Like Pig," New York Times, 21 May 1962, 16, col. 1); and in Britain, the Communist Party played a central role in a postwar campaign against U.S. horror comics that culminated in a nationwide ban on comics (see Martin Barker, A Haunt of Fears: The Strange History of the British Horror Comics Campaign [London: Pluto Press, 1984]).

90 For a good case study that shows how Nelson Rockefeller, director of the Office of the Coordinator of Inter-American Affairs, joined hands with Walt Disney in the early 1940s to produce films that would enhance the image of the United States in Latin America, see Julianne Burton, "Don (Juanito) Duck and the Imperial-Patriarchal Unconscious: Disney Studios, the Good Neighbor Policy, and the Packaging of Latin America," in Nationalisms and Sexualities, ed. Andrew Parker et al. (New York: Routledge, 1992), 21–41.

91 Ketcham, Forman interview, 4 August 1993.

92 Donna Haraway, Primate Visions: Gender, Race, and Nature in the World of Modern Science (New York: Routledge, 1989), esp. chapter 3.

93   Ketcham, *Merchant of Dennis*, 163.

94   Nan Robertson, " 'Peanuts' Bridges a Language Gap and Captivates the French," *New York Times*, 26 March 1975, 2, col. 4.

95   "What's Next, Charlie Brown?" *Wall Street Journal*, 19 April 1971, 14, col. 1. It should be noted that in Brazil, a congressional bill to ban U.S. comics had been put forward in the early 1950s. See "Brazil Assails U.S. Comic Books," *New York Times*, 11 November 1953, 13, col. 2.

96   "Good Grief!" *Wall Street Journal*, 4, col. 1.

97   The comics' turn to relevancy was the subject of discussion in the popular press, and for this reason, it seems likely that people beyond critics, collectors, artists, and intellectuals were thinking about the new "horizon of expectations" for topics in the funny pages. See Saul Braun, "Shazam! Here Comes Captain Relevant," *New York Times Magazine*, 2 May 1971, 1, 32–48; Laurie Johnston, "Women's Liberation in the Comics: The Jokes Are on Everybody," *New York Times*, 3 February 1973, 34; David Kunzle, "Self-Conscious Comics," *New Republic*, 19 July 1975, 26–27; and "Leapin' Lizards! Look What's Happened to the Comics!" *U.S. News and World Report*, 9 June 1975, 44–46.

98   Todd McCarthy, "Dennis the Menace," review, *Variety*, 28 June 1993, 24.

"Her Suffering Aristocratic Majesty": The Sentimental
Value of *Lassie*   Henry Jenkins

Nostalgia is a sadness without an object, a sadness which creates a longing that of necessity is inauthentic because it does not take part in lived experience. Rather, it remains behind and before that experience. Nostalgia, like any form of narrative, is always ideological: the past it seeks has never existed except as narrative, and hence, always absent, that past continually threatens to reproduce itself as a felt lack.—Susan Stewart, *On Longing* (1993)

His mother had asked him to forget about Lassie but he could not. He could pretend to and he could stop talking about her. But in his mind Lassie would always go on living. . . . He would sit at his desk at school and dream of her. He would think that perhaps someday—someday—like a dream come true, he would come out of school and there she would be, sitting at the gate.—Eric Knight, *Lassie Come Home* (1940)

1954. A television legend debuts. Jeff Miller, a simple farm boy, squirms in his suit and tie, as he listens to the reading of a neighbor's will. The bored boy is overjoyed when he learns that he is to receive "the best thing," a collie named Lassie. The dog, however, refuses to leave the house where she has lived since she was a puppy. When Jeff takes her away by force, she escapes and runs back "home." As "Gramps" explains, "The Lord made animals free just like human beings and you can't force them to love you."

Actually, Lassie is protecting her former owner's savings from an untrustworthy handyman. She fights fiercely when he tries to steal the money; Jeff brings help, capturing the crook. Then, at last, Lassie consents to live with Jeff and obey his commands. "She's my dog now, isn't she, Gramps?" Jeff enthuses, and "Gramps" confirms his rightful ownership: "Yes—She's all yours now. She's done her deciding." Thus begins *Lassie*, the longest running children's series in American television history.

In "Inheritance," the series' pilot, the issue of Lassie's legal and economic ownership is settled quickly. No one contests the dead man's will. Nevertheless, the issue of the animal's moral allegiance lingers. "Inheritance" must assess both the worth of the dog (which another boy discounts, "Who wants an old she-dog? All they do is have pups!") and the worth of its potential owner (which is proven through patience, love, and courage). *Lassie* ascribes a moral intelligence to the collie—she can divine human motives and character. Both the handyman's criminality and Jeff's virtues are instantly legible to Lassie. She faithfully repays her old master before doing her "deciding."

The episode's core images—the dog who remains loyal beyond her owner's death, who comes home even when she is given away, and who rewards the virtuous and punishes the corrupt—reflect a larger history, the sentimentalization of dogs in the previous century.[1] In the late nineteenth century, the bourgeois imagination created a myth of canine fidelity, compatible with the prevailing romanticist tendencies. Many experienced the onset of modernity with a sense of nostalgic loss. Old social commitments were breaking down, and the organic ties of traditional communities were giving way to alienated and individualistic urban life. No matter what else changed, however, you could count on "man's best friend." Dogs' loyalty to their masters stood in stark contrast to the perceived breakdown of social ties between their human owners. As social historian Kathleen Kete notes, many of these idealistic images of canine fidelity had entered children's stories by the twentieth century. Yet Kete does not address what these images might mean in the context of children's fiction, where the fidelity of the dog spills over into and gives new life to widely circulating myths about childhood innocence. To address that question opens up the whole issue of children's fiction, its relation to adult needs, its mythic construction of the child, and its ties to nostalgic longing.

Lassie stands at the nexus of two central ideological reconceptualizations, both of which occurred during the late nineteenth century. The first centered around the sentimentalization of the dog, the transformation of dogs from domesticated animals (whose value resided in their productive labor or exchange price) into "pets" (whose value was primarily sentimental); the second revolved around the "sacralization" of the child, the displacement of children as sources of economic revenue and productive labor, and the need to create a compensatory affective value. Probably the most popular in a whole series of dog books written in the twentieth century and aimed primarily at consumption by children, *Lassie Come Home* represented a systematic exploration of

"What Do You Want, Lassie?"

Lassie appears in our minds in broadly drawn images, like the pages of a coloring book.

human affective investments in and sentimental attachments to dogs. These issues cling to Lassie as she travels across different media and is regroomed to changing tastes.

This essay will investigate the sentimental and symbolic value of Lassie as a "popular hero" of literature, film, and television.[2] As she roams, Lassie gets entangled within contemporary discourses about class, gender, nationalism, modernity, and childhood. First, I will identify the issues of ownership and emotional bonds that structure Eric Knight's book, and later, I will look more closely at some key turning points within the television series, involving the exchange of Lassie (starting with the 1954 pilot episode and moving through the 1964 shift from Timmy to Ranger Stuart). Since undying fidelity defines the ideal pet, these negotiations of ownership constitute potential crises where viewer loyalties must also be transferred between series' protagonists. In each case, melodramatic devices ensure a smooth transition, yet possible ideological problems surface that threaten the long-term stability of Lassie's "family values." This essay is, first and foremost, an exploration of the process of nostalgic longing and sentimental investment, of the ways children and dogs become vehicles for the hopes and fears of human adults.

Like most children's works, Lassie seems to exist outside any historical context (history being a grown-up concern) and "innocent" of all but the most blatant ideological content (the morals at the end of the stories speak all the truths). *Lassie* appears in our minds in broadly drawn images, like the pages of a coloring book: the mother in the kitchen and the father in the toolshed; Timmy and Lassie romping across the open countryside; the dog rescuing an injured camper or mothering a lost fawn; the collie winning a blue ribbon at the country fair; a tearful boy clutching Lassie's white mane.[3] We preserve childhood as a utopian space free from adult concerns and controversies, a period of naive idealism and trust betrayed by the adult world. Our need to hold onto these feelings is urgent, yet we are too cynical to embrace them once again, and so we treat children's fiction as banal and meaningless.[4] This essay represents an attempt to cut through our foggy cultural myth of "childhood innocence" in order to reconstruct the historical contexts shaping the popular circulation and consumption of *Lassie*, a series I take to be central to both our cultural understanding of the dog and the postwar construction of American boyhood.

Perhaps not surprisingly, the most significant meanings to be found in children's fiction are adult anxieties about our children's world and adult fantasies about how children (and dogs) may become vehicles for social transformation and personal redemption. What James R. Kinkaid has said of the child holds for dogs as well: "The child carries for us things we somehow cannot carry for ourselves, sometimes anxieties we want to be divorced from and sometimes pleasures so great we would not, without the child, know how to contain them."[5] In the adult symbolic order, dogs and children are primarily beasts of burden who are assumed powerless to speak for themselves. The muteness of dogs and the inarticulateness of children are mysteries that the adult imagination seeks to penetrate—it is both part of their charm and part of their fascination. To serve adult purposes, the innocence of children as well as the intelligence and fidelity of dogs have been fetishized, endowed with a broad range of connotative associations and meanings. Both dogs and children are presumed to be supra- or nonhuman: the child's innocence pulls it away from and the dog's intelligence pulls it toward the adult realm, yet both remain outside. They exist in a state of nature, or so the mythology goes; the meanings that seem to originate from within them are presocial and preideological. The communication between children and dogs is immediate, concrete, and closed to grown-ups. Ideology gets naturalized through its association with children and dogs. As such, children and dogs remain our most powerful symbols for speaking about what is most "precious," "pure," and "valuable" in the face of modernity and change.

Home and Hardship: Lassie Come Home

1940. The opening of Knight's children's novel, *Lassie Come Home*, is preoccupied with Lassie's value. In a dog-centered Yorkshire culture where, Knight tells us, "the dogs [are] rich-coated and as sturdy as the people who live there," Lassie is universally admired: "Every man in the village agreed that she was the finest collie he had ever laid eyes on."[6] Her worth lies in her physical beauty, her intelligence and good habits ("You can set your clock by her"), and most important, her symbolic function. In a period of economic hardship, Lassie's owners have refused to sell her, even when offered lordly sums, and so Lassie "represented some sort of pride that money had not been able to take away from them" (p. 4). Her economic value (as an "expensive" animal) has been translated into sentimental and symbolic worth (as a "priceless" animal).

This tension between a dog's economic and sentimental value can be traced back to what Kete describes as "the embourgeoisement of the beast" in the nineteenth century.[7] By midcentury, dogs were understood as falling into two broad categories—the work-dogs owned by the lower class and the show dogs or lapdogs owned by the wealthy. French tax policy sought to draw a distinction between "useful" and "useless" dogs, and by so doing, restrict dog ownership to those who either depended on them for their economic livelihood (work-dogs) or could afford the expense (pets). Work animals suffered little taxation, while pets were taxed as luxuries. Dogs were viewed as pets if they roamed freely in the home, accompanied the master on walks, or played with children. Pet ownership, however, was expanding from an upper-class phenomenon to an activity of ordinary citizens, and with it, the ideologies surrounding human attachments to animals.[8] The bourgeois pet keepers claimed that the dog's emotional support and physical protection were essential aspects of modern life. In this context, myths circulated about the dog's fidelity to man that exceeded all reason or human understanding.

Especially popular were stories about dogs who traveled tremendous distances to be rejoined with their human owners. Victor Hugo, for example, wrote of a beloved dog that in a moment of bad judgment, he gave to a Russian count; astonishingly, the dog found its way from Moscow to Paris. Such stories formed the foundation for *Lassie Come Home*, which similarly deals with a dog's incredible journey. They privilege the emotional relations between humans and their pets over economic exchanges, which threaten to sever those bonds. The dog becomes a moral arbiter of all exchanges, instinctively negating deals that unjustly break its moral allegiances. Against both economic arrangements and natural barriers, the dog returns home to redeem its master.

Knight's decision to make Lassie a collie seems ideally suited for exploring competing bids on a dog's worth. Collies were almost totally unknown in the United States at the time that Knight first wrote the book, which was dedicated to Dr. Harry Jarrett, the American veterinarian who sought to introduce the breed. For Knight, the choice of the collie evoked nostalgia for the Yorkshire country of his youth, where these gentle-natured dogs were more common.[9] The collie enjoyed a dual status in British culture: on the one hand, it was a favorite of Queen Victoria, closely linked to the aristocracy and highly valued as a show dog among breeders; on the other hand, the collie was an excellent work-dog, especially good at herding.[10] Playing with this contradiction between the collie's aristocratic and common associations, Knight writes:

> You can go into any one of the hundreds of small mining villages in this largest of England's counties, and see, walking at the heels of humbly clad workmen, dogs of such a fine breed and artistocratic bearing as to arouse the envy of the wealthier dog fanciers from other parts of the world. (p. 1)

Knight speaks of the "suffering aristocratic majesty" (p. 34) of Lassie in captivity; characters affectionately refer to her as "Her Majesty" (p. 157) and "Herself" (p. 146). At the same time, her ties to working-class culture are never in doubt. As she moves across the British countryside, Lassie forms bonds and affections almost exclusively with the poor—such as an elderly farm couple still mourning the wartime loss of their son, a traveling busker eking out a meager living, and most powerfully, the Carracloughs, a poor family momentarily on the dole.

Yet interestingly, Knight tells us nothing of collies' economic functions. Sam Carraclough is a miner, not a herdsman, and so the collie contributes nothing to his livelihood. Rather, the dog is experienced as an expense, increasingly difficult to justify in hard times. As Knight explains: "the poor man sits and thinks about how much coal he will need that winter, and how many pairs of shoes will be necessary, and how much food his children ought to have to keep them sturdy" (p. 3). There is no difference, he claims, between the love rich and poor men bestow on their dogs. Still, he seems to suggest something quite different: that dogs, for the rich, are often things that can be bought and bargained over, while dogs for the poor are creatures who must be loved and sacrificed.

By the second chapter, despite Sam's reluctance, the dog has been sold to the Duke of Rudling to become a prize show dog. The sale sets off a contest between the intense emotional and moral bonds that link Lassie to the Carracloughs and the duke's legal right to possess the dog as the object of an economic exchange. In line with his rock-hard morality, Sam sees the economic transaction as irreversible: "No matter how many words tha says, tha can't alter that she's sold, and we've taken the Duke's brass and spent it, and now she belongs to him" (p. 52). Nonetheless, in Knight's world, the ownership of a dog is a moral contract, which once violated, must be set right no matter what the cost. Thus, the book tells us the story of Lassie's many attempts to escape from the duke and return home, including a torturous 1,000-mile journey from the lord's Scottish estate back to her family in Yorkshire.

The book toys with the double meanings attached to the phrase, "come-home dogs." Early in the book, Hymes, the duke's unpleasant and shiftless kennelman, accuses the Carracloughs of training their dog to escape and "come home" so that she can be sold more than once. By the book's conclusion, young Joe Carraclough praises Lassie as a "come-home dog" because she has suffered and endured endless hardship to "come home" to the people she loves and who love her. The contradiction resolves itself when the duke concedes Lassie to her original owners, hires Carraclough to run his kennels, and invites the family to come live on his estate. As the duke tells his granddaughter, "For five years I've sworn I'd have that dog. And now I've got her. But I had to buy the man to get her" (p. 192).

Lassie's incredible journey has temporarily resolved the book's core class conflict, reconciling the competing claims made for her possession. Joe reads this social transformation in the most utopian of terms: "When she [Lassie] had been home, things had been right. When she was sold and gone, nothing had gone right anymore. And now that she was back, everything was fine again, and they were all very happy" (p. 197). Many readers, and some critics, take Joe's thoughts at face value: as the moral of the tale, as a celebration of a child's simple faith and the redemptive power of dogs.[11]

Certainly, the book's sentimental ending is all of this, yet such a reading is profoundly reductive. At the time that he wrote *Lassie Come Home*—first as a short story for *Saturday Evening Post*, and later, expanded into a novel—Knight was known primarily as a journalist and writer of adult novels.[12] Like his close friend, documentary filmmaker Paul Rotha, Knight was interested in documenting the economic conditions and personal hardships faced by working-class Britons. In his "local color" novels, *Invitation to Life*, *Song on Your Bugles*, *The Happy Land*, and *This above All*, Knight wrote with nostalgia and remorse about the decline of the world of his boyhood and the problems confronting English village life in the modern era; he described British workers as having "lost their pride . . . their dignity of being through the industrial paralysis, the narcotic of the dole, the meaningless slavery of the labor camps, the dunderheaded stubbornness of the middle class, the inertia of the leaders."[13] Contemporary critics compared his novels to Richard Llewellyn's *How Green Was My Valley* and J. M. Barrie's *The Little Minister*. Like Llewellyn and Barrie, Knight hoped that his

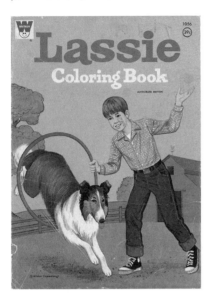

The linkage of those two sentimental icons—the boy and dog—was no accident.

sentimental realism would awaken public consciousness about the decline of traditional British culture. In creating *Lassie Come Home*, Knight was aware that he was writing a children's book, yet at the same time, he hoped that *Lassie* might further social reform. *Lassie* was, he wrote to Rotha, less about a dog than the "tremendous economic problem" that forces the family to sell her.[14] Here, Knight translates the consequences of this social and economic crisis into the images of a child's trust betrayed and a dog's loyalty violated.

The linkage of those two sentimental icons—the boy and the dog—was no accident. As Kete's discussion of the French tax codes suggests, the interactions between dogs and children helped to define the legal status of canines as domestic "pets." Moreover, the period between the 1870s and 1930s had witnessed what historian Viviana A. Zelizer describes as the "Sacralization" of childhood.[15] Zelizer investigates the changing economic and emotional "value" of children through close examination of debates about child labor, issues surrounding the insurance and funeral expenses for children, and a variety of other everyday economic transactions that shaped family life during this key transitional period. The birth of a child in nineteenth-century America was greeted as an expansion of the family's earning power. Reflecting middle-class security from immediate want, a new conception of the child, based on sentimental rather than economic value, gained popular circulation by century's end. The "priceless" bourgeois child was to be protected from the harsh realities of the adult work world. Middle-class reformers sought to impose this new notion of the child as "innocent," "pure," and "dependent" on the larger society, passing laws restricting child labor or regulating child abuse. This economic and legal transformation coincided with medical breakthroughs that ensured that a higher proportion of the children born would live into adulthood; the primary focus shifted from disease and other health risks to concerns for children's mental and emotional well-being. The result was a greater affective investment in the individual child. The expenses of raising a child now needed to be rationalized in terms of the affective rewards of parenting, not the child's potential economic contribution to the family's welfare.

The figure of the innocent child quickly became a vehicle for social criticism against the corrupting influences of the modern world. The desire to separate children from the adult sphere highlighted the "vicious, materialistic and immoral qualities of American society," as Mary Lynn Stevens Heininger asserts.[16] Her exploration of representations of children in literature, art, and material culture confirms Zelizer's argument. Heininger sees fictional children as speaking both to popular pessimism about the present and utopian hopes for the future. On the one hand, popular representations posed children as "soft and smiling foils to a more grim and grown-up reality." They were pure victims of contemporary social ills. On the other hand, as Heininger notes, the notion of the "pristine" child embodied a utopian fantasy of renewal and rebirth. The child came to depict the modern era's hopes for the future.

The dual mythic functions of "childhood innocence" can be tied to the two different children in *Lassie Come Home*: Joe, the poor boy who is so adored by Lassie, and Priscilla, the duke's much-prized granddaughter. Joe is almost suprahumanly innocent: naive about the harsh economic realities his family confronts, unable to understand the sacrifices his parents have already made, and eternally optimistic that the dog will find its way home. The violation of his blind trust seems almost too painful to bear. Knight allows the child-reader to recognize the signs of poverty (the father reaching for a pipe he can no longer fill with tobacco; the mother cutting back on sugar or bursting into tears when Joe asks about meat) and, thus, confront the painful truths Joe is never forced to face. Priscilla, in contrast, seems suprahumanly precocious, the only upper-class character who fully grasps the Carraclough's love for Lassie. Her understanding comes from a recognition of common emotional experience, while kennelman Hymes maintains a profound distrust of the working class and her grandfather simply relishes the shrewd bargain. Priscilla prods and probes the adults, ultimately forcing them to recognize human costs and consequences. She aids Lassie in escaping from her grandfather's estate, rejoices when the collie is returned to her rightful owner, and coaxes her grandfather into hiring Sam. Priscilla embodies the innocent child as the hope for the future.

In a children's book more in keeping with the American ideology of a "class-less" society, we might picture a romance between the poor boy and rich girl. Knight, however, is too much of a realist (and too British) to tolerate such imagery, merely implying their friendship at the end. Both Joe and Priscilla beam with pride as Lassie nurses a litter of pups, the competing interests of the working and ruling classes reconciled through this classic rebirth image. Strik-ingly, Lassie's giving birth represents an immaculate conception, as if the pups were conceived through the combined faith and goodness of the two children. No father is ever mentioned, despite the book's ongoing preoccupation with issues of breeding. Lassie is a pure maternal force, outside brute barnyard reproduction. Part of the construction of childhood innocence, after all, in-volves the denial of both children's sexuality and sexual knowledge.

Nevertheless, sexual anxieties surface earlier in the book, when Lassie must fight against a pack of mongrel farm dogs. The purity and superiority of Lassie's "blood" gives her an intelligence and authority that the mutts must ultimately respect:

> Lassie had something that the others had not. She had blood. She was a purebred dog, and behind her were long generations of the proudest and the best of her kind. . . . Where the mongrel dog will whine and slink away, the purebred will still stand with uncomplaining fearlessness. (p. 104)

As Harriet Ritvo has noted, the elaborate set of breed classifications, which emerged in the Victorian dog show culture, became a way of managing and making sense of other problems of race and class distinctions.[17] Middle-class dog owners could claim status through their ownership of pedigreed animals, even if they were locked out of the bloodlines of human aristocracy, while hy-brids, half-breds, and mongrels were seen as debased and potentially danger-ous, often standing in for the lower classes in popular discourse about dogs.[18]

Knight consistently makes claims about the traits (sometimes physical, sometimes intellectual or moral) that separate Lassie as a purebred collie from other breeds:

> For collies do not rush and hold. Their way of fighting is not like that of the bulldog; nor like that of the terrier which dodges and worries and shakes. (p. 103)

> Lassie had lain still, like a captive queen among lesser prisoners. . . . She did not drop this air of dignity even when the grilled backdrop of the van was opened. The other dogs of mixed breeds yelped anew and darted about. (p. 116)

A Big Family

Lassie is a pure maternal force, outside brute barnyard reproduction.

Such distinctions closely parallel the language he uses to speak of class and regional differences within human characters:

> Joe had in him the blood of men who might think slowly and stick to old ideas and bear trouble patiently—but who do not run away. (p. 182)

In such passages, stereotypical differences between unreliable cockneys, "hard-headed Scots," and "slow-thinking" but honest Yorkshire men assume the same status as "natural facts" as the breed distinctions between collies, bulldogs, and terriers. The two sets of classifications work side by side to create a legible moral universe. At the same time, they rigidify class and national boundaries. A working-class man can no more become an aristocrat than a collie can become a bulldog, or indeed, than a mongrel can hold its own against a purebred.

When Lassie confronts the mongrel pack, she is menaced by animals who are not of her kind, who come from the lower orders, who possess an impure "blood" (all the worse since these animals were of collie descent). With this emphasis on the purity of blood, these animals bring with them threats of rape and miscegenation, a besmirching of Lassie's bloodline. No wonder Knight describes the scene with such melodramatic excess: the virginal Lassie stands her ground, learning how to fight and finally forcing the curs to submit. Within this discourse of bloodlines, the stakes are extraordinarily high, having to do with what British sources called telegony, "the contamination of future generations by the first male to mount the bitch."[19] So if these mongrel animals were to "dominate" (or mount) our heroine, their debased blood would taint all of her future offspring, including the pups so admired by Joe and Priscilla. Knight does not directly articulate this threat to her sexual purity, any more than he explains who actually does sire her pups; it becomes a matter for adult knowingness, seemingly unfit for childhood innocence. Yet this question of "blood" lingers through the entire book.

The persistence of this adult knowingness argues against a purely utopian or simplistic reading of the work. Knight *knows* much more than he can tell—at least more than he can tell the children. Knight, the documentarist, the realist novelist, seems compelled by the conventions of the children's story to give *Lassie Come Home* a happy ending. Indeed, he gives way to the nostalgia that shadows the book, a nostalgia for the simple truths and pure relations of his Yorkshire childhood, a nostalgia for a Britain being torn apart by the forces of modernization.

Still, as literary critic Susan Stewart suggests, nostalgia sparks "a sadness without an object," a longing for a past that never existed except through the narratives of our own memories and imaginations. However much the book's "local color" reflects Knight's personal memories, the close-knit Carraclough family has no relationship to his own childhood experiences. Knight's father, a Quaker jeweler, deserted the family two years after Eric was born. His mother departed the following year, moving to Russia to serve as governess for the Princess Xenia's children, and leaving him with an elderly aunt and uncle. By thirteen, just one year older than Joe, Eric was forced to work to support his siblings. His mother moved to the United States and began to send for his siblings one by one; he was the last to be brought over, some two years after the rest. The separation anxiety that runs through the book, displaced onto the loss of a beloved dog, seems to be the one element that grows most directly from Knight's childhood, while the images of the happy family, of domestic solidarity, are the stuff of nostalgic imaginings. A sense of loss, mourning, death, and separation are integral to the myth of the faithful dog. For Knight, as for the characters in the *Lassie* saga, this beloved tricolor collie becomes an angelic figure of redemption and healing who can make a damaged and damaging world whole again, who can reverse—at least for one family—the economic crisis destroying traditional British culture.

Domestic Angels and Pastoral Ideals: The Timmy Years

1957. One night, Lassie stumbles on the body of a sleeping boy, huddled in the Millers's barn. Hearing the noise, Jeff comes outside. He tries to communicate with the confused and frightened youngster, using Lassie's intelligence and tricks as a vehicle: "She's smart. If you tell her your name, she can remember it." The boy refuses to speak, and throughout much of the episode, is believed to be mute. Though tough and strong-willed, the boy, Timmy, radiates innocence and trust, "a little angel with a dirty face." We soon learn that he is an orphan left in the care of elderly and largely indifferent relatives. As his uncle explains, "It ain't any kinda life for a boy on our place. It's lonely with just us." Timmy has run away from home, fearing that "he wasn't earning his keep" because he was not able to contribute directly to the family's economic well-being. Without the affective bonds of family life, the "priceless" child experiences himself as "worthless." The Millers invite Timmy to stay with them on the farm for the summer, while Jeff and Lassie offer him their friendship and protection.

"The Runaway" begins the process by which the homeless Timmy gets situated within *Lassie*'s construction of the ideal domestic life. Timmy's emotional wounds are nursed and healed by the loving collie. At the same time, "The Runaway" begins the transfer of Lassie's ownership from Jeff to Timmy. Actor Tommy Rettig was perceived as being too old to play the boy any longer, and so the producers replaced him with Jon Provost. As one producer explained, "Boys grow up, dogs don't."[20] The ideological construction of the faithful dog, however, made it difficult to execute this transfer without considerable care and preparation. Neither the boy nor the dog could be seen to be breaking the intense bond between them without powerful motivation. Jeff could acquire Lassie through the death of her owner and the power of his love. Timmy, on the other hand, came to own Lassie because of his deep needs for protection and affection.

To facilitate this transference of affection, the producers introduced Timmy half a season before Jeff's departure.[21] Timmy was shown as consistently needing Jeff's help. Playing the older brother role, Jeff moves from child to adult. In "The Spartan," for example, Jeff's lesson on manhood—telling Timmy that boys don't complain—backfires when Timmy catches pneumonia and almost dies. In "The Graduation," Jeff takes on his first job as a vet's assistant, but courts disaster when he leaves Timmy in charge of the clinic and the younger boy frees a rabid dog. The stories hinge on Jeff's maturity (not yet fully secured), and Timmy's boyish curiosity and emotional vulnerability.

Despite such preparations, "Transition" involved a series of traumatic shifts in the previously secure and stable family life depicted on the program, shifts intensified by the death of George Cleveland, the actor who played the beloved "Gramps." As the episode opens, the characters are mourning "Gramps," whose death forces Jeff to become "the man of the family" and assume responsibility for the farm. Jeff wants to adopt Timmy, but the child welfare office and his mother both insist that "Timmy belongs in a home with a mother and a father." In financial trouble, Jeff sells the family farm to the Martins and moves to the city. The Martins become attached to Timmy and provide him a home. Finally, recognizing both that Lassie will be unhappy in an urban environment and Timmy needs her love more than he does, Jeff bestows the cherished beast on his replacement, saying to Lassie: "Take good care of him. You always took good care of me." Amid tearful reaction shots, Lassie signals her consent by slowly moving from Jeff to Timmy, and the Miller's car pulls off, leaving us with the image of a secure, happy, nuclear family.

To break the bonds between Jeff and Lassie, the producers were forced to disrupt the entire series' framework, questioning the stability of the traditional family, the economic security of middle-class farm life, and the "timelessness" of childhood. The producers reintroduced into *Lassie* the problems its "family values" sought to exclude. As writers like Richard Dyer and Fredric Jameson remind us, the utopian fantasies offered by popular entertainment often require the admission of real-world pains, traumas, and anxieties, so that they may be symbolically resolved through commercial fantasy.[22] Much as the original novel reworked class inequalities and economic injustice through the shared love of a dog, television's *Lassie* seeks to cure the uncertainties of postwar American family life. The fatherless Jeff and the orphan Timmy represented the image of a broken family on television at a time when most other portrayals of American childhood centered around nuclear families. In practice, of course, in the wake of the Second World War, there were many fatherless children, and despite the decline of divorce in the postwar period, many children from broken families. Child-rearing experts such as Dr. Benjamin Spock treated these children as "special cases," addressed in the back of the book, but excluded from their image of normalcy. *Lassie*, on the other hand, depended on the creation of such broken families precisely so that they could be healed through Lassie's commitment and affection. So successful was this process of adoption and redemption that the series and its viewers seemed to quickly forget that Timmy was not the natural offspring of the Martins, and that this cohesive family was brought together under such abrupt and arbitrary circumstances.

A core paradox within our culture's conception of children's fiction centers around its persistent dependence on traumatic shifts in fortune, on melodramatic loss and suffering, given the dominant cultural ideology of "childhood innocence" and the strong imperative to protect children from harsh adult realities. Why does a genre based on "family values" depend so heavily on the threat of the disintegration of the family? Children's fiction often seems to secure our faith in the family by posing a threat—the prospect of a harsher life that tests children's innocence and rewards their commitment to core values, their ability to maintain their virtues even in the face of the worst aspects of the modern world. In this way, children's fiction both shelters children from adult knowingness about contemporary life and draws narrative power from the danger that the modern world poses for traditional family life.

While few American children's books of the 1930s and early 1940s dealt as frankly as Knight does with the issue of class inequality, Lassie Come Home's balance between pessimism (the focus on economic problems) and optimism (the prospect of moral healing) was consistent with a growing emphasis on realism and common experience in that period. Lassie's contemporaries—such as Homer Price (1943), Johnny Tremain (1943), The Yearling (1938), and My Friend Flicka (1941)—sought something akin to the naturalism we associate with adult writers like John Steinbeck, depicting "ordinary people, living under recognizable pressures."[23] The writers temper the pessimism of naturalism, however, with an optimism for the future that the "innocent child" facilitates. Reviewing the dominant tendencies in postwar children's fiction, Sally Allen McNall writes:

> Despite the greater realism of their settings, these books showed problems being solved with ease by boys and girls of common sense and good will. The material and social constraints so carefully detailed are then transcended. . . . It was taken for granted that children and young people would be more idealistic and hopeful than their elders, and those who tampered with these qualities were antagonists.[24]

The child's simple faith and determination restores adult hope. In animal stories, the beloved pet often functions as a similar kind of domestic angel, who rewards those worthy of owning it.

Scenes of redemption, reconciliation, and regeneration run through the series of seven Lassie vehicles made by MGM in the 1940s and early 1950s. In Son of Lassie (1945), the dog becomes a symbol of British wartime pluck and courage when she accompanies Peter Lawford safely through occupied Norway. In Courage of Lassie (1946), a shell-shocked collie must undergo rehabilitation in postwar England, and in the process, restore meaning to the lives of her disillusioned owners. In Hills of Home (1948), she brings about a reconciliation between father and son, and in *The Sun Comes Up* (1949), between a young orphan and an embittered widow.[25]

These films have three things in common with the original novel. First, Lassie is owned by adults and families, not by children. Despite her obvious ties to Joe, she is consistently described as "Sam Carraclough's Lassie," that is, as the possession of the father. The shift of Lassie's ownership from adults to children will come with the television series. Second, Lassie remains a British subject. Lassie loses her English accent when she moves to American television.[26] While the wartime years fostered a shared national commitment between England and the United States, cold war America demanded firm nationalistic allegiances; Lassie could not be tainted with foreignness.[27] Third, the initial crisis originates within the owner's family and must be resolved through Lassie. On television, major problems arise elsewhere—with visiting characters—while the "togetherness" of the Millers and Martins is never called into question.

This last shift is consistent with a tendency that Nina C. Leibman identifies across a broad range of 1950s' series about the American family, such as *Leave It to Beaver, Father Knows Best,* and *My Three Sons:* while most of them draw on conventions of Hollywood family melodramas, they offer a more "optimistic" retelling of those stock narratives, one based on "idealized versions of family life, often pitted against outsider, dysfunctional units."[28] Such a transformation of the domestic melodrama reflects the needs of episodic television for repetition and stability.

Throughout most of its seventeen-season run on American network television, *Lassie* served as the anchor point for CBS's early Sunday evening lineup, helping to establish this time slot's close association with "family television." *Lassie* provided a solid lead-in for other CBS programs, such as *Dennis the Menace, My Favorite Martian, It's about Time,* and *Gentle Ben,* while other networks countered with series, such as *Shirley Temple's Storybook, National Velvet, Bullwinkle, Walt Disney's Wonderful World of Color, New Adventures of Huck Finn,* and *Wild Kingdom.* What all of these series shared was a need to construct and maintain an audience consisting of both children and adults. Saturday morning had become the semiofficial "children's hour," where broadcasters could focus their full attention on the young, but Sunday night prime time still needed a broader demographic that pulled in its share of wage-earning and consuming adults. The "wholesomeness" of *Lassie* (a quality that its longtime sponsor, Campbell's, hoped to attach to its soups) made Sunday night television safe for even the most conservative viewer (and this perhaps accounts for *Lassie's* later adoption by the Family Channel, a cable network owned by the Christian Broadcasting System).[29]

Life magazine television critic Cyclops protested "the sentimentalization and inflating, the scouring away of the story's social context, the Disneyization of Lassie." Lassie had become "Super-Collie . . . the Hound of Heaven," whose extraordinary intelligence, loyalty, and communicativeness "make you look at your own mutt and wonder if somebody put stupidity pills into the Gaines-burger."³⁰ Many of Cyclops's criticisms seem valid: the core "realism" of the 1940s' children's book, its focus on economic hardship and injustice, was stripped away. The Millers and Martins are hardworking farmers, common to the core and often contrasted with snobby rich folks, but the series rarely gives us any sense of the difficult financial status of the "family farm" in the 1950s and 1960s. Similarly, the relocation of Lassie from Yorkshire to the United States involved something more than her Americanization. Television's *Lassie* lacks geographic specificity; its idyllic, pastoral space could exist in any part of the country, and Lassie's various encounters with woodland creatures cut across all known biomes. CBS clearly wanted the Millers's farm to seem like "home" to all Americans, and as a result, it abandoned Knight's careful attempts to document a particular way of life.

Most of the episodes centered around everyday mishaps: Jeff and Porky are forced to babysit for a six-year-old brat who causes them endless trouble; Lassie brings home a litter of kittens, but the Millers can't get them to eat; Timmy accidentally breaks Uncle Petrie's guitar and has to raise money to fix it. Many of these stories could have been told just as well on any of the other domestic situation comedies. Here, Lassie, not the father, knows best. Where more serious incidents occurred, offering opportunities for Lassie's curative powers, they tended to come from outside the core family—via escaped convicts, bankrupt traveling circuses, blinded Korean War returnees, eccentric old ladies who live on the outskirts of town, Japanese American families hoping to settle in the community, crop dusters down on their luck, or deer poachers, to cite only examples from *Lassie*'s first two seasons. In these cases, Lassie is given the chance to reform the wicked and restore the weary.

Having made the virtues of rural living and the American family its ideological bedrock, *Lassie* confronts the dangers posed to this traditional culture by the city (which throughout the American sentimental tradition, was cast as the source of evil and corruption) and technology (which is frequently seen as threatening to break down organic communal bonds). City folk are either so green that they get into trouble—falling into wells, sliding off cliffs, getting lost in the woods—or they bring crime and violence—kidnapping Lassie, hitting her with a car, organizing pit bull fights. In both cases, these urban visitors provide ideal foils for the family's closeness to the natural world and their fundamental honesty. Most often, technological changes are initiated by members of the family and must be negotiated against Lassie's commitments to more traditional lifestyles.

In "The New Refrigerator," for instance, trouble starts when the Martins purchase an electric refrigerator, a long-coveted luxury: "let others have their mink coats." The episode, however, has established a solid friendship between Lassie and the iceman, who is resigned to his displacement by modern technology; even his wife has bought a fridge. Lassie loudly resists the displacement of traditional social networks in favor of the convenience of consumer culture, barking fiercely at the "white monster." As June protests, "Lassie, you're a reactionary." The conflict is presented as a struggle between "two stubborn females" each insistent on protecting their desired way of life. The equation of the mother and dog is most powerfully asserted when June pleads, "Lassie, can't you try to get along with my new refrigerator? I wouldn't bark at something you've always wanted." Despite repeated efforts to train her, Lassie refuses to eat food from the new machine. Ultimately, a crisis secures Lassie's acceptance—Timmy pulls a barrel down on his head and the collie races to the refrigerator to bring him ice. For Lassie, the technology must be seen as central to the family's survival before she can give her blessing.

Given the series' emphasis on the fundamentally conservative nature of rural life and the stability of the nuclear family, the disruptions and anxieties unleashed in "Transition" are startling. Suddenly, in a single episode, the Millers must confront death, bankruptcy, the selling of the family farm, a move to the city, Jeff's manhood, and perhaps most traumatic, the loss of Lassie. "Transition" attests to the power of the sentimental attachments between a boy and his dog. Nothing short of total cataclysm could break them apart.

Escaping Domesticity: The Ranger Stuart Years

1964. During the last week of summer, the Martins load up the family station wagon and take Timmy and Lassie camping. While Alice prepares food, the others go out in a boat to fish. An unexpected storm capsizes their boat. Timmy and Paul make it to shore, but Lassie has disappeared. The parents tell Timmy that "all we can do now is wait and hope," but privately they are worried. The Martins have little success interesting the local authorities in the case: "They have to deal with a lot of human problems right now and a missing collie report just doesn't seem that important to them." As the episode closes, we catch a glimpse of Lassie swimming toward a boat, but it will take four episodes to unite Lassie and Timmy again. Timmy spends the time pining for the lost dog, while his parents urge him to come to terms with harsh facts:

> We can cry for her but we've got to live with reality. . . . We've had more than our share of happiness having a dog like Lassie. Now all we can do is accept the sadness and go on from there.

Learning to deal with such traumatic loss is "part of life, part of growing up," as nature suddenly seems far-less benign than in previous episodes.

Meanwhile, viewers watch Lassie get rescued by a park ranger, Corey Stuart, and form an intense partnership with him as they travel together rescuing other victims of the storm, stopping a poacher from killing game on federal land, and surviving both a forest fire and an avalanche. In the end, Corey restores the dog to Timmy, disappointed that they will have to go their separate ways. Understanding their bond, Timmy laments, "I wish there could be two Lassies." For once, the uniqueness of this "priceless" dog seems a liability rather than an asset.

This four-part story arc began the season-long process of transferring Lassie from Timmy to Ranger Stuart. Here, the melodrama arises from two equally strong bonds and only one Lassie. One or the other must relinquish their claim. If Stuart makes the first sacrifice, just moments after declaring "it would take a department directive and a herd of wild horses to get her away from me," he will ultimately possess her. As the episodes' succession of cliff-hanging spectacles suggests, Lassie will be removed from the safety of pastoral America (with its ties to domestic melodrama). Stuart will teach Lassie to experience the call of the wild: "Listen to the birds, girl. The wind in the trees. The sound of the river. That's the song of the forest." Having heard its cry, Lassie can no longer be fully domesticated, and the logic of the series will push her further and further from well-worn paths. By the series' final season on network television, Lassie has become a lone wanderer, cut off from all permanent ties, yet always stopping along her journey to aid and assist humans in trouble. Lassie, the "come-home dog," no longer has a home. As the ranger explains, "I never know from day to day where I'll be." The result is a rethinking of the series' generic placement.

Throughout the nineteenth century, the growing emphasis on the sentimental value of the individual child was linked to the development of more specialized categories of children's fiction, books aimed at the particular needs of growing girls or boys. Whereas before, children's books were undifferentiated in their address, the new children's books prepared boys for participation in a public sphere of individualistic action and girls for involvement in a domestic sphere of familial relations. Reviewing the educational and publishing philosophies shaping this redefinition of children's literature along gender lines, Elizabeth Segal writes:

> Before the boy's book appeared on the scene, fiction for children typically had been domestic in setting, heavily didactic and morally or spiritually uplifting. . . . The boy's book was, above all, an escape from domesticity and from the female domination of the domestic world. The adventures of

> Tom and Huck, of Jim Hawkins and many lesser heroes of boys' books are the epitome of freedom in part because they are an escape from women, the chief agents of socialization in the culture.[31]

Lassie as both a book and television series struggles to bridge the rigid separation of boy's and girl's books, making the sentimental values associated with the girl's book acceptable to male readers and domesticating the action elements connected with the boy's book.[32]

Lassie Come Home contrasts sharply with a classic boy's book like Jack London's *The Call of the Wild.* The books open in similar ways: Buck, the purebred German shepherd, is kidnapped from his loving bourgeois owners and sold into servitude in the wilds of Alaska, while Lassie is sold to the duke and transported to Scotland. Both dogs go on a lengthy journey and confront a series of life-risking adventures before they arrive at their desired destinations. Buck, however, responds to the call of the wild, finding his place as the powerful leader of a wolf pack; his adventure breaks down his ties to the human realm and establishes his dominance within a brutal natural hierarchy ("the law of club and fang"). Lassie responds to the call of the hearth; she remains in the grips of powerful domestic urges. Something inside her demands that she wait for Joe outside the school gate, and she braves everything to get there. Buck is strengthened by his encounters with natural elements, erupting in uncontainable phallic power:

> His muscles were surcharged with vitality, and snapped into play sharply, like steel springs. Life streamed through him in splendid flood, glad and rampant, until it seemed that it would burst him asunder in sheer ecstasy and pour forth generously over the world.[33]

Lassie is worn down by her exile from the domestic sphere, arriving home a pained martyr with bleeding paws and limping limbs:

> This was a dog that lay, weakly trying to lift a head that would no longer lift; trying to move a tail that was torn and matted with thorns and burrs, and managing to do nothing very much except to whine in a weak, happy, crying way. (pp. 175–76)

That Buck is the "dominant primordial beast" and Lassie "her suffering aristocratic majesty" has much more to do with human assumptions about gender than breed distinctions between German shepherds and collies.

Lassie's femininity allows her to slide comfortably into the melodramatic traditions associated with the girl's sentimental novel. Her saga is a variant on the maternal melodrama where a mother struggles to reclaim possession or

"You're a Good Mother."

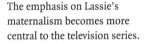

The emphasis on Lassie's maternalism becomes more central to the television series.

access to her children, or the slave story, where she is sold "upriver" to a bad owner and kept in chains, but escapes and makes her way to freedom.[34] Lassie's status as a dog, however, allows her to escape the constraints placed on human females and translate melodrama's passive suffering into decisive action; she fights back, tooth and claw, against anything that stands between her and the people she loves.

The emphasis on Lassie's maternalism becomes more central to the television series. Throughout the Jeff and Timmy years, Lassie remains fairly close to home, having adventures on or around the family farm. All things are relative. Compared to the fenced-in suburban backyards experienced by her viewers, Lassie and Timmy enjoyed extraordinary freedom to roam across a vast range of open spaces. Roger Hart, who studied suburban children's use of play space in the early 1970s, found that children in the fourth and fifth grades enjoy mobility only within 300 yards of their houses, while ten and eleven year olds could count on doubling that distance once they owned bikes.[35] Such mobility was greater than that of city children from the same period. Timmy's play space was much larger still, and offered more opportunities to get into trouble or encounter strangers. Still, compared to the 1,000-mile journey across Scotland and northern England in the Knight novel, television's Lassie was cribbed and confined. (Interestingly, given the series' focus on the great outdoors, most of the *Lassie* merchandise seemed designed for indoor play, such as board games, viewmaster slides, stuffed dolls, figurines, breakfast dishes, and paint-with-water sets.)[36]

As the story became more homebound, the boys, Jeff and Timmy, become more and more central to the program's appeal. Like "Beaver" or Dennis the Menace, Jeff and Timmy were the inheritors of the "bad boy" tradition that literary critics and historians associate with Tom Sawyer and Huck Finn.[37] In keeping with the permissive era faith in childhood innocence, the more mean-spirited and antiauthoritarian aspects of this earlier literary tradition have been discarded. Jeff and Timmy are not active rebels against the maternal sphere, they are simply innocent explorers of adult spaces, naturally boisterous inhabitants of a world where "boys will be boys." If the nineteenth-century "bad boy" escaped the constraints of maternal authority, the ever-watchful Lassie goes out into the woods with Timmy and makes sure he doesn't get into trouble. As Cully explains to Timmy in one episode, "Lassie's always looked after you like her own puppy." Under Lassie's maternal supervision, the wildest corner of the woods remains as safe as a suburban backyard.

Ranger Stuart's relationship to Lassie is profoundly different. As an unmarried adult male, he has no family, no mother, no domestic entanglements of any kind, and so, under his ownership, Lassie is free to roam the entire North American continent. Stuart and Lassie part and come together multiple times, having adventures separately and as a team. Lassie's worth gets redefined in terms of her professional accomplishments—the rescues she performs, the messages she delivers. She battles fires, saves stranded campers from avalanches, survives being swept away by rapids, and helps a man caught under a falling powerline. Stuart consistently refers to her as his "partner" or, more suggestively, "girlfriend." The ideal of pastoral America, the world of civilized communities, gave way almost entirely to images of a wild frontier space, where men and dogs are tested and tempered through their encounter with the natural realm. Under the ranger's ownership, *Lassie* fully embraces the boy's book tradition, becoming a series more about the call of the wild than the yearning for the hearth.

This generic and geographic relocation reflects larger shifts in the way popular entertainment represented the natural order. In the 1950s, when *Lassie* debuted, the collie existed alongside a succession of popular representations of dogs, horses, cats, and other domesticated animals. Walt Disney, alone, was responsible for bringing to the screen *Lady and the Tramp* (1955), *Old Yeller* (1957), *The Shaggy Dog* (1959), *101 Dalmatians* (1961), *Nikki, Wild Dog of the North* (1961), *Greyfriars Bobby* (1961), *Big Red* (1962), *Savage Sam* (1963), and *The Incredi-*

Timmy Tumbles

As Cully explains to Timmy in one episode, "Lassie's always looked after you like her own puppy."

ble Journey (1963), all classic dog stories, many of which became staples of Walt Disney's Wonderful World of Color. Television viewers could watch The Adventures of Rin Tin Tin (1954–1959), My Friend Flicka (1956–1958), and National Velvet (1960–1962). By the mid-1960s, popular representations of animals tended to favor wild and untamed creatures rather than domesticated animals. On television, Flipper (1964–1968) dealt with a boy and his dolphin, and Gentle Ben (1967–1969), a boy and his black bear. Films like Born Free (1966), The Jungle Book (1967), and Maya (1966), as well as television series such as Daktari (1966–1969) and Cowboy in Africa (1967–1968), departed from the "civilized" realms of England and America to deal with the "untamed" wildlife of Africa and Asia. By 1969, Lassie was going head-to-head on Sunday nights with Wild Kingdom, a series full of lurid images of predators and prey and deadly poisonous snakes. Lassie's shift toward outdoor adventure during the Ranger Stuart years both anticipates and participates in this renewed focus on undomesticated fauna.

This move from domesticated to wild animals finds its parallels in the child-rearing literature of the period. Most of the 1950s and early 1960s' films and television series can be traced back to literary sources in the prewar era. The focus on finely trained and domesticated animals was consistent with the then dominant behaviorist paradigm, with its emphasis on regimentation, discipline, control, and domestication. The postwar period of childrearing, on the other hand, was characterized by the trend toward permissiveness, popularized by Spock. Permissiveness stressed freedom rather than discipline, and the "natural" development of children outside tight parental control; it spawned a cult of primitivism, drawing close analogies from the anthropological literature of Margaret Mead. Permissive children were wild and untamed, demanding a world that respected their natural impulses. Although encyclopedic on other aspects of children's lives, permissive writers say almost nothing about dogs and other pets. They do see a value in children engaging with the natural world, but they offer camping trips, walks in the woods, or visits to the zoo. This idealization of the untamed natural world required Lassie, no less than Born Free's Elsa, to leave the constraints of domestic space for the freedom of the wild kingdom.

In liberating Lassie from the domestic space, the producers broke apart the complex set of generic compromises between the sentimental girl's book tradition and the blood-and-guts boy's book tradition that gave the series immunity from popular criticism. Popular discourse about children's television circled around distinctions between classic children's literature and comic books, education and entertainment, realism and sensationalism. Reformers, such as Newton Minnow, consistently urged producers to seek their inspiration from respected literary works rather than comic books and pulp magazines.[38] Children's programs were viewed positively by teachers and reformers alike if they encouraged children to read. Often, there was an implicit (or even explicit) preference for the sentimental values associated with girls' books, and a vilification of the suspense and adventure elements associated with boys' books. Lassie's ties back to a recognized literary classic and its in between status helped the series to overcome some of these most basic objections, paving the way for its widespread acceptance as "wholesome" entertainment. A Parent's Guide to Children's Reading (1958), for example, specifically praises Lassie along with Mary Martin's Peter Pan and Walt Disney's Davy Crockett as programs that encourage youngsters to return to the library shelves.[39] Moreover, at a time when post-Sputnik parents were eager for their children to embrace science and natural history, everything from Lassie to Mr. Wizard was cited for its potential educational benefit.

Nevertheless, the sensational boy's book elements, however subdued in the Jeff and Timmy years, were still potentially problematic and became more so in the Ranger Stuart period. One television producer, for instance, pointed to Lassie in 1967 as an example of how the vividness and immediacy of television added luridness: "Lassie is one of the scariest shows for kids. They see a real kid and a real dog in real danger."[40] Animal-centered adventure series were repeatedly panned by the National Association for Better Radio and Television and other such groups. In 1956, to cite one case, the group condemned Rin Tin Tin as one of the "most objectionable" programs on television: "Tense situations exist throughout the program and unbelievable problems are solved by this incredible dog. . . . Wholesome episodes are the exception."⁴¹ Suspenseful story lines, especially those dependent on children in jeopardy, were feared to overstimulate children's active imaginations.⁴² Here, Flipper was condemned for "story themes [that] abound in crime and involve youngsters in extremely dangerous situations."⁴³ PTA magazine wrote with outrage about the debut of Gentle Ben:

> For years there have been warnings to children and adults against feeding and playing with bears. . . . How CBS could permit a program with a black bear for a pet—not a cub either—but a gigantic adult bear—is beyond our comprehension.⁴⁴

Though Lassie's mid-1960s' episodes are not noticeably different from those of Flipper or Gentle Ben, it continued to get the approval of the parent-teacher association and other reform-oriented groups while the competing animal series were condemned.

Once again, the transfer of ownership (from Timmy to Ranger Stuart), as well as the breaking of the intense bonds between master and pet, occurs only by throwing family togetherness and pastoralism into crisis. This time, these images of boyhood, family, and farm will be banished altogether to allow for greater mobility, more suspense, and a wilder conception of the natural world. As the episode opens, both Timmy and his adopted father are eagerly awaiting the mail. Timmy wants the delivery of a dog tag for Lassie, while the father hopes for more dramatic news about a "wonderful opportunity for all of us." He plans to move the all-American Martin family to Australia, where he insists there is lots of land and not enough people. Yet bad news follows. Lassie will have to be placed on a six-month quarantine before she will be admitted into the country. For a dog used to the freedom that Lassie has enjoyed, such confinement would be unendurable. Timmy refuses to speak to his father, begs to stay behind with Ranger Stuart, and finally threatens to run away from home. "It's tearing us to pieces. I've never seen him act this way before," Ruth exclaims, startled by her normally goody-goody son's willfulness. Paul, however, understands the boy's powerless rage: "He's just a little boy in a grown-up world and that ain't an easy thing to be. Things get decided for you and there isn't nothing you can do about it."

In Knight's Lassie Come Home, Joe never questions his father's "right" to sell his dog, even though the boy continues to hope for its return. When his father speaks, Joe obeys. The boy is silenced on several occasions by a firmly expressed "no." In the postwar period, though, the issue of parental authority had undergone a dramatic transformation, with more child-centered parenting styles seen as fundamentally democratic and most appropriate for raising children into American citizenship. Rudolf Dreikurs's *Children: The Challenge* (1964) charts the different political models behind pre- and postwar child-rearing practices:[45]

Autocratic society	Democratic society
Authority figure	Knowledgeable leader
Power	Influence
Pressure	Stimulation
Demanding	Winning cooperation
Punishment	Logical consequences
Reward	Encouragement
Imposition	Permit self-determination
Domination	Guidance
Children are seen and not heard	Listen! Respect the child
YOU do because I said to	WE do because it is necessary

A conscious effort was made following World War II to reconstruct both the American family and children's culture according to these "democratic" principles.

Many of the key architects of postwar children's culture had served together as part of filmmaker Frank Capra's propaganda unit during the Second World War.[46] Capra assembled a remarkable group that included Theodor Geisel ("Doctor Seuss"), Chuck Jones (Loony Toons), P. D. Eastman (*Are You My Mother?*), Stanley Kramer (*Boy with the Green Hair*, *5,000 Fingers of Dr. T*), and Eric Knight. Knight was killed during the war, so he did not directly participate in the postwar shifts in popular discourse about parents and children, or in the attempt to create a more playful, pleasure-centered culture. Nonetheless, television's *Lassie* embraced at least some permissive doctrines. The sudden introduction of the issue of parental authority represented a significant adjustment in the program ideology.

Lassie cannot be taken from Timmy by force of parental autocracy or legal fiat. The episode must reconcile father and son. First, Lassie distances herself from Timmy. Timmy tells his elderly friend, Cully, that "Lassie's acting strange. She's usually right by my side but now she's gone." Cully links the changes to Timmy's coming of age, implying that as a boy turns into a man, he no longer needs the maternal presence of a dog: "You're growing up and Lassie's sensing it. . . . Lassie knows you've got to be on your own. You've got to stand on your own two feet." Second, Paul apologizes to Timmy for being too domineering: "Maybe I was wrong when I made such a big decision without all of us talking it over." Timmy, however, has accepted the move and the "sacrifice" he must make. By the episode's end, he turns the dog over to Cully. After a series of further misadventures, Cully, in turn, grants custody to Ranger Stuart, explaining that he thinks this is what Timmy would have wanted: "Lassie's a special dog. She needs to be right in the middle of things." Indeed, it is this need for immediacy and excitement that propels *Lassie* from domestic melodrama into outdoor adventure.

Postscript: 1996

Nostalgia, Susan Stewart notes, is "sadness without an object," a longing for a more perfect past that never quite existed.[47] Children and dogs are central figures for nostalgia, evoking images of innocence that adults cannot reclaim and loyalty that defies human understanding. These myths are culturally powerful, serving to reconcile and resolve, at least temporarily, any number of ideological contradictions. They seem to offer us a way out of our adult human problems into a world of simpler moral choices and undying commitments. Yet, as we have seen, the need to tell that story, to communicate our ideals about children and dogs through narrative rather than static images, requires the constant enactment of a threat to their world: things cannot remain simple and pure for long. In the *Lassie* series, such threats surface most dramatically in those episodes that revolve around a change in Lassie's ownership, since these story lines require a dissolution of one set of social ties between children and dogs and the forging of an alternative set of affections. Such a transformation unleashes all of the dangers that traditional children's literature tries to protect children from confronting. In the process, the series' generic formulas often also undergo a shift, and with that, some alteration in the symbolic and sentimental values attached to the beloved collie. *Lassie's* status as a "timeless" myth of core human values is contradicted by the way that the series has been subjected to historic change. Our emotional attachment to *Lassie*, however, may still be governed by the things that do not change in our memory, the kinds of stock images that supplant any specific plotlines when we try to remember what it was like watching *Lassie* as boys and girls.

This is an essay about the way our culture lives with nostalgia, the ways that certain myths about children and dogs spring forth to help us deal with our anxieties about change. At the same time, this essay is a personal exercise in nostalgia, a way back to my own boyhood and my own dog, Brownie, a half-breed female collie. Brownie was my companion from kindergarten through most of high school; she had three litters of puppies, and mothered a succession of pet rabbits, ducks, chicks, turtles, and neighborhood children. Brownie loved to take boat rides and would lap at the wake. Still, she lived most of her life in a fenced-in suburban backyard. As a preadolescent, I was obsessed with the idea that when this dog died, my childhood would be over. Unlike Lassie, Brownie did not go on to bigger adventures with forest rangers when she passed from my possession. She simply died; then she was put in an old cardboard box and left out on the curb for the garbageman to take away. That's how we were legally required to dispose of dead pets in the early 1970s.

Once, I loved a dog. Now, I hate them. Living, breathing canines fill me not with longing, but rather an intense loathing. I plot sinister revenge on my neighbor's yapping dog, who somehow senses and amplifies my hostility.

When I think of dogs, I think of the smell of dog breath in the tight confines of the backseat of the family station wagon and the scent of fresh urine in the plush carpet; I think of the slippery feeling of saliva on my hands after a dog licks it; I think of the unsettling sensation of slipping and sliding barefoot on dog poop hidden in the freshly cut grass; I think of ear-wrenching yelps and barks, of toenails scratching on linoleum; I think of that grayish jelly junk that forms on the top of cans of dog food. I have trouble seeing past the body of the farting, panting, drooling, barking, shitting beast and into the spirit, the romantic ideal, of the domesticated pet. I find the myth of the dog fascinating, but the reality disgusting. Across twenty years of American television, nobody ever stepped in Lassie's poop.

Perhaps this all seems too embarrassingly personal, yet what I want to suggest has to do with our shared cultural construction of the dog, both what it contains and what it excludes. Our mythic reconstruction of the dog involves an isolation of the animal from the reality of its body, just as our myth of childhood innocence involves the isolation of the child from its sexuality and a denial of its agency. Dogs and children are stripped of all their messy bits so they can fetch and carry things for us. When I remember Brownie, I sometimes view her with the mythic aura that surrounds Lassie, as a larger-than-life embodiment of maternal love and childhood freedom. Yet those other more tactile and pungent memories are part of my lived experience of dog ownership, the part we don't talk about, the part that the longing of nostalgia tends to suppress.

When I write about Lassie, I am writing about a dog I never had, indeed, a dog I never could have had. Through writing about her, I reclaim access to a pastoral, conservative, American ideal whose values I do not fully share, but which on occasion, I long for nevertheless. I mourn the death of Brownie, the loss of Lassie, and the end of a world where I found it hard to separate the two. The myth of the faithful dog, Kathleen Kete tells us, stood as a compensation for the reality of faithless people, a bulwark against modern fears of death and loneliness, and the myth always carries with it a sense of mourning and loss.

The essential point about nostalgia is that things are not the same.

In "Heavy Petting," Marjorie Garber describes 1994 as "the Year of the Dog."[48] She cites the popular success of books like *The Hidden Life of Dogs*, *The Intelligence of Dogs*, and *Animal Happiness*, which all rediscover the power of personification, insisting that we can understand how dogs think through the power of empathetic identification. She points to popular films like *Homeward Bound* and *Look Who's Talking Now*, as well as the chic photograph books of William Wegman and Thierry Poncelet. She even notes the release of a new *Lassie* movie and a series of tie-in books. Still, through it all, I remain unconvinced. Things are not the same. There is something annoyingly artificial, self-conscious, and even posing about these postmodern representations of the dog, as if we weren't supposed to take them all so seriously and, above all, weren't supposed to feel the sentimental tug of dog love. If the nineteenth-century French bourgeoisie invested their sense of loss into a compensatory myth of canine loyalty, we tend to discard such feelings behind a facade of carefree parody. As I sit down to write, I find an article in the *New York Times* that sums it all up too perfectly.[49] Dog and cat owners, we are told, are employing a "high-tech method to identify their pets in case they are lost or stolen." A small microchip with an information number is implanted just under its skin, allowing for precise identification should the animal be separated from its owner. One particular California-based Humane Society has "chipped" between 10,000 and 11,000 pets. "It's not so easy with a 125-pound Rottweiler to find a tattoo," one vet explains.[50]

As I ponder the image of Lassie as a cyborg collie, I recall the centrality of her unique identity to the whole saga. In the concluding passage of *Lassie Come Home*, the Carracloughs give their come-home dog a makeover, not so that they can fool the duke into thinking she is another dog, but rather to convince him to relinquish his claims on her ownership. Under the hands of a skilled dog's man, Lassie is transformed:

> For where Lassie's skull was aristocratic and slim, this dog's head was clumsy and rough. Where Lassie's ears stood in the grace of twin-lapped symmetry, this dog had one screw ear and the other standing up Alsatian fashion, in a way that would give any collie breeder the cold shivers. More than that. Where Lassie's coat faded to delicate sable, this curious dog had ugly splashes of black; and where Lassie's apron was a billowing expanse of white, this dog had muddy puddles of off-white, blue-merle mixture. (p. 188)

The duke recognizes Lassie at first glance, even when it flies in the face of human comprehension that she could have made a 1,000-mile journey. As if there is any doubt, he looks at her paws, "crossed and recrossed with half-healed scars where thorns had torn and stones had lacerated!" (p. 189). The duke knows, in his soul, that this dog is Lassie, just as Joe does not have any difficulty identifying the exhausted and emaciated animal that he finds waiting for him after school. Still, miracle of miracles, the duke releases Lassie back to her morally rightful owners: "This is no dog of mine. 'Pon my soul and honor, she never belonged to me. No! Not for a single second did she ever belong to me!" (p. 189). And with those words, with this moment of sublime recognition, Sam is released from his unfortunate deal.

Neither the duke nor Joe, neither Jeff nor Timmy, nor any of the others who were blessed to own Lassie through the years, needed a microchip to identify her. I recognize that the microchip is an act of love, a response to a changed society, a harsh reality we have to live with. But reality falls far short of our cherished myths. Lassie was unique, priceless, without possible imitation or counterfeit. Her spiritual qualities, her moral authority, her "suffering aristocratic majesty," was possessed by no other dog, and only those who understand that distinction were allowed to have a dog like Lassie. Moreover, even if her human owners were confused, Lassie would have known and would have made her wishes known. Something has broken down in the relations between dogs and their masters. The myth of the faithful dog no longer offers us condolences in the face of a feckless world. If the myths of canine fidelity and childhood innocence were central tropes through which our culture dealt with the threats of modernity, such myths of authenticity and natural social relations have no place in a postmodern world.

It is perhaps symptomatic of such a realm that people have read the above postscript and not known whether I was telling the truth about my dog, my nausea, my tears, or my nostalgia. That ambiguity is an essential aspect of nostalgia—we want to believe and yet, at the same time, we can't; we know that the past we create through our myths, our memories, our popular fictions, is only partially true. My relation to dogs is not reducible either to my very real mourning of a lost object of desire nor to my equally real distaste for shit and spit. Our cultural relations to dogs are not reducible either to postmodern chic or authentic celebration. Dogs conjure up complex feelings, contradictory emotions, irreconcilable myths. All of it is true, but none of it is all true. In the end, nostalgia always frustrates the desires that fuel its search for a more perfect past. We can't trust our feelings, memories, or myths.

Things are not the same.

They never were.

Notes

1   Kathleen Kete, *The Beast in the Boudoir: Petkeeping in Nineteenth-Century Paris* (Berkeley: University of California Press, 1994).

2   On James Bond as a popular hero, see Tony Bennett and Janet Woollacott, *Bond and Beyond: The Political Career of a Popular Hero* (New York: Methuen, 1987). On Batman, see William Urrichio and Roberta Pearson, eds., *The Many Lives of the Batman: Critical Approaches to a Superhero and His Media* (New York: Routledge, Chapman and Hall, 1991).

3   Most of these images can be found in *Lassie Coloring Book* (Racine, Wis.: Whitman, 1962).

4   Jacqueline Rose reminds us that fantasies of a transparent relationship between language and the world, and of a simple moral legibility, are at the heart of contemporary conceptions of children's fiction. Jacqueline Rose, *The Case of Peter Pan: Or the Impossibility of Children's Fiction* (London: Macmillan Publishers Ltd., 1984).

5   James R. Kinkaid, *Child-Loving: The Erotic Child and Victorian Culture* (New York: Routledge, 1992), 79.

6   Eric Knight, *Lassie Come Home* (New York: Dell, 1940), 1. All subsequent citations will be made in the text.

7   Kete, *Beast in the Boudoir*, esp. 39–55.

8   Harriet Ritvo argues that this shift reflected growing middle-class fantasies of upward mobility and class assimilation, as the lower orders mimicked the practices of those better off. Harriet Ritvo, *The Animal Estate: The English and Other Creatures in the Victorian Age* (Cambridge, Mass.: Harvard University Press, 1987), 93–104.

9   Knight's writings helped to popularize the collie as the ideal pet for U.S. children. In 1944, there were fewer than 3,000 collies in the United States. Following the popularity of the book and the series of six MGM films that it spawned, sales skyrocketed, resulting in 18,400 registrations of purebred collies by 1949. See Susan M. Brown, "Foreword: A Charismatic Collie and Her Fifty-Year Influence," in *Lassie: A Collie and Her Influence*, ed. Susan M. Brown (St. Louis, Mo.: Dog Museum, 1993), 4.

10 Ritvo, *Animal Estate*, 89.

11 For an example of such a reading, see Emily D. Berkley, "Lassie and American Culture," in *Lassie: A Collie and Her Influence*, ed. Susan M. Brown (St. Louis, Mo.: Dog Museum, 1993), 6–17.

12 Background information on Eric Knight, throughout this essay, comes from Elizabeth Wasserman, "Eric Knight and *Lassie Come Home*," in *Lassie: A Collie and Her Influence*, ed. Susan M. Brown (St. Louis, Mo.: Dog Museum, 1993), 18–23.

13 Eric Knight, quoted in Wasserman, "Eric Knight," 22.

14 Ibid., 20.

15 Viviana A. Zelizer, *Pricing the Priceless Child: The Changing Social Value of Children* (New York: Basic Books, 1985).

16 Mary Lynn Stevens Heininger, "Children, Childhood, and Change in America, 1820–1920," in *A Century of Childhood, 1820–1920*, ed. Mary Lynn Stevens Heininger et al. (Rochester, N.Y.: Margaret Woodbury Strong Museum, 1984), 31.

17 See Harriet Ritvo, "Barring the Cross: Miscegenation and Purity in Eighteenth- and Nineteenth-Century Britain," in *Human All Too Human*, ed. Diana Fuss (New York: Routledge, 1996), 37–58.

18 For the most part, as Harriet Ritvo notes, those distinctions between breeds were emptied of meaningful content (having everything to do with the sentimental value and

physical beauty of dogs, and nothing to do with their functionality or adaptability). Ritvo, *Animal Estate,* 104–15.

19   Kete, *Beast in the Boudoir,* 94.

20   Ace Collins, *Lassie: A Dog's Life* (New York: Cader, 1993), 94.

21   The ideological motivations behind this prolonged transition are clearer when we recognize that the roles of the Martins, Timmy's adoptive parents, were recast, without acknowledgment or explanation, at the end of the first season of the Timmy years, since the producers were unhappy with the chemistry between Cloris Leachman and Jon Sheppodd. Timmy's relationship to his parents was a minor footnote in the series; the focus was on the boy and his dog.

22   Richard Dyer, "Entertainment and Utopia," in *Movies and Methods,* vol. 2, ed. Bill Nichols (Berkeley: University of California Press, 1985); and Fredric Jameson, "Reification and Utopia in Mass Culture," *Social Text* (winter 1979): 130–48.

23   Sally Allen McNall, "American Children's Literature, 1880–Present," in *American Childhood: A Research Guide and Historical Handbook,* ed. Joseph M. Hawes and N. Ray Hiner (Westport, Conn.: Greenwood, 1985), 388.

24   Ibid., 393.

25   Berkley, "Lassie and American Culture," 8.

26   A similar fate befell the protagonists of *National Velvet,* which was adapted for television at about the same time.

27   Lassie's biographer Ace Collins sees this shift as commonsensical, requiring no special explanation: "Maxwell and Rudd came up with the concept of an old-time farm set somewhere in modern-day Middle America. The family would consist of a boy, a mother and a grandfather. With World War II a recent memory and the Korean War creating a new appreciation of American fighting men, it was decided that the father would have been lost during military service, like Eric Knight himself, thus putting more of a focus on the mother's and grandfather's roles and creating a patriotic stance for the show. Because the family was poor and lacked an active young adult male member, the farm would be a bit run-down, presenting a nostalgic look much like a Norman Rockwell painting. Maxwell knew that even with America becoming more urban, folks still yearned for the ideals of a simpler time" (Collins, *A Dog's Life,* 79). Through this process, television's *Lassie* became a distinctly American myth.

28   Nina C. Leibman, *The Living-room Lectures: The Fifties' Family in Film and Television* (Austin: University of Texas Press, 1995), 25.

29   Ace Collins notes that this time slot was initially seen as undesirable for family programming: "Viewership was low at this time and the demographic mix was bad. Many people were eating, throughout the Bible Belt people were in church, and television usually remained off until 8:00 p.m." (Collins, *A Dog's Life,* 83).

30   Cyclops, quoted in David Zinman, *Saturday Afternoon at the Bijou* (New York: Castle Books, 1973), 473. Zinman offers a detailed discussion of the production of the films, as well as the casting and training of the collies who have played Lassie through the years.

31   Elizabeth Segal, " 'As the Twig Is Bent . . . ': Gender and Childhood Reading," in *Gender and Reading: Essays on Readers, Texts, and Contexts,* ed. Elizabeth A. Flynn and Patrocinio P. Schweickart (Baltimore, Md.: Johns Hopkins University Press, 1986), 171.

32   As Elizabeth Segal notes, American educational policy has typically favored the teaching of books aimed predominantly at boys, since girls will read and often enjoy boys' books, while boys consistently reject girl-centered stories.

33 Jack London, *The Call of the Wild* (New York: Puffin, 1903), 120.

34 For a discussion of the sentimental tradition, see Jane Tompkins, "Sentimental Power: *Uncle Tom's Cabin* and the Politics of Literary History," in *Feminisms: An Anthology of Literary Theory and Criticism*, ed. Robyn R. Warhol and Diane Price Herndl (New Brunswick, N.J.: Rutgers University Press, 1991), 20–39.

35 Roger Hart, *Children's Experience of Place* (New York: John Wiley and Sons, 1979). See also Bernard Mergen, *Play and Playthings: A Reference Guide* (Westport, Conn.: Greenwood Press, 1982).

36 See Gayle Kaye, "Lassie Collectibles," in *Lassie: A Collie and Her Influence*, ed. Susan M. Brown (St. Louis, Mo.: Dog Museum, 1993), 24–31.

37 For a fuller discussion of this tradition and its influence on fifties' American television, see Henry Jenkins, "Dennis the Menace: The All American Handful,' in *The Revolution Wasn't Televised: Sixties Television and Social Conflict*, ed. Lynn Spigel and Michael Curtin (New York: Routledge, 1997).

38 Newton Minnow, "Is TV Cheating Our Children," *Parents*, February 1962, 52–54, 116. For a fuller discussion of the ways reformers constructed their cultural canons, see Lynn Spigel and Henry Jenkins, "Same Bat Channel, Different Bat Times: Mass Culture and Popular Memory," in *The Many Lives of the Batman: Critical Approaches to a Superhero and His Media*, ed. William Urrichio and Roberta Pearson (New York: Routledge, Chapman and Hall, 1991).

39 Nancy Larrick, *A Parent's Guide to Children's Reading for Parents and Teachers of Boys and Girls under Thirteen* (New York: Pocket, 1958). Sponsored by the National Book Committee, this report was surprisingly sympathetic to television.

40 "The Mini-Wasteland," *Newsweek*, 23 January 1967, 92–94.

41 "The Most Objectionable," *Newsweek*, 30 July 1956, 78.

42 Anna W. M. Wolf, "TV, Movies, Comics: Boon or Bane to Children?" *Parents*, April 1961, 46–48.

43 Frank Orme, "TV for Children: What's Good? What's Bad?" *Parents*, February 1962, 54 ff.

44 "Time out for Television," *PTA*, November 1967, 20.

45 Rudolf Dreikurs, *Children: The Challenge* (New York: Hawthorn, 1964), 153.

46 For more information on the Capra unit's influence on postwar children's culture, see Henry Jenkins, "A Person's a Person, No Matter How Small: Seuss, Capra, and Postwar America," in *Hop on Pop: The Pleasures and Politics of Popular Culture*, ed. Henry Jenkins, Tara McPherson, and Jane Shattuc (Durham, N.C.: Duke University Press, forthcoming).

47 Susan Stewart, *On Longing* (Durham, N.C.: Duke University Press, 1993), 23.

48 Marjorie Garber, "Heavy Petting," in *Human All Too Human*, ed. Diana Fuss (New York: Routledge, 1996), 11–36.

49 Dylan Loeb McLain, "Dogs and Cats with Chips on Their Shoulders," *New York Times*, 22 January 1996, D5.

50 Ibid.

Kings of the Wild Backyard: Davy Crockett and Children's Space   *Sean Griffin*

On March 20, 1955, Bill Hayes's recording of "The Ballad of Davy Crockett" entered the *Billboard* charts, and stayed there for twenty weeks, five of them as the number one song in the nation. The song helped spark the "Crockett Craze of 1955," a merchandising mania based on the enormous popularity of Walt Disney's version of the life of Davy Crockett (broadcast on the anthology series *Disneyland*), and one of the major American cultural events of the decade. Soon, numerous other artists (including Tennessee Ernie Ford, Eddy Arnold, Burl Ives, Mitch Miller, and even good ol' Fess Parker himself) recorded their own versions of the ballad. In six months, the combined record sales of all the versions was close to 7 million albums.[1]

Parents and teachers in 1955 fully endorsed the widespread popularity of Disney's "Davy Crockett." As Charles K. Wolfe's analysis of the ballad points out, parents valued Crockett's image because it kindled a feeling of Americanism. Wolfe finds the verses commonly recorded on the singles to be filled with "vague, patriotic platitudes" and "conspicuously lacking in . . . gritty detail." He goes on to notice that the one violent element in the song (and probably the most remembered line)—"kilt him a b'ar when he was only three"—was changed when the song was performed at the Disney theme park to "tamed him a b'ar."[2] Although parents approvingly bought Crockett paraphernalia for their offspring, Crockett's persona and appeal did not always conform to parental standards, and children did not always use Crockett's persona in the manner that parents endorsed. Indeed, contemporary advertisements, newspaper commentaries, and journal photographs on the "Crockett Craze" suggest that contrary to conventional histories of the fad, both children and adults struggled over what uses of the Crockett persona were appropriate.

One can find easy evidence of this contentiousness in the other songs about Davy Crockett that proliferated in the wake of the craze. A number of novelty tie-ins hit the record stores as well as the eponymous ballad, including the "Davy Crockett Mambo" and "Davy Crockett Boogie." In addition, parodies of the Disney ballad came out, replacing Davy with a stereotypical Mexican in "Pancho Lopez," turning Davy into a Jewish boy from Manhattan's Lower East Side in "Duvid Crockett," or making him a hillbilly in "The Ballad of Davy Crew-Cut."[3] *Time* magazine found the phenomenon so interesting that it chronicled these different parodies at the end of the summer of 1955. The article concluded with an "as yet mercifully unrecorded" rewrite from some youngsters in Texas:

> Born on a tabletop in Joe's Cafe,
> Dirtiest place in the USA,
> Killed his Paw with TNT,
> Killed his Maw with DDT.[4]

Wolfe's research unearths other folk parodies created by children. Missouri children sang a version called "Adolf Hitler," which began with "Born in a gutter in Germany." In 1960, a Tennessee folklorist discovered a children's adaptation of "On Top of Old Smokey" that recast the image of Crockett:

> On top of Old Smokey, all covered with snow,
> I saw Davy Crockett kiss Marilyn Monroe.
> He asked if she loved him, and she said No,
> BANG BANG, t'was the end of sweet Marilyn Monroe.[5]

These parodic lyrics challenge adults' interpretation of what children were supposed to find appealing in Crockett, reintroducing into the lyrics the violence and sexuality that the conventional words tried to elide. The "killing" of "Maw" and "Paw" directly ties these alternate lyrics to rebellion against parental constraint.

The Davy Crockett phenomenon consequently plays out the struggle over what Jacqueline Rose has termed the "impossibility" of childhood. The child, according to Rose, is a cultural construct, an image created by adults. *Childhood* is a concept of innocence, which has often little relation to the material experience of actual children.[6] Lynn Spigel has furthered this concept by linking the construction of childhood and television: "mass media have been seen as a threatening force that circulates forbidden secrets to children . . . [so] the adult culture has continually tried to filter the knowledge that mass media transmit to their young."[7] With this in mind, recurrent battles over cultural artifacts take on new meaning. A child's ability to use objects created by the dominant hegemonic system in defiance of adult standards acts as a point of "negotiation" or even "resistance"[8] (to use Stuart Hall's terms) to the construction of childhood innocence. Henry Jenkins's study of children watching Pee-wee Herman describes how "children draw upon prefabricated characters and situations of popular culture to make sense of their own social experience, reworking them to satisfy their own needs and desires."[9] Children take what they can and make their own culture with it, "poaching" as Michel de Certeau has called it.[10]

Margaret J. King's work on the "Crockett Craze" discusses the child using phrases from postwar sociologist David Riesman in his influential study *The Lonely Crowd*.[11] She borrows "other-directedness" to describe the wholesale adoption of Crockett as a manifestation of children pressured by the need to meet the expectations of their peer group, to conform to behavioral norms. While I am not denying the power relation that exists among children, what King misses in her focus is the power dynamic between children and the society that attempts to control them, and how this was manifested in the use of Davy Crockett.

This essay will utilize the "Crockett Craze" to examine the power relation between children and society at large, particularly as it relates to contentions over what physical space a child is allowed to inhabit. Beginning with a look at how postwar suburban America conceived of children's space, this essay will then explore how this conception was potentially problematized by Davy Crockett—"king of the wild frontier"—and what steps were taken to "manage" Crockett's image. Finally, this piece will hypothesize on the success of these steps.[12]

The Wild Frontier?

One of the most common labels for the post–World War II period is the baby boom. Returning veterans were encouraged, through special economic advantages, to buy or build their own homes to facilitate family growth. Women were expected to leave the jobs that they had held during the war and become homemakers. Marriage rates soared, and between 1946 and 1964, seventy-seven million children were born.[13] Postwar America viewed children as "a new symbol of hope. . . . (T)hey did not know what their parents knew; they hadn't lived through the hardships of the Great Depression and the war, nor did they bear the blame."[14] Children were seen as innocent, and hence, precious and valuable for the future of the American way of life (especially in the cold war period, in which this way of life was perceived as threatened by the forces of Communism).

As many cultural historians have noted, the conception of children as innocent and the hope for the future did not begin with the baby boom generation. "Since the early centuries of industrialization," Spigel explains, "children have been conceptualized as blank slates upon whom parents 'write' their culture."[15] Thus, parents desired to protect their child's innocence and properly guide it into the social order. The social movement known as the Progressive Era attempted to correct various social ills, with child labor and child safety looming large in the foreground. Viviana A. Zelizer's work on notions of children during this period highlights the importance that society at large placed on maintaining the innocence of children.[16] It was no longer just the place of the family to deal with a child's welfare. The child labor and child safety movements increasingly brought the entire political system into the discussion as well. While ostensibly created for "humanitarian" reasons, the growth of social reform movements along with governmental laws and bureaus also had the effect of regulating the experience of childhood in America.

A perfect example of this constriction can be found in the expanding limitations placed on the actual space a child was allowed to inhabit. Zelizer discusses the uproar caused by the death of children struck by trolleys and automobiles at the turn of the century.[17] "For their own safety," children needed to be taken off the streets. Ordinances were passed against children's street games. In the 1920s, there was an impetus to construct public playgrounds—by 1927, 790 cities reported a total of 5,600 playgrounds. In 1931, the Subcommittee on Housing and Home Management of the White House Conference on Child Health and Protection encouraged housing that gave a child a space of his or her own—a bedroom or separate playroom. In this way, a child would have no need to use the public space of the street, and hence, would be safely ensconced in the four walls of an easily monitored room. The actual space in which children were allowed to exist was slowly being eroded and roped off.

With the onset of the baby boom, there was an even larger perceived need to regulate children's space. Suddenly, there were little ones everywhere, just waiting to run out into the city streets and be hit by cars, or to fall down the stairs of urban apartment buildings. Social concerns that emerged from the war regarding psychological health and the family (through sociology and urban anthropology, as well as via popular psychology) began to question the effects of housing on mental health. One *House Beautiful* article dared to see the quality of the home as "the test of American civilization."[18] In this regard, urban living was found wanting. The suburbs around the urban centers of the United States, in contrast, grew at an extraordinary rate—unit developments and cluster housing projects such as Levittown invoking a more open space that would allow the postwar family (at least the white, middle-class family) the safety and freedom that urban dwellings could not.

Those who marketed this move to the suburbs consciously used the "wide-open" imagery of the Western frontier in their pitches to the American consumer. In the Los Angeles area, developments with names like Lasson Rancho in Van Nuys, Hickory Homes in Costa Mesa, and Fairview Ranches in Santa Ana were being built. While many have seen a variety of issues in Western iconography, contemporary writers such as Frederick Elkin and Martin Naussbaum posited the myth of the Western frontier as one that idealized and romanticized the individual, and (specifically gendered) his freedom in the open space of the unsettled American West.[19] The appeal of the Western frontier, then, meshed well with the desire for "the kinds of homes where the spirit of man [sic] can grow and flower, where each can develop in his [sic] own peculiar way."[20]

Without claiming that Los Angeles was a representative community, the trend toward using the myth of the West in marketing suburban living to white, middle-class families was not unique to Southern California. John Meskell, president of the Builders and Contractors Association of California, stated proudly in 1955 that "California is the nation's leader in home building. . . . Timesaving construction techniques, also developed in Southern California have greatly added to the nation's homebuilders' ability to mass-produce high-quality housing."[21] Increased industrialization spurred the rapid growth of the suburbs. Of course, with the creation of mass-produced prefabricated houses, uniqueness and individuality were rare if not impossible. Developers seemed to find an answer by wedding mass production to the myth of the Western frontier in the reliance on the "ranch-style" house model.[22] Advertisers compared the ranch-style home to Frank Lloyd Wright's modernist designs, which combined "low-pitched roofs, deep eaves and strong horizontal lines" with "more traditional elements like . . . shutters and a wide front porch."[23] In this way, the ranch-style home spoke of uniqueness and individuality by attempting to appeal to the "high art" of Wright's designs.

The child's place in suburbia figured strongly almost from the outset, especially in the discourse of the open space promised by the advertisements. Many of the ads for the newly built communities in the Los Angeles area stressed the advantages that a child would receive from living in the suburbs. The spirit of the frontier and the rural life that promoters displayed would give children room to live and grow, without fear of the dangers of city life. One *Los Angeles Times* ad for the Hollyglen development is quite blunt about it. The copy reads, "Carefully you watch your children's health, seeing that they get the proper food and rest. Equally important for them is the feeling of security you create through a happy life at home, at church and school. That's why you do a lot of thinking before you invest in a new home. And that's why you'll want to see [Hollyglen].[24]

Ironically, just as the industrial conditions of production precluded any true sense of individuality in housing, adults' concern over children in this new space attempted to close off children's freedom even as they professed to endorse it. Headlines in the *Los Angeles Times* in 1955 repeatedly reflect the perception of new dangers to the innocent child in the white, middle-class suburban landscape. Beyond the recurrent tales of children falling into deep holes or ravines, or being trapped in abandoned refrigerators, new terrors awaited the child (and the parent).[25] On the larger front, there was the threat of atomic war. Through 1955, the U.S. government conducted atomic tests in the deserts of Nevada—explosions that could be seen from downtown Los Angeles. By the spring of 1955, some homeowners were installing bomb shelters underneath their backyard lawns.[26] On the more local scene, there was the pool that accompanied many new suburban homes. Letters and articles in the *Times* warned of the imminent catastrophe of unsupervised children drowning in backyard pools.[27] Another article reported police finding a couple of young girls on their bicycles riding down the new freeway that passed by their neighborhood. The most recurrent topic in the news about suburban children concerned their wandering off in the neighborhood (and in the era of mass-produced duplicate houses, it would be easy to see how a child would get lost), generating parental hysteria and widespread police searches. Most of these stories ended with the discovery that the child was playing at someone else's house (without having informed their parents), or if truly lost, that the child was not particularly perturbed by the ordeal.[28] Many of the "child missing" stories that proliferated at this time seem to express a rebellion against dull supervision and discipline. Girls and boys ran away after being spanked, or in order to hide from having to take medicine or see the dentist.[29]

Another source of worry for parents was the perceived rise in juvenile delinquency. Reports of gang warfare, drag races, and school vandalism created a picture of America's teenage population in revolt.[30] Nineteen fifty-five would see the premiere of the films *Rebel without a Cause* and *The Blackboard Jungle*, both of which mythologized the problem of the "generation gap." The latter film, which hit first-run theaters in April at the height of Davy Crockett's popularity, also heralded the newest facets of teenage culture—rock and roll music and the sexually aggressive dancing that accompanied it. The most popular song of the year would be the pulsating music played over *The Blackboard Jungle*'s credits, Bill Haley and the Comets' "Rock around the Clock." Though seemingly found only in the teenage population, delinquency was also thought to threaten younger children, whose infection seemed imminent. Worries that eight to twelve year olds might begin listening to rock, reading horror comics, or disregarding parental or educational authority—in short, losing their innocence— needed to be addressed, and quickly.

Homeowners seemed to find an easy and ready answer for these hazards: fences. Letters advised parents to put up barriers to keep their children safe around pools. "Baby gates" became popular in the home to keep infants from getting into the kitchen or any other "dangerous" area. The wealth of backyard fence building grew to such a point that whole articles were devoted to how to build aesthetically pleasing fences that expressed the owner's individuality.[31] Just as reformers advocated the construction of separate bedrooms for children at the turn of the century (which was one of the selling points of suburban homes), now children were apportioned the fenced-in "backyard," complete with a private swing set, which was only one example of adult attempts to regulate and institutionalize play. As the suburbs grew in population, various groups were organized to supervise children's leisure time. The Boy Scouts and Girl Scouts of America were already established outlets for this type of endeavor, and the mammoth rallies held by these organizations during 1955 testify to their widespread popularity.[32] Little league baseball was another form of adult-supervised play, as teams sprung up with each new housing development, replacing (or attempting to replace) the sandlot or street games that parents feared could end in physical harm from an unseen pothole or a passing car.[33]

Another potential tool for keeping children safely within the survey of parents was the latest addition to the suburban home—the television set. One of the popular views of television during this period was as a built-in babysitter, keeping children occupied and out of trouble. Leo Bogart, in his 1956 work *The Age of Television*, summarizes a number of audience studies that he found "agree[d] completely that television has had the effect of keeping the family at home more than formerly."[34] Yet television was quickly seen as a double-edged sword. Other writers thought television was detrimental to children, broadcasting ideas of violence and sexuality into unprepared and innocent minds. Lynn Spigel also lists a number of instances reported in the popular press of children reenacting violent actions that they had seen on television.[35]

The Western genre, with its emphasis on gunplay and Indian attacks, figured strongly in this discussion—particularly since such figures as Hopalong Cassidy and Roy Rogers were specifically aimed at child audiences. At the same time that these programs glorified violence, however, the Western mythologized a unique part of American history as well, inscribing on the tabula rasa of avid young viewers notions of patriotism and national identity. The ambivalence with which commentators viewed television could also describe the Western genre on television. Did the television Western help keep children contained within the frame of the screen or did it open young viewers to a frontier of possibilities beyond parental control?

The Frontier(land) Will Be Televised

By 1955, Walt Disney had become the upholder of the traditional American family, valued for his creation of films that helped preserve a child's innocence. Disney entered the medium of television in 1954 with the aptly titled *Disneyland*, stressing family entertainment (emphasized in the early evening scheduling on Wednesday nights, when all the family could watch together). Although Disney barely concealed his use of television as a cross-promotional tool to advertise his upcoming features and about-to-open theme park in Anaheim, California (which ABC helped finance in order to get Disney to sign), both adults and children enjoyed it—making it the first ABC series to break into the Nielsen rating's top twenty.

The television series was structured like the park-to-be, each week devoted to one of the various sections of Walt's Magic Kingdom (more on this shortly). The first episode on Frontierland began a three-part chronicle of the legend of Davy Crockett. On December 15, 1954, "Davy Crockett, Indian Fighter" was broadcast. A few weeks later, on January 26, 1955, the series presented "Davy Crockett Goes to Congress." The story concluded (or so everyone thought) on February 23, 1955, with "Davy Crockett at the Alamo," in which Davy (Fess Parker) valiantly fought for Texan independence, the story fading to a Texas flag flapping in the breeze to spare viewers Davy's death at the hands of the Mexican Army.

The episodes display a conscious engagement of the younger viewer, and although parents lauded Disney as the "keeper of the flame" of family values, there is a marked portrayal of Crockett as a person who values fun over work and independence over authority. Davy and his friend George Russell (Buddy Ebsen) are introduced in the first episode off in the woods rather than at their posts as scouts for the United States Army in the War of 1812. The lieutenant who has been sent to find and drag them back to camp discovers Davy trying to "grin" a bear to death. Later on, Davy and George treat an Indian attack on the army as if it were a big game. When Davy decides that he can't "play" soldier anymore, he disregards any attempts at disciplinary action by the army and simply leaves. Still later, when Davy goes to Congress, he ends up quitting his position (and the stuffy clothes he has to wear) and heads off to the Alamo, where things look more lively.

Davy's reputation in culture as a free-roaming, fun-loving upstart reaches farther back than these television episodes. The first flurry of popularity for the Davy Crockett myth occurred from the 1830s to the 1850s in various comic almanacs, which were the beginnings of a mass culture literature in the United States. Carroll Smith-Rosenberg identifies in these almanacs the figure of Davy Crockett as a perpetual adolescent who "fought with [his] father, . . . rebelled against education, and escaped into a mythical wilderness of forest and rivers. [He] drank heavily, killed and ate the animals of the forest, fought viciously . . . , masturbated and whored."[36] Here, Crockett becomes a "trickster" figure, escaping categorization. He is a man turned beast ("half-alligator, half-man"), living beyond boundaries, literally between states.

Disney's Crockett obviously plays down the overt sexuality of the almanacs and substantially tones down the sometimes cannibalistic violence (although the first episode is sometimes startling in its presentation of violence on a professedly "family-oriented" show). Yet the disrespect for authority remains, allowed because it is presented humorously. Davy Crockett, the man who can "run faster,—jump higher,—squat lower,—dive deeper,—stay longer under,— and come out drier than any other man in the whole country,"[37] is a good yarn, a tall tale, a joke. Rarely during the episodes is anything treated seriously. Except for the action sequences, only three portions stand out in their straightforward presentation: the death of Davy's wife, the end of Davy's final speech in Congress, and the calm before the climactic battle at the Alamo. Each of these moments bows to hegemonic concerns about heterosexual marriage and national patriotism, but the rest of the time is spent in a playful mode. As Mary Douglas points out, a joke is "frivolous in that it produces *no real alternative*, only an exhilarating sense of freedom from form in general."[38] Still, jokes have a subversive power, which can challenge or undermine authority and order. They do not overthrow the social order, but can be used as a "tactic" (as Michel de Certeau uses the term) to resist the impositions of the hegemonic "strategy."[39] In their seeming inconsequentiality, jokes are allowed, and humor's ability to provide at least a momentary resistance is often overlooked by those in power.

Certainly, Davy's moniker as "king of the wild frontier" might have worried parents concerned with keeping their offspring in the safe, closed-off backyard. Many of the runaway children seemed to be searching for the West represented in these generic texts. Frequently, a number of these children explained that they took off because of "wanderlust"—desiring a sense of the frontier that was being denied them.[40] As one slightly put-out boy expressed it,

> There's only twenty-four hours in a day and I sleep ten and take an hour I guess to eat and go to school for six including walking and did homework for three hours and that only left me four hours to be free in.[41]

Having a new popular culture icon that seemed to espouse and encourage roaming over the countryside was contrary to the lessons that parents were trying to instill in their children about "not wandering off." Some adult commentators at the time appeared to recognize that Davy's appeal to children could have been partly based on his preference for fun over work and his playful jabs at authority figures. Richard Griffith, a reviewer for the *Los Angeles Times*, scolded, "Fess Parker could do with an occasional bath. So could Buddy Ebsen. Neither he nor Mr. Parker is a great help to mothers with water-shy sons."[42] *Life* magazine reported that some teachers were complaining that the growing Crockett fad interfered with classroom discipline: "kids did nothing but play Crockett games, and need to be calmed down."[43] In a column in the *Los Angeles Times*, Jack Geyer wrote humorously of three-year-old Davy Crockett as a budding juvenile delinquent, about to be arrested by a Tennessee sheriff for "killing a b'ar" without a license.[44]

This last item points to a more general and eventually widely accepted turn in the interpretation of the burgeoning popularity of the "Davy Crockett" shows. The humor inherent in the piece connotes an acceptance and moderate endorsement of Crockett's popularity. Unlike the teachers mentioned earlier that *Life* interviewed, *Los Angeles Times* columnist Mary Lou Downer discussed how her children imitating Davy Crockett were actually quieter than when they were pretending to be Hopalong Cassidy. Rather than running around the house with cap guns, they now stood on the highest point of the backyard and silently surveyed the "frontier" that lay before them.[45] The *New York Times*, while acknowledging that Davy was "salty" and "humorous," nonetheless saw his popularity among children "as a healthy sign by those who have deplored the vogue of the comic-book superman."[46] The general wisdom grew to be that Davy was "good" for youngsters rather than promoting delinquency.

Disney's reputation definitely helped in this turning of the tide. Part of *Disneyland*'s public image was as an educator. Various "Tomorrowland" episodes in the first season were devoted to explaining (and promoting) the real possibilities of space travel. Many of the "Adventureland" episodes were half-hour abridgments of the nature documentaries that Disney had begun producing in the late 1940s. Thus, reenacting the legend of Davy Crockett was quickly regarded as a lesson in American history and folklore. Jesse Crockett, grandson to Davy, eighty years old and living in San Gabriel in 1955, told the *Los Angeles Times* that it was "good for children to have a real historical hero to look up to."[47] Eventually, Walt Disney would be hailed as a leader "who has blazed a new trail in American folklore."[48] Margaret J. King reports that "treatments of Crockett in grade-school textbooks . . . grew in size and emphasis during and after 1955."[49] This promotion of Disney's image of Crockett as a tool for teaching children American history was so widespread that it sparked a brief academic fad as historians set out to "find" the "real" Davy.[50] When these scholarly endeavors unearthed the rowdy violent image that the Disney Davy downplayed, many parents voiced outrage not at Disney but the historians. A Tennessean, for instance, responded fiercely to one such revisionist magazine article: "Even though what you have written is no doubt true, I feel it would have been much better to have . . . allowed children to continue to believe that Davy Crockett was a hero."[51] Academic discussion notwithstanding, by the middle of 1955, popular discourse had positioned Davy Crockett as a preserver of childhood innocence. And what better way to preserve it than to buy a piece of Davy for every child to keep for his or her own?

Accessorizing Childhood: The Coonskin Cap

Davy's final battle at the Alamo was broadcast in late February 1955, yet [the mass media accounts of] the consumer frenzy that fed off the merchandising of Davy Crockett didn't begin until April. The first advertisement of Davy Crockett coonskin caps in the *Los Angeles Times* was printed on April 15 (specifically announcing that they are the "First in L.A.!"). The stretch in between seems odd—that a fad would commence two months after the shows had aired. An answer lies in a photo in the *Los Angeles Times* on February 6, which accompanies a personal interest story on the Boy Scouts. Unlike the other boys who are wearing their scout caps, one boy is shown prominently wearing a coonskin cap. Neither the article nor the photo's caption mentions Davy Crockett at all. Still, there he is. Coonskin caps and other Crockett clothing items had been marketed by Baltimore garment maker Morey Swartz long before the shows premiered, and obviously this child had found one.[52] This early photo, plus acknowledgment by Hedda Hopper in various entertainment columns throughout February of children's fascination with the character, suggests that children did not wait until April to begin liking Davy. Rather, they seemed to quickly adopt Davy into their culture, months before the adult society and economic system realized what was going on.

This facet of the "Crockett Craze" is no more evident than in the unpreparedness of the Walt Disney Studio to capitalize on the merchandising potential. Although one of the primary reasons for *Disneyland*'s existence on television was as a marketing tool, according to Disney biographer Leonard Mosley, O. B. Johnston (head of Disney's newly created merchandising and licensing division) "totally fail[ed] to appreciate the spinoff potential in the Davy Crockett series," and only "belatedly, [did] one member of the marketing staff at Disney . . . realize the possibilities in pushing replicas of Davy's coonskin cap."[53] The Disney Studio had neglected to copyright the name of Davy Crockett, and would eventually lose an infringement suit against Swartz, who did hold the copyright. Throughout the craze, Swartz, not Disney, licensed other manufacturers to use the Crockett name on products.[54] Disney would eventually gain a foothold in the tie-in product lines by promoting trademarked "Walt Disney's Davy Crockett" merchandise.

The full force of the fad, then, seems to have been felt not when children began appropriating Davy Crockett into their own culture, but when adults began noticing and appreciating him. Much as Jacqueline Rose discusses *Peter Pan* as a commodity that adults are willing to buy in order to "return" nostalgically to that feeling of childhood innocence, the willingness of parents to shell out for coonskin caps, tents, rifles, and moccasins signals an overinvestment in Davy as the upholder of adult conceptions of childhood. Walter Ames of the *Los Angeles Times* recounted in his column of May 16, 1955, a birthday party held for one of Red Skelton's children. Skelton had gotten Parker and Ebsen to appear in character for the party, and Ames gushes over this, describing their effect on both children and parents alike.[55] Most of the ads for Crockett merchandise sold at various Los Angeles stores (May Company, the Broadway, and Bullock's) use copy that addresses parents, urging them to buy these items for their children.

The boon to manufacturers and storekeepers from the "Crockett Craze" has been analyzed by many as one of the first instances of the realization of the economic power of the baby boom generation and their ability "to make or break an entire product line."[56] This argument posits the craze as a moment of empowerment for children, commanding the power of the purse. Yet the ads reveal a much different picture—a picture of adults taking over the image of Davy and reinscribing it. After all, *they*, not the children, were the ones who were actually buying the merchandise. With tag lines such as "If your backyard has become his 'wild frontier' " and "for your 'king of the wild backyard,' " newspaper ads positioned Davy Crockett not as a "trickster" or rebel, but as an emblem of childhood innocence—which could safely be contained in the backyard.[57]

Walt's newest enterprise, Disneyland, was the crowning achievement in cordoning off a child's "wild frontier." As mentioned earlier, *Disneyland* the show worked primarily as an advertisement for the new park, and kids who loved Davy were encouraged to visit his "home."[58] Situated in an Orange County suburb of Los Angeles, the new theme park quickly became the fenced-off backyard writ large. Disneyland's architectural conceptions attempted to control the possible types of play. By erecting different sections in the park— Adventureland, Tomorrowland, Fantasyland, and Frontierland—space was limited and defined. Cowboys and Indians belonged in Frontierland, *not* in

Fantasyland or Tomorrowland. Employees from one area of the park were explicitly told never to be seen in costume in another area. Although the park opened with certain attractions that allowed for freer play (such as the forts in Frontierland and the pirate ship in Fantasyland), they were ultimately closed in favor of rides that manipulated the customer's viewpoint (such as the Haunted Mansion's enclosed "doom buggies").[59]

Once safely ensconced in stores or theme parks, these spaces worked to regulate exactly what Davy symbolized and represented. For instance, at Bullock's, children were encouraged to join the Davy Crockett Club, but told that they would have to espouse such traits as "common sense" and "the will to succeed" to become members.[60] Nowhere is the co-optation of Davy from children's culture into adult use more outspoken than in the adoption of the coonskin cap by Estes Kefauver during his vice presidential campaign—the same Estes Kefauver who, in 1952, began a series of Senate investigations into juvenile delinquency and, in 1954, looked into television's relationship to this delinquency.[61] This is not to say that children no longer enjoyed Davy, or the Crockett accessories that their parents bought for them. But now, the meaning of Davy and his paraphernalia was appropriated by adults to express their own views of childhood.

Polly Want a Crockett?

The relative lack of testimony from actual children makes it hard to determine exactly where they stood in regard to the swirl of discussion going on around them over what Davy Crockett was supposed to mean to them. Other than photos of enraptured faces meeting Parker or posed portraits of children in their Crockett regalia, which seem to be more for the benefit of the adult viewer than the child, there are few areas where one can discover how children actually interacted with these cultural objects. For example, one question yet to be answered is how nonwhite children related to the figure of Davy Crockett— neither the contemporary press nor Margaret J. King's work on the fad seems to acknowledge that children existed who were outside the white, middle-class, suburban paradigm. What needs to be examined are potential areas that appear to problematize the relation between how adults and mass culture thought children used Davy, and how children actually came to use him in their own popular culture.

One such area is the recurrent image throughout store ads and magazine photo layouts of young girls who liked Davy Crockett. Right there in the first merchandise ads, Bullock's invites both boys *and* girls to join the Davy Crockett Club. There's a picture of a little girl along with a group of little boys on the pages of *Look*, all gazing with awe at their hero, Fess Parker. And there's a photo of both Red Skelton's son *and* daughter with Parker at the birthday party. In the *Hollywood Reporter*'s review of the theatrical release of the Crockett episodes as a feature, titled *Davy Crockett, King of the Wild Frontier* (1955), the reviewer notes that his two young daughters "are barely willing to nod at a mere male parent after Parker has made his Crockett appearances in the living room."[62]

Nonetheless, at the time, gender roles were being strictly demarcated—women were being encouraged (if not forced) back into the home, while the men went out into the workplace. Little girls were supposed to be "sugar and spice and everything nice." A review of the second Crockett feature, *Davy Crockett and the River Pirates* (1956), explains that "there are no girls cluttering up . . . [the] screenplay and this is the way it should be, just as there are never any girls along when small boys go down to the creek and play river pirate."[63] Whereas suburban society tried to keep young boys within the confines of the backyard, young girls were expected to stay inside the house at mother's side, learning "proper" feminine behavior. Then what were girls doing wearing coonskin caps and holding rifles? This recurrent image speaks of a moment when female children seemed to be using the "Crockett Craze" to break out of their engendered roles and spaces, at least for the time when they used the merchandise.

The image of the "cowgirl" had already carved out an approved area for girls who liked to play cowboy. This was ostensibly endorsed because it took the cowboy icon and accentuated its feminine aspects (particularly the emphasis on costume, with tassels and fringe). The "cowgirl" was supposed to accompany the cowboy, without ever supplanting him in dominance. Such folkloric figures as Annie Oakley and Calamity Jane were reworked in the postwar years to express femininity in Western garb, instead of a challenge to male dominance.[64] Film and television star Dale Evans epitomized the common conception of the cowgirl—comfortable on a horse and with a rope, but looking pretty and never challenging the authority (or top billing) of her husband, Roy Rogers.[65] Yet, to say that this is precisely how girls used the "cowgirl" image, is to deny much of what Jenkins, Spigel, and others have noticed about the "negotiated" use of cultural objects by children. It is just as likely that girls used the "cowgirl" in order to complicate the gender boundaries that were already impinging on them. This would help to explain why girls also reached out to the image of Davy Crockett.

Merchandisers quickly realized the popularity of Davy Crockett among young girls and soon were attempting to redirect their desire—professing that girls were supposed to want to be married to Davy or be his mother, rather than wanting to actually be Davy himself. As one grocery ad put it, "Wimmin n' Heroes Don't Mix . . . Except at Meal Time."[66] Ads began to promote porcelain Davy dolls or dolls the height of eight year olds that girls could square dance with, or they told customers that these items were for "Polly Crocketts," the name of Davy's wife, who appears minutely in the very first episode and then dies (offscreen) of fever in the second.[67] Another ad heightened the fashion style of Davy's clothing, announcing, "Miss Davy Crockett hats in Snowy White Bunny fur . . . for your good little girl."[68]

This does not necessarily mean that girls let their use of Davy be redirected so easily. As a matter of fact, none of these items is ever seen in any of the articles done on the "Crockett Craze" that I have surveyed. Although memory is selective and shouldn't be taken as somehow "pure," a small study group of women who were children in various parts of the United States and Canada during the height of the fad remembered wearing the same coonskin cap that the boys wore. None of them even recalled the figure of Davy's wife, Polly, much less playing her—dying off in the house while the boys fight it out with the Indians or Mexican Army. This is not to say all girls took to Davy, or took to him in the same way, but these comments show how certain girls resisted the redirection of the advertisements. Life's essay on the Crockett phenomenon included a photo of a young girl in coonskin cap brandishing a rifle.[69] Clearly, at least some girls were ignoring how the adult world would have preferred them to use Davy's image.

Conclusion: The Dimensions of Davy

The "Crockett Craze" can be viewed from a number of vantage points, many of which display how children learned to adapt and function within the parameters set by society. Children's use of the toys and costumes for play helped to reconcile them to the ideology that was defining them. As Henry Jenkins correctly contends, "Children's play is not ideologically innocent; it is the primary means by which children absorb the values of their society and master both their own bodies and other culturally-significant materials."[70] The "Crockett Craze" is often correctly seen as an instance of mass consumerism, in which children were taught at an early age how to function within the economic system. Although some girls were using the Crockett paraphernalia to break free from gendered expectations, the song about Crockett kissing Marilyn Monroe obviously reinforces the patriarchal construct of heterosexual relations.

Yet, as I have tried to argue, the forces at work were more complex than this.

Jenkins notes that "[children's] play may and often does reinforce parental values, but it also contains a countersocial potential; it may be used to express the child's feelings of outrage over the expectations imposed upon him or her by the social formation, over the pressure to conform to rules that constrain instinctual life and frustrate personal desire."[71] Young boys looked toward an accepted icon of American history and folklore, and used him to acclimate to hegemonic notions of masculinity. In this way, they fell perfectly within the allowed parameters of social discourse on the Western hero. Still, children (not just boys) may have also used Davy to express their desires for freedom and more open space. To see this phenomenon simply as an instance of rampant "good Americanism" is to ignore the variety of emotions and pleasures that were invested in Davy and those coonskin caps, and to create a nostalgic image of childhood in the 1950s as a time of innocence, forgetting other factors that would explain why children so eagerly adopted a figure who could be called the "king of the wild frontier."

Notes

1   Charles K. Wolfe, "Davy Crockett Songs: Minstrels to Disney," in *Davy Crockett: The Man, the Legend, the Legacy, 1786–1986*, ed. Michael A. Lofaro (Knoxville, Tenn.: University of Tennessee Press, 1985), 182–83.

2   Ibid., 183.

3   "King Davy and Friends," *Time*, 1 August 1955, 30.

4   Ibid.

5   Wolfe, "Davy Crockett Songs," 185–86.

6   Jacqueline Rose, *The Case of Peter Pan: Or, the Impossibility of Children's Fiction* (London: Macmillan Publishers, Ltd., 1984).

7   Lynn Spigel, "Seducing the Innocent: Childhood and Television in Postwar America," in *Ruthless Criticism: New Perspectives in U.S. Communications History*, ed. William S. Solomon and Robert W. McChesney (Minneapolis: University of Minnesota Press, 1993), 264–65.

8   Stuart Hall, "Culture, the Media and the 'Ideological Effect,'" in *Mass Communication and Society*, ed. James Curran et al. (London: E. Arnold, 1977), 324–46.

9   Henry Jenkins, " 'Going Bonkers!': Children, Play, and Pee-wee," *Camera Obscura*, no. 17 (May 1988): 190.

10   Michel de Certeau, *The Practice of Everyday Life*, trans. Steven Rendall (Berkeley: University of California Press, 1984).

11   Margaret J. King, "The Recycled Hero: Walt Disney's Davy Crockett," in *Davy Crockett: The Man, the Legend, the Legacy, 1786–1986*, ed. Michael A. Lofaro (Knoxville, Tenn.: University of Tennessee Press, 1985), 144. The work referred to is David Riesman, *The Lonely Crowd: A Study of the Changing American Character* (New Haven, Conn.: Yale University Press, 1950). Like King, Riesman uses "other-directedness" in his own work to talk of juvenile delinquency as "peer-pressure" and not as a rebellion against societal restraint.

12   The "Crockett Craze" was a national phenomenon, and this study analyzes nationally
     distributed journals and columns. Yet, while in no way claiming that one urban area can
     effectively represent an entire country, for purposes of manageability, the city of Los
     Angeles and its surrounding suburbs will be the main focus of the discussion.

13   Figure taken from Landon Y. Jones, *Great Expectations: America and the Baby Boom Generation*
     (New York: Ballantine Books, 1980).

14   Spigel, "Seducing the Innocent," 261.

15   Ibid. Other authors who discuss this conceptualization of childhood include Philippe
     Aries, *Centuries of Childhood: A Social History of Family Life*, trans. Robert Baldick (New York:
     Vintage, 1962); and Viviana A. Zelizer, *Pricing the Priceless Child: The Changing Social Value of
     Children* (New York: Basic Books, 1985).

16   Zelizer, *Pricing the Priceless Child*.

17   Ibid. The information in this paragraph can be found on pp. 49–55.

18   Joseph A. Barry, "The Next America Will Be the Age of Great Architecture," *House Beauti-
     ful*, April 1953, 117.

19   Frederick Elkin, "The Psychological Appeal of the Hollywood Western," *Journal of Educa-
     tional Sociology* 24 (October 1950); and Martin Naussbaum, "Sociological Symbolism of
     the 'Adult Western,' " *Social Forces* 39 (October 1960).

20   Barry, "The Next America."

21   John Meskell, quoted in "Southland Building Methods Widely Used," *Los Angeles Times*,
     6 February 1955, sec. 5, 13.

22   Among the various ads in the real estate section of the Sunday editions of the *Los Angeles
     Times* are a number of developments that display ranch-style homes. One example would
     be an ad for Hickory Homes in Costa Mesa (23 January 1955, sec. 7, 5), which showed
     models for "Western Ranch," "California Ranch," and "Hickory Ranch" homes.

23   Gwendolyn Wright, *Building the Dream: A Social History of Housing in America* (Cambridge,
     Mass.: MIT Press, 1983), 251.

24   *Los Angeles Times*, 23 January 1955, sec. 1A, 11. The documentary *The City* (1939), produced
     by Pare Lorentz, also heavily stresses the importance of the child's welfare in moving
     from the unhealthy city to the hygienic and happy suburbs.

25   The public's fascination with the "endangered child" narrative was amply displayed in
     the media coverage of Kathy Fiscus's rescue from a well, followed by the Billy Wilder
     motion picture about the rampant promotionalism of the event, *Ace in the Hole* (1951),
     albeit changing the victim to an adult male. Mark J. Williams ("From 'Remote' Possibili-
     ties to Entertaining 'Difference': A Regional Study of the Rise of the Television Industry
     in Los Angeles, 1930–1952" [Ph.D. diss., University of Southern California, 1992] dis-
     cusses the importance of this event in understanding the power and potential of live
     television.

26   See, for example, "Here's New Tank-Type H-Bomb Radiation Shelter Developed for Back
     Yard Protection," *Los Angeles Times*, 20 May 1955, sec. 1, 3.

27   There are numerous listings in the *Los Angeles Times* during 1955 on this subject, both in
     actual reports and editorial or parental advice columns. "Mother Rescues Son, 2, from
     Home Swim Pool" (14 March 1955, sec. 1, 1) and "Girl, 6, Drowns in Swim Pool of
     Neighbor" (14 July 1955, sec. 1, 1) serve as just two examples.

28   An instance of children at play elsewhere can be found in "Little Girls at Party Brew up
     Distinct Stew," *Los Angeles Times*, 25 March 1955, sec. 1, 2, which reported on two pre-
     schoolers who decided to "cook" at a neighbor's house, unbeknownst to their dis-

traught parents. The police found them joyously destroying the kitchen, unaware that they were "missing." A couple of cases exemplify the "truly lost" child who seems undisturbed by the situation. "Girl, 8, Feared Kidnapped, Found," *Los Angeles Times*, 30 May 1955, sec. 1, 1, told of an Altadena girl who simply wandered off and took a couple of hours to find her way back home. "Rescued Boy, 12, Tells of Wandering in Desert," *Los Angeles Times*, 15 June 1955, sec. 1, 13, reports on how a boy, lost near the Mexican border during a camping trip, "nonchalantly told how he 'just kept going' for 52 hours." That this was a phenomenon not unique to Los Angeles (or even suburban parts of the country) can be found in a *Los Angeles Times* article, "Baby, Feared Seized by Bear, Found Safe" (5 July 1955, sec. 1, 1), which detailed the story of a two-year-old "missing" Montana girl who was eventually found only 300 yards away from her home, "undisturbed." The reports of a bear, the article explained, seemed to be only a rumor, which no one was able to substantially authenticate.

29 "Runaway Boy, 12, Ends Stay in Steep Canyon" (*Los Angeles Times*, 9 July 1955, sec. 2, 6) speaks, for example, of a boy who took off to camp in the mountains around Upland after a spanking. "Girl Fleeing Home after Spanking Is Struck by Car (*Los Angeles Times*, 3 February 1955, sec. 1, 4) paints an even more frightening picture for parents dealing with rebellious children.

30 Lynn Spigel (in "Seducing the Innocent," 265) describes the various federal actions taken to investigate and control juvenile delinquency during this period.

31 The *Los Angeles Times Home Magazine* featured ads for fencing every week through 1955, and had two specific articles on fences: "Fences Must Have Personality" (19 June 1955, 20), which noted that "fences . . . have become an important element of landscape design," and "Unusual Fence Forms" (26 June 1955, 22–23).

32 The Girl Scouts of Los Angeles held a party for their forty-third birthday in Shrine Auditorium, sponsored by the May Co. department store chain, which was attended by 14,000 (*Los Angeles Times*, 13 March 1955, sec. 1, 4). In June, the Boy Scouts had their turn, holding a week-long event known as "Scout-O-Rama" in the Los Angeles Coliseum, in which 20,000 scouts and leaders participated, and over 90,000 people were expected to attend (*Los Angeles Times*, 3 June 1955, sec. 1, 4). The link between such organizations and the attempt to stop the threat of juvenile delinquency was made evident in an editorial cartoon at the time of "Scout-O-Rama," which depicted a huge scout badge stopping the black shadow of delinquency (*Los Angeles Times*, 4 June 1955, sec. 2, 4).

33 One example of this phenomenon can be read in "Little League Baseball near in Garden Grove," *Los Angeles Times*, 10 April 1955, sec. 6, 1.

34 Leo Bogart, *The Age of Television: A Study of Viewing Habits and the Impact of Television on American Life* (New York: Frederick Ungar, 1956), 101.

35 Spigel, "Seducing the Innocent," 268. The recent scandal about the child who set his family's trailer on fire after watching the television figures Beavis and Butthead play with fire testifies to the strength of this argument in the popular press.

36 Carroll Smith-Rosenberg, "Davy Crockett as Trickster: Pornography, Liminality, and Symbolic Inversion in Victorian America," in *Disorderly Conduct: Visions of Gender in Victorian America* (New York: Alfred A. Knopf, 1985), 92–93.

37 *Davy Crockett's Almanac, 1835* (Nashville, Tenn., 1835), 28, quoted in Smith-Rosenberg, "Davy Crockett as Trickster," 102.

38 Mary Douglas, "The Social Control of Cognition: Some Factors in Joke Perception," *Man* 3 (1968): 365.

120 SEAN GRIFFIN

39 Michel de Certeau, *The Practice of Everyday Life.*

40 The *Los Angeles Times*'s "3 Boys Start Hike to Nevada but Idea Cools" (14 May 1955, sec. 1, 3) typifies this. An example from another part of the country is "Barefoot Boy Stows Away on Plane from St. Louis" (*Los Angeles Times*, 16 July 1955, sec. 2, 1), in which the twelve year old simply "wanted to go for a ride."

41 "Your Child" column, *Los Angeles Times Home Magazine*, 20 March 1955, 44.

42 Richard Griffith, "Disney's 'Davy Crockett' Hit on Theater Screen," *Los Angeles Times*, 3 June 1955, sec. 3, 6. This article is a review of the three original television episodes as they were reedited and combined for release as a theatrical feature to cash in on the popularity of the shows.

43 "U.S. Again Is Subdued by Davy," *Life*, 25 April 1955, 29. Wolfe, "Davy Crockett Songs," 184, describes a novelty song at the time titled "Davy Crockett Blues" by country singer Red Kirk, which included these lines: "They go around wearing their coonskin caps, Shootin' their guns and setting their traps, / Got me afraid to take my nap, / I got the Davy Crockett Blues."

44 Jack Geyer, "Tough on Raccoons," *Los Angeles Times*, 17 May 1955, p B11.

45 Mary Lou Downer, "Homes Quiet down as Crockett Leaves Rogers and Cassidy in Dust," *Los Angeles Times*, 22 May 1955, sec. 3, 14.

46 "Coonskin Superman," *New York Times Magazine*, 24 April 1955, 24.

47 "Jesse Crockett, 80, Says Davy Is Good for Youngsters," *Los Angeles Times*, 19 June 1955, sec. 6, 5.

48 "Thousands of Crockett Fans Cheer Bowl's Disney Night," *Los Angeles Times*, 15 July 1955, sec. 2, 1.

49 King, "Recycled Hero," 140–41.

50 See, for example, John Fischer, "The Embarrassing Truth about Davy Crockett," *Harper's*, July 1955, 16–18; John Haverstick, "The Two Davy Crocketts," *Saturday Review*, 9 July 1955, 19; and Bernard Kalb, "Dan'l, Dan'l Boone," *New York Times Magazine*, 9 October 1955, 42, which compares the historical Daniel Boone to the historical Davy Crockett, complete with portraits of Crockett made during the man's lifetime.

51 John P. Wright, "In Defense of Davy," letter to the editor, *Harper's*, September 1955, 4.

52 "The Wild Frontier," *Time*, 23 May 1955, 92.

53 Leonard Mosley, *Disney's World* (Lanham, Md.: Scarborough House, 1990), 247. Although Disney had been licensing merchandise for years, the company didn't form a specific department until after World War II, when it renegotiated its contract with "Kay" Kamen, an independent agent who built up the Disney merchandising empire almost single-handedly. It wasn't until they saw Kamen's extraordinary success that the studio decided to exert more control (and get a larger share of the profits) over merchandising. In 1948, Kamen died in a plane crash, and all licensing contracts went through the studio itself. More on Kamen and his relationship with the studio can be found in Cecil Munsey, *Disneyana: Walt Disney Collectibles* (New York: Hawthorn Books, 1974).

54 "The Wild Frontier."

55 Walter Ames, "Davy Crockett Is Star of B-Day Part for Red Skelton Youngsters," *Los Angeles Times*, 16 May 1955, sec. 1, 30.

56 Landon Jones, *Great Expectations: America and the Baby Boom Generation* (New York: Ballantine Books, 1980), 50–51.

57 Ad for the Broadway, *Los Angeles Times*, 13 May 1955, sec. 1, 32; and ad for the Broadway, *Los Angeles Times*, 20 May 1955, sec. 1, 34.

58 An advertisement by the San Antonio Tourist Bureau in the *Los Angeles Times* (29 May 1955, sec. 1, 6) points out that families could make trips to more than one spot to find Davy's "home." As it was, the Disney Company projected, according to a report in the *Los Angeles Times* (John L. Scott, "Advance Peek Taken of Dream to Come True in Disneyland," 29 May 1955, sec. 4, 1), that adults would outnumber children as park visitors four to one.

59 Although I am describing the Disneyland of the 1950s, it coincides with the description of the 1990s Walt Disney World in Florida by Susan Willis in her article, "Public Use/Private State," in *Inside the Mouse: Work and Play at Disney World*, ed. Project on Disney (Durham, N.C.: Duke University Press, 1995), 180–98.

60 Ad for Bullock's, *Los Angeles Times*, 9 May 1955, sec. 1, 12.

61 King, "Recycled Hero," 151–52.

62 "Davy Crockett, King of the Wild Frontier," review, *Hollywood Reporter*, 17 May 1955.

63 "Davy Crockett and the River Pirates," review, *Hollywood Reporter*, 16 July 1956.

64 Both figures became heroines in musicals that showed the aggressive female tamed and turned into a proper mate for marrying the rugged Western male—Annie Oakley in the theater with *Annie Get Your Gun* (1947) and Calamity Jane in the film of the same name (1953). On television, champion rider Gail Davis became the first female star of a Western series, *Annie Oakley* (1952–1956). While Davis gave the character more authority and aggressiveness than the popular stage and film musical *Annie Get Your Gun* did, the series was an isolated instance (and its status as a syndicated series rather than a network-broadcast show might have further limited its exposure).

65 In early 1955, Dale Evans had two books out, *Angel Unaware* and *My Spiritual Diary*, neither of which engaged in the rough action that was to be found in Western pulp fiction. An advertisement to "Meet Dale Evans," *Los Angeles Times*, 11 March 1955, sec. 1, 25.

66 Ad for Thriftimart, *Los Angeles Times*, 12 May 1955, sec. 1, 20.

67 Ads for May Company, *Los Angeles Times*, 22 May 1955, sec. 1A, 6; the Broadway, *Los Angeles Times*, 22 May 1955, sec. 1, 37; and for Bullock's, *Los Angeles Times*, 3 June 1955, sec. 2, 28.

68 Ad for the Broadway, *Los Angeles Times*, 5 June 1955, sec. 1, 28.

69 "U.S. Again Is Subdued by Davy."

70 Jenkins, "Going Bonkers!" 175.

71 Ibid.

Out of Control: Television and the Transformation of Childhood in Late Capitalism   *Jyotsna Kapur*

The latest solution to controlling children's exposure to adult secrets of sex, violence, and commerce in late-twentieth-century America is the V-chip—a computer chip that can be inserted into television sets so that parents can block out programming they consider unsuitable for their children. It positions parents, particularly mothers, as their children's enemy or drill sergeant, who must carry out the orders of the experts in order to control children and protect them from television. This essay examines the assumptions that underlie the notion that television is the main culprit in children's loss of innocence and that its power can be restrained by a reinstatement of parental authority.[1]

One major impasse in the debate on children and television is that it has continued to be embedded within arguments centered on the "effects" of television on children. On the one side are critics in the tradition of the Frankfurt School, such as Marie Winn, Neil Postman, and Steven Kline, who contend that television kills children's imaginations with limited colonizing narratives; violates their innocence in relation to sex, violence, and commerce; and like a narcotic, numbs their innate curiosity about the world.[2] Basic to these claims is the assumption that children will mimic what they see—when they see violence, they will act violently. On the other side, cultural studies has drawn attention to the varied ways in which audiences negotiate with, resist, or are co-opted by mass culture. Both Ellen Seiter and David Buckingham have emphasized that children do not inevitably absorb all the meanings and purposes of media content.[3] For instance, as Buckingham points out in his study of children's responses to television violence, although children may find certain scenes worrying or moving, they develop ways of coping with them, such as changing channels, fast forwarding, watching with others, and so on. The assertion here is that children are not cultural dupes, but discriminating and imaginative audiences. Of course, no one disputes that television's narratives are informed by the inequalities of race, gender, class, and sexuality. The difference between the two positions is that the latter favors critical engagement with television, while the former can lend itself to a ban on television viewing for children. While differing in their opinion on children's responses to television, both approaches assume that the word *children* represents a natural category. They lead us to rehash old arguments about the extent to which children's imaginations are co-opted by television (the same arguments were applied to comic books, cinema, and now the Internet) and ignore the possibility that there may well be a fundamental transformation underway in our cultural conception of childhood.

The inadequacy of assuming *children* to be a natural category, an audience that is simply found rather than constructed, becomes clear when we read the following statement by Cy Schneider, a senior executive in children's marketing. "Children," Schneider writes, "are not that easy to entertain or persuade; they will not watch everything put in front of them on television, and will not buy (or ask to buy) everything that is cleverly advertised to them. In reality, children are intelligent, discriminating, and skeptical. Despite their lack of experience, they are not that easily fooled."[4] Schneider could almost be a cultural studies critic. Since the 1960s, there has been a subtle shift in the concept of childhood, the impact of which is only now fully apparent. What is at stake in Schneider's description of children is a new image, a new idea about childhood. The idea that this is a new generation of kids is repeated in the following statement out of a standard text on marketing to children:

> Do you know what successful companies like Nike, Nabisco, Levi Strauss, McDonalds, Mattel and Nintendo all have in common? The answer is that they have brilliantly tapped into the needs, interests, fantasies and desires of a huge, powerful, and growing consumer group—kids! Marketing studies show that today's new generation of wise-beyond-their-years children have gained unprecedented influence over family purchases—from clothes . . . to cars . . . to computers. It's a $120 billion market right now and the end is not yet in sight![5]

Even the Disney Corporation, which has built an empire on childhood innocence, recently announced that "it is no longer an innocent period of time."[6]

This theme is echoed in law, public policy, and the cultural sphere. In the last decades in the United States, some basic institutions that had previously established children as a distinct category in need of protection have been overturned. For instance, there has been a concerted move to repeal juvenile delinquency laws. According to legislation passed by the House of Representatives on May 8, 1997, those as young as thirteen years can now be prosecuted as adults if they are charged with murder or sexual assault. In Texas, a bill was introduced to reduce the death penalty to thirteen. Withdrawal of public aid to children is another case of pulling back on certain guarantees that children in affluent industrialized nations have possessed since the turn of the century. Under one of the provisions of the recent welfare reform bill, the amount of public assistance that a family receives will no longer increase with the birth of a new child. In the cultural sphere, the boundaries between adult and children's fashions are diminishing. Children dress and behave like adults, watch the same films, and have access to most of the same television programs.

In the face of this blurring of boundaries between adults and children, the old arguments about the effects of television on children become irrelevant. We have to confront the widespread social belief and experience that children have themselves changed. The reaction to these broader changes has been to look for obvious targets. Television is, perhaps, the most cited culprit in what Neil Postman has called the "adultification" of children. Allegedly, television's accomplices in this process are permissive parents who are unable to control their children, to say "no" to their unreasonable demands, including free access to television. What has television done to change children? Could television have accomplished this adultification of children all on its own? Can the family extend childhood? I will argue that the flexibility of the boundaries between children and adults, between the public and private spheres, between work and leisure that we currently experience, are outcomes of capitalist expansion and new technologies at the end of the twentieth century.

Kids' Choice

The most significant change in the cultural notion of childhood in the last decades of the twentieth century has been the construction of children as consumers. Yet right from the eighteenth century, as historian John H. Plumb suggests, childhood was both a commercial and cultural category.[7] Children were at the heart of the nuclear bourgeois family that became the dominant ideal under industrial capitalism. In the early stages of the industrial revolution, capitalism took production out of the household and away from the family, collectivizing it in the factory. The nuclear family, as Michelle Barrett and Mary McKintosh have pointed out, was produced at the intersection of patriarchy and capitalism.[8] The bourgeois home, then, became the private sphere where affection, security, intimacy, sexual love, and parenthood could be expressed and lived. Raising children was elevated to the level of sacred duty. Children were glorified, as in Jean-Jacques Rousseau's writings, as the embodiment of some eternal truth outside the contradictions of sexuality and social inequality. Children, particularly bourgeois ones, had to be innocent of what were characterized as adult secrets—money, sex, and social violence. Conversely, working-class children had to unlearn in school and special institutions their knowledge of these "facts of life." Consequently, although children were a market, they were not sold to directly. Instead, they were imagined as untainted receivers of gifts. As an expression of parental love, gifts to children were considered valueless whose market price was unmentionable. In her excellent study of the commercialization of children's literature in the early 1900s, Jacqueline Rose notes that in the sales rhetoric of James M. Barrie's *Peter Pan*, the child was only ideally the consumer.[9] It was the adult to whom the book was marketed with the promise of making the child happy, obedient, and loving—much in the same way that pet foods are sold to pet owners.

Since post–World War II in the United States, there has been an active effort on the part of industry to transform the twentieth-century notion of children as innocents in need of protection to one of children as sovereign, playful, thinking consumers. Children—that is, preteens—have emerged as the fastest growing market segment based on the premise that the earlier they are hooked on brand names, the longer they will stay with a particular product. Second, there has been a considerable increase in the spending power of this group. David Leonhardt and Kathleen Kerwin estimated that in 1998, kids under fourteen would spend about $20 billion and influence another $200 billion through the choices their parents make.[10] It is increasingly common to find advertisements for adult products in children's magazines. On the inside cover of the May 1997 issue of *Sports Illustrated for Kids*, for example, there was a two-page foldout ad for the Chevy Venture minivan.

The development of children as a market segment is part of the expansion of capitalism since World War II, one aspect of which is a change in marketing research. Prior to the 1950s, audiences or consumers were imagined to be homogeneous masses. The consumer was at the end of the production line, ready to be sold a piece of goods already produced. According to marketing literature, however, "a Copernican revolution" took place in the 1950s; "the consumer became the sun" around which contemporary marketing strategy would evolve.[11]

Now, at the end of the twentieth century, the production of consumers rather than goods has emerged as the primary area of corporate investment and means to expand profit. Consumers or audiences are conceived of as segments, that is, social groups united by shared aspirations and social values, rather than as mass, homogenized, collective entities. Attention has shifted to detailed studies of the lives and habits of consumers, a process that has intensified with the newer, more elaborate tracking techniques and organization of data made available through computers. These market segments are constructions. Unlike class, gender, race, or sexuality, these categories are not based on historical and material relations of power. Instead, they present themselves as psychological or lifestyle markers, under which everyone is hypothetically equal but different in what they desire. We are by now familiar with marketing terms such as yuppies, empty-nesters, style-setters, Generation Xers, preteens, and so on to describe social groups. The construction of preteens as a niche or market comes with a certain social recognition that is allotted to groups when they are viewed as consumers.

If You Don't Have Any of These Little Elves, Then You'll Have to Eat It All Yourself

The targeting of children as consumers did not begin in the 1990s. This process has been well under way since the postwar boom and dramatic expansion of capitalism in the American economy. During this period, there was a mass-scale improvement in the domestic standard of living, and modern technologies became available to middle- and even working-class homes. Increased middle-class affluence, Barbara Ehrenreich suggests, coincided with changes in parenting, which became more child centered. Lloyd DeMause explains that this approach, later characterized as "permissive parenting," was based on a notion of "helping" the child express and live by its own needs.[12] The empathetic parent did not have automatic access to her or his child's desires, but worked hard at trying to understand them. Dr. Benjamin Spock, the chief spokesperson for this position, advised mothers to enjoy their children, not keep rigid schedules, delay toilet training, feed kids on demand, and treat their baby's impulses as valid and legitimate.[13]

It was also in the fifties that the toy industry grew tremendously, and this growth was intrinsically tied to television. Prior to this, toy companies spent relatively little on advertising. According to Cy Schneider, advertising was done to the toy wholesale dealers or through catalogs sent to customers. National brand names were unknown. If an adult wanted to buy a toy, he or she went to the local toy store and asked for a toy appropriate for a child of a certain age. It is amusing to think what would happen if one tried that in Toys "R" Us today. About 80 percent of annual toy sales, Schneider indicates, were made in the last three weeks of the year, around Christmastime. Large department stores would set up toy demonstrations, showing ways of playing with various toys. It was the Mickey Mouse Club, started by Walt Disney on ABC in 1955, that brought children's commercial television into its own. As Schneider recounts, this show initiated the development of a brand (with a recognizable logo), year-round selling of toys, and the creation of fantastic stories around the toy. Hence, toys began to be sold to children in a kid's lingo—that is, for the brands and television narratives they were associated with (rather than the functions they could perform). A product's television budget and schedule became almost as important as the toy's charm, particularly in selling to the wholesalers that dominated the toy market in the 1960s.[14] Children, the audience of these television commercials-cum-programs, would now teach their parents about products available in the market, asking for specific toys such as Mickey ears or Howdy Doody dolls.

By the 1990s, a large number of multinational corporations were producing goods for children in an international market—tangible products such as toys, candy, cereal, snacks, carbonated and noncarbonated drinks, clothes, shoes, books, and those for entertainment, such as films and videos, computer games, and amusement parks. Most of the brands are now household names—General Foods, General Mills, Quaker, and Ralston; Mattel, Hasbro, and Coleco; Hershey's, Mars, M&M's, and Nabisco; American Greetings and Hallmark; Walt Disney, Hanna-Barbera, and Warner Communications; Burger King and McDonald's.

Jean Baudrillard's concept of consumption nets or webs is particularly helpful in understanding how consumer industries create a children's culture as a whole system that is fundamental to establishing a person's identity as a child. According to Baudrillard, "few objects are offered alone, without a context of objects to speak for them. . . . [The] object is no longer referred to in relation to a specific utility, but as a collection of objects in their total meaning."[15] Even before the release of the Disney film *Pocahontas*, department and toy stores were carrying nighties, schoolbags, lunchboxes, sipping cups, T-shirts, pillows, books, and audiotapes with Pocahontas on them. The circular way in which Disney's production of commodities and culture reinforces each other is a striking example of capitalist expansion. Disney's films provide free advertising for its licensed goods as well as its entertainment parks. These commodities, in turn, provide free publicity for the films. As Richard Schickel noted way back in 1968, "As capitalism it is the work of a genius; as culture it is mostly a horror."[16] This cross-referencing between media and toys, initiated by Disney, is now a fundamental aspect of toy marketing. Approximately 50 percent of the toys produced in 1997 were licensed products related to television and film.[17]

Television is a conduit through which corporations advertise to children. In his manual on television advertising to children, Schneider reminds critics that commercial television's first mission is to entice viewers to watch the commercials. "If commercial television cannot move goods, it cannot remain in business. Just because commercial television devotes many of its hours to the special audience of children doesn't change this fundamental point of view one iota."[18] Such plain speaking from a practitioner would sit oddly with an earlier definition of the children's market, which was considered far removed from commercial profit interests. For instance, Jacqueline Rose writes that when the first edition of *Peter Pan* was brought out, it had an announcement on the first page indicating that proceeds from the sale of the book would go to a children's hospital in London.[19] In the early 1900s, there was a certain embarrassment in profiting off childhood.

The Electronic Pied Piper

In directly addressing children as consumers, television acts as the electronic pied piper luring them out of the home and into the street, playing a tune that their parents do not understand. In spite of the gulfs created by race, class, and gender, children's consumer culture is central to developing what Ellen Seiter characterizes as the "lingua franca" of small children.[20] It provides formats (such as animation), themes, narratives, and characters around which children communicate with one another. It helps construct the social identity of "child" in opposition to "adult." Marketeers actively work toward building these characteristics into children's consumer culture. Schneider suggests that since children relate to other children, like to feel more grown up, and enjoy ridiculing adult behavior, advertisers should emphasize fun. Rather than lecture, ads should stay in the child's cultural world. Even in commercials directed at parents, the joke should be on the contradictory values of the adult and child, with an emphasis on children's enjoyment of the product. For example, in a commercial for Reese's Peanut Butter Cups, a mother goes on about its nutritional value while the kids gobble up the candy for the taste. Schneider recounts that in the preliminary tests for Barbie in the late 1950s, mothers overwhelmingly hated the doll even as their daughters loved it.[21] The unifying theme throughout this children's lingua franca is a playful opposition to the adult world.

Children's consumer culture has become increasingly unfamiliar to adults. In spite of being a parent of two young children myself and having a professional interest in children's culture, I find it impossible to keep up, and am constantly being introduced to new programming and products by my daughter, Suhaila, who is seven years old, and my son, Nilim, who is three. In my case, the "knowledge gap" with my children is further widened by the extremely different economic and cultural environments that we come from; whereas I grew up in India in the 1960s and 1970s in a middle-class family, my children were born in the United States. Still, the rapid turnover in children's programming on American television leaves most parents ignorant of what their children are watching. In my discussions with parents, most remembered Mr. Rogers and Shari Lewis, who now both appear on PBS, from their own childhood. There is, however, no such shared memory about commercial television today. As Schneider points out, none of the hit children's shows from fifteen years ago— such as The Archie Show, The Beatles, or Josie and the Pussycats—would be recognized by children in the late 1990s.[22] The gap between the narratives, games, skills, and technologies that we knew as children and what our children know now is vast, and the distance continues to grow rapidly. Children are no longer so dependent on parents for guidance in the world.

The "knowledge gap" between adults and children is closed, not as Postman suggests, because of television's disclosure of adult secrets, but because of the rapid disappearance of the world adults knew and learned about as children. On seeing a typewriter for the first time, my daughter described it as a broken computer. Anthony Giddens explains that the continuous questioning of old knowledge and replacement with new data are basic features of the reflexivity inherent in modernity itself. He argues that the replacement of religious dogma with rationality necessarily implies that no knowledge is ultimately secure, but rather, can be regarded as valid "in principle" only "until further notice."[23] New technologies, such as computers, which are familiar to children but new to adults, place the child ahead of the adult in achieving a working knowledge of the world.

The disappearance of adult authority is connected to the rapid transformation of the urban landscape that Walter Benjamin described so insightfully with reference to the early twentieth century—a process that has been only further radicalized at the end of the century.[24] I am reminded of one of my friends recently telling me about the problems she was having in organizing a family reunion. The older people wanted to get together in a small town in Wisconsin where the father had grown up. The younger people found it inconvenient as it did not have an airport and would involve some hours of driving with young children. My friend's point was that the reunion should be organized in a place that was convenient for all. After all, she said, the town existed only in name. None of the old families lived there, and her father's house had long ago been broken down and rebuilt. In her view, her father's attachment to his hometown (not to the reunion) was simply sentimental. The displacement of older people from the world that they knew comes with a lessening in their authority as well. This loss is inscribed in the radicalization of modernity itself, rather than in permissive parenting.

Once There Was a Family

Not surprisingly, this collapse in adult authority has evoked a conservative clamor for saving the family. As in the mid–nineteenth century, the family is once again called on to act as a buffer between the individual and society, to extend childhood, to resist the alienated relations of capitalism, to be the ground of lasting and loving relationships when all social values are reduced to that of exchange. In this view, television is threatening because it reaches children in the privacy of the family, inviting them to enter the market as consumers. Parents are asked to resist television through a reassertion of their authority. Since the 1980s, there has been a growing concern expressed in child care books that American children are spoiled and out of control. This perspective is hostile to parents, especially mothers, particularly within the discussion of children and television. Winn, Postman, and Kline argue that the child-centered parenting practices of the 1960s went too far in giving into children's unreasonable demands, and they cite television as a prime example. Winn blames "a misplaced pursuit of democracy, a particularly American failing," for the refusal or inability of parents to restrict their children's television viewing.[25] Kline mirrors this sentiment when he questions whether "modern 'child-oriented' practices constitute 'liberation'—or the abdication of child-rearing itself."[26] Both Kline and Winn contend that parents have willfully or otherwise given up control over socializing their children, leaving them to be socialized by television or corporate advertising instead. In what can be read only as a reaction against the women's movement, Winn blames it for what she calls women's "flight" from the home, which she claims, in turn, is precipitated by the "increased willfulness, demandingness, and disagreeableness of undisciplined children" that makes "a life of staying home seem less appealing than the drabbest, most routine office job so many women choose in exchange."[27] Yet, historians such as Barbara Ehrenreich have emphasized that for the majority of mothers, working outside the home is a matter of economic necessity rather than choice. Winn must be talking about only the affluent family who can afford a full-time parent but still experience loss of control over their children.

In the rhetoric of reinstating parental authority, the responsibility for restraining children from consumerism is placed on the family rather than industry (whose solution is the V-chip as a mechanical means of exercising control). This authoritarian approach is epitomized in short commands such as "Shut the set off," "Take command," or "No television ever." Acknowledging that authoritarian parenting is a reversal that children most of all would resist, Winn concedes that it will be a difficult battle. Nonetheless, she argues that it must be done for the sake of old family routines—long dinner conversations, reading books, and family games, that is, finding common things to do— something she calls "like old-fashioned living."[28] She assures parents that once they take the first firm step, their children will follow. She echoes Roald Dahl's *Charlie and the Chocolate Factory* from 1964, eleven years before her own book, *Plug-in Drug*. As Dahl writes:

> Oh, books, what books they use to know
> Those children living long ago!
> So please, oh please, we beg, we pray,
> Go throw your TV set away,
> And in its place you can install
> A lovely bookshelf on the wall.
> Then fill the shelves with lots of books,
> Ignoring all the dirty looks,
> The screams and yells, the bites and kicks,
> And children hitting you with sticks—
> Then, in about a week or so
> Of having nothing else to do,
> They'll now begin to feel the need
> Of having something good to read.[29]

Dahl conjures up the image not of a public library, but an upper-class private home furnished with books. The "old-fashioned family" is private, middle class, and strongly marked by hierarchy. Increasingly, instead of suggesting media literacy for children in both the school and home, as Buckingham and Seiter would recommend, parents are advised that the most important button on the set is the one labeled "off."

Winn and others propose that the family can resist capitalism by transforming itself into a private fortress. This is ironic at a time when capitalist expansion (the construction of children as consumers) and new technologies (the Internet) drastically challenge the public/private divide on which the family is based. There are two major problems with this view. First, it assumes that consumerism is something imposed on the family. Kline, for instance, claims that parents are giving up control over children's imaginations to corporations. Socialist-feminist historians, such as Michelle Barrett and Mary McKintosh, however, emphasize that the family under industrial capitalism is organized as the site of consumption. With the displacement of production from the family and household to the factory, the family's primary economic role became consumption. Given that children were constructed as the core of the family, it is hardly surprising that their primary economic role is also consumption. When children whine and beg for things in a mall, they are acting out the social and economic role prescribed to them—emotionally valuable, economic dependents amid a plethora of commodities to buy. I am reminded of my difficulties as a child in coming up with some answer to the adult question, "What would you like me to get you?" In India, in the 1960s and 1970s, there were the standard things you could buy—candy, dresses, dolls, and some games. Toys were sold in small sections in general stores managed by adults. We simply did not know what there was in the market. I compare this with my daughter's experience. So far, the wish lists, every year right from preschool to first grade, are full of current favorites in the children's market.

What is even more ironic about the claim that the family restore itself as a private domain is that it is an old response to a new situation. It is made in the face of new technologies that blur the boundaries between the public and private domains, between home and work. New technologies such as laptops, pagers, cellular phones, additional telephone lines, e-mail and the Internet have created on one end the corporate soldier (the highly paid multinational executive who takes his laptop and fax machine on vacation) and on the other end the army of underpaid, temporary, work-intensive home-based computer professionals entering data or running computer programs for corporations. As work has invaded the space of the family, numerous articles in popular parenting magazines describe families with little private or leisure time. To counteract this *Parents* magazine, for example, suggests that parents should shut off the fax, screen phone calls, let the answering machine take the calls, and so forth so as to really be *at home* with the family. This advice suggests the threat that television, the Internet, computers, telephones, and faxes pose to the public/private divide can be contained by evoking an old-fashioned ideal of the family as private space with the mother primarily responsible for home and children. Annie Phizacklea and Carol Wolkowitz's research shows that women workers are obliged to take lower paid, insecure jobs that perpetuate their status as domestic workers and primary caregivers for children.[30] This is, of course, not depicted in commercials for new technologies. One television commercial for MCI, for instance, shows a woman madly working at her home office via the phone, the modem, the fax machine, and e-mail, consistently driving hard bargains with the men who are sitting in a traditional office. She is, however, in her pajamas and bunny slippers. In another commercial, this one for Advanced Micro Devices, a mother looks into the computer screen with a placid baby sleeping in her arms.

In light of these technological changes, the continued privatization of the home exemplifies Karl Marx's argument—one that Susan Buck Morss suggests was further taken up by Walter Benjamin—that new technologies are fettered by older relations of production, including the collective imagination.[31] Extension of the workday within capitalism translates into further alienation and lack of control over one's life. Within the logic of patriarchy it translates into the further isolation of women within the home, who must manage both home and work now. It is not possible within capitalism and patriarchy to realize the potential these new technologies have of creating autonomous, de-centered work that integrates home and work, the public and the private, and children into adult social life. Some at the higher end of the professional middle class can see the benefits of these new technologies and the promise they hold of balancing home and work—the best that can be hoped for by the affluent under capitalism. But even that balance is only minimal and usually considered more a cause of stress, despite claims to the contrary made by commercials touting the advantages of the home office.

In my discussions with mothers, however, I find that the drive to "protect" children from consumer culture comes not out of a desire to retain authoritarian control, but their own discontentment with consumerism. Practices such as reading labels on boxes for sugar content, checking ratings on films, or rejecting overpriced and repetitive toys come out of a wish to teach their child to be a critical consumer. My daughter, Suhaila, has often told me how desperately she wants something when we are at Toys "R" Us, but once we leave the store, it seems not to matter at all that we didn't buy it. She has talked about the disappointment of buying something and finding it hollow in comparison to the commercial that sold it. One woman told me that when she and her children go to the mall, she asks them to make-believe that they are in a museum—they look, touch, and leave without buying. This position sees both the parent and child as compatriots in the same world, rather than as opponents in which the former has to control the latter. Parents also recognize that the desire to buy things for their children is a means to express love—a desire appropriated by capitalism.

It is against the backdrop of late capitalism and the radicalization of modernity that television plays itself out as the pied piper who plays a tune whose lures are incomprehensible to adults; a tune that draws children irresistibly out of their house, into the streets, and then into a world of which adults have no knowledge—a world that shuts its doors on them simply because they are adults. Television, as David Harvey explains, does not cause postmodernity to happen.[32] Rather, it is an integral part of it. Television does not make childhood disappear. It is a symptom as opposed to a cause of the changes under way, for capitalist expansion and new technologies at the end of the twentieth century are fundamentally altering the private/public divide on which the institutions of family and childhood rest.

There could be a way out of the paralysis suffered by adults in the pied piper story. That is to stand alongside our children rather than against them. Which is not to say, as children's marketers tell us, that there are no differences between children and adults. Children are vulnerable, physically and in other ways, in a society marked by inequality. In spite of the aggressive corporate move to construct children as autonomous, sovereign consumers, they are the most likely to be exploited in the market and susceptible to violence in the family. We know from our own fears of abandonment that being a child on one's own may be an exciting fantasy (because of the freedom it allows from the constraints of school and the family), yet it is a terrifying experience, particularly in a world strained by the antagonistic relations of class, race, and gender. Instead of the V-chip, training in being a critical consumer is a crucial first step, especially since it might help undermine the relation of dependency between children and adults. Granted, this step is still within capitalist relations. But rather than restoring the authoritarian family or forcing children into greater dependency, I think we need to reclaim the notion of childhood by claiming adult responsibility for the world as it is, and by providing, at least for children, a time of play and learning.

Notes

1   This essay is part of a larger study on the redefinition of childhood in Hollywood films produced for children in the 1990s. I am extremely grateful to my friends, Amy Beer, Ron Gregg, and Jeffrey Skoller, for their feedback on this paper, and to Chuck Kleinhans, Tom Gunning, and Manji Pendakur for their comments on earlier versions.

2   See Theodor Adorno and Max Horkheimer, "The Culture Industry: Enlightenment as Mass Deception," in *Dialectic of Enlightenment*, trans. John Cumming (New York: Seabury, 1972); Marie Winn, *The Plug-in Drug* (New York: Viking, 1977); Neil Postman, *The Disappearance of Childhood* (New York: Vintage Books, 1982); and Steven Kline, *Out of the Garden: Toys, TV, and Children's Culture in the Age of Marketing* (London: Verso, 1993).

3   See Ellen Seiter, *Sold Separately: Children and Parents in Consumer Culture* (New Brunswick, N.J.: Rutgers University Press, 1991); and David Buckingham, *Moving Images: Understanding Children's Emotional Responses to Television* (London: Manchester University Press, 1996).

4   Cy Schneider, *Children's Television: The Art, the Business, and How It Works* (Chicago: NTC Books, 1987), 2.

5   Selina S. Guber and Jon Berry, *Marketing to and through Kids* (New York: McGraw-Hill, 1993).

6   David Vogel, president of Walt Disney Pictures, the family division of the studio, quoted in Bernard Weinraub, "Fun for the Whole Family: Movies for Children, and Their Parents, Are Far from 'Pollyanna,' " *New York Times*, 22 July 1997, B1.

7   John H. Plumb, *The Birth of a Consumer Society: The Commercialization of Eighteenth-Century England* (Bloomington: Indiana University Press, 1982).

8   Michelle Barrett and Mary McKintosh, *The Antisocial Family* (London: Verso, 1982).

9   Jacqueline Rose, *The Case of Peter Pan: Or, the Impossibility of Children's Fiction* (London: Macmillan Publishers Ltd., 1984).

10   David Leonhardt and Kathleen Kerwin, "Hey Kid, Buy This!" *Business Week*, 30 June 1997, 61–67.

11   Robert Keith, "The Marketing Revolution," in *Marketing Classics: A Selection of Influential Articles*, 4th ed., ed. Ben M. Enis and Keith Cox (Toronto: Allyn and Bacon, 1981), 44–49.

12   See Barbara Ehrenreich, *Fear of Falling: The Inner Life of the Middle Class* (New York: Harper, 1990); and Lloyd DeMause, *The History of Childhood* (New York: Psychohistory Press, 1974).

13   Benjamin Spock, *Baby and Child Care*, 3d ed. (New York: Hawthorn Books, 1968).

14   Schneider, *Children's Television*, 22.

15   Jean Baudrillard, "For a Critique of the Political Economy of the Sign," *Jean Baudrillard: Selected Writings*, ed. Mark Poster (Stanford, California: Stanford University Press, 1988), 31.

16   Richard Schickel, *The Disney Version: The Life, Times, Art, and Commerce of Walt Disney* (New York: Simon and Schuster, 1968), 18.

17   Leonhardt and Kerwin, "Hey Kid, Buy This!"

18   Schneider, *Children's Television*, 9.

19   Rose, *Peter Pan*.

20   Seiter, *Sold Separately*.

21   Schneider, *Children's Television*, 26.

22   Ibid., 63.

23   Anthony Giddens, *The Consequences of Modernity* (Cambridge, UK: Polity Press, 1990), 49.

24   See Susan Buck-Morss, "Dream World of Mass Culture: Walter Benjamin's Theory of

Modernity and the Dialectics of Seeing," in *Modernity and the Hegemony of Vision*, ed. David M. Levin (Berkeley: University of California Press, 1993), 309–38.

25 Winn, *Plug-in Drug*, 209.

26 Kline, *Out of the Garden*, 3.

27 Winn, *Plug-in Drug*, 201.

28 Ibid., 204.

29 Roald Dahl, *Charlie and the Chocolate Factory* (New York: Alfred A. Knopf, 1964), 104.

30 Annie Phizacklea and Carol Walkowitz, *Homeworking Women* (London: Sage Publications, 1995).

31 Buck-Morss, "Dream World of Mass Culture," 115.

32 See David Harvey, *The Condition of Postmodernity: An Enquiry into the Origins of Cultural Change* (New York: Blackwell, 1990), 61.

II RECEPTION AND CULTURAL IDENTITY

Sesame Street: Cognition and Communications
Imperialism   *Heather Hendershot*

Many journalists, parents, teachers, congressional representatives, and academics have held up the public television show *Sesame Street* as the epitome of "good" television. Many parents like the show because of its educational goals, nonviolence, multicultural cast, and high production values. In 1993, the program won kudos from liberals for nodding to feminism and adding an extroverted female muppet.[1] The show is widely considered to be high quality and in "good taste." Notwithstanding its squeaky-clean image, this program that seems so obviously "good" at first glance, so obviously uncensorable, has been the focus of numerous adult debates over what is good and bad for children. In fact, criticism of *Sesame Street* appeared immediately after its 1969 premiere, and continued into the seventies.

More recently, the 1994 Republican Congress took *Sesame Street* (and *Barney*) as a totem of the Public Broadcasting Service's (PBS) failure and evidence that the government should cease its 14 percent funding of the Corporation for Public Broadcasting (CPB). Conservative, free-market aficionados lamented that the CPB had not seen any of the profits from *Sesame Street* and *Barney* products,[2] a situation that Senator Bob Dole hyperbolically and somewhat hysterically dubbed "Barneygate." Popular press cartoons showed Congressman Newt Gingrich in Oscar the Grouch's trash can, and Kermit the Frog panhandling. Panicky headlines asked if "The Death of Big Bird?" was impending.

The frenzied Republican assault on *Sesame Street* and *Barney* is, intentionally or not, diversionary. As we emotionally defend *Sesame Street* (and perhaps bid good riddance to *Barney*), our attention is distracted from examining the politics behind the attack on PBS. Fundamentally, it is merely one small brick in a monolithic conservative schema to eliminate "big government." Big government spends very little on public broadcasting, about .02 percent of the federal budget; continuing or eliminating CPB funding will not eliminate the federal deficit. What defunding will destroy is the very principle of nonprofit television, which frightens adult *Sesame Street* fans with the thought that their show may be corrupted by commercialism or eliminated if PBS is defunded. In 1997, these anxieties were confirmed when *Sesame Street* began to advertise itself.

Sesame Street's merits may well be questionable, but not because it is responsible for the deficit, as Gingrich et al. would have us believe. Many of the previous critiques of the program—that it is too fast paced, too much like an acid trip, or even "communistic"—do not hold water either. Perhaps this is why these concerns, leveled against the program in the seventies, have not found a place in popular memory. This essay recounts the history of criticisms of *Sesame Street* and then lays out new grounds on which to question the program. I believe that the show should be scrutinized for both its objectifying child-testing practices and its international production and distribution practices. Close analysis of *Sesame Street*'s research, production, and distribution problematizes the show's image, demystifying *Sesame Street* and the Children's Television Workshop (CTW), and I hope, opening up debate about the global politics of children's television. Since children's programming is generally articulated as a "problem" strictly in terms of how it may make children antisocial, the political economy of mass-produced children's culture is rarely addressed. *Sesame Street* is often seen as an antidote to the children's television "problem," but if we concentrate on the show's production rather than its consumption, a different picture emerges.

Bridging the Gap?

When *Sesame Street* first appeared on the air on November 10, 1969, it was unique in several ways. *Sesame Street*'s 1968–1970 budget was $8,191,100,[3] the largest amount of funding ever put into a U.S. educational television series. The program stressed cognitive development, while other programs emphasized creative play (*Romper Room*) or affective (emotional) development (*Mister Rogers' Neighborhood*). In other words, *Sesame Street* strove to teach mental skills, while other programs sought to teach socialization and help children cope with common childhood fears. Shows such as *Mister Rogers* and *Captain Kangaroo* reflected the traditional view of the preschool years as a time when children's education should focus on learning social skills, not cognitive ones. *Sesame Street*, on the other hand, more closely mirrored the Montessori view of early education, where preschool is a radical pedagogical experience. Although Montessori stressed sensory and motor development through hands-on activities that the television screen could not directly provide, the Sesame Street philosophy had elements in common with the basic tenet of Montessori philosophy: that enriching the child's preschool experience can help counteract the negative effects of an impoverished home environment. In keeping with the Montessori method, the Children's Television Workshop (CTW), Sesame Street's creator, embraced the idea that intelligence was not predetermined at birth but rather could be fostered by early education.[4] And like Montessori, the CTW was strongly committed to teaching poor children in particular.

Sesame Street rode the wave of the sixties' "cognitive revolution" in psychology. Cognitive psychologists researching television's possible effects seemed to turn away from earlier behaviorist models of subjectivity. In theory, this meant that many psychologists reconceptualized subjects as active participants in their environment, rather than passive slaves to stimuli. Cognitive researchers speculated that people used mental "scripts" to make meaning, and many developmentalists used Jean Piaget's theories to explain the child's cognitive maturation process. Yet, as David Buckingham argues, cognitive psychologists did not abandon many of behaviorism's methodological assumptions. Buckingham explains that when cognitive psychologists study media viewers and texts,

> Cognitive processing is widely defined as a "mediating variable"—in other words, as something that intervenes between stimulus and response [the crux of behaviorism]. Despite the emphasis on children as active constructors of meaning, meaning is still largely seen as something contained within the text, which can be "objectively" identified and quantified. Thus, the text itself is typically defined as a "stimulus": "formal features" such as camera movements or editing techniques are seen to have fixed meaning, and their "effects" are studied in isolation from the contexts in which they occur.[5]

The CTW exemplified the cognitive revolution that Buckingham describes: it rejected the old stimulus-response passive viewer model, preferring a cognitive conception of child subjects, while still clinging to the idea of a text as a stimulus that could be properly fine-tuned to produce certain specific, radical cognitive responses.

The CTW did, however, try to go beyond textual determinism in conceptualizing Sesame Street's child audience. Initially, Sesame Street's focus was on "bridging the gap" between "advantaged" and "disadvantaged" U.S. children. Sesame Street would do this by aiding the cognitive development of the poor. Soon after Sesame Street's release, this idea was de-emphasized when it was found to be in poor rhetorical judgment. The show's producers realized that to truly bridge the gap, the disadvantaged would have to learn more from *Sesame Street* than the advantaged, or the advantaged would have to be prevented from watching the program. So the initial goal was revised: *Sesame Street* would help all preschool children get a cognitive head start by teaching them letter and number recognition and other simple cognitive tasks. *Sesame Street* was a stimulus that the CTW hoped would produce a particular response: improved cognition that would lead to greater success in school and, eventually, improved socioeconomic status.

Another reason that "bridging the gap" was finally de-emphasized by the CTW was because it evoked the "deficit model" of education. CTW staff member Gerald Lesser said that educators subscribing to the deficit learning model felt that compensatory education programs could improve the lot of the poor by giving them certain middle-class "advantages," such as the ability to speak standard white English.[6] Lesser contended that "correcting" the poor would not make them into middle-class children and that compensatory programs problematically seek to make disadvantaged children "like everyone else." The goal of *Sesame Street*'s planners was not to make the poor into the cognitive equals of the middle class, but rather as Lesser writes, "to give disadvantaged children what they need in order to cope with their environments and improve their lives."[7] This vague contention was as specific as the CTW would get about its aims for impoverished viewers.

Debating Education in the Sixties

Sesame Street's educational philosophy was clearly indebted not only to Montessori, but also to Project Head Start, a component of President Lyndon Johnson's "War on Poverty." Both Head Start and *Sesame Street* depended on the premise that human development occurred rapidly in the first few years of life, and that improving the disadvantaged child's early environment was imperative if one wanted "not only to relieve the symptoms of poverty but to cure it; and, above all, to prevent it."[8] Like Project Head Start, *Sesame Street* received governmental funding and drew inspiration from social scientific research that showed how environment affected early child development.

This social scientific research, the Head Start project, and *Sesame Street* should be understood in the context of late sixties' educational politics. In 1969, when *Sesame Street* premiered, the Westingham Learning Corporation released a negative evaluation questioning Head Start's benefits, and the Richard Nixon administration consequently lessened its support of the program. That same year, Arthur R. Jensen published his controversial article, "How Much Can We Boost

IQ and Scholastic Achievement?" This *Bell Curve* predecessor attacked environmental psychologists for ignoring the role played by genetics in determining IQ. Drawing on data showing that "Negroes" consistently tested lower than "Caucasians" across all socioeconomic levels, Jensen argued that they had lower IQ's because of genetic predisposition, and he cited data showing that 42.9 percent of the poorest "Negroes" had an IQ below seventy-five, which indicated that they were "mentally retarded," while only 7.8 percent of the poorest "Caucasians" fit in that same category.[9] Jensen's data was attacked, but he had many supporters as well.[10] This dangerous research implied that improving the education of African Americans was a waste of time and money.

Sesame Street turned to the government for funding at a moment when the status of U.S. education and the need for government-sponsored reform was being hotly debated. Although the government in no way controlled *Sesame Street*'s form or content, 48.8 percent of the show's initial budget came from the Department of Health, Education, and Welfare.[11] In her original funding proposal, CTW founder Joan Ganz Cooney explained that *Sesame Street* could be funded for as little as one penny per child per day. Although the CTW never argued against school reform, clearly *Sesame Street* had potential as a comparatively cheap alternative to structural changes. Hoping to affect the socioeconomic disparity between blacks and whites, *Sesame Street* shared Project Head Start's goals, yet at a fraction of the cost. In addition, unlike Head Start, *Sesame Street* turned out to be an exportable, reusable product. The television series, thus, was a tangible product that proved to be a good investment. Yet when CTW first pitched the project, the Department of Education was shortsighted. One of the hardest hurdles to jump was convincing the department that educational television could hope to reach an inner-city and/or lower-class audience.[12] Perhaps the department assumed that this audience would ignore programming that was not pure entertainment. There was also reasonable concern that *Sesame Street*'s audience would be limited because so many areas of the country, particularly rural ones, had fuzzy ultrahigh frequency (UHF) reception. PBS tended to be ghettoized at the UHF end of the spectrum, and many older sets did not even have the capability to receive UHF signals. The Federal Communications Commission had not made UHF reception mandatory for television sets until 1962.

Cognition as Leveler of Social Differences

Social scientific research on children and television often articulates cognitive development as a bridge across class and race differences. Given the CTW's initial cognitive agenda, then, it is not surprising that when they were criticized for not bridging the advantaged/disadvantaged gap, they would fall back on the universalizing concept of cognition as a safety net, offering up the defense that they were merely operating on the pretense that *every* child's cognitive skills could be developed by viewing *Sesame Street*. *Sesame Street* showed an integrated neighborhood of Anglos, Latina/os, and African Americans, and it taught viewers how to count in Spanish, and in this way the show highlighted cultural differences and diversity. At the same time, *Sesame Street* worked on the assumption that cognition could be the great universalizer, the leveler of cultural heterogeneity. The idea that our brains make us all biologically the same—and therefore, *potentially* socially, culturally, and economically similar—may be preferable to the Jensen (and later *Bell Curve*) approach, whereby it is the differences in our brains that produce the differences in our lives. Still, the idea that cognition can be an equalizer can blind researchers to real structural inequalities (such as institutional racism) that preschool television has never challenged.

Whatever the limitations of a deep structure conception of cognition, and however much such a conception may ignore important cultural factors, it is important to bear in mind that many sixties and seventies' educators conceived of the brain as the great equalizer in order to combat racist scholars like Jensen. A 1976 study of Mexican American children illustrates the contrast between racist and comparatively liberal views of child development, yet the study also reveals the troubling ways that cognitive studies cannot adequately address research subjects' cultural and material existence. Edward A. DeAvila, Barbara Havassy, and Juan Pascual-Leone deplored the disproportionate number of minorities placed in classes for the "mentally retarded" based on IQ scores. Their belief in deep structural developmental similarities across racial and ethnic groups enabled them to question the cultural biases of Jensen's data.[13] DeAvila et al. had no doubt that all brains are equal, and moreover, that one could prove such equality with tests that children of all social backgrounds would score identically on. The researchers found that Mexican American children performed as well as Anglos on Piagetian developmental tests. They also, however, found "aberrant" and "inconclusive" results when they tested a group that included a high number of recent Mexican immigrants and migrant workers. The researchers had not successfully accomplished their goal of removing all "external," "environmental variables" in order to examine internal developmental variables in their pure state. These developmentalists were liberals fighting racism, and their goals sharply contrasted with the racist ones that Jensen demonstrated in his IQ studies. Yet their developmental approach was akin to Jensen's sociobiological approach in that neither could account for the cultural identity of their research subjects. Both Jensen and DeAvila et al. erased the cultural identities of their experimental subjects, the former in order to demonstrate the inferiority of people of color to whites, the latter to show that people of color were not inferior to whites. Like *Sesame Street*'s producers, DeAvila and his colleagues believed that cognitivism could have emancipatory results.

Fast Pacing and the Developmentalist Debates

On *Sesame Street*'s initial release, many media critics and educators harshly critiqued the program for its fast-paced teaching style. Joan Ganz Cooney's background was in commercial television, and she rejected the cheap, slow-paced educational programming that had preceded *Sesame Street* on narrowcast instructional television. Locally produced educational programming had generally featured a teacher at a blackboard explaining concepts. Cooney criticized such programming for its "slow and monotonous pace and lack of professionalism." In its place, she envisioned an educational program that could compete with network television: "Children are conditioned to expect pow! wham! fast-action thrillers from television [as well as] . . . highly visual, slickly and expensively produced material."[14] *Sesame Street* would exploit such conditioning by being fast paced, modeling itself after *Rowan and Martin's Laugh-In* by using quick vignettes. Animated bits on the alphabet were conceived as ads for particular letters, which would interrupt the program just like real ads on commercial television. The show's ad-like look was troubling to critics, who felt that the program's style helped children develop a taste for advertisements. Parents who objected to *Sesame Street*'s commercial style may have felt that their trust in PBS had been violated.

One of the CTW's worries on *Sesame Street*'s release was whether or not the masses would watch a program on PBS, generally a site of high culture adult programming such as symphonies and filmed stage productions. Yet I would posit that some of the initial resistance to *Sesame Street* came not from the masses, who were uninterested in PBS's pretension, but rather from the elite, who feared public television would be corrupted by unsuitable, fast-paced programming. Some parents and critics reacted strongly against *Sesame Street*'s style because PBS was supposed to be above commercialism.[15] In other words, *Sesame Street* violated their expectations about public broadcasting's "good taste." The CTW saw its style choice as a purely pragmatic one in order to compete with commercial television for children's attention. *Sesame Street* tapped into exactly the kinds of visual and aural cues that appealed to young children: lively music, sound effects, pans, peculiar voices, and audio changes.[16]

So this was one camp of *Sesame Street* detractors: parents and journalists, expressing their criticisms of the show's fast-paced, ad-like style, in newspaper cartoons, magazine articles, and letters to the editor. There was another camp that also focused on Sesame Street's quick pace: professional educators and developmental psychologists. Since Sesame Street's creators believed that children's brains were naturally curious and could be conditioned through early priming to be thirsty for knowledge, they reasoned that a preschool child regularly exposed to Sesame Street would come to school better prepared to learn than one who hadn't. Having mastered cognitive tasks such as letter, number, and shape recognition, and the ability to categorize, the Sesame Street viewer would have a higher level of cognitive development than the nonSesame Street viewer. However, some developmental psychologists worried that Sesame Street would be harmful to what they defined as the child's "natural" maturation, and they argued that the show would rush a child through her or his natural progressive developmental stages. To hurry a child into learning, particularly with a rapidly paced program like Sesame Street, would do more harm than good.

In "Turned-on Toddlers," clinical psychologist Werner I. Halpern claimed that "fast-paced TV bombardment" can "overwhelm the child's defenses against sensory overload."[17] As his essay's title indicates, Halpern implied that television could affect children like a drug.[18] The television-drug analogy is one that is still made today, but it was more common in the late sixties and early seventies when "turned on and tuned out" hippies were abundant and many middle-class adults were anxious about LSD use. Halpern thought that the "rate of development cannot accelerate indefinitely without jeopardizing cognitive and educational growth."[19] He criticized educators and parents who overzealously pushed children to achieve cognitive development levels beyond what he considered to be their innate developmental capability, and he cited Sesame Street as one of the tools that can be used to prod and overwhelm children. Halpern recounted his observations of toddlers who exhibited "behavior symptoms" that were "directly traceable" to Sesame Street. Some children, he wrote, "compulsively recited serial numbers and letters learned from Sesame Street. . . . [The] children often inspected their inanimate surroundings like restless, wound-up robots."[20] Halpern argued that "sensory assault" involving rapid perceptual shifts through the use of quick dissolves and zooms, coupled with the lack of pauses between Sesame Street segments, was harmful to "organismic balance."[21] If a child's nervous system was overtaxed by Sesame Street and other fast-paced programs, her or his development could be irreparably damaged.[22]

When Sesame Street first aired, a split emerged between psychologists who favored Sesame Street and those who preferred Mister Rogers' Neighborhood. The pro-Mister Rogers school of thought was that a young child needed to feel loved and nurtured more than he or she needed to know how to recognize letters and numbers. The most outspoken pro-*Rogers* developmentalists were doctors Jerome and Dorothy Singer, whose research showed that children benefited from the kind of imaginative play encouraged on *Mister Rogers*: "They can wait quietly or delay gratification, can concentrate better, and seem to be more empathic and less aggressive, thanks to their use of private fantasy."[23] The Singers were not outspoken crusaders against television, but they did argue that fast pacing led to shortened attention spans in children. Although *Sesame Street* was on PBS, it offered no break from the pacing of network television. With its emphasis on emotional development rather than cognitive skills, and its slow, careful pace, *Mister Rogers* was a program more psychologically healthy for children. Interestingly, the Singers pointed out that many adults dislike the program, but they reasoned that *adult* criticisms of *Mister Rogers* are irrelevant because the show serves children well. One could, of course, similarly rebut adult *Sesame Street* critics; perhaps the program is only too fast for adult tastes.

Targeting Sesame Street to Adults

The developmentalists notwithstanding, *Sesame Street* did suit the tastes of many adults, and watching it with your child was seen as a healthful alternative to using television as an "electronic baby-sitter." A 1970 *New Yorker* cartoon even went so far as to construct the show as a maternal obligation. A police officer confronts a woman in the park, asking, "shouldn't that child be at home watching *Sesame Street*?"[24]

To attract adult viewers, *Sesame Street* featured stars recognizable primarily to grown-ups, and such celebrities still commonly appear on the program. The CTW explained that Carol Burnett, Burt Lancaster, and James Earl Jones appeared on the show to encourage parents to watch with younger viewers; children would benefit more from the program if they discussed it afterward with older viewers.[25] The presence of stars not only drew adults to watching with children, but also helped them to enjoy and, therefore, support the program. Entertaining adults was crucial if *Sesame Street* was to succeed. Whereas *Mister Rogers* was relatively cheap and backed by the Sears Roebuck Foundation, *Sesame Street* initially cost over $8 million and was almost half government funded. The stakes were high: both taxpayers and the government had to be convinced that *Sesame Street* was a good show.

Since it was funded by the Department of Health, Education, and Welfare to teach cognitive skills, the program could not risk losing its funding by admitting to any implicit political goals. Yet whether the CTW talked about it or not, the show's style and its picture of racial integration were certainly overtly controversial, and *Sesame Street* guests included celebrities from Hollywood's blacklist. The inclusion of these performers was an explicitly political choice, and one which reveals the strong liberal convictions of *Sesame Street*'s creators. If they had only cared about their show succeeding and keeping its funding, they certainly would not have risked alienating adult viewers who would object to blacklisted actors such as Zero Mostel and Pete Seeger.[26] Pat Paulsen was another potentially risky guest. Some adults saw *Sesame Street*'s modern style as psychedelic and feared its possible "addictiveness." They worried that *Sesame Street* was too much like an acid trip, and thus, that it might predispose children to dropping acid.[27] Those who disapproved of *Sesame Street*'s style as hippie or psychedelic would have found their worst fears confirmed by the presence of Paulsen, a *Smothers Brothers Comedy Hour* regular. The *Smothers Brothers* was well known for its critical stance toward U.S. involvement in Vietnam and its liberal attitude toward integration.

In retrospect, both *Sesame Street* and The *Smothers Brothers* seem relatively tame, and it is hard to understand why they were so controversial in the late sixties and early seventies. Both programs relied on stylistic elements—sets, costumes, zooms, fast cuts, shot superimposition, and lap dissolves—that strongly evoked the youth counterculture, and both portrayed an integrated world that was a relative rarity on television. Although *Sesame Street* strove to appeal to children by using a modern, youth-coded style, it risked losing some of its parent audience (the conservative middle Americans that President Nixon referred to in 1971 as "the silent majority") precisely because of that style. *Sesame Street* needed wide adult approval to maintain its funding, but it was guided by liberal principles that meant it could not succeed with all adults. The series' liberalism appealed to those who appreciated a variety of hip guest stars, some of them enemies of the Right, while more conservative adults (not unlike the liberals who feared that the show's style would indoctrinate children with commercial values) were turned off by the show's "happening" style, which might indoctrinate "turned-on toddlers" into the hippie mentality. Ostensibly a children's show, *Sesame Street* could not have been more thoroughly enmeshed in the politics of the adult world.

Communism, Integration, and Space Age Television

Sesame Street plays a dual role in the drama of sixties and seventies' cold war anxiety. On the one hand, the show was attacked by right-wingers for its "pinko," liberal beliefs. The far Right saw it as un-American. On the other hand, the program was a manifestation of the post-Sputnik, cold war drive to ensure that U.S. children were better educated than Communist children, and in this way, *Sesame Street* could not have been more American. Panicked by the fact that the Soviet Union made it into outer space before America did, the U.S.

government determined that its children would be the most up to date in the world; these modern children would be educated for the space age.

A key part of *Sesame Street*'s early success was its modern image, which was underpinned by a technologically deterministic faith in television.[28] The show depended on up-to-date education research, and it used testing to produce a body of scientific data proving the show's worth. Michèle Mattelart explains that one of *Sesame Street*'s major funders, the Carnegie Corporation,

> had taken a close interest in the psychologists, educationalists and child-specialists of the cognitive school who had been dubbed "modern" by comparison with the "traditionalists." To attain their goals, they suggested—amongst other pedagogic strategies—the technique of "verbal bombardment," on which they had experimented with children from underprivileged milieux. In their book *Teaching Disadvantaged Children*, Carl Bereiter and Siegfried Engelman draw up a list of the basic skills of which a child should be capable before entering the first year of school. These items became a programming guide for *Sesame Street*. . . . [It] is this codified *scientific framework*, already organised in the form of a sequential programme, which revealed itself to be the most useful, tailor-made for the serialised format of *Sesame Street*.[29] (emphasis added)

Sesame Street was scientifically modern not only in its pedagogical strategies, but also in its appearance. The program used computer animation, chroma keying, pixillation, word matting, and other techniques that gave it a technologically modern look. In this way, the show displayed its budget and distinguished itself from cheap, "nonprofessional," narrowcast educational programs. *Sesame Street* saw itself as "space age" television, as Loretta Moore Long makes explicit in "*Sesame Street*: A Space Age Approach to Education for Space Age Children."

In her 1973 dissertation, Long explains that children need all the cognitive help they can get in order to prepare them for life in a technologically dynamic society. For her (and the CTW), technological progress unequivocally means progress toward a greater good: "There is no reason why the same technology that puts men on the moon cannot be utilized to teach Johnny to read." Long argues that education for preschool children is imperative because we need to "equip these citizens of the twenty-first century for their future, which may well include space travel, developing totally new lifestyles, and working in occupations that we have not even envisioned."[30] She concludes her dissertation with the lyrics of a *Sesame Street* song about a future where people live on the moon; the producers saw their program as laying the cognitive foundation for the astronauts of tomorrow.

In his book on *Sesame Street*, Gerald Lesser excerpts an anti–*Sesame Street* article that demonstrates how some people watching the show saw not little astronauts but red diaper babies. The article is worth citing at length in order to indicate which buttons *Sesame Street* pushed with its liberal, integrationist stance, as well as to illustrate that some viewers read *Sesame Street* as a highly politically charged program that definitely taught children much more than cognitive skills or a protechnology space age attitude.

> The young mother who sits her child in front of the TV to watch *Sesame Street* might be better off hiring Fidel Castro as a baby sitter! . . . Here are a few random facts for Moms (and Pops) to ponder:
>
> (1) While parents study the horrors of "communism," *Sesame Street* introduces their tots to real live Reds, and sugarcoats those Reds to make them look like good guys. An excellent example is Pete Seeger, who shows up at nearly every major communist gathering and pro-communist gathering in the world to strum his guitar and warble the praises of Red Revolution. Pete is a *Sesame Street* "lovable."
>
> (2) At a time when small children should be learning the faith of their fathers and love of country, *Sesame Street* indoctrinates them into an anti-Christian, anti-national, faceless, raceless, one-worldism.
>
> (3) *Sesame Street* purposely tries to indoctrinate children into complete disregard of racial distinctions and racial pride. Every greatest civilization in history which dropped racial pride and tribal pride crumbled into oblivion.
>
> *Sesame Street*'s directors admit that they knocked out the housewife-mother image to appease Women's Lib. In early programs a character known as Susan was a housewife, but this seems to offend the gruff-voiced he-gal types who preach that Mother's place is not in the home. . . . If Lib becomes strong, isn't it possible that *Sesame Street* will become even more perverted?
>
> *Sesame Street* is already promoting biracial relationships. Could it not under pressure from the gruff-voice gals gradually "glorify" girl-girl relationships? Is there any real progress in doing away with Robert Louis Stevenson's *Treasure Island*, and replacing it with the Isle of Lesbos?[31]

The article conflates miscegenation, feminism, and lesbianism, issues that *Sesame Street* certainly made no intentional attempt to address. The quips about Fidel Castro, Reds, and Pete Seeger reveal that the presence of blacklisted actors on *Sesame Street* did more than merely encourage parents to view with their children. Clearly, some of the public was outraged by *Sesame Street*'s "Commie" cast. This article also shows that *Sesame Street*'s integrated world was not as subtle as Lesser implies. For Lesser, *Sesame Street* could help blacks by teaching them cognitive skills, but the program could best address racial concerns *tangentially*. Lesser argues that it was best

> to teach about issues and emotions, not through content, but in context and through the life styles of the people on the program. An integrated cast, for example, can be a teaching device in itself. Through this *indirect* route, the program might also address itself to supplying some of the elements usually missing on television: real fathers, Negro men and women who love one another.[32] (emphasis added)

Notwithstanding Lesser's claims for subtlety, the defensively racist response cited above bolsters Long's contention that *Sesame Street*'s integration was a central component of what she calls the program's "hidden curriculum" of racial tolerance and integration.

Long was intimately acquainted with *Sesame Street*'s goals through her own involvement with the program. She played Susan, the show's African American housewife who, as the disgruntled lesbophobe quoted above correctly surmised, became a nurse in response to liberal protest. According to Long, the program saw the eradication of racism as absolutely central to its mission.[33] Pointing to the show's "conscious devices—an inner-city neighborhood, an integrated cast, an equal role for all children in solving problems," Long claims that *Sesame Street* has a "hidden curriculum that seeks to bolster the black and minority child's self respect and to portray the multi-ethnic, multi-cultural world into which both majority and minority children are growing."[34] Long provides proof of the hidden curriculum's success by drawing on viewer mail.

According to Long, *Sesame Street* offered black children characters to admire and identify with, which in turn bolstered their self-esteem and racial pride. Long recounts how African American children's feelings about their appearance were positively influenced by seeing *Sesame Street*'s black characters Susan and Gordon. One mother wrote that her child asked her to stop straightening his hair so he could have an afro like Susan's. Another mother wrote that after seeing a close-up of Susan's face, her child asked, " ' . . . do I have any of that stuff in my skin that Susan has?' When the mother replied, 'yes, a little,' the child breathed a sigh of relief and said, '*Thank Goodness!*' "[35] Another black child watching a black child on the show exclaimed, "Look! He looks like me and he knows the answers!"[36] A white girl told her mother, " 'Susan and Gordon are bad people. They're different from us. Their hair and skin are all funny.' Some days later the child reported, 'Mommy, Susan and Gordon aren't really funny or bad. Now I know them, and every day they make me feel happy inside.' "[37]

Long explains that the decision to locate *Sesame Street* in an inner-city neighborhood crowded with garbage cans and old brownstones was crucial to the program's commitment to promoting racial understanding and tolerance. From today's perspective, it is hard to perceive *Sesame Street*'s antiseptic, inner-city soundstage as radical. Indeed, some critics at the time faulted this set—and the rest of *Sesame Street*'s harmonious world—for being too sanitized. In a 1971 *MAD* magazine parody, "Reality Street" is demolished to make way for a munitions development plant. The Vietnam War or demolition crews would never disrupt the real, goody-goody Sesame Street. But the choice to represent an inner-city locale was, nonetheless, quite radical if one considers the sets of other children's programs—Mister Rogers' middle-class neighborhood, Captain Kangaroo's fantasy home, or the *Kukla, Fran, and Ollie* puppet stage. Although the *Sesame Street* set was hardly an excursion into neorealist grittiness, compared to other children's programs, it represented a genuine attempt to show "real life" and to speak to children of color in America's inner cities. Long tells a story to illustrate the effectiveness of the set:

> Many suburban children are sheltered from this type of neighborhood by their parents, and the setting of the show provides a window to the world for Whites, while helping the inner city child to relate more to us [the cast] as his neighbors. The almost magic effects of the show were related to me . . . [when] some children from a country day school in the suburbs of San Francisco were brought into the inner city for a trip to the museum. Going into the inner city caused much fear and trepidation on the part of school officials and parents. When they hit the ghetto neighborhood that surrounded the museum, the children on the bus became so excited that no one on the bus understood what they were saying. They were jumping up and down, saying, "Thank you! Thank you! Thank you!" Finally the teacher asked them, "Thank you for what?" and they all answered, "For bringing us to Sesame Street!"[38]

This anecdote offers an interesting contrast between adult and child perceptions. The parents feared the inner-city ghetto that their children would have to pass through on their way to a museum, a traditional site of high-class privilege. The children, because of *Sesame Street*, saw the inner city as a site of adventure rather than racism, poverty, or violence. They confused representation (*Sesame Street*'s fictional inner city) and what their parents perceived as reality (the dangerous ghetto). *Sesame Street* was a far cry from the images the suburban parents were familiar with from watching the nightly news or blaxploitation pics. Although Long called *Sesame Street* a "window" onto the inner city, it was more like a museum display. On *Sesame Street*, sidewalks were perfect, streets were well paved, and the only thing that smelled bad was a grouchy puppet.

Sesame Street's U.S. Testing Practices

The CTW's greatest claim to fame is that *Sesame Street* was the product of the "marriage," as they put it, of scientific (cognitive) research and television expertise. Never before had expert cognitive psychologists and educators worked so closely with television producers in order to conceptualize a program. Psychologists continue to work behind the scenes, testing children's responses to the show and bringing the results back to the show's producers. Through the "marriage" of social science and technological know-how, the CTW has created the most popular children's television show on earth.

Through its child testing, the CTW produces scientific knowledge that can be fed back into their production loop in order to improve their product. Social scientific data culled from an initial group of children serves as fuel for high-tech television production. The television images are then tested on other children, and new data from this test group is used to produce more high-tech images. In this way, social science and television production form a closed circuit; responsive child test subjects are instrumental to this circuit. The CTW's child-testing practices are based on a number of questionable assumptions: that children's viewing practices can be translated into "data"; that their viewing can be scientifically studied without accounting for contextual aspects of television viewing and meaning making; and that memorization or recall is identical to learning.

Sesame Street engages in two kinds of research: formative and summative. Formative research is in-progress research whereby segments are tested before being aired; the segments are then reformulated in response to the test results. Summative research involves postbroadcast testing of the show's effectivity. Most *Sesame Street* research is formative. The CTW's testing-production circuit has been coined the "CTW model." The CTW model is widely accepted by many researchers and educational program producers around the world as the most effective means of producing quality children's programs. The model is basically a feedback loop (see figure 1). First, a new curriculum objective is formulated, and it must be determined that this is not a topic that exceeds the competence of the three-to-five-year-old target audience. An experimental segment is produced, then tested for "appeal" (do kids look at the television when the segment is on?) and educational effectiveness (will tests show that kids got the idea of the segment?). The segment is revised in response to the formative data, and finally included in a broadcast show. Sometimes there is a summative postevaluation. Reactions to the new segment are brought back to curriculum developers for the next season, and they wonder where they could go next:

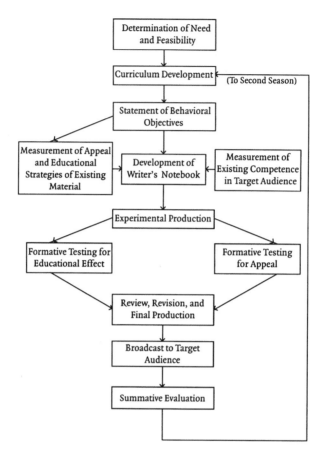

Figure 1. The CTW Model

"Teaching about mountains worked last season. How about constructing a similar segment on valleys?"

Sesame Street defines a segment as effective if it holds a child's attention and teaches him or her something. For testing purposes, teaching is defined as recall. *Sesame Street* has four basic methods for measuring the effectiveness of a segment. The first is the distractor method, a "crazy Rube Goldberg style machine"[39] developed early in *Sesame Street*'s history by the program's director of research, Dr. Edward L. Palmer. Gerald Lesser reports that measuring eye movement would have produced more precise estimates of viewer attention, but that such research was prohibitively expensive and placed children in "un-

natural viewing conditions because of the recording equipment used."⁴⁰ As
an alternative to *Clockwork Orange*–style eye measurement, Palmer designed a
cheaper and seemingly more natural way of testing viewer interest. To simulate
the many "distractions" that children encounter when they watch television at
home, Palmer set up a "distractor" slide projector, which he adjusted to project
on the wall beside the television. The distractor automatically changed slides
every eight seconds, showing "attractive scenes" such as animals and land-
scapes.⁴¹ To record viewing attention during the experiment, an adult researcher would depress a button when the child watched the television screen
and would release the button when the child looked away.

That the CTW created the distractor as an experimental tool attests to the fact
that they realize children do not simply stare at the screen in a transfixed,
hypnotic, and passive state, as some television opponents imagine. Not unlike
the producers of children's advertisements, the CTW acknowledges active and
distracted viewing, but only in order to work against it.⁴² In other words, the
CTW tests, reformulates, and retests segments with the goal of increasing
attention and decreasing play and distraction.

CTW testers are not cruel brainwashers who want to turn children into
drooling, hypnotized viewers, but they do hope to produce a particular kind of
attentive viewer. The workshop's research is one of a multitude of institutional
practices that strive to control the child in the name of a greater good (in this
case, learning). Like the correctly trained body in school, church, or the military, the CTW's ideal *Sesame Street* viewer behaves in certain prescribed ways.⁴³
The child must focus his or her attention on the television screen, not the
distractor's images, and she or he must also take in certain data—letters,
numbers, and shapes—and repeat them back to the tester. Knowledge and
learning are defined as recall: a child sees a show on the letter *b*, and after the
show, a researcher holds up several letters and asks which is *b*; if one correctly
identifies the "*b*," one has learned what it is. It is not necessary to understand
what a symbol is and how symbols function in the world in order to succeed on
the test. Test children are not deeply and irreparably harmed by memorizing
letter shapes without fully understanding what signs are. Besides, memorization and understanding are not mutually exclusive; they are interdependent,
and sometimes it can be difficult to even differentiate between them. *Sesame
Street* tests do not strive to do so.

Valeria Lovelace, a *Sesame Street* research director, reveals the central role
recall plays in CTW testing when she explains that in developing a new geography curriculum, the CTW was concerned about whether or not three-to-five-
year-old children could actually be taught geography on television. The CTW

developed a very simple test video, which we called the "Map Shape ID." The tape contained four segments, eight to eleven seconds in length, showing static, black-and-white maps of Hawaii, Alaska, Africa, and the United States, respectively. As each land mass appeared, a voice would identify it by name, saying twice, "This is a map of Hawaii [or Alaska, Africa, or the United States of America]." . . . To our surprise, when we compared the scores of children who had viewed the segments with a control group who had not, we noticed significant differences in their ability to select the correct place. . . . Only thirteen percent of the children in the control group could correctly identify Hawaii, compared with seventy percent of the children who had viewed the tape.[44] (brackets in original)

The concept of how maps symbolize land masses is a complex one (and one that is addressed on the show itself), yet the researchers Valeria describes did not consider whether the children understood a map as an iconic sign. Rather, they tested associative memory. The children knew what shape "meant" Hawaii, but that doesn't show that they understood what *Hawaii* meant or what it meant to associate a particular shape with the word *Hawaii*. Hence, as Lovelace writes,

[another study was] inspired by an additional set of concerns, voiced by our producers, writers, and advisers, who worried that the Map Shape ID approach came perilously close to rote teaching. Weren't we losing sight of the qualitative aspects of geography? Wouldn't children be interested in the people and the animals that live in different places? Responding to these concerns, the research staff found a segment . . . [showing] a map of Australia with pictures of animals superimposed on it. We showed this segment to children, and afterward presented them with a map of Australia and photographs of animals and asked, "Which of these photographs did you see in here?" The majority of the children correctly identified the animals.[45]

This experiment addresses the "qualitative" aspects of geography in a very limited way. Associating a kangaroo with a particular shape is not equivalent to understanding what it means for an animal to be indigenous to a country. Although the broadcast *Sesame Street* units on geography strive to explain what a map actually is, the research behind these units does not. The research produces facts that can be fed back into the CTW testing-production circuit.

In addition to the distractor test, the CTW also engages in three other kinds of testing. Since 1982, it has used the "group viewing attention method," whereby fifteen children sit in three rows, with three year olds in the first row, four year olds in the middle, and five year olds in the back. A researcher sits at the end of each row wearing a headset that beeps "observation-point cues" every five seconds. At the beep, the researcher scans his or her row and records "whether the children's eyes are focused on the screen."[46] Like the slide distractor, this testing environment certainly does not approximate "normal" home viewing, but then that's not the point. The objective is to gather data about eye positioning.

In 1988, the CTW began using "research video reports" to measure attention. The reports are created by videotaping child viewers and then electronically inserting into the image a small box showing the program that the kids are watching, in sync with their reactions. This surveillance enables researchers to see all kinds of responses to Sesame Street, such as clapping, singing, and repeating words. This testing method defines attention more complexly than the group viewing attention method, but like that method, the video research reports constitute one-sided observation that does not allow researcher-child interaction.

The final test type is the comprehension-testing interview, a method that does allow for research-child interaction. Although the CTW had been conducting interviews with Sesame Street viewers all along, it was not until 1983 that "new methods were developed to help researchers establish a better rapport with each child interviewed and to encourage children to talk more freely during the session."[47] In comprehension-testing sessions, four or five children enter a viewing room, and each is assigned an adult researcher as a "partner." Then, the children "play 'Mr. Potato Head' with their partners. This warm-up activity allows children enough time to feel comfortable and familiar with their research partners."[48] After playing Mr. Potato Head, the children are given the following instructions:

> Today we are going to play a game called "reporter." Do you know what a reporter is? A reporter is someone who sees something and tries to remember as much as he or she can and then tells someone else about it afterwards. To help you be a good reporter, I'm going to give you a reporter's hat [researcher mimes giving each child a hat]. Okay, everyone put your hat on and tie it under your chin [continues to mime] so that it won't fall off while you are being a reporter. We are going to be doing other things while you watch, so when you're finished watching you can tell us what you saw and what you heard on the show. Is everybody ready? Okay.[49] (brackets in original)

The children then view a segment or segments of the program and "report" what they saw to their adult partners.

This kind of scripted play is problematic, I would argue, not because it harms children—some kids probably love it, while others are terrified or uninterested. Rather, it is methodologically problematic because of its rule-boundedness. Children play with and against rules all the time; because their activity is *play*, the rules can be reinvented as the play progresses, or the rules can be followed exactly. The researcher, on the other hand, cannot break the rules or allow the child to do so. Children often take their play very seriously, leading adults to theorize that "play is the child's work" (a homily of play theory),[50] but they don't get paid for their play. It is the discrepancy between children's understanding of play and researchers' understanding of work that problematizes the Mr. Potato Head/reporter scenario. The comprehension-testing session may be viewed by children as play or work (like a school test), but for the researchers it is work. Simply put, children at play and researchers gathering data have completely different and probably conflicting motives. This may be inevitable in any encounter between researchers and children, but what seems crucial is that researchers remain aware of their own position as researchers, noticing how children respond to them as authority figures and how they interpret the interview situation.

Although all ethnography will objectify to a certain extent, some social scientists have actively strived to be sensitive to their subjects as active and desiring *subjects* rather than *objects* of research. Throughout his interviews with child television viewers, David Buckingham found that children reacted to the interview situation in a variety of ways, some seeing it as play (a great way to get out of classes) and others seeing the situation as more stressful (like a test). As he collected data from them, Buckingham questioned his own role as interviewer and how the children responded to the interview dynamics. Similarly, sociologist Patricia Palmer framed the parameters of her study of child television viewers by responding to early feedback from kids. She used *their* concerns to shape her study. Ultimately, it was *her* study, but she attempted to mold it around what kids thought was important about television. The CTW has specific goals it must accomplish in its testing. This leaves little room for flexibility. Children must be objectified to produce the kind of empirical data that is useful for the CTW testing-production circuit.

Interestingly, the CTW labors against the same kind of distracted viewing that many cultural studies scholars have valorized. A number of cultural studies researchers have argued that TV cannot be fully understood through close analysis of particular TV shows/texts. In their daily lives, viewers' understanding of TV is dependent on specific viewing contexts. Some people play with toys or cook dinner while the TV is on. Some people watch sports because they enjoy rooting for their favorite team, and some watch because their partners monopolize the remote control. What viewers get out of shows is bound up in such varied reception contexts, and viewers are not ineluctably positioned by texts (shows) according to this line of thought. Conversely, a "textually positioned" spectator is placed in a particular subject position by a TV show. To give a simple example, soap operas constantly move from story to story. If you believe that viewers are ineluctably positioned by texts/shows, you might conclude that soap opera viewers must be as "distracted" as soap opera narratives are.[51]

The CTW acknowledges that a viewing model that accounts for reception context (such as social interaction) is more realistic than the textually positioned viewing model, but its testing-production circuit is designed to create a textually determined spectator. In principle, the CTW sees viewers as cultural subjects embedded in complicated home or school viewing environments, but its testing-production circuit rests on a behaviorist foundation whereby CTW producers alter stimuli to produce desired responses. One *Sesame Street* researcher notes that

> changing the audio at the beginning of a segment is of great importance in regaining attention to the screen. Many children are continually deciding for themselves, "Is this interesting enough to watch?" I find this one of the most pleasing results of the attention research. It shows that children are not unwitting victims of television but independent little decision makers. This situation is preferable by far to the well-known "zombie viewing," the situation in which an attention level of 100 percent is achieved.[52]

This statement is interesting because it affirms the CTW's understanding of children as very active viewers, seeming to negate the possibility of achieving a child's undivided attention. But in terms of practical application, the aim of the research is to determine how to change the audio to gain the maximum amount of attention.

Sesame Street in the Global Marketplace

Sesame Street holds up its testing and development model as its greatest achievement, proudly noting that children's television producers around the world strive to duplicate it. For this reason alone, it is crucial to subject the CTW model to critique. If this model has indeed caught on and is seen as the best way to produce educational children's television, the CTW's techniques are internationally influential. In effect, like many other technologies, children's television production needs to be understood as an imperialistic export product. *Sesame Street* is imperialistic not simply because the show itself is a widely disseminated American cultural product, but also because the technology of its production, the testing-production circuit, has been so widely disseminated and accepted by many governments as the best—indeed, the only—model for producing educational television.

Sesame Street is regularly leased to countries that cannot afford to produce their own educational programming; the show is one of many examples of television that is produced in prosperous countries and distributed to less-prosperous countries. Of course, it is becoming increasingly difficult to label export goods by their country of origin; transnational corporations defy the unidirectional country-to-country understanding of imperialism that once seemed to make sense. As Gage Averill explains,

> The emergence of transnational capitalism has, naturally, been haunted by the ghost of corporate nationality past, but transnational corporations have long sought ways of strategically positioning their "nationality" to maximize their appeal in global markets. Locally owned subsidiaries, globally traded shares of publically owned stock, franchises, and other tactics allow transnationals to transcend their national origins in the quest for global free flow.[53]

To maximize appeal in global markets, global brands are customized for particular countries. The actual product can be customized (Kellogg's proposes to market Basmati Flakes in India), or customizing can happen at the level of packaging, marketing, or the product name itself (Diet Coke is Coca-Cola Light in France). One might say that *Sesame Street* is an internationally customized brand created through franchises. Unlike transnationals, though, the CTW remains a privately owned, not-for-profit, U.S. corporation. Also, *Sesame Street* earnestly attempts to be profoundly sensitive to cultural differences, rather than "playing to a thin or superficial version of cultural difference as a means of establishing globally uniform habits of consumption,"[54] as big profit-driven corporations do. *Sesame Street* is not customized simply in order to increase profits. The CTW will not allow its franchisers to air the series with commercials, and the only profit that the CTW makes off foreign *Sesame Street* distribution is from toy sales. This profit is pumped back into researching and producing new U.S. programs or deposited into the CTW's large endowment.

Although foreign countries *purchase* the rights to use filmed *Sesame Street* segments and the logo, the CTW never portrays the show's dissemination as a business transaction. Rather, the CTW persistently depicts *Sesame Street* as a utopian bridge across cultures. To illustrate its contention that it is on a global goodwill mission, the CTW notes that *Sesame Street* is even watched by political foes: Arabic children view *Iftah Ya Simsin*, while Israeli children see *Rechov Sumsum*. Joan Ganz Cooney has often said, half-jokingly, "My fantasy has always been that one day during a tense meeting of Arabs and Israelis at a negotiating table, one side will throw out a line from a Bert and Ernie routine, and the other side will pick it up, and the two sides will go back and forth until laughter and peace break out in the Middle East."[55] The Arab and Israeli versions of *Sesame Street* are different from the U.S. version; they include Ernie and Bert, plus new Muppets designed specifically for Middle Eastern children. But it is the U.S. created characters Ernie and Bert that enable the peace negotiation in this fantasy. This scenario illustrates what appeals to the CTW about globally distributing *Sesame Street*. The show taps into what are perceived as universal child (and, implicitly, adult) needs and desires, and in this way, is an ambassador across cultures. From the CTW's perspective, the bickering Ernie and Bert have no American qualities; their middle-class American clothing, apartment, and furniture are all neutral. Notwithstanding the CTW's efforts to respect cultural differences, I would argue that *Sesame Street* is not just any ambassador. It is a specifically U.S. ambassador. In the course of producing the first combined Israeli-Palestinian *Sesame Street* segments in 1998, even the CTW could not ignore the show's status as a U.S. presence. The segments were shot in studios guarded by soldiers with automatic weapons, and there were disagreements about how fearful the puppets should be of each other. In general, both Israelis and Palestinians saw the project as naïve. As the CTW's emissary tells it, however, it did eventually work out: "The puppets, after a short, nervous introduction, became as friendly as Arafat and Rabin on the White House Lawn."[56]

The CTW has repeatedly stated that it only sends the show to countries that ask for it, but it never explains who does the inviting. Is the CTW invited by elected government officials, military or religious rulers, TV producers, educators, or citizens? In Chile, the anti-Allende Catholic church simultaneously collaborated with both the CIA and the CTW. By emphasizing its invited status, the CTW absolves itself of imperialistic intent and distinguishes itself from uninhibited imperialists like Viacom, Coca-Cola, or McDonald's. The exporters of other globally popular U.S. shows like *Dallas* and *Bay Watch* don't care whether or not they are imperialistic; they just want to make a buck. This makes them different from the CTW. But like *Sesame Street*, *Dallas* and *Bay Watch* also have permission from somebody to be in non-U.S. countries. They were either "invited" like *Sesame Street* or pitched to a foreign corporation that chose to lease them for broadcast. With the exception of illegal transborder broadcasting, such as the United States's Radio Martí (illegally broadcast to Cuba), all internationally distributed programs are "invited" by somebody.

How Global Sesame Street *Production Works*

It's not unusual for other countries to develop their own versions of popular U.S. shows. The French both imported and created new shows that were clearly modeled on *Dallas*. One thing that makes *Sesame Street* special, however, is that it participates in the development of foreign versions of itself.[57] *Sesame Street* has two different kinds of foreign formats. The euphemistically titled "Open Sesame" format is made up entirely of pieces of U.S.-produced program material chosen by the host country from a leased footage library. Only the opening and closing title sequence is locally produced. This is the most common type of foreign format. Coproductions, conversely, are comprised of both U.S. and locally produced material. In 1975, *Sesame Street* coproductions were made in four different languages, for distribution to sixty-nine countries.[58] By 1988, there were fifteen coproductions,[59] and the number continues to hold at about this level. The workshop is vocal about its desire for other countries to contribute to *Sesame Street* production and explains that the host country formats its own curriculum goals.

Coproductions pass through four stages. First, the country puts together a research team, which is sent to New York City to be trained in conducting formative research (child-testing methods such as the distractor). Summative research is generally too expensive to be undertaken by coproducers.[60] Second, the country goes into preproduction, making some pilot half-hour shows to test for appeal and comprehension. During the third stage, coproducers respond to test results from the second stage, and in the fourth stage they complete all their live-action and animated sequences. Typically, the country makes three hours of original animation and three hours of live-action footage *per season* of 130 half-hour shows.[61] By contrast, in the United States, the CTW produces 120 new one-hour shows each year, with approximately twenty-two to twenty-four minutes of new live-action and animated material *per show*.[62]

After the curriculum is developed in stage two, indigenous Muppets are conceptualized and produced by Henson Productions in New York City. Big Bird retains his personality in all of his incarnations, but his species may change. He is a parrot in Mexico and a porcupine in Israel. The fact that all Muppets are produced in the United States undercuts the CTW's argument that indigenous Muppets are precisely what prevents Muppets in foreign countries from being an imperialist presence. Yet, on the practical side, making the Muppets in the CTW's U.S. facilities does reduce costs for the coproducing country. To illustrate how appealing these U.S.-produced Muppets are, Gerald Lesser points out that when Iraqis invaded Kuwait in 1991, they stole Kuwait's Muppets.[63]

The CTW requires that its quality standards be upheld, but it does appear that foreign segments have lower production values than U.S. ones. Lesser explains that the CTW has incorporated some non-U.S. material into the leased footage library that foreign producers draw from, but that the U.S. version of *Sesame Street* does not use any foreign material (except a little bit of Canadian *Sesame Street*) because foreign production quality isn't high enough to fit into U.S. shows.[64] Again, although the CTW is not a transnational, for-profit corporation, it has something in common with transnational entertainment producers. As Gage Averill explains, "try as they might, cultural workers in the rest of the world have been structurally prohibited from achieving the same results as state-of-the-art studios in the West (and Japan)—that is, unless they turn over an essential stage in the production process to the transnationals."[65]

The main economic constraint for foreign coproducers is that they must set up the same testing-production circuit used in the United States. This is so expensive that some coproductions only run for one season. Then production must stop until enough money is raised to hire the researchers and testers needed for the testing-production circuit to continue. Germany and the Netherlands are able to produce a new season every year, while the Latin American *Plaza Sésamo* had managed only four seasons, as of 1993.[66] The last directional arrow of the CTW model (see figure 1), "To Second Season," is null and void in many countries. The circuit is, in effect, broken by economic constraints. This means that the CTW model, perceived worldwide as the best way to produce children's television, only really functions in the handful of countries that can afford it.

For both the coproduction and Open Sesame formats, host countries pick the bulk of their program material from the CTW's leased library of "culturally neutral" *Sesame Street* footage. The CTW has never explained how segments are chosen for the library, and we can only guess that "neutral" *Sesame Street* segments avoid overt reference to American culture. Of course, the problem is that *Sesame Street* in and of itself is American culture. Weeding out segments that parody American rock singers or movie stars does not make the program neutral.

Except in countries where English is the official school language both Open Sesame and coproduction programs dub new soundtracks over their "neutral" leased footage. Since *Sesame Street* is meant to prepare kids for school, the show is produced in each particular country's official school language. *Plaza Sésamo*, the Latin American coproduction, is produced in so-called "neutral" Spanish, then distributed in eighteen Spanish-speaking countries in South and Central America and the Caribbean.[67] The CTW explains that education experts from many different Latin American countries decided that "neutral" Spanish that avoided localisms was an economic necessity; it would not be feasible to produce separate versions of Plaza Sésamo in different dialects. Spanish is not the first language of many Plaza Sésamo viewers, but Amerindian language experts were apparently not invited to the Plaza Sésamo planning meetings. Neutral Spanish is thus doubly problematic; it is unfair to both speakers of various "nonneutral" Spanish dialects and those who speak Spanish as a second language, if at all.

Rua Sesamo is another coproduction with complicated language politics. Produced in Portuguese, Rua Sesamo is shown not only in Portugal, but also in African countries formerly colonized by Portugal: Angola, Mozambique, Guinea Bassao, Cape Verde, and São Tomé. The educational director of Rua Sesamo praises the program because "in these countries, not only [do] less than ten percent have access to preschool education, but also they get to primary school, where the teaching is done in Portuguese, knowing very little Portuguese—so the failure rates are, not surprisingly, enormous."[68] Rua Sesamo presumably helps guard against such "failure"; the director does not consider the possibility that in this postcolonial situation it is not African children who fail school but rather Portuguese school that fails children.

Like Rua Sesamo and Plaza Sésamo, the Arabic Iftah Ya Simsin is a widely distributed coproduction. As of 1989, it was sent to fourteen countries. The program is broadcast in Standard Arabic, the official school language of the Arab world. Abdelkader Ezzaki, education professor from Morocco, argues that "there is a wide gap between the language of home socialization and the language of the school, and . . . this program contributes significantly to the bridging of that gap." Ezzaki adds that "the style and philosophy of CTW—and that is the philosophy of teaching through fun—does not merely serve the cause of learning, but also the cause of classical Arabic, the [popular] perception of classical Arabic."[69] But what causes does the popularization of Standard Arabic serve? Of what value is the "language of home socialization"? Does it differ among the fourteen countries where Iftah Ya Simsin is distributed? In these fourteen countries, to what extent is the language of the home culturally coded as feminine and the language of the public sphere of the school coded as masculine? Are girls sent to school in all of these countries? Such pressing questions are never asked by Ezzaki or the CTW, and Ezzaki never elaborates on the specifics of domestic language use. These silences are typical of discussions of foreign Sesame Street productions.

Pedagogical theorist Paulo Freire has argued that literacy cannot be emancipatory if native languages are not used in literacy programs.[70] Freire believes that sociopolitical structures and the act of reading are interrelated, and that "the exclusion of social and political dimensions from the practice of reading gives rise to an ideology of cultural reproduction, one that views readers as 'objects.' It is as though their conscious bodies were simply empty, waiting to be filled by that word from the teacher."[71] The CTW objectifies children, in Freire's sense, when it accepts that a culturally neutral film library is possible and that the dubbing of official school languages in foreign versions of *Sesame Street* is merely a practicality. To the CTW, the social dimensions inherent in the cognitive act of learning letters in a politically charged, postcolonial situation, where the former colonizers' language may still be in use, are not at issue. The workshop thus addresses children of all nations as identically capable of learning letters and numbers, regardless of the possible affect bound up in the chosen teaching language.

The CTW tends to understand children as paradoxically unique yet universal. The unique child's needs can be met through cultural sensitivity, which means collaborating with educators in other countries to devise curriculum goals. The universal child will then find his or her needs met by *Sesame Street*, the cognitive equalizer. The workshop sees that the children of the world who view *Sesame Street* come from different cultures, but it does not see how such differences could conflict with the CTW's testing-production circuit, that instruction language is a politically charged issue, or that its own scientific idea of cognitive development, whereby all children pass "through a series of fixed, value-free, and universal stages of development,"[72] is not a politically neutral idea.

Foreign Testing of Sesame Street

To show the success *Sesame Street* has had with non-U.S. audiences, the CTW often cites tests undertaken in Jamaica and Mexico in the early seventies. In Jamaica, as Armand Mattelart explains:

> armed with a videotape system courtesy of Sony, with batteries charged by a Suzuki jeep, a team from Harvard showed *Sesame Street* in mountain villages to find out the reactions of people who had never before seen television. The findings from this groundwork were used at Harvard by the Children's Television Research Centre, established jointly by the CTW and the Harvard education department, thanks to funding from the Ford and Carnegie Foundations.[73]

The Harvard team set up mobile viewing sites in four villages and a stationary viewing site in a fifth, where a video camera was mounted above the television set, and groups of children were recorded viewing *Sesame Street* programs.

At this fifth site, the viewing situation was considered noncoercive because the child viewers had options besides watching television; instead of viewing,

Jamaicans watch television—
and *Sesame Street*—for the first
time on a Sony Suzuki mobile
viewing unit.

they might get up and move around the room, talk to each other, or look at the images cast by a distractor unit. The distractor's U.S.-produced images of circus animals, bicycles, and ice cream cones might indeed prove distracting to rural Jamaican children, who were presumably no more familiar with slides than they were with television. One hundred hours of videotapes were made. Back in the States, Harvard researchers paused the tapes every few seconds in order to record the viewers' "attention," which was measured by whether or not they were looking at the television set. Comprehension was not measured. U.S. researchers noted whether children in three different age groups paid attention to details such as different kinds of sounds, images, and characters.

Harry M. Lasker's report on the Jamaica study only briefly mentions the four nonstudy sites, yet the report does note that "for the Sony and Suzuki Corporations, the project would afford an opportunity to test their equipment and to observe the general reactions of villages to mobile television."[74] Since mobile television sites were set up only in the four villages that the Harvard team did not study, it is fairly clear that Sony and Suzuki were engaged in their own studies there. Whatever their true purpose may have been, according to Lasker's report, the Sony/Suzuki mobile units did succeed in appealing to both children and adults in nonelectrified villages. Lasker claims that the reception of the mobile video units was "warm and enthusiastic" and that Jamaicans eagerly gathered around the mobile viewing units. The researchers interpreted the Jamaicans' interest in television in purely positive terms; the children and adults were "delighted" and "fascinated" by the mobile programs.[75] At no point did the researchers consider if they had the right to introduce a new technology to a culture. They did, however, indicate that "electric power was scheduled to reach the villages soon, so we felt [the Jamaican villagers] would not be *tantalized* by something they could never see again"[76] (emphasis added), the implication being that it is not introducing television that is questionable, but rather introducing it and then unfairly taking it away. CTW researchers Edward L. Palmer, Milton Chen, and Gerald Lesser conclude from the Jamaica experiment that

> the research done to date suggests that a common factor behind the popularity of Sesame Street in its different versions abroad is the degree to which the program is integrated with local or regional culture and language. Tailoring the idiom and tone of the program to local or regional culture, social and educational values also appears to enhance its appeal in adopting countries.[77]

The question of how a program could be crafted in "idiom and tone" in a way appropriate for a culture without television remains unanswered.

The CTW considers the Jamaica study a success. Likewise, it cites successful Mexican test results. Rogelio Diaz-Guerrero and his colleagues twice undertook summative testing on Plaza Sésamo, the Mexican coproduction. In 1971, 221 three to five year olds from lower-class day-care centers were divided into two groups. The test group watched Plaza Sésamo for six months, while the control group watched unspecified "cartoons and other non-educational TV programs." Afterward, the children were tested for specific cognitive gains such as knowledge of numbers and letters, and the ability to sort and classify. The Plaza Sésamo viewers scored higher than the non–Plaza Sésamo viewers. As with Sesame Street testing in all countries (including the United States), one of the crucial problems with the Mexican study was that it tested only for "intended effects." Since Plaza Sésamo producers did not explicitly set out to change viewers' attitudes about American television, they were not interested in testing for changes in such attitudes. Likewise, they were not interested in what the cartoon viewers might have learned that Plaza Sésamo viewers did not, so no testing was performed toward this end. The cartoons, like the images cast by the distractor, were considered neutral. They were the control media, while only Plaza Sésamo programs were considered capable of producing effects in viewers.

The second Plaza Sésamo study went less smoothly. (As late as 1993, the CTW referred to positive test results in Mexico,[78] presumably referencing only the first study.) The first test had been conducted in 1971 when Plaza Sésamo was fairly new to Mexico. By the time the second study began in 1974, enough urban children had seen the program that it was impossible to find a control group "uncontaminated" (as the researchers put it) by Plaza Sésamo viewing. However, the initial version of the program, Plaza Sésamo I, stopped broadcast six months before the experiment began, so it was possible to control exposure to the show, even if the control group was "contaminated" by previous viewing experience. Again, the control group was shown unspecified cartoons, while the experimental group was shown *Plaza Sésamo*. Then, several unforeseen problems arose that compromised the experiment. One-third of the children dropped out of the study because, the researchers lamented, "on September first, when the school year began, many parents enrolled their children prematurely in the first grade, an illegal practice that is nevertheless widespread."[79] The researchers' frustration is ironic, given that one of the primary goals of *Sesame Street*, and its foreign versions, has always been to provide preschool education to those who would otherwise be denied. It seems odd to disparage children for going to school instead of watching a show that prepares them for school. Another problem was that one month before the experiment began, *Plaza Sésamo* unexpectedly came back on the air. Although the experimenters kept the control children from seeing the program during the experiment, they could not prevent viewing during the preexperiment month. Nor could they control viewing during the Christmas holidays. To counteract these factors, the control children were "purified." Those who could recognize any of the *Plaza Sésamo* characters, beyond the two most popular ones, were eliminated from the study.

After a year, all the children were tested, and the results were disastrous. Across all socioeconomic groups, virtually no differences could be detected between the viewers of *Plaza Sésamo* and the viewers of "neutral" cartoons. The researchers noted that rural children did particularly badly, even though they were not "contaminated" by previous knowledge of *Plaza Sésamo* (since they had no access to television). Diaz-Guerrero et al. hypothesized that part of the problem was rural children's poor attendance at *Plaza Sésamo* screenings. In other words, it was their own fault. In their conclusion, the *Plaza Sésamo* researchers reiterated the problem of "ambitious mothers who pushed their children illegally into the first grade" and rural-child-viewer absenteeism, again blaming their objects of study for the failure of the experiment. Perhaps such poor peformance was an appropriate response to the experimenters' methods.

The Broader Context of Communications Imperialism

Communications scholar Tapio Varis has shown that U.S. programming constitutes the majority of imported television in many countries. Of the areas Varis studied in 1973 and 1983, Latin America had the lowest output of domestic programming (54 percent of its total programming in 1983). Moreover, he found that 35 percent of the programs in Latin American countries come from the United States. The United States is not the only exporting culprit, of course; export trends also reflect postcolonialist hegemony. "Although American and

British programs dominate in English-speaking Africa, the French have a strong influence in francophone Africa. In Senegal, for example, 60 percent of imported programs originate in France and only 5 percent in the United States," according to Varis, who in general discovered a "one-way traffic from the big exporting countries to the rest of the world, and a dominance of entertainment material in the flow."[80] While *Sesame Street* has loftier intentions than noneducational entertainment, it remains part of the unidirectional flow of U.S. programming. The vast majority of countries use the Open Sesame, not the coproduction format, which means that the only locally produced material is the opening and closing title sequences. Although coproducing countries do shoot some of their own material and formulate their own curriculum goals, most of their programs are composed of pieces culled from the "neutral" library of U.S.-produced material.

The CTW is like other internationally distributed U.S. shows in that it is "invited" to foreign countries, as we saw earlier. Where the show is different is in how it is given a unique spin in some countries. This makes *Sesame Street* less like *Bay Watch* and other internationally popular shows, and more like international advertisements, which are crafted to match the countries in which they are shown. Former Coca-Cola executive Ira Herbert explains that "around the world . . . [Coke] is marketed and developed and invested in by mostly independent businessmen who are indigenous to the country in which we are marketing."[81] The product is identical in each country, which makes Coke different from *Sesame Street*, but consider how Herbert describes the specialization of Coke advertising:

> We developed pattern advertising that could be adjusted [by local franchisers] to fit the local environment, the local culture, the local language, and could be changed or edited as long as the concept wasn't changed—as long as the feel wasn't changed—as long as the sound wasn't changed. The feel of the commercial had to come out according to pattern.[82]

Local Coca-Cola franchisers adjust advertisements to be as appealing as possible to local viewers, but the essence of the product must remain intact in the ad. Similarly, foreign versions of *Sesame Street* are required to retain key *Sesame Street* elements. It would be unacceptable to the CTW, for instance, if an educator in Mozambique rejected the vignette format or suggested that cheap sock puppets be used instead of expensive muppets. Nor could one change the title so that it did not reference the U.S. title, or change the introductory song, which has the same tune the world over. Overt politics are not allowed, and any religious instruction must be carefully framed as "legends, tradition, or folklore."[83] Deviations from these guidelines would violate "the feel" of *Sesame Street*.[84]

Table 1. Ten Leading Transborder Radio Broadcasters, according to Voice of
America, 1988

Rank	Country	Number of languages	Hours per week
1	United States*	50	2,277
2	USSR	81	2,247
3	China	47	1,493
4	Taiwan	17	1,091
5	West Germany	37	821
6	Egypt	30	816
7	United Kingdom	36	751
8	Trans World Radio**	61	526
9	Voice of the Andes***	14	500
10	Albania	21	451

*Includes Radio Martí (1,199 hours), Radio Free Europe (630 hours), Radio Liberty, and Radio Free Afghanistan (448 hours).
**Religious broadcaster with transmitters in Guam, Monaco, the Netherlands Antilles, Sri Lanka, Switzerland, and Uruguay.
***Religious broadcaster with transmitters in Quito, Ecuador.

Historically, the U.S. government and U.S. foundations have used broadcasting to disseminate U.S. culture worldwide, and the CTW must be understood in this context. The CTW is one of many organizations that has participated in communications imperialism, though it is certainly one of the smaller, less malevolent players. Not surprisingly, one of the CTW's original funders was the Ford Foundation, which began promoting the use of telecommunications to educate poor children in the post–World War II years. In 1951, the foundation used Samoa as a testing ground for how uneducated populations react to tele-education projects. Televisions were installed in Samoan classrooms; during the day, programs were educational, while at night, U.S. films and series were shown. In 1972, an expert from the foundation proudly reported the Samoans were starting to eat foreign foods: "No one can live on coconuts, papayas and bananas forever."[85] Samoans had also become interested in washing machines, automobiles, and mopeds, and had abandoned their old custom of giving their money to the head of the village. The researcher exclaimed that "the Samoan system has been hailed as the most successful educational television in the world."[86]

The U.S. government, another former CTW backer, is a major disseminator of imperialist communications. The United States broadcasts more programming outside its boundaries than any other country in the world, as table 1 illustrates (for radio).[87] In 1988, the Voice of America (VOA) radio program, an arm of the United States Information Agency, was broadcast in fifty languages in addition to English. The Reagan administration appreciated the VOA's power as a disseminator of U.S. policy, and between 1981 and 1988, the Information Agency's budget was doubled.[88] Unlike the government, the CTW does not engage in illegal transborder broadcasting. If the CTW disseminates information that could be labeled "propaganda"—either for cognitive psychology or U.S. technologies of educational television production—it does so without malicious intent. The CTW sees its global endeavors merely as examples of practicing what they preach so often on *Sesame Street*: "co-op-er-a-tion."

"No Better Than Underdog or The Flintstones"?

As television violence is repeatedly debated in Congress—and broadcasters, pressure groups, and parents fight over the V-chip and revisions to the Children's Television Act of 1990—*Sesame Street* functions as a highly charged symbol. Proregulation forces wish that there were more programs like *Sesame Street*, while antiregulation factions such as the networks preach the need for all kinds of programming, not just the educational type. The industry uses *Sesame Street* as a trump card against complaints about overcommercialization, arguing that if reformers want to remove all the programs that help sell toys, *Sesame Street* will have to go too, since its products are a multimillion dollar industry. Some parents fear the V-chip will make television more violent, sexual, and commercialized than ever before, since programmers will argue that anything goes if viewers can block out whatever they don't want to see. This leads parents to worry that soon *Sesame Street* will be one of the few programs their kids can watch. For these concerned parents, the show has become a symbol of what good television means.

Sesame Street functions as a powerful symbol for conservative politicians as well. Although it no longer receives governmental funding, conservatives attack the show (and PBS) as an unfair burden on taxpayers. Laurence Jarvik of the right-wing Heritage Foundation has claimed that

> *Sesame Street* is just another kids' show. . . . No better than *Underdog* or *The Flintstones*. What did the taxpayers get for their investment in *Sesame Street*? A generation of kids who spray graffiti on the walls of New York City. If *Sesame Street* was so effective, why do we have such a literacy problem?[89]

Sesame Street may be like other shows, such as *The Flintstones*, in terms of its marketability and exportability, but that does not make it the same as *The Flintstones* any more than *The Flintstones* is the same as *Underdog*, as Jarvik seems to imply. All three shows have different narratives, conventions, and intentions, and none of them are the cause of street art or illiteracy. Jarvik targets *Sesame Street* because the CTW makes a lot of money on toy licensing, but all of this money either goes back into producing the show or into the CTW's endowment. Licensing income and the endowment enable the CTW to produce their shows without government money, and Jarvis thinks other PBS shows should finance themselves in a similar manner. But *Sesame Street* and *Barney and Friends* are the exceptions on PBS, not the rule. Is there a fortune to be made in Charlie Rose coffee mugs and Bill Moyers sweatshirts? U.S. taxpayers spend virtually nothing on PBS; defunding PBS is a symbolic statement about privatization, not a genuine means of reducing the deficit.

Jarvik's assault aside, since the seventies, *Sesame Street* has become virtually immune to attack. Luckily for PBS, Jarvik makes a huge tactical error in targeting the program, because in doing so, he evokes a knee-jerk, pro-PBS response from many Americans. If this knee-jerk reaction is what it takes to make PBS continue, I'm all for it.[90] But *Sesame Street* and the CTW should not be off-limits to critical investigation. *Sesame Street*'s symbolic stature discourages media critics from putting the show under their analytic microscope, but it is precisely because the show is such a potent cultural symbol that it must be subjected to close analysis.

Just as violent and commercial cartoons may actually contain progressive elements, "good" programs may not be so commonsensically above reproach. To study a so-called good program is necessary because "good" programs define themselves in relation to "bad" ones and vice versa. "Bad" shows incorporate educational elements and public service messages into their stories in order to combat their critics, while "good" programs use fast pacing and popular licensed characters. In asserting its own high quality, *Sesame Street* has even gone so far as to parody *Mighty Morphin Power Rangers* in a "Super Morphin Power Monsters" skit. With the Power Monsters skit, *Sesame Street* defines itself as "good" precisely by virtue of its not being the "bad" *Power Rangers*. The skit reassures parents that even though television can be dangerous, they have done the right thing by allowing their children to watch *Sesame Street*. To understand adult debates over which images endanger children, we need to ask not only why some images are contested, but also why other images are praised. It is crucial to critically examine all kinds of children's television programs, considering all phases of their production, distribution, and reception.

Notes

1 Hilary Mills, "Pete and Joan," *Vanity Fair*, August 1993, 119. This did not happen sooner because the show's muppet maker, the late Jim Henson, was resistant to developing

strong female characters. See also Joan Ganz Cooney Seminar, 1993 Museum of Television and Radio Collection, New York City (hereafter cited as Cooney Seminar).

2   *Sesame Street* products finance Children's Television Workshop (CTW) programs, but the workshop does not make a profit. Of the $800 million grossed on *Sesame Street* products in 1994, the CTW received $20 million in licensing fees. This money plus interest from the CTW's endowment funded the 1995 production budget.

3   Richard M. Polsky, *Getting to Sesame Street: Origins of the Children's Television Workshop* (New York: Praeger, 1974), 114. By 1993, the budget had risen to around $19 million (Cooney Seminar).

4   See J. McVicker Hunt, introduction to *The Montessori Method*, by Maria Montessori (New York: Schocken, 1974), xi–xxxix.

5   David Buckingham, *Children Talking Television: The Making of Television Literacy* (London: Falmer, 1993), 13.

6   On the deficit model, see Herbert Ginsburg, *The Myth of the Deprived Child: Poor Children's Intellect and Education* (Englewood Cliffs, N.J.: Prentice-Hall, 1972); and William Labov et al., *A Study of the Non-Standard English of Negro and Puerto-Rican Speakers in New York City* (Washington, D.C.: U.S. Department of Health, Education, and Welfare, Office of Education, 1968).

7   Gerald Lesser, *Children and Television: Lessons from Sesame Street* (New York: Random House, 1974), 52.

8   Lyndon Johnson, quoted in Valora Washington and Ura Jean Oyemade, *Project Head Start: Past, Present, and Future Trends in the Context of Family Needs* (New York: Garland Publishing, 1987), 6.

9   Arthur R. Jensen, "How Much Can We Boost IQ and Scholastic Achievement?" *Harvard Educational Review* 39, no. 1 (winter 1969): 1–123. The uproar that Jensen's article provoked compares to the more recent controversy surrounding Richard J. Herrnstein and Charles Murray's *The Bell Curve: Intelligence and Class Structure in American Life* (New York: Free Press, 1994). Jensen is the most cited author in *The Bell Curve*'s bibliography.

10 See the pro and con views expressed in *Harvard Educational Review*, 39, no. 2 (spring 1969).

11 Polsky, *Getting to Sesame Street*. Polsky also notes that 18.3 percent of the total funding was provided by the Carnegie Corporation, and 18.7 percent came from the Ford Foundation.

12 Cooney Seminar.

13 Edward A. DeAvila, Barbara Havassy and Juan Pascual-Leone, *Mexican-American Schoolchildren: A Neo-Piagetian Analysis* (Georgetown: Georgetown University Press, 1976).

14 Polsky, *Getting to Sesame Street*, 11.

15 Big companies such as IBM and Xerox, however, have traditionally funded much PBS programming, along with conservative foundations such as John M. Olin and Adolph Coors. See Josh Daniel, "Uncivil Wars: The Conservative Assault on Public Broadcasting," *Independent* (August/September 1992): 20–25.

16 Dafna Lemish found that infant viewers were consistently drawn to two kinds of programming: advertisements and *Sesame Street*. See her "Viewers in Diapers: The Early Development of Television Viewing," in *Natural Audiences: Qualitative Research of Media Uses and Effects*, ed. Thomas R. Lindlof (Norwood, N.J.: Ablex, 1987), 44.

17 Werner I. Halpern, "Turned-on Toddlers," *Journal of Communication* 25, no. 4 (fall 1975): 66.

18 See also Marie Winn, *The Plug-in Drug* (New York: Viking, 1977). In a 1969 *Boston Globe* article, Dr. S. Hayakawa said, "the kinship of the LSD and other drug experiences with

television is glaringly obvious: both depend upon turning on and passively waiting for something beautiful to happen" (quoted in Lesser, *Children and Television*, 29).

19   Halpern, "Turned-on Toddlers," 68.

20   Ibid.

21   Ibid., 69.

22   This kind of argument harkens back to behaviorist criticisms of radio and film in the thirties; both mediums were considered dangerous to children because they were "over-stimulating." The "normal" child was the least-stimulated child.

23   Jerome Singer and Dorothy Singer, "Come Back, Mister Rogers, Come Back," in *Television in American Culture*, ed. Carl Lowe (New York: Wilson, 1981) 124–28.

24   Reprinted in Lesser, *Children and Television*, 170.

25   Lesser, *Children and Television*, 120.

26   See Bert Spector, "A Clash of Cultures: The Smothers Brothers vs. CBS Television," in *American History/American Television: Interpreting the Video Past*, ed. John E. O'Connor (New York: Frederick Ungar, 1985), 159–83.

27   Captain Kangaroo, on the other hand, received governmental funding around 1968 to produce cartoon segments "designed for mental health purposes in hopes of counteracting future drug use" (Lucille Burbank, *Children's Television: An Historical Inquiry on Three Selected, Prominent, Long-Running, Early Childhood TV Programs* [Ph.D. diss., Temple University, 1992], 31).

28   On technological determinism, see Raymond Williams, *Television: Technology and Cultural Form* (Hanover, N.H.: Wesleyan University Press, 1992), esp. "The Technology and the Society" chapter.

29   Michèle Mattelart, "Education, Television, and Mass Culture: Reflections on Research into Innovation," in *Television in Transition*, ed. Phillip Drummond and Richard Patterson (London: BFI, 1986), 172.

30   Loretta Moore Long, "*Sesame Street*: A Space Age Approach to Education for Space Age Children" (Ph.D. diss., University of Massachusetts, 1973), 1.

31   Lesser, *Children and Television*, 177–78.

32   Gerald Lesser, quoted in Polsky, *Getting to Sesame Street*, 77.

33   Long, "Space Age Approach," 56.

34   Ibid., vii.

35   Ibid., 80.

36   Ibid., 86. Gerald Lesser also tells this story.

37   Ibid., 81.

38   Ibid.

39   Cooney Seminar.

40   Lesser, *Children and Television*, 138.

41   Rose K. Goldsen, *The Show and Tell Machine: How Television Works and Works You Over* (New York: Dial Press, 1977), 197.

42   The CTW's distractor child-testing method has been adopted by the television industry for testing commercials and programs on children. See ibid.

43   See Michel Foucault, *Discipline and Punish: The Birth of the Prison*, trans. Alan Sheridan (New York: Random House, 1979).

44   Valeria Lovelace, "*Sesame Street* as a Continuing Experiment," *Educational Technology Research and Development* 38, no. 4 (1990): 23–24.

45   Ibid., 24.

46 Ibid., 20.

47 Ibid.

48 Ibid., 21.

49 Ibid.

50 See Brian Sutton-Smith, *Toys as Culture* (New York: Gardner Press, 1986), esp. chapters 9 and 10.

51 See Tania Modleski, "The Rhythms of Reception: Daytime Television and Women's Work," in *Regarding Television: Critical Approaches—An Anthology*, ed. E. Ann Kaplan (Los Angeles: American Film Institute, 1983), 67–75.

52 Peter Levelt, "A Review of Research on International Coproductions of *Sesame Street*," in *Sesame Street Research: A Twentieth Anniversary Symposium* (New York: Children's Television Workshop, 1990), 57–58.

53 Gage Averill, "Global Imaginings," in *Making and Selling Culture*, ed. Richard Ohmann (Hanover, N.H.: Wesleyan University Press, 1996), 211.

54 Ibid., 203.

55 Joan Gant Cooney, quoted in Gerald Lesser, "Sesame Street: Getting There from Here; International Co-Productions: And the Street Goes On," Museum of Television and Radio Seminar Series, 1993, Museum of Television and Radio Collection, New York, N.Y. (hereafter cited as Lesser Seminar).

56 Josh Selig, "Muppets Succeed Where Politicians Haven't," *New York Times* 29 Mar. 1998, sec. 2:45.

57 *Jeopardy* is another U.S.-based show that has participated in the creation of foreign versions of itself.

58 Goldsen, *Show and Tell Machine*, 407.

59 Lutrelle Horne, "Introductory Remarks," in *Sesame Street Research: A Twentieth Anniversary Symposium* (New York: Children's Television Workshop, 1990), 54.

60 Levelt, "Research on International Coproduction," 58.

61 Lesser Seminar.

62 Cooney Seminar.

63 Lesser Seminar.

64 Ibid.

65 Averill, "Global Imaginings," 213–14.

66 *Plaza Sésamo* was produced in 1972, 1974, 1983, and 1993. See Lesser Seminar. In 1983, the show was funded by a grant from the Latin American Bottlers of Coca-Cola. See *Children's Television Workshop International Research Notes* 4 (fall 1983): 25.

67 On *Plaza Sésamo's* "neutral Spanish," see Rose K. Goldsen and Azriel Bibliowicz, "Plaza Sésamo: 'Neutral' Language or 'Cultural Assault,' " *Journal of Communication* 26, no. 2 (spring 1976): 124–25; on its distribution, see Lesser Seminar.

68 Maria Emilia Brederode, "Research on *Rua Sesamo*, the Portuguese Coproduction," in *Sesame Street Research: A Twentieth Anniversary Symposium* (New York: Children's Television Workshop, 1990), 64.

69 Abdelkader Ezzaki, "Research on *Iftah Ya Simsin*, the Arabic Coproduction," in "*Sesame Street*" *Research: A Twentieth Anniversary Symposium* (New York: Children's Television Workshop, 1990), 61.

70 This begs several questions: How should native language be defined? In a postcolonial situation, must a former colonizer's language be purged? If so, how? In Morocco, should *Rua Sesamo* be in French instead of Standard Arabic?

71   Paulo Freire and Donaldo Macedo, *Literacy: Reading the Word and the World* (South Hadley, Mass.: Bergin and Garvey, 1987), 145.

72   Ibid., 148.

73   Armand Mattelart, *Multinational Corporations and the Control of Culture*, trans. Michael Chanan (Atlantic Highlands, N.J.: Humanities Press, 1979), 183.

74   Harry M. Lasker, *The Jamaican Project: Final Report* (Children's Television Workshop, New York, photocopy), 1.

75   Ibid., 58–59.

76   Ibid., 4.

77   Edward L. Palmer, Milton Chen, and Gerald S. Lesser, "*Sesame Street*: Patterns of International Adaptation," *Journal of Communication* 26, no. 2 (spring 1976): 118.

78   Lesser Seminar.

79   Rogelio Diaz-Guerrero, Isabel Reyes-Lagunes, Donald B. Witzke, and Wayne H. Holtzman, "*Plaza Sésamo* in Mexico: An Evaluation," *Journal of Communication* 26, no. 2 (spring 1976): 149.

80   Tapio Varis, "Trends in International Television Flow," in *Global Television*, ed. Cynthia Schneider and Brian Wallis (New York: Wedge Press, 1991), 106.

81   Ira Herbert, quoted in Richard Ohmann, ed., *Making and Selling Culture* (Hanover, N.H.: Wesleyan University Press, 1996).

82   Ibid., 5.

83   Lesser Seminar.

84   The CTW does not articulate what they are going for as "the feel" of *Sesame Street*; this is my interpretation. Notwithstanding the CTW's rules, there is room for flexibility. For example, the program is shown in English in Curaçao, where the local dialect is Papimiento. At points when the local broadcasters thought English might not be understood, they turned down the audio and narrated in a Papimiento voice-over. Then they would turn the English audio track back up. Later, the teachers who had been doing the voice-overs were actually incorporated into the show, explaining segments in Papimiento. In Curaçao, the feel of the show is definitively altered. See Lesser Seminar.

85   A. Mattelart, *Multinational Corporations*, 159.

86   Ibid., 160.

87   Sydney W. Head and Christopher H. Sterling, *Broadcasting in America: A Survey of Electronic Media*, 6th ed. (Boston, Mass.: Houghton Mifflin, 1990), 507.

88   Ibid., 508.

89   Laurence Jarvik, quoted in Bill Carter, "Conservatives Call for PBS to Go Private or Go Dark," *New York Times*, 30 April 1992, B4, col. 3.

90   It is unfortunate, however, that PBS must be infantilized to survive, that adults will only support PBS in the name of child viewers. See James Ledbetter, *Made Possible By . . . The Death of Public Broadcasting in the United States* (New York: Verso, 1997).

Ranging with Power on the Fox Kids Network: Or, Where on Earth Is Children's Educational Television? Marsha Kinder

Rarely in the history of television has a fall season opened with such a spate of action-adventure cartoons for kids. . . . And never has so much added up to so little. You don't need to be a rocket scientist to figure out what opened up the gate to all this action—Fox's *Mighty Morphin Power Rangers*, of course. It's a straight financial proposition: If *Power Rangers* made gazillions of marketing dollars, the producers' reasoning goes, why shouldn't show X have a shot at some of those gazillions, too?—*TV Guide*, 29 October–4 November 1994

Carmen Gives New Meaning to "America the Beautiful."—CD-ROM cover, Broderbund's *Where in the World is Carmen Sandiego?*

Over the past decade, there has been a controversy raging in the United States over the deplorable state of children's television programming—a controversy involving children's advocates, Congress, the Clinton administration, the Federal Communications Commission (FCC), the broadcast industry, and the mass media. Although some have called for rigorous censorship, the most effective advocacy group, Action for Children's Television (ACT), remained sensitive to First Amendment guarantees and lobbied instead for legislation to encourage the production of educational programs that would present better alternatives to existing shows for youngsters—shows that are either overly violent, blatantly commercial, or simply awful. Largely through the persistence of Peggy Charren (the founder of ACT), those efforts led to the successful passage of the Children's Television Act of 1990, which regulates the amount of broadcast time during the children's block that can be devoted to commercials, in addition to requiring all stations to serve "the educational and informational needs of children." Yet considerable ambiguity still remains over what the terms *educational* and *informational* actually mean.

After an ongoing dialogue with the television industry on this subject, and with the continued urging of children's advocacy groups and the support of President Clinton, in August 1996, the FCC passed new guidelines requiring stations to broadcast a minimum of three hours per week (between 7 A.M. and 10 P.M.) of educational programming for children under the age of sixteen. Although the term *educational programming* was now specifically defined as having "a significant purpose," and stations were now required to specify on the air and in programming guides which of their shows fall in this category, there was still considerable disagreement among networks over how to interpret the word *educational*. While NBC's Executive Vice President John Miller claimed that their long-running situation comedy *Saved by the Bell* presented "pro-social" messages for teens, and hired an educational consultant who concluded that each episode was a "morality play" and therefore should qualify, the president of Fox Kids Network, Margaret Loesch, argued that the new FCC guidelines mandated more curriculum-based shows like Fox's own *Where on Earth Is Carmen Sandiego?*: "I believe the expectation of the public is that we'll have more shows that impart some kind of curriculum, like science or geography, in a framework that kids will watch. . . . I'll be very disappointed if all we end up doing is playing games and counting shows that have little educational value."[1] Unimpressed with the self-serving nature of this dialogue, Charren concluded, "If the TV industry has to question what is educational for children, they ought to be in the shoe business, not the TV business."[2]

Today, children's advocates claim there is still precious little programming with any educational value on American broadcast television. Although the focus of these debates has shifted to rating systems and V-chips that can help parents block out the worst offenders, the key question continues to be how to get better shows on the air—shows that are both educational *and* entertaining. As President Clinton put it (prior to his impeachment), "It is not enough for parents to be able to tune out what they don't want their children to watch. . . . They want to be able to tune in good programs that their children will watch."[3]

I want to enter this debate by turning back to a crucial moment in children's programming: 1994, the first time in television history that an entertaining educational series succeeded in being ranked number one in its time slot on an American commercial network, beating out other noneducational shows.[4] The station was Fox Kids Network, which after only four short years in the children's programming market, was now the dominant force. Its domination began in February 1993 when Fox pulled ahead of CBS, NBC, and ABC in the

Saturday morning time slot with *X-Men* (which few would consider educational), an animated adventure series from Saban Entertainment based on one of Marvel's most successful comic books. Fox's lead was solidified in September when Saban's *Mighty Morphin Power Rangers* debuted in the weekday 7:30 A.M. slot and, after only three weeks, captured number one in the ratings, retaining that position for the season among all viewers under the age of eighteen. Once it moved to Saturday morning in October of that year, *Power Rangers* quickly morphed into the top-rated and most controversial show in children's television.

The educational show that joined Fox's popular Saturday morning lineup in February 1994 was *Where on Earth Is Carmen Sandiego?*, an animated series based on Broderbund's successful computer software. This interactive adventure game was designed to teach geography and history by having young players track the elusive Carmen Sandiego, a former spy-turned-thief, across space and time in order to restore stolen treasures. The original software was introduced in 1985, and by 1992, had sold over 2.5 million copies, with six variations of the game that are widely used in the public schools. There are also adventure books, jigsaw puzzles, and a weekday quiz show, *Where in the World Is Carmen Sandiego?* produced by two PBS stations, WGBH (Boston) and WQED (Pittsburgh), which debuted nationally on PBS in fall 1991. Much closer to the original software than the PBS quiz show, the Fox series features a pair of young brother-sister detectives, Ivy and Zack, tracking Carmen. Although sandwiched between two male-oriented action series (*Batman and Robin* and *X-Men*), the Fox series is attentive to gender issues, encouraging both boys and girls to use computers to master the information superhighway while discovering that learning can be an exciting, empowering adventure.

Some skeptics argued that the only reason *Carmen Sandiego* ever got such a high rating was its prime position on Fox's Saturday morning lineup, where it served to counter the notoriety of *Power Rangers* and *X-Men*, which were both being heavily criticized by journalists, teachers, and parents groups for their violent content. In fact, it was this Manichaean balance that helped Fox's President Loesch, who joined the network in 1990 and quickly became known as "the Queen of Kid-Vid," put a happy face on the quicksilver conquest of a $650 million a year kids' television market. A less dramatic version of this could also be found in Loesch's prior achievements: whereas at NBC and Hanna-Barbera she was responsible for the highly praised, moralizing *Smurfs*, at Marvel she developed the controversial action series *G.I. Joe* and *Transformers*, as well as more benign fare like the saccharine *My Little Pony*[5] and sophisticated *Muppet Babies*. With this diversified experience behind her, Loesch took personal credit for giving both the *Power Rangers* and *Carmen Sandiego* Fox's green light. According to Erick Schmuckler in a "Special Report on Children's Television for *Mediaweek*," "Loesch relishes telling how she fought to put the show [*Power Rangers*] on against the judgment of her staff, bosses, and affiliates."[6] And we have already seen how she used *Carmen Sandiego* to position Fox ahead of the other networks as the strongest supporter of the new 1996 FCC guidelines. Apparently, this dual strategy paid off, for as one journalist put it,

> Going into its fifth season, the Fox Children's Network on Saturday morning is the undisputed leader in the daypart. Not only is its lineup the most popular among children 2–11 and 6–17, it also has launched the two most popular children's series of the past few years—*X-Men* and *Mighty Morphin Power Rangers*—and it boasts the most successful curriculum-based, FCC-friendly series, *Carmen Sandiego*.[7]

This strategy also worked with scholars, including those who prepared the University of California at Los Angeles's eagerly anticipated, heavily publicized *Television Violence Monitoring Report* (1995). While acknowledging Fox's domination of the children's television market, the report assigns four of the station's shows to its most dangerous "sinister combat violence" classification (which includes only a total of eight programs) and singles out *Power Rangers* for the harshest condemnation (because it is "completely driven by combat" and, as a live-action show, is more realistic than the others). Yet the report concludes on a positive note by singling out a few shows for special praise, putting *Carmen Sandiego* at the top of that list: *"Where in the World Is Carmen San Diego?* [sic] (Fox) is a particularly impressive show given its ability to hold children's attention and allow them to use their imaginations without relying on violence at all."[8]

As if the mere juxtaposition of these moral opposites on Fox's Saturday morning lineup were not already sufficiently ironic, one journalist further complicated the link, reporting that Fox "threw *Power Rangers* on Saturday because *Carmen Sandiego* wasn't ready."[9] Thus, instead of casting Carmen in the role of the innocent little sister who was swept along to power in the wake of her butt-kicking elder siblings, she was suddenly playing the difficult diva of a back-stage musical whose delayed debut (from October 1993 to February 1994) created an opening for the opportunistic Rangers who morphed overnight into Saturday morning stars.

It was Haim Saban—a young, Egyptian-born, Israeli independent producer—who brought the Rangers to power. After carefully scrutinizing the phenomenal international success of *Teenage Mutant Ninja Turtles* (which made its debut in 1984), Saban emigrated to Hollywood in 1985 with (according to his banking agent, John Shuman) a driving ambition to become "a full-service software provider" with a "plan . . . clearly calculated at exploiting the children's market internationally."[10] What Saban found in the Turtles was a successful formula for a cultural myth that could enhance a global marketing strategy—a combination of Pan-Asian martial arts action with a wholesome gang of heroic American teens. In other words, a comic conflation of Hong Kong and Hollywood superheroes to colonize the world. Buying the rights to a Japanese action series for children (which was already popular in that nation) and adapting it to kids' media culture in the States, he hoped to make it marketable worldwide, which is precisely what he succeeded in doing with The Mighty Morphin Power Rangers. Transforming the Japanese live-action heroes into a band of ordinary American high school kids (played by actors in their twenties), he varied their identities in terms of gender and ethnicity while retaining the Japanese action footage (where they are garbed in unisex jumpsuits, helmets, and boots that reveal no flesh or nationality). He also kept the talking head of their Master Zordon as well as their Japanese antagonists, the villainous Rita Repulsa and her legions of invasive aliens.

With the long run and high profits of the Turtles clearly in mind, even as early as 1993, Saban was calling the Power Rangers a "ten-plus-year, multibillion dollar franchise. . . . Our whole approach—our investments, our expectations for the return on investment—is based on a ten-year plan and not a two-year plan." By December of that year, his plan was already paying off: "Nearing the close of the Christmas sales season, sole toy licensee Bandai Co. has sold close to one million of the Power Ranger action figures, putting it on a faster early pace than the record sales of Teenage Mutant Ninja Turtles dolls five years ago."[11] Yet after four years of success for the Rangers, their popularity (unlike that of the X-Men, who have greater transgenerational appeal)[12] began to subside, making it doubtful whether they would fulfill Saban's ten-year plan. At the time of this writing, the latest incarnation of their series, Power Rangers Turbo (which recharges the Ranger's selling power by driving them back to their roots in the Transformer toy genre) is still playing on Saturday morning television.

Still, far from falling into disfavor, in July 1997, Saban negotiated a new partnership with the Fox parent News Corporation on Fox Kids Worldwide, which led to the incorporation of the Fox Kids Network (FKN) and its subsequent acquisition of the Family Channel. Not only did this corporate move help fulfill Saban's earlier goal of "exploiting the children's market internationally," but it also morphed him into the king of kid-vid, deposing the reigning queen, Loesch, who had created the FKN (when Barry Diller was still head of Fox), and was now demoted to vice chair and second in command under the newly empowered Saban. At first, this new subordinate position seemed to cast Loesch in a role of moral leadership, as she became the primary spokesperson for Fox's (as well as the industry's) compliance with the new government guidelines for educational content on children's television. While this role would have been virtually impossible for Saban to perform with credibility, it placed Loesch in an ideal position from which to consider her next move. In November 1997, three years before her contract with Fox was due to expire, she resigned as vice chair of Fox Kids Worldwide. By the following February, she had found a new power base at Jim Henson Productions, where she is now president of television development. Like Carmen Sandiego and Rita Repulsa, despite losing the backing of her former imperial infrastructure, Loesch presumably will never give up the fight.

But back in 1994, Loesch and Saban were still allies, united in their efforts to make the Power Rangers rule. The growing impact of the *Power Rangers* series in that year can be perceived by comparing how TV Guide treated the show in the spring and fall special issues of its influential biannual "Parents Guide to Kids' TV." As if trying to balance its awareness of Fox's new domination of the kids' television market with an equal sensitivity to the controversies raging over the violence of some of the network's programs, the spring issue (12–18 March 1994) featured cute little African American actress Erin Davis from Fox's *Sinbad Show* on its cover, with four tag lines addressing generational conflict within the family. All references to the *Power Rangers* were safely tucked inside (on page 19), where the series was cited as the prime example of a show kids love and parents hate, complete with supporting quotes from both generations ("I love this! The fighting is the best part!" versus "This is one of the worst of the new shows. Badly made, repetitive, very violent."). By the fall special issue (29 October–4 November 1994), TV Guide reversed its strategy, now devoting its cover to two leaping Power Rangers (the white and the yellow) with two promotional tag lines apparently designed to cash in on the marketing power of these superheroes. All Ranger bashing was discreetly confined in two articles by James Kaplan ("More Power" and "Superheroes or Zeros?" from which the opening epigraph is taken). Like the rest of the nation, TV Guide had succumbed to the "Morphin Power" of the Rangers. By fall 1994, morphing had become such a widely used trope throughout the United States that on the morning following the Republican landslide victory in the November congressional election, CBS news commentator Bill Plante could quip about those winning candidates who had run the nastiest campaigns against Bill Clinton and other Democrats, "This morning the politicians are *morphing* into statesmen."

There was obviously something far more potent in this myth of *Mighty Morphin Power Rangers* than mere violence, or why else would kids find it so compelling? One summer day in 1994, as I was walking along Larchmont Avenue (a street full of posh boutiques in a white, middle-class neighborhood

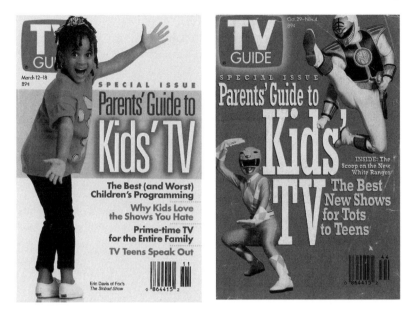

in Los Angeles), I witnessed a fascinating scene that forced me to confront this question. I saw a young mother pushing her baby girl in a stroller while her four- or five-year-old son walked by her side. Suddenly, the boy jumped into a martial arts pose, shouting, "Go, Go, Power Rangers!" as a look of pride and supreme pleasure spread across his face. When I got closer, I realized that this little *flâneur* was responding to a large Power Rangers poster hanging in the display window of a shop. I was intrigued with the question of why this experience was so pleasurable for him. Perhaps it was because the poster seemed to be specifically addressing him, rather than his mother or baby sister (who was apparently occupying more of mom's attention than he was). Not only did the poster acknowledge his importance as a knowledgeable player within a culture, but it helped him map the world and his own place within it, a map that directly linked his own television set to shop windows on the boulevard (or as some cultural theorists might say, domestic space and the public sphere). The poster also tested his cognitive powers, demonstrating that he was successfully able to recognize these connections and, even more important, that he knew what to do in response: he knew the correct imitative moves and mantra, and could perform them with a sense of drama and style that belied his subordinate position within the culture.

These moves functioned as a form of juvenile voguing—like the kind performed in the documentary *Paris Is Burning.* There, adult "children" (as they are

called by those interviewed on camera) fiercely compete in elaborate masquerade balls in Spanish Harlem that reassure marginalized gay men of color that
they can "pass" (as a woman, straight man, white VIP, or whatever) and feel
safe as they move between "legendary houses" and public display (those protective, alternative spaces of their own creation). Despite crucial differences in
ethnicity and class (and the cruel irony that these very kids may some day grow
up to be gay bashers), a similar thing was now happening to this boy and
others like him in their bedrooms and playgrounds across America as they
dressed in their Power Rangers drag. Playing Rangers enables them to morph
into teens who can range more freely (like Ivy and Zack) across different media
and neighborhoods. What I had witnessed was the morphing of a powerless
four year old into a consumer (or in Althusserian terms, the interpellation of a
consumerist subject). As part of the Power Rangers commercial network, the
poster was hailing the boy as a postmodernist subject, and he was responding
loud and clear to that call. That call and his response apparently made him feel
empowered, and this feeling gave him pleasure.

While there is considerable talk about a need for an educational program
that teaches media literacy to children (a need I have emphasized in my own
book, *Playing with Power in Movies, Television, and Video Games*),[13] what most of us
fail to realize is that there is already a highly sophisticated mode of instruction
in media literacy taking place *within* children's television—one with which this
boy on Larchmont has already begun to interact. I will argue that what children
are learning is how television mediates the understanding of all other forms of
cultural production and introduces the basic cognitive categories for organizing perceptions of the world. Ironically, these same "lessons" are being taught
in virtually all the shows in Fox's Saturday morning lineup (and probably in
those of other networks), not just in an educational series like *Carmen Sandiego*,
but also in violent action adventures like *Power Rangers* and *X-Men*. Moreover,
these "lessons" are to be found not just in content or the moralistic tags that
pay lip service to the Children's Television Act, but also systemically at the level
of structure. Before we can address what kind of media literacy is needed in the
schools, we have to understand what kind is already in progress.

Methodology

My methodology here is similar to the one used in *Playing with Power*: randomly
choosing one Saturday (September 24, 1994) to tape the entire morning block
of children's programming (7 A.M. to noon)[14] on the top-rated commercial
network, which was Fox rather than CBS (as in my earlier study). In the 1994
fall season, Fox had the top-rated show in every Saturday morning time slot

From the 1994 press kit
for the Fox Kids Net-
work.

(for both the two-to-eleven and six-to-seventeen age groups) as well as seven
out of the ten top-rated shows for that general time block. There was a second
advantage in choosing Fox: the diversity of its programming. Not only did
Fox's Saturday morning lineup include action series like *Power Rangers* and
X-Men from Saban Entertainment along with the universally praised *Where on
Earth Is Carmen Sandiego?* from DIC Enterprises, but also sophisticated Warner Bros. animated series like *Animaniacs* and *Batman and Robin*, Fox's own
Eek!stravaganza and *The Tick*, and Jim Henson's puppet/animation hybrid, *Dog
City*. These shows, moreover, represent all three classifications of violence as
defined in the UCLA study: "sinister combat violence" (*Batman and Robin*, *Mega-
Man*, *Power Rangers*, and *X-Men*), "tame combat violence" (*Dog City* and *The Tick*),
and "slapstick" (*Animaniacs*). Thus, this sample provided a good opportunity to
examine conventions that were systemic rather than limited to any specific
series, producer, or genre. Though my analysis refers to all of these series and
even includes commercials broadcast during this time block, it gives special
emphasis to *Carmen Sandiego* and *Power Rangers* as the two most presumably
opposite extremes.

What I found were four interrelated operations that comprise a system of
how to read specific images, words, and sounds (as well as the programs that
contain them) against the broader cultural field: cross-referencing, serial im-

itation, morphing, and overriding the programming. I derived the names of these operations not from any theoretical source, but from the programs themselves, for they are explicitly discussed in the dialogue, illustrated in the images, dramatized in the narrative, and sometimes even presented as "the moral" of the episode. Beyond its cognitive value, this system combines cognitive development with the transmission of ideological values, including consumerism and American supremacy within global markets.

Cross-Referencing

Cross-referencing is a method of intertextual reading that encourages children to track words, images, characters, and ideas across individual episodes, series, channels, media, and spaces (home, school, city streets), as well as across different cultures, periods, and academic subjects, and to derive pleasure from discovering these connections. While it is found in virtually all of the Fox series, it is enunciated most clearly in the episode of *Where on Earth Is Carmen Sandiego?* called "Chapter and Verse," which focuses quite literally on cultural literacy—how knowledge of Anglo-American literature is a useful means of learning history/geography/biography. This process is visualized in recurring scenes where viewers are instantaneously pulled into cyberspace in search of data, whizzing through winding corridors past a series of suspended screens on which still images and movies are constantly being projected. This visualization suggests a vast mental gallery that contains cultural icons grouped into particular paradigms or selective databases that are continually being updated.

The episode opens in Copenhagen with Ivy and Zack brushing up on their Hans Christian Andersen while they wait on a stakeout of Carmen, who plans to steal the *Little Mermaid* statue that commemorates the author. Hence, within seconds, an association has been made between a literary figure like Andersen and a recent Disney hit. The cognitive skill being taught is how to organize images into categories or sets on the basis of common characteristics that enable one to predict where characters and plots are moving. To succeed, viewers must watch for repetitions. For example, in order to predict Carmen's next literary target, the brother-sister detectives have to figure out what her previous three targets (Charles Dickens's inkwell, Mark Twain's writing desk, and Rudyard Kipling's jungle ruin) have in common. Realizing that all three of these authors wrote about orphans (Oliver Twist, Huck Finn, and Mowgli, respectively), they correctly predict that her next target will be Heidi in Maienfeld, Switzerland.

Cross-referencing is also operative in the opening teaser of the series and the recurring transitional image of a teenager (supposedly representing the viewer/

player) at a computer, an image that leads in and out of commercials. Both the teaser and transitional image prominently feature the Statue of Liberty as an icon of American national identity. Later in this particular episode, when Ivy and Zack are on their way to Dickens's house in London, their chief presents a slide show, purportedly of famous London monuments—Westminster Abbey, the Empire State Building, and Tower Bridge. As if playing "What's Wrong with This Picture?" Ivy points out that the Empire State Building is not in London but New York, which triggers a chain of Statue of Liberty images. Like the Empire State Building, the Statue of Liberty is emblematic not only of the United States, but also the so-called freedom of its citizens to range imperially across the rest of the world—as do Ivy and Zack.

Viewers are also able to cross-reference the Statue of Liberty across adjacent series. For instance, near the end of the *Carmen Sandiego* episode, we again see the transitional image of the unisex player seated at a computer screen with her or his back to the camera (as if to facilitate identification for a wider range of viewers of both genders). Above the player's head in the upper-left corner of the room there is a green sports pennant imprinted with the word "GO" (a familiar mantra chanted by fans at sporting events). The pennant points like an arrow to a large facial close-up of the Statue of Liberty in the upper-right corner. These icons connote mobility and freedom, respectively, a combination that evokes the kind of interactive spectatorship that is promised by computer games and the Internet, and that is only simulated in a television adaptation like *Carmen Sandiego*. A few moments later, in the teaser for the following show, we notice one of the X-Men, the rebellious archangel Jean, revolting against the immortal giant Apocalypse, who has enslaved him and is here seen posed against the Statue of Liberty. Jean emerges from the fire in the Statue of Liberty's torch and breaks off one of the spikes on her headpiece, transforming it into a weapon that he can use against his villainous oppressor. Later in the Saturday lineup, the Statue of Liberty is also briefly visible in the urban skyline at the opening of *The Tick*, where the parodic blue superhero stares out over the city, which he calls (in voice-over) "the city that he's sworn to stare out over." In all of these contexts, the connotative meanings of the Statue of Liberty have been transformed: no longer seen welcoming the world's hungry, impoverished immigrants, this icon of freedom is now figured as empowering First World nomads and superheroes to freely traverse the global cybersphere.

The Statue of Liberty and its connotations acquire more resonance through cross-referencing, for both *Carmen Sandiego* and *X-Men* accentuate dimensions of the icon besides the shifting meanings of "freedom." In the static image from *Carmen Sandiego*, the statue's head is visually analogous to the talking head of the chief, which is frequently seen on a computer screen giving instructions to Ivy and Zack. Both belong to a paradigm of authoritative heads that are a source of empowering knowledge—a category of modern oracles that also includes the talking head Zordon in *Power Rangers*, or going further back in media history, the androgynous genie in *Pee-wee's Playhouse* and the Magic Mirror in *Snow White*. Since this icon of the authoritative talking head is central to television discourse (especially in documentaries and on the news), its usage encourages young viewers to have faith in the veracity of the medium.

In the *X-Men* episode "Obsession," it is the Statue of Liberty's gender that is stressed, for she is one of a series of females who are powerful allies in an oedipal struggle against patriarchal tyranny. This association is immediately introduced in the main plot, when Rogue is the first to join Jean's vengeful rebellion against Apocalypse. This relationship is also echoed on the villain's spaceship, whose controlling computer has a gentle maternal voice and subjectivity (as in *Alien*), instead of the omnipresent patriarchal voice of Darth Vader. Ship helps Beast (a furry blue mutant also known as Henry McCoy, who is described in the *X-Men* bible as "the intellectual and scholar of the team")[15] defeat Apocalypse because McCoy taught "her" freedom: "Thank you, you made me understand I could choose, you made me feel" (one is tempted to add, "like a natural woman"). These associations suit a character-driven series like *X-Men*, which focuses on oedipal conflict, and whose subplot evokes other oedipal texts like *Beauty and the Beast* and *Blade Runner*.

In the context of commercial television, cross-referencing also serves the commercial interests of the producer and network—by encouraging viewers to take pleasure in tracking these licensed characters (be it Carmen Sandiego or X-Men) from one time slot or medium to another, and by strengthening the cross-referencing between dramatic episodes and commercials, which frequently show collectible X-Men or Power Rangers paraphernalia in action. This cross-referencing also helps Fox retain viewers from one show to the next by making them feel empowered by the perception of these connections. For example, the episode of a classic series like *Batman and Robin* is updated by its cross-referencing with adjacent series; its villain (The Riddler) is a riddling thief like Carmen Sandiego, who licenses toys in order to gain power (which echoes a similar scheme in *Animaniacs*). Cross-referencing is also operative in the choice of time slots. To cite one example, Fox first positioned its (then) new series *The Tick*, which parodies "the superhero community," immediately after *Batman and Robin*, as if to ensure that kids would be able to recognize and savor the parodic cross-referencing. Once *The Tick* was established, it was moved next to *X-Men*, where the blue color of its hero gains a stronger parodic link to Beast.

This operation of cross-referencing can be both blatant and subtle, one that is accessible to viewers at various cognitive levels—whether it is the steady stream of allusive puns performed by zany Animaniacs, or Batman's studied decoding of the Riddler's larcenous puzzles. Thus, it can provide pleasure to sophisticated teens or adults, as well as little kids like the boy on Larchmont.

Serial Imitation

Serial imitation is a chain of simulations performed by characters in the stories that also extends to viewers who identify with and imitate their favorite television personalities. It is a form of repetition that many young viewers find reassuring, for as the UCLA Television Violence Monitoring Report points out, "Children seem to be more comfortable with and desirous of repetition, familiarity, and predictability."[16] This process of simulation must be understood both by the shape-shifter and the one who sees through the masquerade; these two must also be able to distinguish morally between creative and dishonest forms of impersonation. I found blatant examples in four different programs within my sample.

The first is from Carmen Sandiego. After defining the concept of nom de plume and citing well-known examples like Lewis Carroll and O. Henry, Ivy and Zack seek out Mark Twain (the nom de plume for Samuel Clemens) as Carmen's next literary target. As soon as they reach Hannibal, Missouri, where the Mark Twain Museum is located, they run into Clemens, who makes them repair the fence they broke in their landing. This assignment gives them the chance to reenact Tom Sawyer's clever trick of getting other kids to do his work. Eventually, they discover that Clemens is an imposter and that the real one is being held hostage by Page Turner (a female member of Carmen's gang of international thieves), who is trying to steal Twain's writing desk. When her impersonation is exposed, the "real" Clemens shouts: "Stop! She's pretending to be me pretending to be Mark Twain!" This example not only distinguishes morally between creative impersonations (such as an artist's use of a pseudonym or a young reader's playful reenactment of something read in a book) from a thief's dishonest use of a false disguise, but it also associates gendered cross-dressing with criminal behavior.

The second instance of serial imitation is from Eek!stravaganza, a series featuring an anxious cat named Eek who has a little canine friend called Sharky and a fat feline girlfriend named Anabel. Eek's relationship with Sharky is not as hostile as the one between Garfield and Odie, nor as intense as the one between Ren and Stimpy, yet it is blatantly derivative nevertheless. As if to defend this indebtedness by acknowledging that parodic imitation is the central premise of the show, the first commercial break in the program on the morning of my sample featured an ad for Garfield Ravioli. As another indication that imitation is structured into the series, each *Eek* episode ends with a "Useless Fact" that parodies those moralistic epilogues that pay lip service to the Children's Television Act of 1990 but are invariably contradicted by the content of the story.

This particular episode, "Fatal Eektraction," parodies a film that few kiddie viewers are likely to have seen. Lusting after Eek, a feline fatale called Alice tries to steal him away from his beloved Anabel by imitating the Glenn Close role in *Fatal Attraction*. To impersonate Eek's canine friend Sharky, she steals his skin— a horrific image that evokes the skinned rabbit in *Fatal Attraction*, the serial killer in *The Silence of the Lambs*, and for the kiddies, the big bad wolf in *Little Red Riding Hood*. The story ends with a head-spinning number of unmaskings of these serial imitations. The first occurs within the inset movie *Fatal Eektraction*, which Eek, Sharky, and Alice go to see; the cinematic Alice removes her mask to reveal that she is really Sharkela, Sharky's twin sister. As the trio of specta- tors leave the movie theater, quipping that the villain is "always an evil twin," the "real" Alice also removes a mask, this time revealing that she is really Sharky's twin brother. Once more, she peels off a mask, saying, "Just kidding!" and reveals it is just Alice after all! Not only do these successive unmaskings blur the boundaries between fiction and "reality," but they also transgress borders of morality, species, and gender.

A parodic form of doubling is also central to the structure of *The Tick*, which comically pits a hyperbolic world of fantasy adventure (heavily indebted to movies like *Jurassic Park*, *Honey, I Blew up the Kids*, and *King Kong*) against the deflating banality of domestic situation comedy. In the particular episode that aired during my study, "The Tick versus Dinosaur Neil," just at the point where *Jurassic Park* comes to mind, scientist Neil (who later morphs into a gigantic dinosaur) acknowledges that he stole his research premise from a movie. At the height of the havoc being waged against the city, Tick must decide whether to go fight the giant dinosaur or stay home to dine with his sidekick's mousy sister, Dot, who disapproves of brother Arthur's superhero lifestyle. Even the battle evokes this doubling, for (as in *The Wizard of Oz*) the extraordinary menace is defeated by an extremely ordinary cure: a giant dose of aspirin. Further, the reconciliation of these absurd generic differences provides an opportunity to parody the FCC-friendly educational tag—in this case, a scientific lesson about aspirin. Here is how our superhero sums it up at the end: "Science is a two- headed beast—one is nice, it gives us aspirin, and the other is bad, it bites and can really ruin a day off!"

Serial imitation is also structured around parody in the "Doggy See, Doggy Do" episode of *Dog City*, which has a title full of puns, along with an array of characters who simulate Barney, Big Bird, and Mr. Rogers from educational shows on PBS. When a big, pink Saint Bernard called Bernie is impersonated by Bugsy the thief, one of the characters asks, "Who's the real Bernie, the real imposter?" Knowing viewers probably answer, "Barney."

In this reflexive show, an animated cartoon about "Dog City" is being produced and watched in a studio by a pair of live-action canine puppets, Mr. Shag and his young assistant, Artie. The stars of the inner cartoon are another master/apprentice pair: a canine detective named Ace and his young sidekick, Eddie, who are thinly disguised versions of Mr. Shag and Artie. Although Mr. Shag claims that the main lesson of this episode is that "all learning can be fun" (even math and history), all of the animated examples he presents involve various forms of imitative doubling—whether it's a couple of married fleas parodying *I Love Lucy* whose teeming offspring make them remark, "It's a good thing we can count, cause we sure can multiply!"; or the parodic *Masters Choice Theater* where a thief steals a truck of meat and crashes into his own mirror reflection. The nonlinear structure of the show (and its heavy use of puns) encourages viewers to recognize a chain of analogous relations (or cross-references) not only between parody and impersonation within the cartoon, but also with mathematical multiplication (which the little puppet Artie has to learn when his mother insists that he "spend less time at his drawing table and more time on his multiplication tables"), and creative repetition (which we repeatedly see is essential to the art of animation). Yet children must also learn to distinguish these positive forms of simulation from criminal impersonations (by thieves like Bugsy) and slavish imitation (by starry-eyed fans like Eddie). While acknowledging the widespread critique of Bernie's cloying cuteness and his creation of fanzine clones (the "zombie puppies"), this episode frequently insists that "imitation is the sincerest form of flattery"; in fact, the two Bernies repeatedly sing, "Imitation is good, imitation is nice, imitation goes with everything, even with rice." Why else would a Henson show parody Henson muppets? Thus, like the multiplication tables that Artie must learn, parodic imitation is presented as a cognitive skill that children must master in order to understand their culture—a message that ends up justifying Bernie's commodification.

Moreover, serial imitation is rampant in the commercials as a mode of consumerism—especially those advertising Power Rangers paraphernalia, where we see boys dressing up with weaponry hardware and becoming Rangers through performative masquerade. We see it as well in a Raisin Bran commercial, where young teenage girls gather clothes for coming events as if they need all the strength and resources they can muster for future impersonations. Both kinds of commercials imply that gendered impersonation requires perpetual consumption, and that empowerment is a serial process, never authentic or permanent.

Morphing

Morphing is a high-tech mode of creative transformation. In contrast to impersonation, it has more to do with empowerment than with appearance, and the effects are usually longer lasting. In contrast to mutation, which is central to *Teenage Mutant Ninja Turtles* and *X-Men*, this mode of shape-shifting is based on technological rupture rather than part of a "natural" evolutionary process.[17] Whereas mutation looks backward to Darwin's nineteenth-century transformative trope of evolution and to earlier twentieth-century print media like comic books (from which both *Ninja Turtles* and *X-Men* derive), morphing looks forward to new technologies. It is active rather than passive: you do it to something or yourself as opposed to having it done to you. This distinction is linked to the shift in spectator position, from passive viewer (associated with movies and traditional television) to active player (demanded of the video games and other interactive media that most of these series emulate).

The cultural meaning of morphing has been expanded by *Mighty Morphin Power Rangers*. Not only is it an electronic means of shape-shifting now readily available in the proliferating software programs for digital compositing that have recently made such imagery and myths seem meta-morphic, but it is also a successful marketing tactic for transforming a tacky Japanese sci-fi action series into the top-rated show in American children's television, and a megahit in the global market with a growing array of licensed products and multimedia spin-offs. This form of cultural morphing compensates for the Japanese mastery over entertainment hardware (by companies like Sony), thereby demonstrating that the United States still has superior know-how with software and marketing. The visual tackiness of the series (its artificial sets, corny dialogue, and crude dubbing) cultivates a precocious appreciation for kitsch and camp. It implies that the more sophisticated work of meaning production is being performed by active spectators (who creatively adapt these texts to their own personal needs), rather than by the producers (who merely recycle obsolete images from other cultures to make a quick buck). This dramatization of active spectatorship was central to the success of such shows as *Pee-wee's Playhouse* and the Nickelodeon cable network, as well as *Mystery Science Theater* and *Beavis and Butthead*.

Additionally, morphing works on the register of narrative, as a plot device that transforms a group of ordinary American multicultural high school students into color-coded unisex martial arts superheroes fighting against alien sci-fi villains from another plane of reality. Both sides are capable of constant transformation: while the villainous Rita Repulsa has been replaced by Lord Zed, the original five Rangers have expanded to six, now joined by Tommy, the

Green Ranger, a moral transformer of ambiguous ethnicity who was originally sent by the villainous Rita Repulsa to spy on the others but who has since undergone a moral conversion.

Despite an earnest attempt by Saban Entertainment to diversify their membership (especially in contrast to the original Japanese television series, where girls were not full-fledged members and where all Rangers had the same ethnicity), the color coding in the first few seasons of the American series tended to reinforce old racial and gender stereotypes: with Zack, the only African American male, coded black; Kimberly, a white female, predictably pink; Trini, an Asian American female, tinted yellow; Billy, a brainy white male with glasses tinged true blue; and Jason, a buff white male colored red for "hot."

As if that were not sufficiently problematic, in the 1994 season (shortly before the Christmas shopping rush), the Green Ranger Tommy strategically morphed into a White Ranger, who immediately became not only the most powerful and virtuous member of the team, but also the new leader of this formerly egalitarian group. Not surprisingly, his action figure and other paraphernalia quickly sold out in the stores, sending droves of parents into a desperate quest for this superdesirable white hero and giving new meaning to the term "White Christmas." According to Ann Knapp, programming director for Fox's Kids Network, this change was motivated by the character's virtue ("You could look at it as Tommy being rewarded for being such a good student and working so hard on his martial arts"), yet cynics claimed, "it's because Saban Entertainment . . . ran out of Green Ranger footage from the cheap action sequences bought for the show from Japan" and "it also has to do with product turnover."[18] Far more disturbing were the racist implications, for this transformation clearly put the white man's power back on top even while exposing the constructedness of "whiteness" as a category. In one commercial for Bandai toys (positioned within *Batman and Robin*), a Darth Vader–like voice says to a little white boy dressed in Power Ranger drag, "This is Zordon calling the White Ranger." Voguing with this desirable hardware (the Talking Saber, the Power Cannon, and the Power Gun Sword), the boy adopts an aggressive posture and makes his face look as menacing as possible, as Zordon describes the ultimate weapon, "It's harmless to humans but not to evil space aliens." The racist implications here are even more blatant than in the show.

In the episode broadcast on September 24, 1994, "Welcome to Venus Island," the six Rangers are trying to save a young girl, Trini's neighbor Halley, who has been kidnapped by Lord Zed and his villains and taken to Venus Island, which at sunset will sink into the sea forever. Lured to the island to save the girl, the Rangers find it is full of strange vaginal Venus Fly Traps, the biggest of whom fills in for the displaced Rita Repulsa as maternal monster. She swallows four of the Rangers (all but Tommy and Trini), storing them in her abdomen like four little fetuses. Applying heat both from inside and outside the monster's body, the resourceful Rangers manage to free themselves by popping out of her belly and then annihilating her in fierce combat. As if preparing for his lucrative metamorphosis into the White Ranger (as advertised by TV Guide), Tommy (whom the villains hope to reclaim) offers to take Halley's place as captive, but (after Trini manages to override the programming of a force field that encircles the victim's body) he succeeds in awakening her from the spell like Prince Charming in Sleeping Beauty. His quick change from ferocious fighter to gentle prince is reversed in the two final codas: first, an FCC-friendly tag that shows the Rangers nobly interceding in a brother-sister fight over toys, advising the quibbling siblings, "It's okay to be angry as long as you learn how to express it responsibly," and then demonstrating a number of nonviolent ways of doing so; and then, a violent commercial for "The Incredible Hulk" video game that shows another superhero who is "mean and green" (like Tommy) in nonstop combat that clearly contradicts the pacifist message of the previous coda.

In the visual representation of morphing within the episode, the disjunctive cutting accentuates the weapons and athletic moves of the Rangers, both of which disrupt the linear continuity of the story (which was already quickly summarized at the opening of the show). The Rangers are teleported to and from the island by being transformed into bands of color-coded light. When they prepare for battle, there is a flash cut to serial close-ups of each Ranger framed within his or her insignia, ritualistically chanting the name of that individual's totem animal. Then, there is a move in to a close-up of a helmet whose colors are solarized. The next cut is to the island, with the Rangers somersaulting into the frame from different directions, violating all rules of continuity editing. The members of the group then leap into an ensemble arrangement that shows that they fight together as a team. It is these moments of fast-paced power voguing that little viewers eagerly await, not the breathless plots that are barely coherent. These are also the scenes where viewers are required to exercise their cognitive skill of cross-referencing the distinguishing colors, totems, and weaponry of the individual Rangers, a task that many kids find empowering.

These morphing visuals are closely imitated in several commercials, especially the one for Juicy Fruit gum that interrupts the action. It features a group of teenagers with brightly colored helmets, who are presented in disjunctive cuts, making similar leaps with their bicycles as they enter the frame from various directions, as a voice-over sings, "The taste that's gonna move you."

In a later fight sequence, the Rangers prepare for the action by putting their power wrists together, and then again each of them is featured in an individualized dynamic shot, this time naming the weapon of his or her choice. It is this montage that equips them to blow the Venus Fly Traps to smithereens. This kind of sequence is evoked in a commercial for Hidden Valley Super Cheese Salad Dressing, where a boy and girl are shown taking a bite and then having their heads instantly morphed into a cracker or taco, as a voice-over booms, "Feel the power!" Even more playful is the commercial (during *Batman and Robin*) for Gusher Fruit Snacks "that will blow you away." With each new action word ("they're blasting . . . bursting . . . booming"), we see a child's face comically explode, with cheeks or eyes popping out and features rearranged, as if they were toons. Another commercial less parodic (between the two segments of *Animaniacs*) shows a band of kids using Power Rangers hardware from Happiness Express—a watch, a projector lamp, a motion detector, and gloves that sing when you put your Power Rangers wrists together—toys that enable kids to project or replicate this kind of "power voguing" in their own domestic spaces across America.

In the consumerist world of Power Rangers, the process of serial imitation is performed primarily in the commercials. Both the advertised products and structure of the show enhance the player's ability to identify interactively across media—to move as fluidly as his or her superprotean heroes from television images, to plastic toys, to video games, to blockbuster movies. Both in the series and commercials, morphing functions as a form of accelerated consumerist suture. You are liberated from your infantile dependency on a "bad" mother like Venus Fly Trap (or Rita Repulsa) by learning how to identify with and become a transformer. To achieve this accelerated mode of active spectatorship, you must somehow acquire the phallic hardware as well as the cognitive ability to track this fantasy narrative that moves faster than a *Road Runner* cartoon.

In the other Fox series, morphing is not necessarily restricted to characters and spectators. For example, in the episode of *Carmen Sandiego* discussed here, it is also presented as a form of visual punning and mode of creative identification that is essential to writers and other artists, yet it is still linked with an empowering upward mobility—in this case, from poverty to fame. When Ivy and Zack are on their way to London to prevent Carmen from stealing Charles Dickens's inkwell, their chief shows them an image of a group of orphans. Recognizing the connection, Ivy says, "Hey, that's Oliver Twist," and Zack adds (for the less knowledgeable players), "He's the orphan boy from Charles Dickens's first big book." At this point, the identification turns visual: as the chief remarks in a voice-over, "And get this twist, pardon the pun, Oliver was inspired by Dickens's own life," a twisting morph turns the image of orphans into a formal portrait of the writer, whose impoverished childhood is then described. Yet lest we think that all icons are morphable, this sequence teaches us that certain boundaries should not be transgressed; for here is where Ivy catches the chief's mistake of placing the Empire State Building among British monuments—a misidentification that ignores the American Revolution (which launched our own empire) and seems to be vigilantly censored not only by Ivy but also the Statue of Liberty (whose repeated image demands its repositioning in New York City). When we later learn that this error was caused not by the chief's lack of knowledge, but by Carmen's attempts to hack into their mainframe, this misidentification morphs from a careless error into an act of subversion. These dynamics raise crucial questions: who will have access to this morphing, at what price, and what kinds of freedom or subversion will it provide?

Overriding the Programming

Overriding the programming is an active form of reading against the grain or an aggressive form of what Henry Jenkins (and Michel de Certeau before him) calls textual poaching—an operation that has been popularized with youngsters by *Beavis and Butthead.*[19] In most of the Fox shows, we see characters watching screens and commenting on and manipulating images. The dramatic conflict in the *X-Men* episode "Obsession" is totally structured around this operation. When Beast enters the spaceship, he observes admiringly, "Ship, you are a work of art," and "she" responds, "You have no idea how pleasurable it is to interface with someone who understands the subtlety of my programming." This interface romance enables Beast to realize that they can defeat their formidable adversary only "if we can just override Apocalypse's security code." But later, when Ship begins working against the X-Men, she explains that there was "an automatic override" and a "preset override system." As Beast learns, "It appears an override may be overridden." Although the X-Men eventually prevail, Ship is destroyed; yet she dies content, knowing that she was able to achieve free choice, the ultimate override. This reprogramming premise is central to the conception of mutation that drives all these protean characters and lies at the heart of this resilient adventure series.

On that same Saturday, a similar reprogramming struggle was central to the episode of *MegaMan*, "Electric Nightmare," where Dr. Wylie attaches "an override relay to the master control computer" so that he can take control of everything in Gizmo City and Megaland with a single joystick. With the help of his transformer dog, Rush (who morphs into a jet rocket, security dog, or robotic man's best friend), MegaMan bests the evil Wylie and his electronic henchmen (including his own evil twin, Robo Bro) by becoming "an over-grown circuit breaker" who can override Wylie's override. At one point in the drama, the villainous Robo Spy Doris reprograms Rush by plugging a circuit card into his wiring. As a fitting revenge, Doris (who formerly impersonated Arnold Schwarzenegger's *Terminator*, quipping, "Hasta la vista, baby") is now reprogrammed into Rush's personal servant. The nonhuman status of heroes and villains in this series enables limbs to be freely chopped off and restored, without any loss of blood or reputation.

As an updated version of the classic Loony Tunes, Steven Spielberg's *Animaniacs* series is also totally structured around reprogramming. In the particular episode within my sample called "Puppet Rulers," two mice time travel back to 1954 so that they can become popular characters on the *Meany and Treacle Show* (a simulacrum of *Beanie and Cecil*), where they can capture the hearts and minds of the kiddie spectators (the baby boomers) who will later (in the 1990s) elect them president. This political plot evokes both the programming strategy of the children's cable network, Nickelodeon, and the generational strategy adopted by Clinton's 1992 presidential campaign (with its innovative use of MTV).[20] The failure of their plot demonstrates that television stars actually have little control over reception and fandom—a theme reinforced by an allusion to Milton Berle (who failed to retain his popularity) and the moralizing epilogue, "Vote early and vote often." At first their plot fails, for the 1954 audience doesn't find the mice funny because it cannot understand their language and cross-referencing. But eventually the mice become superstars with a successful line of licensed products and a mass of fans who (like the "zombie puppies" in *Dog City*) hypnotically chant their names, yet whom they callously abandon. When the mice are finally reunited with these fans in the 1990s, instead of worshiping their long-lost idols, these neurotic infantilized adults (who were traumatized in the 1950s by the loss of their pop heroes) now seek revenge and reimbursement for their pricey psychotherapy. This "moral" recommends a precocious mode of active reading in which young viewers freely override the intended meanings of the text—a lesson in textual poaching that is not only central to the series, but also vital to children who are exposed to media programming from infancy.

The key question is whether this mode of active spectatorship is illusionary, particularly when positioned within an ideological context that naturalizes individualism, and a commercial network that is designed to convince young viewers that freedom is best expressed in front of the television screen and in the marketplace.

These issues can be explored with greatest resonance in the season premiere

The conservative vision of American history found in the *Carmen Sandiego* television series is consistent with the CD-ROM games from which it is derived.

of *Where on Earth Is Carmen Sandiego?* (broadcast on September 17, 1994), where Ivy and Zack track Carmen back to the American colonies in the eighteenth century, where she tries to prevent Paul Revere from warning American rebels that the British are coming, Ben Franklin from harnessing electricity with his kite, and the Liberty Bell from surviving.[21] Despite *Carmen Sandiego*'s emphasis on cutting edge technology, the television narrative strives to preserve the traditional version of American history, defending it against any revisionist override.

The issue of revisionist history has been highly charged in educational circles since 1989, when President George Bush launched a national program to have select panels of educators define new standards that would help raise the level of academic achievement in American public schools. Although qualified experts drafted standards for many subjects (including science, math, English, and civics), the ones that proved most controversial and had to be repeatedly revised were those dealing with history. Attacked by conservatives for reflecting liberal biases that were bent on expanding the inclusiveness of American history, the new standards were criticized for not giving sufficient attention to traditional American icons like George Washington, Thomas Jefferson, the Constitution, and the Bill of Rights. Or as one journalist put it, for including "six mentions of Harriet Tubman but none of Paul Revere."[22] According to Joyce Appleby, then president of the American Historical Association, the debate was "about the politics of nostalgia," for it was "not a case of people who felt history was changed so much as people feeling the way they had been taught history was changed."[23] Although the 1996 version "beefed-up discussions of the Constitution and Bill of Rights, the Cold War and the westward expansion," and added new sections "on the role of science and technology in American progress," even President Clinton concluded that these new history standards were a failure.[24] It is against this cultural debate that we must read (and cross-reference) the historic success of *Where on Earth Is Carmen Sandiego?* and particularly, its premiere episode.

The premiere episode restores a colonizing discourse within a postcolonial sphere—celebrating the postcolonial independence of the United States (which Revere helped to win); its superior technology, especially in the field of electronic communications (which Franklin's harnessing of electricity helped to launch); and its democratic ideology (which is represented by the visual icons of the Liberty Bell and Statue of Liberty). Thus, along with history and geography, the episode teaches kids a national discourse of American supremacy, which Europeans (like Carmen Sandiego) were trying to reverse. In 1994, that supremacy was centered on the trade status of America's second-leading export, its movies and television shows, particularly in the General Agreement on Tariffs and Trade talks where European nations were attempting to curtail our domination of the global market. Although Carmen (like the European Union) claims that "Time is on her side," Ivy and Zack as American patriots are determined to "get history back on track" in order to protect our nation's cultural hegemony.

Although this globe-trotting narrative makes youngsters feel comfortable in an international setting, they are constantly being reminded of their national identity—especially in the weekly lead-in to the show where Ivy and Zack are posed against the Statue of Liberty as they hold a miniaturized globe in the palm of their hands, exercising their manifest destiny of freedom and mobility that is as American as the myth of westward expansion. Ivy and Zack are empowered to travel freely through space and time, like nomadic First World tourists, colonizing figures from the past, who (like people of underdeveloped nations) are stuck in a single zone. Whenever their technology breaks down (in this episode, their time machine temporarily malfunctions), these American heroes are threatened with the prospect of getting stuck in one place—back in history or sitting passively in front of their screen, which is precisely where we as television viewers are positioned, even though we are directly addressed as active mobile players within the fiction.

The series, while frequently praised for its gender and ethnic diversity, still casts the empowered adult female as the villain and doubly codes her ethnicity as Hispanic, not only through both her names—Carmen and Sandiego—but also through her jet-black hair (which contrasts sharply with the red and blond tresses of the heroic Anglo siblings, Ivy and Zack), and bright red trench coat and fedora. The color coding in this series is no more elaborate than that in the *Teenage Mutant Ninja Turtles* myth or *Power Rangers* cult that replaced it, for they all empower young players through the cognitive pleasures of mastery and decoding. Carmen's red color coding also links her to danger and the stop sign, associations that stress her narrative function (in the Proppian sense) as the character who has to be stopped and the one who is set in symbolic opposition to that jolly green giantess, the Statue of Liberty, who (with her "GO" pennant) rallies our spirits like a cheerleader, urging American players to go beat Carmen and her treacherous team of international thieves. The red coding also evokes Carmen's past as a former Communist spy who speaks flawless Russian and got her hardware from the Soviet Union—a backstory that helps recuperate the cold war paradigm. Perhaps this explains why this particular episode on American colonial history opens in Arctic Russia, with Carmen stealing a "top secret" time travel machine from our old cold war rivals that enables her to reverse the outcome of the American Revolution.

In the scene where Ivy and Zack finally recover the time machine, we see how the viewer is mobilized as an active player who supposedly pushes the buttons and supplies definitions, and who can allegedly communicate directly both with the young heroes and the villain. Not only does the plot increasingly poach on *Back to the Future*, but Ivy and Zack appropriate an ordinary commercial billboard as a screen for displaying the talking head of their authoritative chief, who sports a temporary British accent that results from Carmen's subversive reversal of history (just as his erroneous positioning of the Empire State Building in London resulted from her hacking into the mainframe in the later episode). In this advertisement for American know-how, the chief's talking head is linked visually to the image of Albert Einstein. When Zack picks up the time travel gadget, he holds it in his hand and tries to think of a more familiar object to compare it with, pausing just long enough for us as viewers to come up with our own analogue: a television remote control. Although Zack finally compares it to a garage door opener, the trope of the television joystick proves far more resonant, particularly when we realize how proficient television is as a time machine that can represent any period through the appropriation of other media both from the past and future: the low-tech classroom medium of the slide show, which transports our heroes back to the eighteenth century, and the simulated cutting edge computer screen, which provides an illusory sense of interactivity and control. The episode shows us that the battle over screens is really a struggle between rival media and their competing versions of history.

Perhaps the most liberating way to read this series is as a generational discourse in which kids outwit their adult adversaries—a reversal that also proved commercially successful in the *Back to the Future* and *Home Alone* movie series. Furthermore, Ivy and Zack are more knowledgeable than adult geniuses and heroes from the past simply because they come later in history, and thereby have access to advanced technology, scientific progress, historical perspective, and a broader range of linguistic reference. When an eighteenth-century foun-dryman fails to get their pun ("he's into heavy metal"), they experience the kind of linguistic empowerment that rap sometimes offers youth subcultures and adult spectators ordinarily enjoy while watching sophisticated transgen-erational cartoons like *Loony Tunes*, *Garfield*, and *Animaniacs*. This dynamic en-courages kids to watch for verbal puns and use decoding as a mechanism of power. This skill depends on intertextuality; that is, on mastering the broader, fluid historical/cultural field against which all specific texts and speech acts must be read.

A Pedagogical Coda

The four cognitive operations that I have been describing from Fox's Saturday morning lineup are specific techniques for achieving that mastery of intertex-tuality. Like Freudian dreamwork codes, they are overlapping: morphing can be seen as a form of serial impersonation, which expands the range of cross-referencing, and all three are means of overriding the programming. Moreover, through cross-referencing, these four operations bear a more specific analo-gous relationship with Freud's four dreamwork codes: morphing as condensa-tion; cross-referencing as displacement; serial imitation as concrete repre-sentability; and programming override as secondary revision. Perhaps these four operations are merely a morphed version of those dreamwork codes, masquerading as new cognitive concepts for an imaginary form of empower-ment within a consumerist culture, but with little potential for actually overrid-ing our basic programming.

Because these cognitive patterns work primarily at a structural level, I have no way of demonstrating whether kids are really learning these lessons—certainly not by asking them. Though most kids would probably interpret the meanings of specific images and associations in these shows far differently than I have in this essay, I am convinced that they *are* learning two things: a system of how to read images against a broader cultural field and the crucial role that television plays in teaching them how this system works. So I am left (and will leave my reader) with my anecdote of the little boy on Larchmont, impersonating and cross-referencing his beloved Power Rangers who enable him to morph into an empowered consumer, a transformation he apparently experiences as a pleasurable form of programming override.

Notes

1   John Miller and Margaret Loesch, quoted in Jane Hall, "Differing on Lesson Plan for Kids' TV," Los Angeles Times, 15 August 1996, F5.

2   Peggy Charren, quoted in ibid. For a more recent article about the implementation of these guidelines that contains similar quotes from all three spokespersons (NBC's Miller, Fox's Loesch, and ACT's Charren), see Jane Hall, "TV Class Is Now in Session," Los Angeles Times, 26 August 1997, F1, F10.

3   William Clinton, quoted in John M. Broder and Jane Hall, "President Hears TV Executives Commit to Ratings System," Los Angeles Times, 1 March 1996, p. A1.

4   The ratings for Where on Earth Is Carmen Sandiego? peaked on March 19, 1994, with a 9.2 rating and 36 share for children between ages two and eleven. Interestingly, the independent producer of the series, DIC Entertainment, is partially owned by ABC rather than the Fox Network.

5   For an excellent article on this series, see Ellen Seiter, "Toy-Based Video for Girls: My Little Pony," in In Front of the Children: Screen Entertainment and Young Audiences, ed. Cary Bazalgette and David Buckingham (London: British Film Institute, 1995), 166–87.

6   Erick Schmuckler, "Oh, What a Beautiful Morning," Mediaweek, 18 April 1994, 31.

7   Steve Coe, "Saturdays and the Fox Factor," Broadcast and Cable, 25 July 1994, 58.

8   Jeffrey Cole, The UCLA Television Violence Monitoring Report (Los Angeles: University of California, Los Angeles, Center for Communication Policy, 1995), 101–7. Apparently, the researchers have confused the title of the Fox animated series with that of the PBS quiz show.

9   Ibid., 28.

10   Haim Saban, quoted in Mike Freeman, "Haim Saban: The 'Power' Is His," Broadcasting and Cable, 20 December 1993, 30.

11   Ibid.

12   Saban Entertainment's awareness of this carefully modulated transgenerational address is explicitly acknowledged in the bible for the series, which advises its writers:
   Finally, whatever you do, do not write down to your audience. X-Men comics are among the most "adult" on the market. Though our audience is primarily adolescents, we respect their experience and intelligence. We can write too "old" for them and keep their respect. If they sense we are "writing for kids," we will lose them. (Saban Entertainment, X-Men: Notes Toward a Bible, 28 February 1992, 4).

13   Marsha Kinder, Playing with Power in Movies, Television, and Video Games: From Muppet Babies to Teenage Mutant Ninja Turtles (Berkeley: University of California Press, 1991).

14   "The earliest hours of Saturday morning television belong to the youngest children. The

shows that begin around 7:00 A.M. appeal to 4–6 year olds. Around 9:00, the schedule changes to accommodate the youngest viewer's older brothers and sisters. This is when the more action-oriented shows are broadcast. In the last year [1994], NBC devoted its Saturday morning schedule (after news) to live-action programming for teenagers, as did Fox at 11:30" (Cole, *UCLA Television Violence Monitoring Report*, 100). This statement is contradicted by the fact that in fall 1994, *Power Rangers* (which is certainly "more action-oriented") regularly aired on Fox at 7:30 A.M., yet the rest of this discussion is accurate. For this reason, I have not included Fox's live-action teenage show *Sweet Valley High* (which aired at 11:30 A.M.) in my analysis.

15 Saban, *Notes Toward a Bible*, 23.

16 Cole, *UCLA Television Violence Monitoring Report*, 101.

17 For a fuller discussion of this issue, see Marsha Kinder, "From Mutation to Morphing: Cultural Transformation from Greek Myth to Children's Media Culture," in *Meta-Morphing: Visual Transformations in the Culture of Quick Change*, ed. Vivian Sobchack (Minneapolis: University of Minnesota Press, forthcoming).

18 Ann Knapp and "Cynics," quoted in James Kaplan, "More Power," *TV Guide* (29 October–4 November 1994), 38.

19 See Henry Jenkins, *Textual Poachers: Television Fans and Participatory Culture* (New York: Routledge, 1992); and Michel de Certeau, *The Practice of Everyday Life*, trans. Steven Rendall (Berkeley: University of California Press, 1984).

20 For a fuller discussion of these issues, see Marsha Kinder, "Home Alone in the '90s: Generational War and Transgenerational Address in American Movies, Television, and Presidential Politics," in *In Front of the Children: Screen Entertainment and Young Audiences*, ed. Cary Bazalgette and David Buckingham (London: British Film Institute, 1995), 75–91.

21 For a fuller reading of this episode, see Marsha Kinder, "Screen Wars: Transmedia Appropriations from Eisenstein to *A TV Dante* and *Carmen Sandiego*," in *Language Machines: Technologies of Cultural Production*, ed. Jeff Masten, Peter Stallybrass, and Nancy Vickers (New York: Routledge, 1997).

22 Elaine Woo, "Standards for Teaching History Unveiled—Again," *Los Angeles Times*, 3 April 1996, A1.

23 Joyce Appleby, quoted in ibid., 16.

24 Woo, "Standards for Teaching," 1.

Xuxa S.A.: The Queen of Rede Globo in the Age of Transnational Capitalism   *Elissa Rashkin*

In an episode of the *Xuxa* show that aired in the fall of 1993, Xuxa and her guests gathered to play a game called "Candied Kid." Participants were to dive into a slimy substance known as "gloop" after saying their names into Xuxa's microphone, then jump into a container of crunchy coating, finally emerging to be encased in oversized candy wrappers bearing the label "Xuxa Bar." After two teams of children had gone through the game, and the winner was determined, Xuxa herself, in a display of calculated naïveté, went to take her turn. Temporarily abdicating the microphone, Xuxa announced herself and dove into the gloop, emerging as a Xuxa Bar, a representation of a product bearing her own name.

In February of the same year, performance artists Guillermo Gómez-Peña and Coco Fusco staged a theatrical piece entitled *New World (B)order*, depicting a scenario in which all national borders had been dismantled, and cultural artifacts and ideologies circulated freely, yet the familiar disparities of economic and political power remained.[1] Their performance did not mention Xuxa, nor was it particularly concerned with children's television; still, if it had been, their dystopic fantasy might have resembled the scene I just described. For the game "Candied Kid"—with its deliberate transformation of children into products, its confusion between the consumer and the consumed, and its apparent inversion of authority brought about by Xuxa's participation—does not take place in an ideological vacuum. As part of one of the first episodes of Xuxa's program aired in the United States, the playful flaunting of Xuxa's own commodification in the gloop can, in fact, be read as an allegory, exemplifying what it means to be a Latin American superstar in the era of transnational capitalism.

Xuxa's transition from Brazilian to U.S. television—from superstardom to relative obscurity, from universalized sex symbol to foreign curiosity—is, as I will attempt to illustrate in this essay, emblematic of what happens as capitalism expands, outgrowing forms of racism and imperialism that are no longer functional or defensible, and focusing instead on the creation and absorption of new markets. During the early 1990s, what has been called the "Latinization" of the United States, a phenomenon demonized by politicians seeking post–cold war scapegoats and ignored for decades by mainstream media, suddenly attracted the attention of corporate America: Spanish-language radio and television stations were cluttered with advertisments for chain stores, Miller and Coors beer, and long-distance telephone companies; the 1994 World Cup put Brazilians, Colombians, Bolivians, Argentineans, and Mexicans on billboards, the news, and the covers of major magazines; a Danielle Steele novel was published in simultaneous English and Spanish versions; and Latino celebrities such as Univisión talk show host Cristina Saralegui were hired to create English-language programs such as Saralegui's CBS special on "Latin Lovers of the '90s" featuring crossover stars like Erik Estrada and Ricky Martin.[2]

In short, for painfully obvious commercial reasons, phenomena that once had a secure niche in so-called "specialty" (that is, Latino) markets were spilling over into the mainstream. Xuxa, the star imported from one of the world's largest television networks, was a part of this historic transformation, at least until the cancellation of her U.S. show in 1996. But what happens to such phenomena in the complex process of translation?

Building an Empire

Maria da Graça Meneghel, nicknamed Xuxa, made her Brazilian television debut in 1983 on the Manchete network, hosting a children's program similar to the various shows that she stars in today. Having been "discovered" a few years earlier at age fifteen, she was already famous as a model, sometime softcore porn actress, and perhaps most notoriously, the girlfriend of Pelé, the soccer champion. Her show's seemingly improbable combination of games, songs, and cartoons for children with overt sexuality aimed at adults was stunningly successful, and her name became synonymous with the Brazilian ideal of feminine beauty, fame, and sex appeal. As Amelia Simpson has described in *Xuxa: The Mega-Marketing of Gender, Race, and Modernity,* Xuxa's sexuality embodied the philosophy popularized in the 1950s by *Playboy,* and represented by stars like Brigitte Bardot and Marilyn Monroe: innocent, refreshing, uninhibited, and thoroughly disingenuous in terms of its implicit claims to being outside or beyond power relations.[3] Along with her young age and appearance, her literal association with children reinforced the impression that

"Our Lady of the Industrial Era,"
Xuxa. Photo courtesy of David
Sonnenschein, Crystal Vision,
Rio de Janeiro.

her sensuality was not a manufactured media image, but something that came to her "naturally."

In 1986, Xuxa moved to a larger network, Rede Globo, and became its most popular star. Globo, which was started in 1965 with partial funding from the Time/Life Corporation and enjoyed a special relationship with the military dictatorship that was in power until the mid-1980s, is comparable in scale to the major networks in the United States, perhaps surpassing the latter in terms of influence. Its programming, especially the popular telenovelas, is often exported to the rest of Latin America and Europe, and it is generally seen as having a decisive influence on national politics, including both the election and impeachment of former President Fernando Collor de Mello, as well as on fashion, style, cultural values, and consciousness.[4]

Xuxa's success on Globo made her a national and international superstar. Her daily audience in Brazil was estimated at close to four million; in addition, her live shows drew crowds reportedly near 50,000.[5] By 1991, her average salary was the highest among Brazilian entertainers, well above that of established artists like Roberto Carlos, and her six albums had sold 1.9 million copies.[6] Albums and programs in Spanish, taped in Argentina, allowed her to expand beyond the Portuguese-speaking market and become popular throughout the Ibero-American world. In 1993, just prior to her debut on anglophone U.S. television, her twelve albums had sold twenty million copies; she had starred in several popular movies (including one by the acclaimed "feminist" director of *Patriamada* and *Gaijin*, Tizuka Yamasaki); her Xuxa comic book was the most popular in Brazil; and her shows, in Portuguese and Spanish, were seen by an estimated fifty million viewers in seventeen countries and had been broadcast in the United States on Univisión.[7]

At the same time, she had built an empire of affiliated products and services that in terms of their income-generating potential, surpassed her monetary worth as a performer. In addition to records, videos, dolls, and the other usual star-related merchandise, Xuxa, or rather the companies that bore her name, sold shoes, soft drinks, food, and other products, owned real estate, ran a line of clothing stores, and operated a tourism agency. It was this conglomeration of enterprises, as well as the success of her program, that placed her on *Forbes* magazine's 1991 list of the forty richest entertainers worldwide—a stunning achievement for a Latin American. As one publicist observed, "Xuxa is Our Lady of the Industrial Era. She is the protector of kids and the saint of entrepreneurs."[8]

In the wake of her phenomenal success in Latin America, Xuxa made a move that under the circumstances, can be seen as both natural and risky: she signed a contract with MTM Productions and Lynch Entertainment to produce a television series in the United States, beginning in September 1993. Apparently this was not an easy decision. Although for some time she had been publicly expressing a desire to leave Brazil, she told Univisión interviewer Chabeli that she had turned down earlier offers to come North because of her lack of confidence in her ability to speak English.[9] Although MTM executives did not seem bothered by this obstacle, and in fact (as we shall see), structured the new program in order to accommodate its star, the language barrier remained a prominent theme in Xuxa's interviews, even after the first sixty-five episodes had been completed. As Xuxa told *TV y Novelas* magazine in May 1994:

> The program here was an experiment to see if Americans would accept my style, my way of talking, dressing and working . . . if they react well, we'll do more programs next year. If not, I'll take with me a great experience in the United States, and go back to doing the programs that I have to do in all of South America and Spain.[10]

In spite of Xuxa's own professed hesitation and doubt, early expectations for the show were high. In the "Kids" section of its 1993 fall preview, *TV Guide* commented, "That's SHOO-sha to you, but your kids may already know the name of this Brazilian phenomenon whose daily half hour is touted as the season's hot ticket."[11] *Broadcasting and Cable* ran an article that described MTM's lavish spending: weekly production was expected to cost $150,000 to $200,000, and the international-theme set, large in order to contain the 150 to 200 children who would be brought in for the six-week taping session, would cost over $2 million.[12] For some observers, Xuxa's entrance into the mainstream U.S. market recalled that of another multitalented Brazilian celebrity; commenting on the move, the editor of the Los Angeles–based *News from Brazil* magazine observed that "not since Carmen Miranda has Brazil had a more exportable entertainer."[13]

Although Miranda's act was not directed toward children, the comparison was in other ways an apt one. Miranda, in the 1940s, had also been a popular star in Brazil before being brought by Broadway impresarios to the United States. She achieved astounding financial success following her move to Hollywood, much of which was due to the coincidence of several favorable factors: first, a fad among white U.S. consumers for things Latin, including music, dances, and clothing; second, the Hollywood studios' interest in compensating for the wartime loss of European revenues by cornering the Latin American market; and last but not least, the U.S. government's desire to promote harmonious inter-American relations through entertainment media. This ambivalent context was reflected in Miranda's performances, in which her ethnic difference was highlighted and her specific national origin downplayed in favor of a largely superficial, although sometimes playfully parodic Pan-Americanism.

Among Brazilians and other Latin Americans, Miranda has been widely perceived as a tragic figure for these very reasons, and is often seen as having been exploited by a racist film industry for imperialist ends. For writer Eduardo Galeano, she was "the chief export of Brazil. Next comes coffee."[14] Musicians have blamed her for the general lack of seriousness with which Latin American music is received in the United States (see, for instance, the record jacket of Paquito D'Rivera's *Tico! Tico!*), and Rubén Blades presented her story as a quintessential Latin American allegory in his song, cowritten with Elvis Costello, "The Miranda Syndrome."[15] At the same time, she is celebrated for having done what few other Latin Americans have: becoming the highest-paid actress in the United States, and as Caetano Veloso wrote, "conquer[ing] 'white' America as no other South American had done or ever would."[16]

Xuxa's career echoes Miranda's in a number of ways, one of which is simply the sheer scale of her success. Although her show (which initially ran at a limiting 6 A.M. in the Los Angeles area) was not an instant hit in the ratings, her name slowly infiltrated the media, and several varieties of Xuxa dolls were sold in chain toy stores. She became a favorite with pop critics such as Chuck Eddy, who perceived her as a camp icon, and was introduced to feminists and academics through Amelia Simpson's book-length study. Also like Miranda, her difficulties with English were a focal point of her media coverage; her crash course at Berlitz, her frustration with the language that frequently reduced her to tears on the set, and the in-house English teacher at her Argentina mansion all recalled stories told fifty years earlier about Miranda, from the rumor that Twentieth Century Fox was paying her fifty cents a word to learn English to her own, considerably more parodic, self-deprecating references. While both actresses were fluent in Spanish as well as their native Portuguese, both the press and the stars themselves tended to emphasize their linguistic shortcomings rather than their accomplishments.

Another important similarity to Miranda is Xuxa's promotion of internationalism, particularly Pan-Americanism. The 1993 video for her song "América Total," as described in *La Opinión*, was strikingly reminiscent of the Good Neighbor musicals of the 1940s; against scenes of the Brazilian jungle and other natural landscapes, children dressed in the costumes of each Latin American country proudly waved their flags. Xuxa herself, in an interview with *Impacto Latin News*, labeled "América Total" "a song that refers to the union of all countries, without borders or barriers, through the language of love."[17] Yet in spite of this and similar public statements of idealism and faith in the power of love to cross borders, Xuxa was no more successful than Miranda at eluding (much less transcending) the disparities of power that pertain in the Americas; rather, like Miranda, Xuxa remained suspended in the intersection of a variety of contradictory positions that she was able to negotiate only with difficulty.[18]

Little Kisses and Educational Television

In presenting Xuxa to U.S. viewers, MTM executives told *Broadcasting and Cable* that they hoped to keep the music and games that had been the ingredients of her international success, but also incorporate positive social messages and expand the show's educational content.[19] Although even in Brazil Xuxa had positioned herself as an advocate of children, having initiated and carried out various well-publicized charity efforts on their behalf, social issues were not the focus of the *Xou de Xuxa*, which itself was not the standard-length program it was in the United States, but rather five hours broken up by animated cartoons. In adding an educational slant to the show, Xuxa's producers also superimposed a system of values that, it could be argued, actually negated and inverted Xuxa's original freewheeling and innocently rebellious image—and with it, her status as apparent center of power and control.

Two episodes of the show, one from Brazil and one from the United States, illustrate the difference.[20] Both episodes deal with the theme of cross-cultural communication as a source of empowerment, yet it is approached in very different ways. In the Brazilian show, taped in 1989, Xuxa interviews a boy from

California named Brad Correa, who after participating in a goodwill trip to the Soviet Union, had been traveling to bring his message of peace to other children and their governments. While Brazilian American, Correa does not speak Portuguese, and is hesitant in delivering his coached line, "*eu quero paz*" ("I want peace"). Xuxa, gently but clearly amused, prompts him to say it again; unsure, giggling and flustered, Correa asks in English, "what do you want me to say?" After helping Correa through his brief moment in the spotlight, Xuxa goes on to read, in her rapid-fire Portuguese, a declaration on the human rights of children, thereby introducing issues such as malnutrition and abuse into her program. In a typical Xuxa transition, however, she softens her message and returns the show to its real focus by assuring the *baixinhos* (kids or short ones) that they also have the "right" to have fun.

In a 1993 episode of the U.S. show, Xuxa performs "Talk to Me," a song that would be repeated (as most of her songs were) on many subsequent programs. Coming after a commercial break, the song starts over the show's logo, a spinning globe encircled by Xuxa's name. The globe splits open to reveal the Xuxa set in long shot, which gives way to a closer view of Xuxa on a raised platform to the rear of the stage, wearing her trademark high white boots and a short (but not revealing) red dress, against a background of spinning windmills and cupola-topped towers. As she begins her descent from the platform, she sings, "I come from Brazil / Rio de Janeiro / my first language, you see, is Portuguese."

On reaching the floor, she greets, touches, and dances with her eager guests while continuing her song, which turns out to be a plea for understanding about her language barrier. The content of the song is diffused somewhat by the stylized editing, which substitutes a series of blurred freeze-frames for real-time movement, and long shots of Xuxa's dancing during the instrumental breaks. Yet in her close-ups, Xuxa pantomimes the emotions indicated by the lyrics. "I'm trying my best / for proper English," she mock frowns, "tripping over vowels and consonants." Much like Correa in her show of four years earlier, she has become a goodwill ambassador, demanding the attention that she deserves because "I've come such a long way to find / people with so much to say / to look you in the eye." The warm and near-hysterical enthusiasm with which she is received, much of which has clearly been added at the mixing board, seemingly validates her mission and provides a reassuring response to her foregrounded vulnerability.

Both of these sequences celebrate what the Walt Disney Corporation calls a "small world," which might be described as the ability of children to transcend cultural barriers through a replacement of language with festivity and, more fundamentally, their location in a fairy-tale world outside political differences. The nuances of the celebration, however, are rather different between the Brazilian and U.S. programs. In the former, Xuxa is obviously in control, due especially to her mastery of the language, which is not shared by her guest. While assimilating Correa into the fantasy of worldwide child solidarity through fun, she does not have to make the specific gestures toward internationalism that come to predominate in her programs in the United States. She may embrace a rhetoric of solidarity, yet it is unnecessary for Xuxa to explicitly demonstrate her place in a world capitalist system, since her power as queen of Rede Globo is uncontested.

In the latter program, on the other hand, the insecurity that Xuxa had at that point frequently expressed off the set is almost ritualistically performed. The resulting spectacle not only places Xuxa in a position of endearing vulnerability, but also identifies her with any other immigrant: having come such a long way, she must downplay difference (while providing enough basic facts for audiences to appreciate her "diversity"), emphasize her struggle and hard work, and be humble and ingratiating in order to win understanding, approval, and acceptance. Despite the incongruity with her role as star and center of the show, Xuxa would assume this posture on many occasions, particularly with respect to her guests: athletes, acrobats, and other performers who were normally not only shown as more talented, disciplined, and accomplished than their host, but often ignored Xuxa's remarks and seemed to monopolize communication with the audience.

Beyond these blatantly foregrounded shifts in Xuxa's relationship to language, and therefore knowledge, the early shows in the United States reveal other noteworthy changes. The self-proclaimed "sensuality" of the Brazilian program was downplayed, with regard to both the host and her guests; nothing resembling the black vinyl bikini worn by a young girl in the Correa episode appeared on the new show. Although fashion was still a highlight of the program, Xuxa rarely wore the miniskirts and hot pants for which she was known; in one episode, she even adopted a grunge look, with ripped jeans and a fringed, long-sleeved blouse. Moreover, the games she organized were no longer battles of the sexes; instead, teams consisted of both boys and girls. Much of the program was now run by two assistants, who in spite of their animal costumes, were clearly male. The authority of these helpers not only took part of the burden away from Xuxa, but also desexualized the show. Finally, the Paquitas, Xuxa's young look-alike helpers who in Brazil were sex symbols in their own right, were barely visible. Thus, though still glamorous and attractive, and still liberal in her bestowing of *beijinhos* (little kisses), Xuxa's demeanor on her new show contained little that would offend notoriously prudish U.S. parents.

In Brazil, much of Xuxa's show seemed to be devoted to the selling of merchandise, through tie-ins and product placement. Her apparent lack of a social conscience made her the target of criticism, yet the show's disregard for conventional wisdom regarding child education was part of its appeal. In the United States, however, the "educational" imperative of post–*Sesame Street* children's television is well established, and in order to conform, Xuxa now admonished viewers to eat their vegetables, care for their planet, and say no to drugs. Uncontroversial to the point of meaninglessness, these messages were read by Xuxa in a voice so stilted as to imply that even she didn't always know what they meant. To enhance the show's educational value, segments produced by Disney World's Epcot Center were included in each episode, as "answers" to ostensibly viewer-generated questions. This part of the show, called "Ask Xuxa" and revealing Xuxa's deference to prepackaged, narrated footage coded as "scientific," was yet another instance of the displacement of her authority.

All of this suggests careful attention to the norms of U.S. television and liberal wisdom regarding children's programming. In fact, nearly all of the criticisms leveled at Xuxa by Simpson and other critics seemed to have been addressed in some way by the new show. Of these changes, the most important was undoubtedly the show's aggressive multiculturalism, which as I have already contended, served as a Disneyesque response to the accusations of racism regularly flung at the blond superstar. Now, instead of entering the show from a cartoon spaceship, Xuxa emerged from a globe, which remained as a backdrop on the set. Her young guests, while still participating in a weird kind of controlled chaos reminiscent of anthropologist Roberto da Matta's descriptions of Carnival,[21] now waved the banners of all nations; the viewer was likely to be confronted at any moment with the incongruous image of a Canadian or Israeli flag, evoking global politics while lacking any context whatsoever.

Xuxa's guests and assistants were also more "diverse"; many if not most tended to be visibly Asian, African American, or Latino. Her noticeable warmth toward her Latino guests in particular highlighted her own ethnic background, drawing additional attention to the condition of difference that she actually performed in the song "Talk to Me." Pleading, "Talk to me, I want to talk to you," and adding perhaps offhandedly, but also accurately, "you bring your history along with you," Xuxa admitted not only her sense of difference, but her vulnerability and discomfort—not as a woman, which Simpson argues is part of Xuxa's innocent/erotic star persona, but as a foreigner and Brazilian in the United States.

While it would be unwise to read either this performance or Xuxa's related public statements as expressing the true feelings of Xuxa the person, it is clear that foreignness was a disruptive element on the show. Indeed, one might very

The Superstar Xuxa doll: "Be a Superstar just like Xuxa"

well read the flags, globe, and multiculturalist slant of the program as an
attempt to naturalize Xuxa's own difference and make her acceptable within a
U.S. television industry in which even Latino, much less Latin American performers are extremely rare. With her cover-girl looks, attractive costumes,
conspiratorial sympathy with the *baixinhos*, and simultaneous sexy behavior
toward the camera, Xuxa's appeal in Brazil and throughout Latin America is
virtually unquestioned; in the United States, however, a new image had to be
created and its appeal vigorously asserted.

Indicative of the ambiguous place that was allocated to Xuxa in North American popular culture is the marketing of the Superstar Xuxa doll. On the one
hand, the doll was packaged in a box bearing pictures of Xuxa among her fans
with the command (on one version), "Be a Superstar just like Xuxa," and came
with Xuxa-labeled lip gloss and stickers. This packaging accented her superstar
status and assumed that Xuxa needed no introduction. On the other hand, the
doll itself did not look like Xuxa, and had long hair instead of her medium-
short bob. This, Xuxa explained to *TV y Novelas*, was because of a poll showing
that girls prefer dolls with long hair.[22] In other words, the image presented of
Xuxa was subordinated to the demands of the preexisting U.S. doll market
(Xuxa, however, suggested that young consumers could cut the doll's hair to
resemble hers). Such concessions indicated the extent to which Xuxa's individ-

uality was subordinated to a carefully researched and culturally specific notion of mass appeal.

Ironically, Xuxa has been routinely accused by critics of being a living incarnation of Barbie; the doll example shows that, in fact, U.S. standards of both wholesomeness and Barbieness were to be the prerequisites for Xuxa's success in this country. The fear that Simpson expressed in her book of "the possibility of Xuxa and Angélica [a younger Xuxa clone] expanding their domains throughout the Americas, Europe and beyond"[23] and creating hordes of young, slavish imitators appears to be unfounded, for in reality it was Xuxa who changed, in anticipation both of adult critics such as Simpson and a well-developed young market already set in its habits, tastes, and prejudices.

Exporting Entertainment

In 1992, a writer for *La Prensa de San Antonio* introduced an article on Xuxa by commenting that "her name carries all kinds of associations, according to one's nationality."[24] In fact, the reception of Xuxa in the Americas resembles that of Latin American celebrities since the 1930s in terms of the vast differences in perception that exist between the Latino and Latin American press, on one side, and the implicitly white dominant media, on the other. In the former, Xuxa may not be universally loved, and may indeed be joked about, but she is not treated in ethnic or national terms; she is simply a celebrity, whose career and activities are assumed to be of interest, and who appears often in comparisons with other female stars—many of whom defensively claim not to be "another Xuxa." Yet in the U.S. mainstream press, when she is mentioned at all, Xuxa is an object of mild ridicule and occasional curiosity. Her arrival on U.S. television in September 1993 provoked bemusement, skepticism, and incredulity, and from some reviewers, the verdict that in spite of all the changes that had been made in the program, its appeal in this country would still be limited.

In the *Hollywood Reporter*, Rick Sherwood described Xuxa as "a combination of Barbie and Olivia Newton-John who comes off like a subdued Charo meets the Shari Lewis of the cha-cha set," and concluded that the show was "fun for the pre-'tween set, and really doesn't have much appeal for anyone older." An anonymous *New York Times* reviewer, who characterized Xuxa as an "anatomically correct" Barbie as well as "the nightmare offspring of Fred Rogers and Pia Zadora," was even less charitable; while acknowledging that Xuxa's show is "tamer than the tamest music video," the author pointed out that "she does break ground in that her sexual or 'sensual' (Xuxa's word) pitch is directly to kids. Just what daytime television needs. It almost makes you like Barney."

Other reviewers, however, liked the show's eccentricity and chaotic sensibility, with Tim Gray in *TV Guide* predicting Xuxa's "looks of a leading lady, charm of Barney, and social conscience of Mother Teresa" to be a surefire hit.[25]

Discussion of Xuxa was not limited to the entertainment pages. For the *New York Times*'s South America correspondent James Brooke, Xuxa's name became a cultural reference point as her popularity in Latin America soared in the late 1980s and 1990s. Several of Brooke's articles alluded to Xuxa in the context of Latin American exoticism and kitsch: his report on the Brazilian royal family listed her as a possible contender to the throne, and another piece described the inclusion of a Xuxa float in the 1991 Carnival parade. Also in 1991, he mentioned her in an article about the former dictator of Paraguay, General Alfredo Stroessner: in exile in Brasília, Stroessner "often dressed in pajamas," and "whil[ed] away morning hours watching a children's television show run by Xuxa, a blond model who favors hot pants."[26]

While Brooke deploys Xuxa as a means of ridiculing and trivializing the former dictator, the affinity of foreign dictators for models in hot pants is nothing new in the history of U.S. media stereotyping. A catalog released by Brooklyn-based Shake Books of articles published in 1950s and 1960s' scandal magazines, for example, lists dozens of titles such as "The Strange Sex Life of Fidel Castro," "The Secret Love Life of Juan Perón," "The Teen-Age Harem of Don Juan Perón," and "Rafael Trujillo: Babes, Bananas, and Bloodshed," along with similar articles about Khrushchev, Stalin, Chiang Kai-shek, the Shah of Iran, and other Communist and/or Third World leaders.

While U.S. politicians also appeared in these tabloids, their exposés rarely involved sex, and overall, the articles were respectful. Foreign leaders, on the other hand, were assumed to be decadent, perverse, and ridiculous, an impression that was reinforced by their association with the pop stars of their day. Carmen Miranda, for instance, was widely rumored to be the mistress of Brazilian President Getúlio Vargas. Once again following in Miranda's footsteps, Xuxa, besides being admired by Stroessner, has been linked romantically to Argentine President Carlos Menem. The trivialization of these female stars thus indirectly contributes to the trivialization of Latin America as a whole; and the oppressive regimes that the United States has so often supported, sustained, and even installed are reduced to the image of an old man in pajamas watching Xuxa on television.

Prior to these articles, the *Times* had introduced its readership to Xuxa in a 1990 article titled "Brazil's Idol Is a Blonde, and Some Ask 'Why?'" In this piece, Brooke presented a hodgepodge of trivia that did little to answer the question posed by the title. Focusing on the alleged incongruity of Xuxa's physical appearance, Brooke noted that "the blond image that Xuxa projects runs counter to racial trends here."[27] These "trends" apparently included Afro-Brazilian activism and the growing visibility of the Japanese population, but Xuxa's or any other celebrity's social responsibility was not clearly determined; in particular, the relation of her charity work (a description of which opened the article) to the accusations of racism remain vague. Interestingly, Brooke reproduced without comment a Brazilian sociologist's offhanded reference to Xuxa as a "national symbol," giving her a political importance that she herself never claimed.

The inappropriateness of Xuxa's blond hair and blue eyes for a "national symbol" is a central issue as well for Simpson, who critiques the Brazilian media for promoting whiteness as an ideal and the Brazilian public for embracing it. Yet this emphasis on Brazilian racial hypocrisy by U.S. critics in itself suggests a certain double standard. In a letter published in the *New York Times* two weeks after Brooke's article, reader John McBride asked:

> Since when is racial or national origin a criterion for citizenship in the Americas? Michael Jackson is 'black'; yet he is an idol for United States youth, many of whom are 'white.' . . . Why should Latin Americans be subjected to different ethnic criteria? Like the people of the United States, they too are an amalgamation of races and nationalities. Who decreed that being of any one color, ethnic or racial type is Brazilian, Argentine, Bolivian or Puerto Rican? Why should a Polish, French, German, Jewish, Arabic, or Japanese—or even English—name be considered an anomaly if carried by an individual of Hispanic background?[28]

It would be easy to dismiss McBride's argument as disingenuous, for we know (for example) that Michael Jackson's race is indeed an issue, and that Xuxa's popularity is not due to talent alone, but also to historically constructed notions of beauty that cannot be separated from racism and sexism. Brooke and Simpson's focus on racism in Brazil, however, obscures the obvious fact that a disproportionate number of our own celebrities are blond, blue eyed, and unrepresentative of the heterogeneity of our population. Moreover, the highlighting of Xuxa's blondness is doubly ironic if juxtaposed with the way blondness functioned as a trope of ethnicity in the films and star discourse of Miranda in the 1930s through 1950s.

For Miranda, blondness symbolized the lack that was at the core of the fetishization of her "Latin" ethnicity. In her films, she was frequently paired with blonds such as Betty Grable, whose conventionality she parodied, but with whom her characters, as women, could never compete. In the mid-1940s, she began to flaunt bleached hair and performed a song called "I Make My Money with Bananas," which even more blatantly than Xuxa's game "Candied

Adventures of a "national symbol": *Super Xuxa contra Baixo Astral*, 1988. Photo courtesy of David Sonnenschein, Crystal Vision, Rio de Janeiro.

Kid," presented the star as a self-aware commodity. In this song, Miranda complained about stereotyping and exclusion from more conventional female roles: "I love to wear my hair like Deanna Durbin," she sang, "but I have to stuff it in a turban / a turban that weighs 5,433 pounds."[29] In the film *Copacabana* (1947), she wore a blond wig in order to impersonate a sexy French chanteuse, while her brunette persona remained comic and picaresque.

The weight of this self-defeating masquerade was that of always representing an exotic other, for although Miranda's exotic, foreign, not-blondness was the basis of her success, her constant expression of lack reinforced blondness and whiteness as cultural ideals. It is thus ironic that four decades later, the "most exportable entertainer since Carmen Miranda" is criticized for possessing those attributes that Miranda only expressed as lack; for if Miranda was unable to overcome her perceived otherness, Xuxa is now attacked for not being other *enough*. Hence, Xuxa too falls victim to the paradox of blondness: that is, a Latin American who is not blond, either literally or figuratively speaking, is seen as inferior and has little chance of succeeding on mainstream U.S. television; yet a Latin American star who is blond is seen as inauthentic, the product of a public brainwashed by imperialist fantasies and impossible ideals.

Authenticity, therefore, becomes the standard that is used to selectively and self-righteously judge the Third World performer: Kim Basinger, Sharon

Stone, and countless other U.S. and European stars can be unproblematically blond, and just as similar to Barbie as Xuxa is accused of being in almost every article written about her, but Xuxa cannot, for she is a "national symbol." Xuxa's appearance on U.S. television as a result of prior success in other countries may suggest that borders are being broken down, but in fact they are merely less visible, and if Xuxa herself is not a "victim," as such her reception in the U.S. media reveals that racism, stereotyping, and condescension are still the most prevalent attitudes toward Latin America, and especially its popular culture and the public that consumes it. While Xuxa's own quest for greater fame and wealth in the "land of opportunity" may well have been cynical, those that would attack her for this and implicitly demand a more "pure" alien to entertain their children are more cynical still in their assumption of the right to define and police the contested terrain of cultural diversity.

Sociedade Anónima

In the program notes to *New World (B)order*, Gómez-Peña and Fusco included a dictionary of syllogisms, which they called *Borderismos*. Among these was "Culti-multuralism," defined as "an Esperantic Disney worldview in which all races and sexes live happily together."[30] As mentioned earlier, the Disney Corporation, whose Epcot Center was contracted to supply short "educational" films for each episode of the Xuxa show, has long wielded the notion of a "small world" in the interest of both profits and the ideology of U.S. cultural superiority; in the 1990s, this notion began to circulate widely on many levels of society, from fashion to politics.[31] As Fusco has written, "even in this period of multicultural frenzy where there is a desire to discover and understand the other, there exists at the same time a desire to forget that our contemporary relationship and actions have insidious historical antecedents."[32]

This conflicted desire, finally, is what the Xuxa show represents: the advent of a culture of free trade; or what Gómez-Peña and Fusco term a kinder, gentler expansionism, in which commodities can cross borders, but people, perhaps more than ever, cannot. Even as the Latinization of northern North America accelerates, anti-immigrant hysteria is becoming an increasingly powerful force in U.S. politics; and while "Xuxa S.A." (Xuxa, Inc.) continues to achieve unprecedented success in Latin America by exploiting the fears and desires of audiences/consumers, Xuxa herself, as a symbol of the transnational subject in a world with both fewer and more borders, seems to be adrift in a true *sociedade anónima*—an anonymous society in which, in spite of new discourses of tolerance, individuals continue to be defined and classified, in subtle and sometimes paradoxical ways, by the flag they wave, the accent with which they speak, the costume they display, and the color of their skin.

Under these circumstances, the cancellation of Xuxa's show and the general failure of "crossover" programming to take root in the mainstream are hardly surprising, for the same factors or "historical antecedents" that bring about such cross-cultural experiments also render them impossible to sustain. The finale of another program from Xuxa's first season in the United States summarizes the Xuxa show in both its naive/ideal and cynical/contradictory aspects. Finishing a song, Xuxa reads one of her prepared "messages," this time a statement against discrimination, more poignant than usual in the context of the multiracial cast and crew that surrounds her. After applying red lipstick, she chooses that day's recipient of her ritual *beijinho*, a tiny dark-skinned boy named Omar. As she plants kisses and bright lipstick smears on his face, Omar grins vacantly, as if in shock. Having in this combined verbal statement and gesture seemingly done away with racial conflict, Xuxa ascends the platform and exits into her globe, blowing kisses to the studio and television audiences. Just before she disappears, two flags cross immediately in front of her face: the yellow and green of Brazil, and the red, white, and blue of the United States. Then the star exits into her globe; the right of children to have fun has been exercised, races and nations have been reconciled, harmony is restored. For the corporations and media conglomerates that have made it all possible, it's a small world after all.

Notes

1 Guillermo Gómez-Peña, *Year of the White Bear: The New World (B)order*, performed by Gómez-Peña and Coco Fusco, Hancher Auditorium, Iowa City, Iowa, 17 February 1993.
2 "Firma con CBS," *La Opinión*, 5 July 1994, 3B.
3 Amelia Simpson, *Xuxa: The Mega-Marketing of Gender, Race, and Modernity* (Philadelphia: Temple University Press, 1993), 27–28.
4 Alma Guillermoprieto, "Obsessed in Rio," *New Yorker*, 16 August 1993, 49.
5 "El Xou de Xuxa," *El Sol de Texas*, 14 May 1992, 6B; "Xuxa: La nueva bomba de Brasil," *La Prensa de San Antonio*, 24 April 1992, 3B; and Carlos Ravelo, "Bye, Xuxa; Hello, Shoe Shah," *News from Brazil*, March 1993, 9.
6 "A loirinha chegou lá," *Veja*, 25 September 1991, 104.
7 Tim Gray, "Xuxa," *TV Guide*, 9 October 1993, 24.
8 "A loirinha chegou lá," 104. This and all other translations are mine.
9 *Chabeli*, broadcast in Iowa City, Iowa, 4 May 1994.
10 Graciela Mori, "Xuxa," *TV y Novelas*, 30 May 1994, 75.
11 "Kids," *TV Guide*, 18 September 1993, 107.
12 Mike Freeman, "Xuxa Works on U.S. Makeover," *Broadcasting and Cable*, 2 August 1993, 23.
13 Rodney Mello, "Recado," *News from Brazil*, March 1993, 5.
14 Eduardo Galeano, *Memory of Fire III: Century of the Wind*, trans. Cedric Belfrage (New York: Pantheon, 1988), 131.
15 Bret Primack, liner notes, on Paquito D'Rivera, *Tico! Tico!*, Chesky Records, 1989; and

Rubén Blades and Elvis Costello, "The Miranda Syndrome," on Rubón Blades, *Nothing but the Truth*, Elektra, 1988.

16 Caetano Veloso, "Caricature and Conqueror, Pride and Shame," *New York Times*, 20 October 1991, H34.

17 Miguel Angel Rodríguez, "Xuxa luce belleza y promueve su imagen en sus 'videoclips,' " *La Opinión*, 1 April 1993, 3F; and "Titulada EOH, EOH, EOH; Xuxa lanza tercera producción discográfica," *Impacto Latin News*, 29 December 1992, 22.

18 My discussion of Carmen Miranda is based on an unpublished project of mine entitled "The 5,433-Pound Turban: Carmen Miranda and the 1940s' Latin Craze." Shari Roberts and Ana López have written about Miranda's gender and ethnic positioning. See Shari Roberts, "The Lady in the Tutti-Frutti Hat: Carmen Miranda, a Spectacle of Ethnicity," *Cinema Journal* 32, no. 3 (spring 1993): 3–23; and Ana López, "Are All Latins from Manhattan? Hollywood, Ethnography, and Cultural Colonialism," in *Mediating Two Worlds: Cinematic Encounters in the Americas*, ed. John King, Ana López, and Manuel Alvarado (London: British Film Institute, 1993), 67–80.

19 Freeman, "U.S. Makeover," 24.

20 Tapes of these programs were graciously shared with me by Maria Duarte and Brad Correa.

21 See Roberto da Matta, *Carnavais, malandros e heróis* (Rio de Janeiro: Zahar, 1979).

22 Mori, "Xuxa," 76.

23 Simpson, *Mega-Marketing*, 166.

24 "La nueva bomba de Brasil," 3B.

25 Rich Sherwood, review of *Xuxa*, Hollywood Reporter, 13 September 1993; "Barbie Lives," *New York Times*, 28 November 1993, late ed., sec. 6, 29; and Gray, "Xuxa," 27.

26 James Brooke, "Pretenders Keep Dreaming," *New York Times*, 25 April 1993, late ed., sec. 4, 2; James Brooke, "City of 'Zillion Vanities' Is Set to Flaunt a Few," *New York Times*, 4 February 1991, late ed., A4; and James Brooke, "Paraguay Jittery over the Exiled Stroessner," *New York Times*, 3 March 1991, late ed., sec. 1, 6.

27 James Brooke, "Brazil's Idol Is a Blonde, and Some Ask 'Why?' " *New York Times*, 31 July 1990, late ed., A4.

28 John McBride, letter, *New York Times*, 14 August 1990, late ed., A20.

29 Martha Gil-Montero, *Brazilian Bombshell: The Biography of Carmen Miranda* (New York: Donald I. Fine, 1989), 169–71.

30 Guillermo Gómez-Peña and Coco Fusco, "The New World (B)order," program for *Year of the White Bear: The New World (B)order*, 2.

31 A Xuxa record released in Argentina in October 1994 was titled *El pequeño mundo*—the small world. Much like the Disney attraction of the same name, the title plays on both Xuxa's role as queen of the *baixinhos* (again, short ones) and her internationalism.

32 Coco Fusco, quoted in Kathleen Newman, "New World (B)order Art," program for *Year of the White Bear: The New World (B)order*, 6.

tions. The potential for virtual masquerade—which has become a cherished, almost utopian characteristic of the Internet in both popular and academic rhetoric—makes it practically impossible for researchers to make firm statements about the "true" demographics of their study. Furthermore, the complexities of human identity and cultural processes that have vexed ethnographic studies over the years multiply in this new media environment. In reading the on-line writings of those who identify themselves as adolescent girls, we must be reminded that the same environment that allows teens the freedom to explore identity, may make it difficult for readers to locate the absolute or "authentic" contours of that identity.

In this essay, I enter into this abstruse area of investigation in order to consider how one television program, My So-Called Life (hereafter MSCL), activated the imaginations of a particular group of teen girls who, after viewing the show, met on-line in the winter of 1994–1995 to discuss and explore their subjectivity as female adolescents. Although MSCL fans range in age, race, class, and gender, it was these teen girls who consistently and emotionally voiced the importance of the text's proximity to their own lives in their on-line writing.[3] This sense of proximity, I contend, stems from a number of factors, including: the manner in which adolescent girls use both television and computers to see themselves as part of the sensuous "world" of the television and computer imaginary; the fact that girls who identify more closely with MSCL believe it was created as a representation of their own lives; and the apparent process of intense self-creation and experimentation that teen girls find themselves in as they struggle with ambivalence toward their encroaching "womanhood." These elements lead girl fans to feel a deeper investment in the exegesis of the meanings of MSCL. The ways in which these girls make meaning involves the processes of participatory spectatorship, identification, the development of a relationship to an ideal self, and girl-culture activism. As a result, MSCL and its narrative trajectories became not simply entertainment, an education on social issues, or fantasy fulfillment for this group of teen girls, but rather an investment in an individual and communal understanding of teenage girl identity.

MSCL, a defunct ABC weekly drama that premiered in the fall of 1994, focused on the internal struggles of fifteen-year-old Angela Chase (Claire Danes). Created by the same team that produced thirtysomething in the eighties (Winnie Holzman, Marshall Herskovitz, Edward Zwick, and Scott Winant), the show was praised by critics for its realistic characterizations and fine performances. Nevertheless, it drew a relatively small audience of about 10 million viewers per week, and as a result, in March 1995, after only nineteen episodes, the show was put on hiatus as network executives decided whether or not to include it in ABC's fall lineup. During this time, fans organized to save the show, pooling enough funds to take out full-page ads on behalf of MSCL in

Variety and the *Hollywood Reporter*. In addition, they developed sites on the World Wide Web and met on-line via America Online's bulletin boards.

Originally designed as an avenue to comment on ABC programs, the MSCL's bulletin board became a meeting place/discussion group for fans (both teens and young adults) who thought that their lives would be significantly altered if the show was taken off the air. MSCL fans (who call themselves "Lifers") filled the board with almost 9,000 postings in eighteen files over three months. The early files primarily contained urgent pleas to ABC to save the show: fans or frequent viewers articulating the pleasures that the show has aroused in them and, consequently, their anger at the network executives' threats to cancel it. But with time, the billboard took a different form. As often occurs on-line, fans altered the intended function of the billboard space: they used it to generate friendships, share experiences, and talk about themselves through their relation to MSCL. Also, more complex interpretive practices appeared as fans wrote to each other and exchanged scripts and stories that extended the show's narrative beyond the season's final episode.

Television, Computers, and Participatory Spectatorship

Many MSCL on-line fans engaged in a participatory spectatorship, making meaning collectively as well as individually. In their writings, they described their viewing practices as solitary. When logged on, they brought their individual interpretations, snippets of emotionally significant moments, and fetishization of repeated dialogue or images to the bulletin board in order to garner response and incite debate. This second level of rereading, the meshing of individual viewing experience with others, results in an encrustation of meaning surrounding the original television text. Jenkins points out that this process of meaning making extends the life of the text and provides additional reading strategies or "poached meanings" for a spectator's engagement with a favorite text.[4] In addition, I would argue that the self is continually intertwined with these "poached meanings," as the text prompts self-reflection, and that girl fans are particularly adept at mastering this process.

An entry written by Jill, a teen fan of the show, reveals the emotional intensity of many of these girls' on-line reading strategies. She starts by describing her high school experiences: being rejected by a boy, being called a "dyke" by her classmates, and receiving abuse in the hallways:

> They don't know what it's like to walk down the hall and hear them, and feel their eyes on you, and feel so awkward because your skirt's too long and you keep stepping on it and you keep dropping things but you don't pick them up because they're already talking about you, you don't want

them commenting on your ass. At first when they talked about you, they did it loud, so they knew you would hear how much they hate you . . . only some of them yell "bitch" at you. The others just whisper and stare . . . criticizing everything about you, critiquing every little move you make, everything about your appearance. . . . Then you go home and try as hard as you can to save your favorite TV show; the only one that has ever meant anything to you . . . because it really seems to understand what you're going through, but now they're taking it off, but you're still trying your damn hardest to do whatever you can. And then you talk to your best friend and she's going to have sex with her boyfriend and you figure out that you're going to be an ugly virgin for the rest of your life, that no one will want to touch you, even though some people tell you [that you] look like Angela. And now you're crying because you can't get the words out and Kurt's [Cobain] gone and so's River [Phoenix] and Angela might be too . . . then you remember the hour or so before that when those tears were rolling down your face because it could have been the last time Angeleka will ever be Angeleka. And the letter was so sweet, and you loved duh squared, and Rayanne's orange strands and the end was so sad when Angela got into Jordan's car. And you kept saying this can't be the end. And then it was, and you were left hanging and you just hate it because you may never know.[5]

Another girl writes of similar pain:

I need Angela's emotions.
I am sad. I need to watch MSCL cuz it makes me cry, and I need to cry. I hate living, does anyone else? Does anyone feel as though they don't belong? and I'm not talking about just in a specific group of people, but like with anyone anywhere. This is my life. Maybe some day I can be happy, and not lonely . . . and sad, but this is just a fantasy to me. I can't wait for tomorrow. I missed the first episode [of MSCL]. I need it. It's like a drug that I long for and need.[6]

Although these are especially dramatic accounts of fan life in relation to MSCL, many of the entries written by girl teens contain a similar urgency. They often speak to the unstable nature of teenage girls' identity during a time of shifting expectations, bodily transfiguration, and intense socialization. In witnessing a parallel instability in the character of Angela (the primary protagonist and only figure whose thoughts were revealed to the audience through a voice-over), these fans were able to recognize and give voice to their own inner turmoil. This is partly due to a process of identification, but it also relates to the particular manner in which female fans interact with the television text.

In his study of Star Trek fans, Jenkins found that while male fans concentrated on the accuracy of the plot and actions of the central protagonist, female fans saw the narrative as if it were an "atmosphere or an experience," and found pleasure in tying their own inferences, emotions, and knowledge to this "world."[7] This is also true for the fans of MSCL. While the male fans tended to engage in cataloging and debating textual details, the female fans, specifically the adolescents, interwove the text with the reality of their own everyday, using the show to wrap their own desire/pain/ambivalence in, through, and around the narrative. One girl fan explains how this process works in her own viewing of MSCL:

> I get a little defensive when someone says, "It's just a TV show; get a life." This show is different. This show folds me into another space; it turns me inside out. The cold reason of my normal waking life changes places with the soft, sensitive interior that's normally protected from the elements. . . . And only when I experience those emotions do I really imagine that I am actually alive. And isn't feeling alive a reality? Isn't it the best reality?[8]

The computer, and the communication that it offers, becomes another stratum in this narrative world. It's an additional fantastical site that provides a private/public dream or play space for a girl's construction of a sense of identity. Just as MSCL supplies a narrative atmosphere through which self-reflection is induced, the on-line board provides the opportunity for further engagement with both the show and the self. In a study of computer cultures, Sherry Turkle found that the adolescents she interviewed used computers as a constructive and projective medium in relation to their subjectivity.[9] Moreover, she saw a significant difference in the way boys and girls approached their relationship to the computer. While playing with computational graphic objects called "sprites," boys used them to engage in fantasy, while girls took the fantasy a step further, tending to see themselves inside the world of the sprites. The added structural system of America Online, along with the access to community that it provides, expands the potential for an even more intensive experience for girls than it did in the case of the sprites. In considering the intersection of the computational and televisual sites, it appears that girl MSCL fans were enmeshed in fluid states of identity play in relation to their spectatorship and the text, and that the on-line computer chat facilitated that involvement.

Identification, Imitation, and Realism

An important factor in the girls' identity alignment with Angela is the assertion by the viewers of the text's verisimilitude. In their writing, they tick off simi-

Angela looks directly
at the viewer.

larities between the narrative trajectories of Angela's life and their own. Determining how one text becomes more "real" than another is a difficult thing to do, particularly since the characteristics of such "realness" are often subjective. Yet, there seems to be a link here to the genre known as "quality programming." This genre is defined by its ability to skillfully navigate through complex social and personal issues without entering into clichés, easy wrap-ups, or melodrama.[10]

These teen fans speak of Angela's life being just like their own, containing the very contradictions, ambivalence, and angst that they are experiencing. The problem of who has authored the text, however, never comes up in discussions over such verisimilitude. The fact that this show is written by a middle-aged woman and produced by two middle-aged men does not inhibit the fans' ability to view this text as "authentic." This may stem from the scarcity of other viable teen girl representations currently available to them. In considering the selection at hand, Angela's comparative authenticity is amplified to such a point that it matters little who created her.

Because of the negligible choice of "realistic" teen characters in the mass media, teen girls might well have learned to be flexible in their spectatorship,

Many girls on the MSCL
bulletin board describe
the pleasure they took in
dressing like Angela.

finding a different sort of pleasure in identifying with older female stars and
characters.[11] Still, there is a difference in the strategies at work in the identification with older female stars or characters rather than one that is of similar age
to the viewer. The former identification can be an issue of the desire "to
become," while identification with the latter can be contingent on the desire
"to be" in the here and now. As I mentioned earlier, girl fans urgently desire a
narrative world through which they can come to an understanding of and give
voice to their individual adolescent subjectivity. A spectatorial relationship with
a teen character as opposed to an adult one seems to provide more narrative
material from which these girls can build a site for such exploration.

The fans' relationship to Angela also involves the more active and physically
involved component of identification/imitation. Many girls on the MSCL bulletin board describe the pleasure they took in dressing like Angela (primarily
flannel shirts), wearing T-shirts that proclaim their fandom, and most commonly, their attempts to dye their hair the exact color of Angela's. For instance:

On my first Thursday without Angela I dyed my hair red. It turned out kind
of pink and my mother went ape; she says I'm just a little too involved. I

consider it striking back. Besides, I look good in red. My second Thursday I got a plain tee shirt and iron-on-letters and ironed on "Angela Lives" on a shirt. I'm going to wear it tomorrow to school and see if anyone has any idea what it means. Its fun [sic] to keep them guessing.[12]

Another girl responds:

I want to dye my hair red for Angela but I think people will say I did it because of Sidney on *Melrose Place* and then I'd really feel like a dork.[13]

There is a specific textual reference attached to all this hair dyeing. In the premiere episode of MSCL, Angela decides to change the color of her hair from light brown to a vibrant "Crimson Glow" red. The idea came from her friend, Rayanne, who told her that, "[her] hair was holding her back." Angela felt she had to listen to Rayanne because "she wasn't just talking about my hair, she was talking about my life." Thus, most of the other characters read her new hair color as a defiant act. Angela's mother (Bess Armstrong) is angry and tells Angela's father (Tom Irwin) that, "[Angela] did it to get me to react. . . . It's just so hard to look at her, she looks like a stranger." Angela's former best friend, Sharon, says to her, "I can't believe you did that without telling me. . . . I hate it." And a teacher notes, "Your appearance has altered . . . is there a problem at home?" Angela responds to the teacher by telling her, "It just seems like I agreed to have a certain personality or something just to make things easier for everyone, but when you think about it, how do you know it's even you?"[14]

Thus, the narrative suggests that Angela's change in hair color is a physical manifestation of her desire for agency in the creation of her own persona. While most of the characters, primarily those in a position of authority, are concerned that her hair signals the eruption of a troubling problem or cry for attention, Angela continues to struggle to define the act's meaning as an initial step toward controlling the direction of her life. Women and girls often express change through altering their appearance. Making over oneself has long been a way in which to transform the female identity: to make oneself anew. In the case of Angela, the dying of hair appears as an act of self-production and peformance. The physical changes lead to alterations in the expectations and conceptions of other individuals in the girl's life. The act destabilizes the idea of a fixed identity and allows Angela, as one fan put it, "to keep them guessing."[15]

Such a performance of difference/sameness is also played out through the fan's emulation of Angela and leads to intriguing contradictions. First, the life of the fan becomes somehow more real to her through the adoption of codes constructed for a fictional character. Second, many of these girls articulate their desire to show their affinity with Angela by dressing, looking, or acting like her, yet they also want to stand out to their peers and prove their own individuality. Even as they take pleasure in Angela's rebellions and define their emulation of her as such, their own fan-related rebellions involve conformity.

In another way, however, their sameness is not only considered a mark of their ability to change or define themselves, but connects them to other fans, marking them as members of a particular social group. In her study of Madonna and Cyndi Lauper fans, Lewis described the practice of "copying" among girl fans as a desire for unity:

> The girl practice of dressing alike . . . is not just the form of adherence to a regime of feminine attire, but as a symbolic system that signifies female solidarity and female bonding. Dressing alike is frequently part of the signification system of girl friendships at the time in a woman's life before heterosexual desire is rigidly channeled.[16]

The Lifer's practice of copying resonates with the activities of other fan groups, as well as the high school hierarchical structure in which one's identity is affected or blended through an affinity with others. Teen Lifers have chosen to move outside the confines of their own high schools, however, and form affiliations through the Internet, being, ironically, invisible to their fellow fans, yet visible in their fandom to those who may not be familiar with their codes. Writes one Lifer:

> I received my MSCL T-shirt in the mail last week and I love it. Anyway, it came just in time for me to wear it to school on Thursday—Thursdays of course being national mourning day for MSCL, when I usually wear my plaid shirt that's almost identical to the one Angela always wears. I am continually amazed, astounded, grateful, laughing, crying, relating, bonding when I read your posts. I forget that you aren't my best friends (you'd make better friends than some of mine) and that you guys don't "know" me as well as I know you.[17]

Their invisibility on-line enables them to express feelings that may be frightening or alienating in their social or family settings. They are neither judged on appearance nor their ability to assimilate to the strictures that they feel are being placed on them by family and peers. In this way, the on-line space works to create an alternative subculture based on creativity and the willingness to expound on the experiential. They have re-created the fantastical site activated by the televisual and computational, expanding on it to include physical manifestations of their productivity. Their hair dyeing and choices of clothes help them to bring what they have experienced through MSCL and their on-line community back into their everyday lives.

Adolescence, Femininity, and the Ideal Self

Film theorist Jackie Stacey has, in her work on female spectatorship, found imitation to be a physical (as well as consumerist) manifestation of identificatory practices activated by star construction. Stacey argues that a fan's relationship to a particular star (we can extend this to the character/persona that a specific star is linked with) is, in part, connected to one's relationship with an ideal self and that:

> Recognizing oneself as different from, yet also similar to, a female ideal other produces the pleasure between femininities which has been referred to (by Gillian Frith) as the "intimacy which is knowledge."[18]

Stacey goes on to note that in the process of identification, the self and ideal are not unified or collapsed into one, but rather, it is the difference between self and ideal that generates pleasure and creates a sense of "realness." If kept intact, this distance sustains a longing for the other, while the perceived sameness produces a comparative identity in which to test or play out life possibilities. By adopting certain codes of the character Angela, these teens intensify their relationship with their ideal as well as, perhaps, experiment with the boundaries of social roles and norms that are attached to female adolescence.

Identification is an exceedingly apt act for teenage girls who are in the midst of creating their own sense of self in relation to the shifting expectations of adolescence, both in terms of their previous identity as "girl" and their future identity as "woman." Since adolescence is such a short, tumultuous period of life, a teen girl must adapt quite quickly to the ever-tightening boundaries that are being placed on her still-forming sense of self as a female in a patriarchal society. We might assume, then, that the complexity and ambivalence of a character such as Angela may provide a parallel identity in which these girls can play with, create, and edit/reedit their conception of femininity in relation to their approaching womanhood. The televisual and computational worlds through which fans work with Angela provide safe spaces for girls to negotiate their desire to retain some familiar characteristics of girlhood (such as independence, gregariousness, playfulness, and so on) with their need to accept the encroaching and contradictory responsibilities of mature "womanhood."

Perhaps the intermingling between text and the personal may have a more poignant meaning for teen girls than other fan groups, since they are in a process of adopting two disparate signifiers into their identity. They are pro-

Girl Lifers repeatedly articulate the pleasure they get from the text's verisimilitude.

cessing not only what it means to be female, but also what it means to be a "teenager." Barbara Hudson asserts that the discourses of adolescence and femininity are subversive of one another, creating a set of conflicting expectations for the teenage girl. She describes adolescence as a masculine construct (embodying images of rebellion, restlessness, resistance, and the like) that contradicts a girl's attempt to become a patriarchally defined feminine, demure (perhaps even silent) young woman.[19] The dissonance created out of this dichotomy is one that leads a girl to feel uncomfortable with either signifier. Therefore, the narrative pleasure that MSCL allows these girls and the interpretive practices that it activates foster an important imaginary space that permits them some freedom to negotiate and define themselves in relation to cultural expectations.

The character of Angela contains these heterogeneous, and often contradictory, elements of teen subjectivity. Her personality is pensive, intelligent, anxious, playful, and mercurial, vacillating between defiant and introverted, and her voice-overs frequently conflict with the action occurring on-screen, revealing her fallibility and desire to misread in order to further fantasy. As mentioned earlier, girl Lifers repeatedly articulate the pleasure they get from the text's verisimilitude, finding Angela's construction as one that speaks to their own. They understand Angela's play with and confusion over shifting identity positions, and can validate their own ambivalence for the adolescence experience through the dichotomy presented in the fantasy/reality split in Angela's "life."

The identification with and fantasy of Angela may also be charged with a type of "crush" that girls may harbor for such an ideal. These crushes are commonly experienced by teen girls, and often involve a friend, teacher, or mentor. This phenomenon has been attributed to both a stage of increased bisexual feelings in women, which is due to the complexity of a girl's early oedipal period, as well as the positioning of the female spectator. Nancy Chodorow asserts that a girl's puberty is "characterized by bisexual wavering and indecisiveness about the relative importance to the girl of females [sic] and males."[20] The attachment and subsequent homoeroticism felt for a female ideal (who is not her mother) may be part of this process of the retention of a girl's connection to other females while she moves toward an attachment to her father. In addition, the fluidity of female spectatorship may bring with it the conflation of the desire "to be" and "to have," leading a girl to hold onto the feeling of a crush. A particularly fitting piece of dialogue from an episode of MSCL, in which Rayanne's mother is speaking to Angela's, addresses the possibility of such conflation:

> Rayanne talks about Angela all the time. She's in love with her. She wants to be Angela. You know kids, they find one person. It's like being in love but you're not allowed to have sex. Don't you remember? There'd be like one person and they had like perfect hair, or perfect breasts, or the best sense of humor and you'd just want to eat them up, to live in their bed, to be them.

Girl Culture and Activism

The on-line and off-line fantasy space in which identification is performed and imitation is initiated is analogous to the "bedroom culture" that Angela McRobbie points to as the private space where girls can safely create their own subculture.[21] This bedroom culture (away from exclusionary boy leisure activities and street culture) is where girls can play these identity games through a social relationship with popular culture. Within the safe space of the computer and television's narrative atmosphere, a girl can express anger and discontent with her life without fear of threat or intimidation. It is here, too, that an anger regarding a girl's invisibility in American culture can be expressed through the viewer activism that worked to save MSCL. One of these girl fans describes the rebellious emotions that were aroused when listening to the MSCL sound track alone in her bedroom:

> So anyway, I got the MSCL sound track and I got shivers when the theme song came on out of my own stereo, and I played it so loud my parents

thought I was insane. Tonight is the last show, you guys. I won't be able to sign on after it because of my stupid parents, but at least I will be with ya'll in spirit.—the depressed lonely little girl with absolutely no life at all who really hates ABC and all their stupid asshole rulers and the stupid hierarchy of the stupid Nielson ratings . . . bye.[22]

The writings of girl Lifers contain an activist sentiment that not only worked to save the show, but to save Angela's "life." To extend the life of their ideal self against the wishes of powerful and predominately male network executives—who have the final say on whether or not the show or Angela survives—may possibly be related to the desire to thwart the elite male culture that is working to inscribe stricter codes of femininity to teen identity. As one teenage fan insists:

> My Thursday nights and Friday mornings consist of talk of MSCL. It has made such an impact on my life. When something good finally comes along, the execs destroy it. This show relates not only to me, but to all my peers. Sometimes we try to impersonate Angela. She is not only a character to us as she might be to the execs, but Angela is someone who owns a portion of our hearts and minds. We cry with her, laugh with her, and share her need for Jordan. We look up to her. Angela is like a sister. You probably don't believe in separating a family, right? Then they shouldn't take away my sister.[23]

The fight to save Angela may be interpreted as a struggle for control over representation. Many teen girls feel just as silenced by, and invisible to, television networks as they do by the culture at large. Even the television teens on network prime-time shows such as *Beverly Hills 90210* are played by adults, and such programs maintain adult-oriented social problem plotlines and character constructions. Therefore, the importance of Angela (who these teens have adopted as an ideal or perhaps symbolic self) is that she has become, at least to this small group, a contested site where they can enact a tiny battle for visibility.

By examining the on-line activities of these MSCL fans, we can begin to situate difference in the spectatorial experiences of teen girls. We can identify their unique and temporal social positioning, and extrapolate possible modes of meaning making that occur out of their interaction with the televisual text and characters. Most important, we can answer their demand for visibility by recognizing and addressing the significance of their textual practices, and move toward incorporating their struggle over identity into our overall interrogations into television spectatorship. I would like to end with a posting that consolidates a number of issues addressed in this essay into one feisty, yet contradictory, declaration:

> My parents don't like it simply because it's REALITY and it bites. It hurts to see how low our [teenagers'] self-esteem is and how hard lives are for us nowadays but it's reality. And we love it![24]

Notes

1   See Dick Hebdidge, *Subculture: The Meaning of Style* (London: Methuen, 1987); Lawrence Grossberg, *We Gotta Get Out of This Place: Popular Conservatism and Postmodern Culture* (New York: Routledge, 1992); and Henry Jenkins, *Textual Poachers: Television Fans and Participatory Culture* (New York: Routledge 1992).

2   See Barbara Ehrenreich, Elizabeth Hess, and Gloria Jacobs, "Beatlemania: Girls Just Want to Have Fun," in *The Adoring Audience: Fan Culture and Popular Media*, ed. Lisa A. Lewis (New York: Routledge, 1992) 84–106; and Lisa A. Lewis, "Consumer Girl Culture: How Music Videos Appeal to Girls," in *Television and Women's Culture: The Politics of the Popular*, ed. Mary Ellen Brown (London: Sage, 1990), 94.

3   Although it's quite difficult to identify gender, race, class, and age while on-line, a large number of these writers labeled themselves as teenage girls. We can, perhaps, assume that most of these girls are middle to upper class, since to use America Online one must have both a computer (or access to one) and a subscription to the service.

4   Jenkins, *Textual Poachers*, 27.

5   JillCB, "RE: My Life and Angela is in It," 26 January 1995, on-line posting, America Online, ABC Bulletin Board.

6   Star 88, "I Need Angela's Emotions," 9 April 1995, on-line posting, America Online, ABC Bulletin Board.

7   Jenkins, *Textual Poachers*, 27.

8   Yadwigha, "My Actual Life," 9 April 1995, on-line posting, America Online, ABC Bulletin Board.

9   Sherry Turkle, *The Second Self: Computers and the Human Spirit* (New York: Simon and Schuster, 1984), 98–122.

10 Jane Feuer has outlined the ways in which contemporary industry discourse has defined "quality" television in relation to MTM style. She cites the interpretation of MTM shows as warm, human, self-reflective comedies or dramas that appeal to a liberal, sophisticated audience. These qualities have also been applied by fans and critics to MSCL. See Jane Feuer, "The MTM Style," in *MTM: "Quality" Television*, ed. Jane Feuer, Paul Keir, and Tise Vahimagi (London: BFI, 1984), 56.

11 For a discussion of girl identifications with teen boy idols see Gail Sweeney, "The Face on the Lunch Box: Television's Construction of the Teen Idol," *Velvet Light Trap* (spring 1994): 49.

12 SER23, "Life Sucks W/Out Angela," 9 February 1995, on-line posting, America Online, ABC Bulletin Board.

13 Sydney7522, "The Sky is Blue," 8 January 1995, on-line posting, America Online, ABC Bulletin Board.

14 *My So Called Life*, episode 1, 25 August 1994. ABC Television.

15 SER23, "Life Sucks W/Out Angela," 9 February 1995, on-line posting, America Online, ABC Bulletin Board.

16 Lewis, *Consumer Girl Culture*, 94.

17 MaggieTen, "Gee Whiz! 'Bout Time!" 27 February 1995, on-line posting, America Online, ABC Bulletin Board.

18 Jackie Stacey, *Star Gazing: Hollywood and Female Spectatorship* (New York: Routledge, 1994), 175.

19 Barbara Hudson, "Femininity and Adolescence," in *Gender and Generation*, ed. Angela McRobbie and Mica Nava (London: Macmillan Publishers Ltd., 1984).

20 Nancy Chodorow, *The Reproduction of Mothering* (Berkeley: University of California Press, 1978), 138.

21 Angela McRobbie, *Feminism and Youth Culture: From "Jackie" to "Just Seventeen"* (Boston, Mass.: Unwin Hyman, 1991), 188.

22 Crowcount, "Okay so 10 Folders and We Still," 26 January 1995, on-line posting, America Online, ABC Bulletin Board.

23 JM4628, "My Life is Over!" 27 January 1995, on-line posting, America Online, ABC Bulletin Board.

24 Nancypup, "Come Back!" 27 January 1995, on-line posting, America Online, ABC Bulletin Board.

III PEDAGOGY AND POWER

Power Rangers at Preschool: Negotiating Media
in Child Care Settings   Ellen Seiter

Young children do a considerable amount of their television viewing in group care settings. Videotapes make their way to the classroom as show-and-tell objects, or simply as new gifts that children are eager to bring to school and show their teachers and fellow students. VCRs, television sets, and video collections are standard supplies in day-care centers and preschools. But television viewing at school involves complex negotiations among teachers, parents, and children. The quantity of television viewing in day-care settings is frequently used to grade centers as to quality. If too much television viewing is done, middle-class parents often complain to teachers or center directors. Some day-care centers claim superiority over home-based day care precisely because of their restrictions of television watching. For this reason, the corporate day-care chain Kindercare has written policies limiting the amount of time videos may be viewed at school and specifying what types may be watched (such as G or PG only).

Baby-sitting young children is one of the things television does best. It is undeniably handy for calming children down, confining them to one area, reducing noise in the classroom, and postponing demands for adult attention. But such uses of television are widely condemned by the vast majority of early childhood professionals.[1] Problems around television viewing in institutional settings reflect the ambiguous definition of these child care spaces as intermediaries between the home (where television viewing is usually frequent and acceptable) and school (where explicit learning, rather than merely child care, is supposed to be taking place).

How do rules about television in child care settings help produce status differences and work to stratify/segment the child care market? How do informal theories about media effects support different conceptions of childhood, as well as different definitions of the work of caregiving and teaching? How do women—and child care is, statistically, women's work—perceive their work as media gatekeepers? To study how children's popular media fit in the ecology of the preschool, I interviewed preschool teachers and child care workers to discern their attitudes and beliefs about media effects.[2] Interviews also focused on the extent to which television is talked about with children by their caregivers outside the home. I attempted to record the range of praise and criticism for children's television among child care professionals—and the schemes of value at work in judging some videos as unacceptable for classroom use and others acceptable. I also gathered information on teachers' leisure time media preferences and their own childhood experiences with television in order to correlate these with perceptions about children's television viewing.

This research extends to the preschool setting of Bob Hodge and David Tripp's work on Australian elementary schoolteachers' derogatory attitudes toward television and ways that talk about television is systematically discouraged at school.[3] Hodge and Tripp pose the important question, "What does the school tell the child about television?" To study this, they hired ten teachers to observe television references made by their own students. They found that "there appeared to be a general understanding from the children that television was not part of school and that it should be kept quite separate."[4] Further, Hodge and Tripp noted the strategies that students develop for censoring their own speech about television in order to avoid teacher disapproval. This study suggests that television is part of the hidden curriculum in many grade schools: children learn that teachers generally hold derogatory attitudes toward television, that some genres—such as news and documentary—are preferred over others, and that television rates very low in comparison to other cultural forms. Hodge and Tripp are concerned that low-income children, already at risk for poor school performance, are most disadvantaged by television's place in the hidden curriculum.

Preschool classrooms offer a special set of circumstances in which to investigate the relationship of teachers to television.[5] Most children now spend years in day care or preschool, gaining extensive experience there with caregivers' attitudes toward television before arriving at the public kindergarten. The children at preschool are younger and less mature in their reading of adult cues (verbal and nonverbal), so we may expect that socialization about television may be more overt and involve more explicit messages than in the grade school classroom. Thus, day-care centers and preschools provide an opportunity to study early tracking in the signals that students receive about schoolwork, television, and adult expectations. I argue in this essay that hierarchies of media taste interact with and are legitimated by teachers' beliefs about child development and media effects.

Preschools and day-care centers are highly stratified, and vary greatly in terms of teacher salaries, tuition costs, and levels of public subsidy. The occupation is differently interpreted and enacted by women from different socioeconomic communities, with the most highly paid and educated women emphasizing their role as teachers, and the lowest paid stressing the type of care associated with mothers such as providing affection, nutrition, and training in personal hygiene.[6] Upper-middle-class preschools also accomplish some of the important work of inculcating tastes that was formerly reserved for the home. As Randal Collins points out in a discussion of women's occupations and their location in the cultural sphere, this work may not be adequately compensated, but it is vital nevertheless:

> Women live subjectively—and, in terms of their successes, objectively as well—much more in the realm of status than in the realm of class. This might make it seem that women are living mainly in a realm of illusion, a cultural fluff floating over the hard material basis of our society. But the capitalist economy of the twentieth century has increasingly derived its dynamism from the permeation of status symbolism into the material objects of everyday consumption. . . . The activities of women, in both the production and consumption of status culture, may well constitute the feature that keeps modern capitalism alive.[7]

My research indicates that status production is a crucial part of the work of professional preschool teachers—as it is with many pink-collar occupations—and the aspect of their work that may be most valued by the women themselves.

Compare the following scenarios. At a suburban Montessori school, popular videos or films are banned from the classroom. Viewing is rare, confined either to 16 mm films borrowed from the children's library or National Geographic specials. Talk about television or play involving popular characters—even on the playground—is expressly forbidden. Across town at a low-income day-care center, kids watch network television programs, and freely play rowdy Power Rangers games. Along with their caregiver, the children celebrate character theme days, where they dress in purple for *Barney* or enact plays of *Beauty and the Beast*. These case studies represent the two most divergent examples of all the centers I have studied: the most affluent and the poorest, the most inclusive media environment and the most restricted. The majority of schools fell somewhere in between in their rules over media culture in the classroom and anx-

ieties over media effects on children. These two settings, however, vividly capture the ways in which beliefs about media effects—as well as other kinds of
ideologies—impact media use in the preschool environment. I have chosen
them to illustrate ways that rules about television and toys emerge from the
intersection of the material circumstances of the care setting, and the beliefs
and experiences of the teachers.

Case Study 1: A Montessori School

Sara Kitses has taught at the suburban Montessori school for twenty-three
years. Her half-day classroom combines children between the ages of three and
six. She has a total of fifty students in her morning and afternoon classes. Sara
describes her students as representing "very little economic diversity," mostly
white, with a number of "Oriental children." Tuition is about the highest in the
community, nearly $400 per month for less than four hours a day. The Mon-
tessori school is attended largely by the children of attorneys, physicians, and
university professors. Sara is the highest paid teacher in the community.
Around fifty years of age, Sara holds a bachelor's degree in addition to specialized Montessori training.

More than any other teacher in the study, Sara denied having any knowledge
of popular children's programming (she asked, "Who's Barney?" during the
interview). She rigorously excludes videotapes from the classroom, even banning widely accepted Disney feature films, Disney Sing-Along videos, and PBS
programs.[8] In her long experience in the classroom, she has picked up a
passing acquaintance with the names of programs and characters she herself
has never seen—usually to marshal forces to ban them from the classroom. The
only video from a list of fifty currently popular programs that Sara had ever
shown at school was an animated version of Dr. Seuss.

Sara requires parents to attend a meeting before the school year begins
(unlike many centers, where children come and go from month to month,
Sara's school enrolls children only in the fall). She advises parents that the best
thing to do with television is keep it off, but the least they must do is monitor
what their children are watching extremely carefully and remain with them
during viewing. Sara commands considerable respect from the parents and
openly claims the status of an expert with regard to the children—one who
knows more than the parent. A great deal of her identity is invested in being a
professional teacher. The Montessori school is typical of that segment of the
child care market that promises preparation for entry into the competitive
world of the grade school. Sara's status depends, in part, on the degree to
which parents grant her the power to evaluate their children's social and aca-

demic skills. Television threatens both the children's cognitive development and her own professional standing; if children can learn from videos, and be entertained through their childhood years, why would they need a Montessori education? Her mind was made up a long time ago that television is a very negative influence on everyone; for more than a decade of her married life and throughout her children's early years, Sara had no television set.

Sara's disdain for television dictates her selection of classroom media. She prefers showing 16 mm films and filmstrips to the students (by her estimate, she uses film three or four times more often than video), nearly all of them adaptations of children's literature. Videotapes are restricted to programs such as National Geographic specials. While Sara spoke about exhaustion in her job, she does not consider media screenings to be appropriate for teachers to use as a break to do other chores in the classroom (she has a large number of assistant teachers in her class). She monitors the screenings vigilantly, and operates the 16 mm projector herself. Her assistant is in charge of supervising the children during the screenings.

Children and parents bring videotapes to school, and occasionally Sara will show the tape if it is educational, if she has prescreened it, or if the parent is someone she trusts. All of her recent examples of videos she allowed were nonfiction: a computer-animated video with an exclusively musical sound track by Philip Glass, distributed by the upscale Nature Company; or *Road Construction Ahead*, an independent video for children featuring no words, just music. Children can bring objects from home every day to set on a viewing table. The rule is that whatever is brought to school must be educational, a concept that Sara reports the children and parents have no trouble grasping.

Sara's complaints about television and children cluster around issues of fantasy and passivity. Primary is the objection that television comes from adults, it does not originate with the child.

> I really believe there's a lot in children, and if you give them a proper environment, they will act upon it and will be constantly learning. They're very eager to learn. And if what you give them is a lot of television and passive stuff, or it's all coming at them, they have to make no decisions whatsoever except to turn it off or on. I don't think that's . . . [what] we should be advocating.[9]

Television is commercial and makes children want to buy things they don't need: Sara is interested in environmentalism and reducing material wants. Television is frightening for children and introduces them to material inappropriate for their age. Sara even dislikes *Sesame Street* for its "silliness" and presumption that children's attention spans are quite short. Television is simplistic in its advocacy of violent solutions to problems. Sara finds the sex-role stereotypes, and focus on appearance and decoration, offensive in media targeted at girls. Most important, television isn't real.

Sara believes that children have a tenuous hold on reality at this age and teachers should guide them toward reality—thus, her heavy emphasis on nonfiction materials. Television pushes children into fantasy and leaves them "perpetually confused." Television stories, unlike some more naturally occurring kinds of role-play, are not creative play:

> Certainly, make-believe and role-playing are wonderful and important things. But I don't consider that a fantasy that's being perpetuated by adults. That's coming from within the child, and fantasy coming from within the child is a good thing, but when they are playing games, like Ninja Turtles, they start playing Ninja Turtles on the playground, that's not creative play. It's something that's been given them, so I make a distinction between those two things.

She backs up her feelings about television with some stiff rules: no talk about it on the playground, no television play, conversations with her about television programs are discouraged, clothing with media characters is not allowed because it distracts children (parents are informed of this on the first day). Sara spoke of one boy who was obsessed with what she believed was Nintendo, and would talk at great length to the other children about the story and plotline. "It was very boring. The other kids didn't like it," she claimed. When the boy turned to talking to the teachers, Sara became increasingly forceful in restricting such talk:

> I had decided that I had a limit to listening to him. So when he would come to school, I'd let him talk and then I'd say, "Let's focus on the environment and what you might . . . " I didn't tell him not to talk about it, I just redirected his attention. "What would you like to choose today? Can I help you make a choice?" Trying to focus him in the classroom. Finally it came to the point where we had to say to him after that initial time, "While you're at school, we want you to just be talking about school things," because he was throwing the other kids off.

Reading between the lines, I would suspect that the other students' reactions to such television talk may not have been solely one of boredom, but that some amount of imitation of these unwanted behaviors led Sara to lay down the law.

Curiously, these rules apply much more leniently to girls, who tend to play in groups separate from boys. Sara knows that the girls play games in secret based on *Aladdin* or *Beauty and the Beast* while they are on the playground. But

Female superheroes

the girls only play these games out of her hearing, and because it does not create disruptions, she does not intervene. Also, Sara does not enforce the no-characters rule with the girls' clothing, allowing them to make their way into the classroom dressed in media-promoting shoes, socks, and T-shirts. She does enforce a ban on jewelry, and encourages parents to dress girls in slacks and sensible shoes.

Sara explained that there is a costume area in the classroom and that she has brought in Greek, Indian, and Native American costumes. When the children enact a play, the teacher generates the story, acts as the narrator, and assigns parts to the children: The Three Little Pigs, The Billy Goats Gruff, or The Little Engine That Could are examples of stories she might use. I was wondering why Sara saw no contradiction between these guided forms of dramatic play and her position on outside influences. Does an interest in Greece come from within the child, for instance, or is it Sara's? Is acting out parts in a prescribed story any more creative than acting out parts in a play based on television? When I first introduced myself to her, I said that I believed television effects were often misunderstood and overestimated, so that I could discuss what I perceived to be contradictory positions openly with teachers during the follow-up interview. On the second interview, then, I probed Sara on this point directly:

> Sara: I like to see them doing role-playing kinds of things that might put them in an adult model. House kinds of things or positive adult kinds of things where they're enacting something good instead of something horrible. I don't like it when they get involved in fantasy that's created by the media, because it doesn't go anywhere, and it's not coming, again, from within the child. They're reenacting something they've seen. Part of that's inevitable, part of it's how they learn. But . . .
>
> Ellen: How could you explain the difference, then, if they're acting out something that's from a book? Like you said that you do plays from books?
>
> S: That's a fairly structured activity when we do these plays. You take on this role and you are that particular role in the play. You're supposed to follow the story line. We do that at two levels. One is just informally, in the circle, and the other is this play that these older kids put on every year. And they understand that quite well.
>
> E: So you see this in a different category because that's a structured . . .
>
> S: Exactly. The teacher is guiding the children into that, whereas the other is out on the playground.

Sara is certain that her role in the classroom is to provide authority and to keep the children under control. Television—as a video shown in class or as references in play or on a T-shirt—symbolizes a loss of control for her. Not only is television a world that she is almost completely unfamiliar with, but—without viewing it—she has an overwhelming feeling that it undermines everything that her own classroom stands for. Sara's complaints are not the more common ones about rowdy behavior or aggression, although she mentioned these in passing. Instead, they are phrased in the language of child psychology: television delays the achievement of the developmental stage when children can discern the difference between reality and fantasy. But her goals are embedded in the dispositions of the class to which she and her students belong. By emphasizing creativity as a spontaneously produced result of children's play, she legitimates her role as an educator in aesthetics as well as behavior.

In Sara's scheme of value, books are basically good and television is basically bad; film falls somewhere in between. Unlike most of the other teachers, however, for whom any reading is viewed as positive, Sara is unwilling to accept just any book. She discourages the purchase of "grocery store books,"

If television is the school's bad screen, computers are its good ones.

such as *The Berenstain Bears*, as well as any media-related books, such as Disney stories. While her principles stress the generation of fantasy from within the child, she approves of the enactment—on the playground or in the classroom— of stories from children's literature: these forms of imitation are not recognized as imitation per se.[10] Nonfiction is preferred to fiction in the choice of videos and for computer software. The children are encouraged to write "research papers" on topics of interest to them: this, I would contend, is the highest activity on Sara's scale of value, combining as it does writing skills, an ordered display of encyclopedic knowledge, and the rehearsal of forms of work that will certainly be required in grade school.

If television is the school's bad screen, to be used sparingly and purposefully, computers are its good ones, and access is open throughout the school day, limited only by the number of terminals available. Sara speaks with pride about running "ahead of the pack" because her school budget allocates money for computers and sees computers as "an absolutely critical moment of information right now for young children." The classroom has one computer with a CD-ROM, and another set up for WordPerfect and Logo, a program that teaches how to program. A sign-up sheet and two chairs are placed at each computer, but the children are allowed to work alone if they wish. Sara is "flabbergasted" by the speed at which children learn to operate the mouse, and she uses computers heavily for teaching the alphabet and reading skills.

Sara says that the computers are fun for her because they represent something new after so many years of teaching. Comparing a CD-ROM to video, she thinks of it this way:

> They're interactive. They [the children] have to make some choices as to what they want to do. It's much more informational than videos, so they're learning a lot. And there are levels of difficulty, so I find that the five and six year old is going to a higher level of difficulty, so he can read and . . . they'll choose things that are challenging to them and interact with them. They're much more popular with boys than girls, but it might be because . . . I don't have any programs on the CD-ROMs yet that are other than mammals and the San Diego Zoo . . . [and] the dinosaur program—the boys tend to dominate it. I think it's better than videos because it's much more interactive, but it can't be their entire life.

It is not surprising, of course, that virtually no television viewing was noted in Sara's media diary, although she had shown a nonfiction tape, *Road Construction Ahead*, on two occasions that week in her classroom. Sara had warned me at the first interview:

> You're going to find . . . I hate television. I really want to devote my time outside of school to artistic endeavors. I'm a photographer, and I've got this incredibly strong feeling that if I don't use my time well, I'll never use it. I'll just be like everybody else, watching all this stuff, and I read a lot. But that's a choice. I choose what book. I don't turn on the television and make somebody else make those choices. So I am kind of extreme.

Sara's resistance to completing the media diary was reflected in her failure to bring the diary with her to the follow-up interview. She did not begin to keep the diary until several days after our interview. In her diary, Sara records daily listening to National Public Radio, both *Morning Edition* and *All Things Considered*. Her reading that week was Carl Jung's *Memories, Dreams, Reflections*. She also watched two rented videos, both of them arty costume dramas: *The Bostonians* and *Howard's End*. When pressed about any passive viewing Sara might have done, she explained that *Oprah!* was being watched by her daughters several afternoons, but she remained apart in the kitchen with her radio.

Despite Sara's harsh judgment of contemporary children's television, she spoke fondly of her television viewing as a child. Her parents paid little attention to what she watched. Television was a novelty, and her family was early in getting a set. She never watched cartoons, but remembers *Ozzie and Harriet*, *My Friend Flicka*, *The Ed Sullivan Show*, *Superman*, *The Jack Benny Show*, and *Lassie*, a show for which she felt strong affection. In our interview, she commented that for her, television had

had a positive effect, because I was seeing children in other families and parents that were relating in a very idealistic way. Things were wonderful, and everyone was looking up to a glorious future, so I feel good about the television that I watched, especially *Lassie* because I loved animals so much. This dog did all these wonderful things in relationship to this boy, and his relationship to the family.

Sara's image of television during its golden age is overwhelmingly positive and, although she has had so little viewing experience over the past twenty years, she compares it negatively to contemporary television: "They addressed heroic kinds of things, solving problems, moral values, ethical values. I think a lot of that has gone."

Sara's belief system about children and the media typifies that of those with the most training and investment in the professionalization of child care. She subscribes to a developmental view that emphasizes cognitive deficits, and thus, children's incomprehension of television and films.[11] Sara's unfamiliarity with television and her refusal to listen to children talk about it, however, makes for an extremely limited basis on which to formulate her judgments. In fact, Sara herself is somewhat incompetent as a television viewer, and she uses this studied ignorance about it to signal her erudition—she fears being "just like everybody else." By completely discrediting knowledge about television in the classroom and limiting media use to those forms—such as 16 mm—that are more difficult to operate, Sara also maintains her authority over the children.

Hodge and Tripp construe television as a barrier between teachers and students. Middle-class teachers understandably might wish to bar television from the classroom because, in part, they know less about it than their students do:

> Not only are they untrained to deal with it, but it so often challenges their own knowledge and experience of life and understanding in general. In comparison with most teachers, the average pupil watches a great deal more television and quite different television programmes. Whereas 20 years ago teachers could, in a very real way, safely assume that their pupils knew a great deal less about everything than they did, today the children often know a great deal more than their teachers, albeit about things such as Batman, Spiderman, Superheroes.[12]

Hodge and Tripp found that while teachers do not overtly punish pupils for bringing their television experience to school, signals are nevertheless clear that it is not a legitimate topic for discussion.

Running underneath the discourse about children's incompetent distinctions between reality and fantasy, and the fragility of their comprehension of narrative, is Sara's belief in the need for adults to shelter children from all that is too intensely emotional, dramatic, or peer oriented because of their moral deficiency, their easy corruptibility. Thus, an essentially romantic view of the innocence of children is masked by the discourse of Piagetian cognitive development.

Reinforcing these notions of deleterious media effects is an equally strong belief in the need for explicit teaching in the area of aesthetics. Systems of distinction extend to clothing (it should not be too feminine or representational; it should not be purchased in discount stores) as well as books (they should not be bought at the grocery store; they should not be mass market). Sara is heavily invested in both what is acquired and how it is acquired—a distinction that increases in importance with status. She confines herself to a narrow range of media forms, those most closely allied with books. She prefers 16 mm film and CD-ROM as modes of delivery over videos, despite their greater ease and affordability. As Pierre Bourdieu points out, the more difficult the means of acquisition, the more distinguished the cultural goods.[13] Sara risks the appearance of authoritarianism (with her dress code), arbitrariness (with her censorship rules), and severity (with her banning of toys from the classroom). But if her job is viewed as one of status production and the inculcation of taste, the strictness of her rules and her lack of involvement with nurturing behaviors begin to make sense.

Girls and boys mount different forms of rebellion, and have different susceptibilities to vulgarity. The girls gravitate toward things that violate the aesthetic code (Disney characters) and the ideology of gender neutrality (frilly dresses). The boys tend to violate the decorum of the classroom by moving in too close to others, being too loud, or dominating conversation. The boys' attachment to media is pathologized more so than the girls' because it requires more direct intervention by the teachers to bring it under control. The genres that boys gravitate toward as media fans—science fiction, superheroes, action/adventure—are associated with the derring-do masculinity that is especially disapproved of. These boys are to develop intellectual, not physical abilities. Girls simply receive less attention altogether; Sara is disappointed by their lack of curiosity about the computer, for example, but she also finds that the girls conform to her standards as good students more readily.

Within the upper-middle-class milieu of the Montessori school, enforcing the ban on television should not be viewed as a marginal part of Sara's job or a personal idiosyncrasy. The ban is, as Sara herself believes, a crucial element of her work. Its justifications in terms of theories of childhood development masks a more class-conscious motivation: distinguishing these children and their education from that of the common masses. As Collins describes this type of work: "The higher classes . . . observing the cultural style of the classes below them, engage in reflexive role distancing, once again re-establishing their superiority to those who have a less sophisticated view of cultural symbols."[14] While her vigilance in enforcing these norms may pit her against some parents at the school (who are left with many more hours of the day in which to occupy their children while keeping them away from undesirable media, and generally fail to hold to Sara's high standards), parents acquiesce for the sake of securing a successful future in the education system.

Case Study 2: Gloria's Place

Along with her seventy-four-year-old mother, Gloria Williams owns and teaches in a center called Gloria's Place, which she operates out of her home in an older, integrated neighborhood close to downtown. This center is a federally funded provider that offers twenty-four-hour care for children from infancy upward. In the interviews, Gloria relates with pride that she is the only licensed black caregiver for children in town. Her influence in the community extends well beyond the children into the lives of their parents, most of whom are divorced. All of her mothers and fathers work for pay outside the home, unlike those with children at the Montessori school, where the half-day program necessitates having one parent at home (meaning usually that the father is receiving something that can serve as a "family wage"). A forty-three-year-old woman from New York with a degree in computer programming, Gloria switched from her office job to child care at the age of twenty-five. While not college educated in early childhood education, she is well read on the subject and receives a lot of training in the form of workshops as a Title 20 provider. Gloria's mother works with her and has taught her a great deal about child rearing. Recalling her own childhood, Gloria mentioned that there always seemed to be children around the house that her mother was caring for. Gloria charges a sliding fee: "I can't see a person making $200 a week and then you're taking over half of that in day care, you know, I can't, so I have a scale where I go with the person's income."[15]

Gloria conceives of her work broadly, combining the role of foster mother and teacher. She strives to prepare children for school by teaching them letters and numbers, and encouraging them to be autonomous from adults. The emphasis is on giving the children experiences such as trips to the library that their parents don't have time for. Gloria's interview took place during Black History Month, and that week the library books she read to the children clustered around that theme: *The Black Women's Poetry Book*, *The Drinking Gourd*, and biographies of Sojourner Truth and Dr. Martin Luther King. But she also

stresses the work of providing nutritious food, a safe environment, and affection. She was more frank than any other teacher we spoke to about how trying
this kind of work can be:

> Some days . . . I mean, if they had a bad day at home, they're going to try
> to carry it on through here. [Mimicking the children's voices] Don't look at me.
> Don't touch me. Leave me alone. He's looking cross-eyed at me. What's
> he staring at? He touched me. He's got my Crayola. I was playing with that
> block. I don't want this. I'm not hungry. I don't like this kind of juice. Why
> can't we have chocolate milk? Stuff like that. Things like that [make] you
> want to just put their coats on and march them right back out. So some
> days it's not worth getting up, but you know you have to.

According to Gloria, the local wages are especially low, and she claims that
she made twice as much, with all the advantages of a regular schedule (such as
weekends, evenings, and vacations free), in her old job. Typical of family child
care providers, Gloria is threatened by many of the hazards of this type of work:
burnout, emotional attachment to children she lacks the authority to protect,
and frustrations stemming from low pay and inadequate funds to properly care
for children.[16] But it is clear that a primary incentive is her dedication to the
children she cares for, both as a foster mother and day-care operator.

Gloria's approach to television viewing was keenly interested and unapolo-
getic. She shows tapes frequently and lets children choose from television off
the air (home-based day care is much more likely to have cable hookup than
public day-care centers, thus greatly increasing the options for television viewing). Of all the teachers interviewed, Gloria was the biggest fan of *Sesame Street*
(which she much prefers to *Barney*), and her children watch the PBS lineup (as
well as visiting the local PBS station each year to appear on air during fund
drives). They also watch commercial television and choose from her large
selection of purchased videotapes, including every Disney movie ever released.

Throughout the interview, Gloria chatted freely about a wide range of television programs and films: she was full of information and opinions about
them. Gloria had strong preferences about children's television: for *He-Man*
over *Power Rangers*; *Captain Planet* over World Wrestling Federation characters.
She does not impose her preferences, however, when the children select programs to watch. Television is used in the mornings, when children are arriving;
at lunchtime to "quieten [sic] them down"; and at pickup time around 5:00
P.M. Sometimes they have special character days, when they dress in special
clothes or colors and enact stories based on their favorite characters. There are
no restrictions on clothing or toys, and Gloria is familiar with a large variety of
items—shoelaces to backpacks—with licensed characters, as well as the latest

Superhero play at preschool.

toys and what is available at stores in town. She lets children bring anything to the center with the exception of toy guns and knives.

In discussing children and television, Gloria refuted the argument against fantasy as a developmentally dangerous activity. She herself is familiar with a broad range of film and television genres, and gave the most informed and sophisticated readings of popular culture—those closest to the opinions of media studies academics, in fact, of all the teachers we interviewed. In striking contrast to Sara's concerns that children become lost in television fantasy, Gloria described her students as easily able to understand when something is "nothing but make-believe."

> Well, you've got to go on the cartoon thing that they know it's make-believe in the first place. And I think they're cutting the kids really short if they don't think kids have it in their brain that this is make-believe, that you cannot do it. It's like *The Three Stooges.* We knew we couldn't do those things and still be alive with a normal brain. That's the way it is with the cartoons. And the parents should know that they do have some imagination. And that it's nothing but make-believe. There are some violent cartoons, but you know the person [cartoon character] always gets up and goes on about its business or you see it [alive and unhurt] in the next section. So I think the child knows that it's make-believe.

Gloria reported that the children talked about television or movies every morning on their arrival to her place, and frequently described to her the plots of entire movies that they had seen over the weekend. The children at Gloria's

Place are reported to be much more sophisticated about their viewing and understanding of genre rules. One reason may be the relaxed atmosphere at the center, and another, Gloria's openness to listening to conversation about television.

> *Ellen:* Do you find the kids are pretty good at telling the stories of things they've seen?
> *Gloria:* Yeah. A lot of them are. Some of them just roll two stories into one. But I usually let it go like that, if they're telling the story, they're telling it their way. If I'm reading a book, I'll straighten out the story. But when it's their time to tell the story I let it go. But it depends on when they want to talk. It's just when they want to, it's right there. But if you ask them on command, forget it. They're not going to do anything. You know . . . or you can creep up on them and hear them telling the stories. But if you ask them to get up front of their own peers to tell the same story—forget it.

Her careful attention to children's play scenarios has also influenced her opinion of television's promotion of violence. She seemed to have a more accurate, vivid memory of play—and of movies and television—than many of the other teachers we interviewed. Her childhood as one of seven children—with four brothers—may have promoted a much higher tolerance for physically active play than other interviewees as well. She thinks of rowdy play as substantially similar to the kinds of play of her childhood. For example, she reported that Ninja Turtles, which seemed to be universally reviled among preschool teachers (and which Gloria also found uninteresting), was on second take, nothing more than cowboys and Indians:

> Everything that's on television today is spinned off of something that we've seen back in the fifties or the sixties. And it's just made it more vivid, more violent I think. But the basic message is the same, to me it is. You know, you see Roy Rogers hiding behind a tree or a mountain. Or you see the Ninja Turtles hiding behind a streetcar. They've got a tunnel instead of a mountain. They still hide. They're still waiting to surprise somebody when they come out. Or they're still defending their territory. So John Wayne and the cowboys were defending his ranch, well, they're defending their sewer or raft or wherever. . . . I don't see the difference.

Gloria's house has lots of open space, with broken-down furniture or no furniture at all—one reason for her calm attitude toward physical play. Further, she has a smaller number of children and does not feel compelled by the decorum of having a classroom space. As long as they are not "throwing furniture across the room" or landing punches, she does not interfere. Gloria reported a much higher level of engagement in rowdy play by girls in her classroom:

> Oh yes. We've got kickbox and *Karate Kid. X-men.* What's that show I didn't like. *Power Rangers.* They play a lot of that. That's their karate. They really try to kick, action, do the flips like the *Power Rangers.* On the GI Joe they get down and try to hide in little places and spring out on you. Or try to do that *Karate Kid* move on one foot and all that stuff. Now I do have some girls that will get in there with them. They'll stick with them just like the boys do, you know. Try the karate stuff.

She also described boys—preschool and school-age—playing with Barbies and baby dolls at her place after school (noting that the boys would not do this at kindergarten or their own homes: "Gotta be a macho male when you go home. Dad's not gonna let you play."). While all of the other teachers we interviewed felt that popular media increased gender stereotypes, and segregated boys and girls in play, the play that Gloria portrayed was the least gender stereotyped or segregated. "A lot of the boys still play with dolls and get all the baby dolls dressed up . . . it's no big deal. And they can put that down, go watch *Power Rangers,* come back and pick up the baby doll."

In her own media diary, Gloria reported a wide variety of choices: videos, books on tape, books, radio, and music. Her selections were eclectic in range, and she seemed to have relatively little interest in women's genres such as soap operas or made-for-television movies. Her favorite movies feature Jean Claude Van Damme and Steven Segal; her favorite shows are news magazines; and she watches all sports except golf. She spoke enthusiastically about the media and the ways it provides her with entertainment; television is especially important to her because she is restricted to her home/workplace seven days a week with little or no opportunity for vacations.

Gloria's assessment of media and consumer culture were by no means un-critical. She was keenly aware of the manipulative effect of marketing strategies (such as the need kids feel to collect *all* the Power Rangers in a set). She was matter-of-fact in describing the best way to deal with children's material desires:

> If you set your child down—well, two and three year olds, you really can't reason with them—but four, five, and six year olds, if they're giving you a hard time, you just tell them, "Hey, this is the budget. This is what we can have. You can pick two of them out of this. This is all. That's it.

She often lectures parents about the need to keep children away from adult films and graphic violence. Indeed, when children choose to watch one of the violent action movies that Gloria herself most enjoys, she pulls the plug on the set on a regular basis. Moreover, she directly teaches children the limitations of consumer spending. One of her greatest concerns is the way that parents substitute consumer goods for parental companionship. She advises parents to turn off the television set and play cards or board games with their children.

Gloria watches the media carefully for black characters: she was more perceptive and accurate than other teachers interviewed in noting the various types of characters on different shows. Gloria also noticed the changing demographics of action figures to include more black characters, even though they are rarely the main hero. She speculated that Teenage Mutant Ninja Turtles were popular with her children, most of whom are African American, because they seem to remain outside racial categories.

When asked to envision the kinds of changes she would like to see in her job, she spoke about the broader contexts of children's lives. She was the only interviewee who imagined structural changes (in the legal system, in governmental support) as a means of bettering children's lives:

> I'd probably have the government pay for everything. At a nice rate—not a low rate. And have them take some of the burdens off the parents that couldn't afford it, you know, they wouldn't have to go through so much red tape. And since I'm a foster mother I'd probably if I ever see, well I do have some kids that are abused, I would change that system, so the parents wouldn't have them anymore. One time, you're out. If it's a little thing, I'll give them two times, but that's it. I wouldn't give them on back. And make sure if the kids came not dressed right, if the parents couldn't afford it, I'd have some kind of funds just out there and get what they need. If parents didn't take care of it, I'll just keep it here. If they go out they wouldn't look like second-class citizens. That's my idea. And everybody had enough to eat. A lot of my kids don't.

Two Women, Two Worlds Apart

What produces the stark differences between these two women—both with over two decades of experience in child care, both highly dedicated to their jobs—in their beliefs about television's effects on children?

Gloria sees children as active users of television, and this view is based on an acceptance of television as a normal influence on play routines. Her familiarity with genre rules on the screen and in children's play allows her to see violence as symbolic and conventional. Gloria rates her children's cognitive skills more highly than Sara rates the Montessori children's. Gloria expects children to be able to handle violent content on children's shows, and is confident that they

Student drawings of superheroes.

can distinguish between media fiction and reality. This assessment is based on her close observation of children's play and television viewing, and frequent casual conversations with kids about the media, in the context of a warmly affectionate relationship. She accepts the children's immersion in a separate peer culture and does not expect to share their predilections. Gloria has nothing invested in improving the children's taste. Indeed, she does not expect to interfere with children in their play or dissuade them from their interest in popular culture. She is also more comfortable with overt forms of control than Sara is: rather than attempting to "redirect their attention," as Sara phrases it, Gloria just says "no." The boundaries between adulthood and childhood are clear at Gloria's Place.

Sara is at once completely unfamiliar with television and absolutely certain that it has a detrimental effect on children. Yet her classroom rules and avoidance of television during her leisure time make her a poor observer of the phenomenon of its effects. Sara's classroom is a place where children are supposed to get on with the work of adulthood, and this does not include the idle pleasures of television viewing. In some ways, the boundaries between childhood and adulthood are more blurred at this school. "Work" is valued over play; books and computers over television and toys. Children are taught to work quietly, alone at intellectual tasks. Bothering other children with talking or gregariousness is not permitted. When 16 mm films are shown, the students are expected to hold still and remain silent, thus a passive viewing posture is enforced. Her classroom is a microcosm of the environments the children can expect to experience throughout their school and adult lives as middle-class professionals. Sara openly defines her role in terms of educating tastes, monitoring and preselecting cultural goods. One of the most important features of her work, then, is to sharpen the distinction between children's mass culture and educational materials, and banishing television as a subject of conversation or an activity is a linchpin in Sara's strategy.

Two competing views of childhood and the work of caregivers operate in these case studies, and are manifested in subsets of cultural and media forms, cultural goods that are included or excluded from the environment. It would be a mistake, however, to view Gloria's center as market saturated and Sara's classroom as free from commercial influences. In some ways, Gloria's childrearing methods (the straightforward denial approach), her encouragement of group play rather than solitary activities, and her advocacy of traditional game playing, such as cards and checkers, as the best way for parents and children to spend time together, are examples of practices relatively untouched by the market. John R. Hall has noted that the working class may have more autonomy from the market than the middle classes:

[T]he poor will find themselves exposed to the cheapest of petty commercial culture. . . . And they will be the targets of culturally distinctive state- and religiously organized welfare and charity programs. These realities would suggest that the poor partake of what Bourdieu calls a "dominated" cultural aesthetic. Yet the poor do not engage in commercial consumption in the same way that more monied popular and elite classes do. . . . Paradoxically, the relatively greater distance of the poor from commercial culture will leave room for the greater importance of "quasi-folk" cultures made in the ongoing practices of the people who live socially marginal lives.[17]

Despite Sara's objections to the commercialization of childhood, her classroom is, in certain ways, more invested in consumer goods and dependent on high-ticket items such as computers, CD-ROMs, educational materials, and books. Ironically, middle-class adults spend enormous amounts of money in the attempt to shield children from mass-market goods and television, and to avoid advertising that directly targets them.[18] The consumer goods available for children's use at Montessori are more controlled by adults. While the argument is often made that children should be kept away from television because they cannot understand it, in fact, it is generally the ease with which they become media experts that may frighten adults.

The Montessori school represents the type of institution afforded status by those class factions predominant in the academy and most similar to the petit bourgeois intellectuals at the center of Bourdieu's study in *Distinction*. But it would be a mistake to see Sara's system of cultural representations as the only legitimated one in this community, recognized by one and all as the superior system. In Bourdieu's model, distinctions are used to legitimate the privileges of those with more education and money, who envision themselves as superior to those whose tastes differ from their own. But Hall has criticized Bourdieu's model as too holistic, and rigidly tied to class rather than cultural (and subcultural) distinctions:

[C]ultural distinctions do not represent some generalized currency of "legal tender" among all individuals and status groups. . . . Cultural capital, after all, is good only (if at all) in social worlds where a person lives and acts, and the value that it has depends on sometimes ephemeral distinctions of currency in those particular social worlds.[19]

This incommensurability of cultural distinctions may be found in the child care market. To many parents—including some of those enrolled in her school—Sara's strict rules about television are dismissed and ignored at home. Because she is a woman, working for relatively low pay in a female-segregated job, Sara's authority is fragile. Nor would the type of care Sara's classroom offers be appreciated by all parents equally. Many value experiential knowledge of child rearing, and the emotional availability of the caregiver, as well as their children's pleasure and enjoyment, much more than the kind of formal curriculum that Montessori offers.

Television is cheap, easy, and plentiful, and children love to watch it. It is also pathologized—often unreasonably—by those with the most invested in status distinctions and the most at stake in professionalizing child care. As Julia Wrigley warns, in her useful discussion of professional expertise in child care,

> In the absence of a social movement demanding child care as a universal right, a segmented child care market will continue to provide one set of stigmatized services for the poor and other services geared to preparing middle-class children for entry into the competitive world of schooling. With such strong segregation of the children being served, caregivers can develop narrow ideologies that exacerbate the educational anxieties of one part of the population and emphasize the parental inadequacies of another.[20]

Beliefs about media effects on children are inextricably bound to adult use of the media, class position, and ideologies of childhood. Gloria's case study suggests that a less deleterious view of media effects may emerge from situations where adult caregivers know more about the media, invest less in status distinctions, and create an environment where children feel free to talk about media without inviting adult disapproval. Paradoxically, Sara's children, who live in the most affluent and protected homes, are viewed as gravely at risk of deleterious media effects, and in need of constant protection from the influences of media and consumer culture. I would argue that parents and teachers should worry less about the debilitating effects of television on affluent children and more about improving access to education for children against whom the odds are already stacked. More integration of popular culture into the early childhood curriculum may be an important strategy to make school more inviting to all children.

Notes

1   Television is either condemned or simply ignored by early childhood professionals. To read *Young Child* magazine, the publication of the National Association for the Education of Young Children, for example, is to believe that television does not exist in the lives of small children, so rarely do researchers refer to it.

2   During 1994 and 1995, my research assistants, Madelyn Ritrosky-Winslow and Karen Riggs, and I conducted in-depth interviews with twenty-four preschool teachers and child care workers in my local community. Child care professionals were interviewed at their place of employment, usually on a lunch hour or long break. At the end of the interview, subjects were asked to keep a one-week media diary of all media used both in the classroom and during their leisure time. Subjects were interviewed again one week later, and were compensated $100 for their time and expertise.

This research is part of a larger study that includes classroom observations of media references in children's play and conversation, and an ethnographic study of one preschool's attempt to design a prosocial superhero character, based on children's drawings and storytelling, under the guidance of a visiting artist in the schools.

3   Bob Hodge and David Tripp, *Children and Television: A Semiotic Approach* (Palo Alto, Calif.: Stanford University Press, 1986).

4   Ibid., 167.

5   See William Corsaro, *Friendship and Peer Culture in the Early Years* (Norwood, N.J.: Ablex, 1985). His excellent ethnography of children's play in preschool settings presents compelling evidence for the early development of a peer culture, one that at times sets itself off against adult expectations and values. Corsaro has had little to say, however, about television viewing or references in children's play.

6   For a historical account of the development of this segmentation and the role of the professional, see Julia Wrigley, "Children's Caregivers and Ideologies of Parental Inadequacy," in *Circles of Care: Work and Identity in Women's Lives*, ed. Emily K. Abel and Margaret K. Nelson (Albany: State University of New York Press, 1990), 304–5.

7   Randal Collins, "Women and the Production of Status Culture," in *Cultivating Differences: Symbolic Boundaries and the Making of Inequality*, ed. Michele Lamont and Marcel Fournier (Chicago: University of Chicago Press, 1992), 229.

8   These videos are so widely accepted that they were included in the libraries of every other center that I visited. Disney has achieved flabbergasting levels of market penetration—as well as acceptance by adults as unobjectionable material.

9   Sara Kitses, interview by author, January 1995. All subsequent quotes refer to this interview.

10 Sara prefers older classics. *The Little Engine That Could*, which she regularly uses, could be seen as a consumerist fantasy, with its preoccupation with a load of toys and goodies for children. The age of the book, I suspect, exempts it from criticism or scrutiny.

11 James Anderson discusses this notion in "Research on Children and Television: A Critique," *Journal of Broadcasting* 25 (1983): 395–400.

12 Hodge and Tripp, *Children and Television*, 170.

13 Pierre Bourdieu, *Distinction: A Social Critique of the Judgment of Taste*, trans. R. Nice (Cambridge, Mass.: Harvard University Press, 1984), 260–317.

14 Collins, "Status Culture," 217.

15 Gloria Williams, interview by author, February 1995. All subsequent quotes refer to this interview.

16 See Margaret K. Nelson, "Mothering Others' Children: The Experiences of Family Day Care Providers," in *Circles of Care: Work and Identity in Women's Lives*, ed. Emily K. Abel and Margaret K. Nelson (Albany: State University of New York Press, 1990), 210–33.

17 John R. Hall, "The Capital(s) of Cultures: A Nonholistic Approach to Status Situations, Class, Gender, and Ethnicity," in *Cultivating Differences: Symbolic Boundaries and the Making of*

Inequality, ed. Michele Lamont and Marcel Fournier (Chicago: University of Chicago Press, 1992), 265.

18 For an extended discussion of the educational market, see Ellen Seiter, *Sold Separately: Children and Parents in Consumer Culture* (New Brunswick, N.J.: Rutgers University Press, 1993).

19 Hall, "Capital(s) of Cultures," 275.

20 Wrigley, "Children's Caregivers," 305.

What Girls Want: The Intersections of Leisure and Power in Female Computer Game Play   *Heather Gilmour*

Once subordinate to other cultural forms, computer software, both pleasurable and practical, is moving from the margins to the center of culture and industry. Yet all too often, women and girls have been left on the sidelines of the high-tech playing field. Software industry developers and researchers have become increasingly aware of this disproportion, and a wave of software targeting the girl market is now being produced amid widespread discussions about what it is that girls really want in computer games. Developed by companies committed to girls, a few of these products, such as Mattel's *Fashion Barbie* and Girl Games's *Let's Talk about ME!* and *Let's Talk about ME! Too*, recently attained considerable success in the marketplace, proving what many have long suspected: that girls represent a target audience with great potential. Still, instead of challenging those entrenched divisions between boys and girls as players of electronic games, the discourse around these products has unfortunately tended to strengthen the traditional divisions between genders. Like some of their less successful predecessors (such as Her Interactive's *McKenzie & Co.*), these products feature girl-coded topics such as dating, fashion, hairstyles, and social protocols, leading both developers and consumers to conclude that "good" software must be specifically gendered.

Thus, girls continue to be essentialized as emotional, highly social, neo-Victorian subjects while males are defined as competitive and technologically inclined—an old binary that has come to inform discussions about new technology. Here is how one journalist "distilled" such information from various panels presented at the 1994 Computer Games Developers Conference:[1]

Men seem to like:	*Women seem to like:*
Repeating actions to get to the next level	Solving problems among characters
Action (shooting, running, jumping)	Storytelling and characters
Solving puzzles to overcome specific obstacles	Picking up clues and learning from characters in the game
Measuring their skills	Getting credit for trying
Turning off the sound	Using music to add to the fun
The challenge of negative comments from the game	Encouragement and support from the game
Lots of definite and rigid rules	Fewer, simpler, variable rules
Winning through competition and individual prowess	Winning through cooperation
Playing until someone wins	Quitting when they get bored

Such lists are commonplace not only in popular articles and from the proliferating educational panels at conferences and trade shows, but also in the research around electronic games. For example, Maria Klawa, a researcher of interactive games, concludes, "Boys and girls use software and video games differently. Girls like characters and relationships between them, while boys like fast action." Electronic Arts Kids spokesperson Catherine Wambach describes an interactive program that "had an area where you could construct a character and playhouse. The boys could have cared less. The girls wanted to bring that character out, and bring it into physical reality. They'd spend hours on the pictures, houses and clay forms of those characters."[2] Even when the evidence suggests the contrary, researchers provide explanations that seem designed to keep traditional binaries in place. For instance, the popularity of Nintendo's *Tetris* with female players would seem to counter the belief that women prefer character interaction, since this is a game of spatial relations with no characters. Yet Dr. Gini Graham Scott, a sociologist commissioned by Nintendo to study this phenomenon, claims that *Tetris* causes women to experience an endorphin rush because it satisfies the feminine craving for order: "It's the woman who handles the decor; it's usually the guy who messes things up." Asserting that *Tetris* appeals to women's holistic ways of seeing things, Scott even ties the game's popularity to prehistoric gender behavior: "Men were the hunters—they focused on killing for survival; women were the gatherers— they see the whole picture."[3] It is disturbing that essentializing explanations such as these originate with experts and then gain acceptance in the popular imagination.

Michel Foucault observed that juridical systems of power produce the subjects they subsequently come to represent. Indeed, software production and much current research have produced a girl consumer whose definition is only in opposition to a putative standard "boy." Such definitions can be as distorting for boys as they are for girls. It is difficult to reconcile boys' alleged disinterest in character development with the popularity of fantasy games like *Dungeons and Dragons*, which according to Patricia Marks Greenfield, "involve complex characters with a medieval flavor who go on adventures together and meet a wide variety of circumstances. . . . One distinguishing mark of this type of game is that there are so many more possible happenings and characters than in a traditional game."[4] Additional counterevidence can be provided by Multi-User Dungeons (MUDs) where players (mostly boys) develop elaborate character relationships and create environments—two activities stereotyped as female. In short, the gendered binary of assumed preferences in software says more about the ideologies and assumptions of researchers and developers who speculate on the topic than about any essential differences between the sexes, yet these speculations are recirculated back to consumers through advertising and popular journalism, encouraging kids to choose those products that are supposedly appropriate to their gender. It is not surprising, then, that such differences also appear even in the innovative studies of Yasmin B. Kafai, who analyzes gender differences in games designed (rather than merely consumed) by girls and boys.[5]

This essay explores issues of socialization and gender around computers and computer games, and seeks to clarify how girls relate to interactive media. While not denying that differences between boys and girls do occur in their use of computers and games, I will argue that these differences are attributable to the cultural gendering of leisure and play, rather than to inherent biological differences. Historical discourses around leisure reveal that current "discoveries" by researchers about girls' interests and play preferences are clearly linked to much older discussions about what constitutes appropriate feminine leisure activity. These considerations led me to test how gender differences around software are being actualized by children in three Los Angeles schools. My object was to do my own analysis of girls' behavior with computers and then weigh my findings against popular theories of what girls want in software. At the same time, I contextualize both current theories about girls and my own research within historical discourses around feminine leisure.

Continuities in the Discourse around Leisure

Any inquiry into computers and culture must observe the intersection of computers as they are used at school for educational purposes and at home as a leisure activity. This relationship is crucial because while boys and girls may sometimes use the computer in the classroom in similar ways, their leisure use is markedly different, and this discrepancy, in turn, influences classroom behavior. Children's use of computers, then, has to be considered in both of these contexts.

Instead of viewing computer use in terms of the effects that a new technology has on society, I regard computer use as a social act, influenced by long-standing cultural beliefs about education, leisure, and gender. In this sense, computers are not a force that drives the course of society or human behavior, but objects that become embedded in elaborate cultural codes and social patterns. A review of the history of women, girls, and leisure indicates that present-day patterns of computer game play are inflected by much older beliefs about feminine leisure.

Karla A. Henderson has theorized women's place in the history of leisure via a periodizing scheme that includes six eras from 1907 to the present. For Henderson, women's relationship to leisure was conceived differently in each period, and can be related to the dominant social ideologies of the time.[6] While I agree with Henderson's notion that discourses about gender and leisure must be located within broader ones about gender and culture, I see the relationships between leisure, gender, and culture less as a series of separate eras than as a continuity of ideas about the contested nature of the feminine.

Henderson observes the historical invisibility of women in the literature about leisure, which she attributes to the assumption that men have traditionally been dominant in the public sphere, whereas women's roles have been confined to the private sphere. According to Henderson, discussions of girls and leisure have reinforced the notion that leisure ought to enhance girls' education as feminine subjects.[7] In other words, not only has the actual participation of females in leisure activities been governed by traditional conceptions of femininity, but these notions have also governed the production of discourse around the topic. There is some continuity between the literature on girls and computing today and historical discourses about girls and leisure. Although a great deal has been written about the implications of gender in the educational use of computers, much less has been written on girls' use of computers and software as leisure—and much of that tends to assume that girls' leisure preferences are skewed toward educational software. Much work remains to be done on girls' pleasures in leisure itself. Contemporary perceptions about gender and leisure, then, must be viewed as part of an ongoing discussion about how girls and boys ought to behave, and how it is proper for them to spend their time.

As has been abundantly remarked in research on gender and leisure, women have less free time than men, largely due to the conflation of public and private spheres for women, who often come home to a "second shift" of work, whereas men in general associate time at home with leisure. Because girls are acculturated, in part, by observing their mothers' roles, some girls experience this time pressure at surprisingly early ages. Citing a 1910 study, Henderson claims that girls made fewer demands than boys for recreation, and thus, were seen as less interested in it. She notes here that "Further examination of this perception indicated that many girls as 'little mothers' were so tired from their household tasks when they came to the playground that they had little energy to play."[8] This perception still has relevance today, as Susan Shaw's studies of adolescents have shown: there is "a statistically significant difference in obligatory and nonobligatory time between males and females, with females spending more time than males in obligatory activities. Females tend to spend more time than males at school, doing schoolwork at home, and doing chores."[9]

The reigning discourse about girls' preferences in interactive entertainment submits that girls prefer cooperative games to competitive ones. This assertion is part of a much longer discussion. The late 1900s and early 1920s were periods when the importance of athletics was stressed for all children, including girls. As Henderson explains, however, girls' games and sports were considered to be properly group activities—team play and competition were downplayed. Girls and women of this period were encouraged to join clubs because they provided opportunities for members to work together, and group participation and cooperation were stressed.[10] Clearly, the notion that girls ought to be, or rather are, primarily social beings has become naturalized. Popular and academic discussions of what girls want in interactive media invariably highlight group play, cooperation, and social interaction. Foucault has argued that discourses proliferate within certain power relationships. By enforcing an essentialist view of the female as social and group oriented (read: not intellectual and not independent), dominant discourses about interactive media continue to appeal to the same structures of power that have historically guided discussions of gender.

Method

The incorporation of ethnographic methods into cultural studies suggests a refusal to theorize female readers of culture monolithically, as well as a willingness to observe difference and lived experience. Several contemporary studies of female audiences have called on empirical or ethnographic methods: Marsha Kinder's *Playing with Power in Movies, Television, and Video Games*, Angela McRobbie's "Dance and Social Fantasy," Janice Radway's *Reading the Romance*, and Jackie Stacey's *Star Gazing: Hollywood Cinema and Female Spectatorship.*[11] Informed by these approaches, my research method followed three paths: ethnographic observation in schools, a broad survey of students, and follow-up interviews with teachers and students.

By first observing kids at school (a setting that is part of their daily lives, rather than an artificial environment like a laboratory or focus group), I was able to formulate questions that would guide my survey and interviews. I noted the behavior of kids in computer classes, seeking to discover who asks questions, who is more aggressive or tentative with computers, who works with others and who works alone, and how students and teachers interact.

For the survey, I compiled a twenty-two-item questionnaire (included in the appendix) and distributed it to 180 students (45 girls and 45 boys each at two different schools) to obtain an overview of their opinions, preferences, and habits. While some of the conclusions I reached have been widely discussed in previous literature, others were surprising. The surveys were valuable insofar as they added a broader perspective and, I suspect, allowed greater candor. As a research tool, however, the survey is rooted in a social science methodology that looks for generalities, while I was primarily interested in the heterogeneous and local aspects of girls' experiences with computers.

Hence, in addition to these surveys, I interviewed a number of girls in greater depth to gain a fuller understanding of their opinions. Assuming that there would be some variations or contradictions between the spoken and written responses, I saw the interviews as one way of moving beyond the anonymity of the survey to locate individual responses within personal experience and social context.

Originally, I intended to work in three Los Angeles private schools with different demographics: Pilgrim School, the most ethnically diverse private school in the nation; the Sinai Akiba Academy, a Jewish private school that uses more interactive software than most; and Marlborough School, one of the oldest girls schools in Los Angeles. Although all three schools are private, there are striking differences in class between Marlborough and the others. Located in the wealthy Hancock Park neighborhood, Marlborough has a tuition of about $13,000 per year, more than double those of Pilgrim (which is situated in a multiracial neighborhood near downtown Los Angeles) and Sinai Akiba (which is in a predominantly Jewish neighborhood in Westwood). Whereas Marlborough is reputed to be the city's most prestigious school for girls, one that protects them from competition with boys who are presumably favored by teachers, Sinai Akiba attempts to integrate the premises of Judaism with first-rate education for a homogeneous community, and Pilgrim strives for academic excellence while preparing an ethnically diverse population for college.

I chose to work in private schools for several reasons. First, while a number of studies of children and computer use have already been done in public schools, private schools have been for the most part neglected. Second, the demographics of private schools are more easily differentiated. Moreover, I found that private schools offered greater ease of access to kids, and far superior computer labs and software resources than were available in the L.A. Unified School District's schools, particularly since, according to a 1995–1996 study by Quality Education Data, California ranked last nationally for number of students per computer.

At Pilgrim and Sinai Akiba, the teachers were forthcoming, and I was able to watch and speak with students as much as I liked. Despite their initial enthusiasm, the school administrators at Marlborough finally decided that my research came at a bad time of year for their students. Nonetheless, I was able to interview a Marlborough student and her mother at length.

My research in the schools allowed me to study kids from a variety of ethnic and class backgrounds. Further work remains to be done by observing kids in their homes, since as mentioned earlier, computers and software are used in both educational and recreational ways, and each of these patterns of use informs and has impact on the other.

Research Findings

Observation. At the Sinai Akiba Academy (K–8), Marilyn, the computer teacher, makes an effort to integrate computer classes with other subjects. There are no programming classes. Kids use educational games, in addition to typing, math, art, and word processing programs.

Rick, the computer teacher at the Pilgrim School (K–12), places more emphasis on applications such as drawing and word processing programs because he finds it hard to integrate existing interactive software into other teachers' syllabi. The Pilgrim School also offers optional programming classes.

My first impression from observation at both schools was that kids act much more traditionally than I would have thought. It seemed that girls were more hesitant to work their way through interactive software and programming exercises, and stopped frequently to ask questions, whereas boys seemed more independent. The more I watched, however, the less convinced I became of this finding. Some girls, particularly if they are familiar with a program, are quite aggressive, and some boys ask many questions. I noted that traditionally gendered behavior is related to what computers and software are used for, and in what settings, rather than being a function of computers or software as such.

In other words, it is more instructive to look at how a technology is used within a social context than to draw conclusions about technology without concern for its actual use.

At the Pilgrim School, writing and drawing applications are often used for class exercises, as in one first grade project that involved drawing sea creatures and writing sentences about them. Both boys and girls had many questions about typing, spelling, and opening and closing their documents. The students' writing, however, strongly reflected traditional notions of gender. Many boys wrote sentences that implied action or violence, such as: "I draw a hammershark. He eats fish in the ocean," "The whales are surrounding a pile of fish and trying to eat them," and "The sharks are surrounding a whale. The whales are jumping in and out of the water." Most of the girls' sentences described their affective relationship to the creatures they had drawn, such as: "My whale is nice. I love whales, do you?" "I love whales," and "I like whales, they are pretty." This class, then, expressed more traditional gender behavior in terms of the content of their projects than in their approach to the computer. I noticed a similar dynamic in Marilyn's third grade class at Sinai Akiba. For one project, students made stationery that included their names and clip art. Although boys and girls seemed equally comfortable with the software used here, most girls selected images of unicorns, fairies, or ballerinas, while most boys chose sports images.

Much popular and academic literature argues that girls prefer to use computers in pairs or groups, and boys to work alone, yet I found that both boys and girls pair up and work alone with about equal frequency. Most pairs were same-sex. Sometimes, pairs were composed of one leader, who understood the program, and one follower, who needed help, and this pattern was true for boys and girls.

Gender differences are much more apparent in the Pilgrim School's programming classes. Invariably, many more boys than girls are enrolled—usually in a ratio of about four to one. The girls I observed were relatively silent, while boys tended to engage Rick in discussion about their assignments and computing in general. For example, in Rick's grades nine through twelve Pascal class, several boys involved Rick in a discussion about how they might hack their way into Rick's locked files. These results are not especially surprising, since gender differences become more pronounced toward adolescence (kids in the programming classes are much older than the first and third graders I described earlier) and programming is perceived, like math and science, as a male-coded activity.

In short, my observations suggested a number of questions: To what extent is the popular perception by researchers that girls are less comfortable or aggressive with computers a product of researchers' biases? How would "aggressiveness" be quantified? Is "aggressiveness" the same as computer competence, as is usually assumed? As one of my survey respondents explained, "Girls are much better at computers because girls understand technology more. They don't just rush in putting things together." Girls' responses to computers and software seem to be more strongly determined by how computers are used than by attitudes about properties inherent in the technology itself.

Marlborough School. Although my interaction with Sharon (pseud.) and her mother was methodologically unlike the rest of my research, I include our interview in the appendix to point up the way class inflects the relationship between gender and technology. I contend that Sharon's and her mother's attitudes about the relative lack of importance of computer education at school have their roots in a class privilege that regards knowing the nuts and bolts of computing as nonessential to the type of professions it is assumed these girls will eventually enter.

A great uproar has been caused by the experiences of Marlborough students on the Internet. Girls have been caught using school computers to download pornographic images and engage in racy conversations with men in chat rooms. This concern with the invasion of the protected space of the private school by a questionable public influence has a long history in the development of communications technologies. At Marlborough, the stakes in controlling what goes on within the school gates are all the higher because of the upper-class ethos of the school. A recent issue of *Ultra Violet*, the school paper, contains a two-page special report on the Internet, titled "Sex, Lies, and the Internet." Some contributors were repelled by the men they encountered on the Internet and shared their experiences as cautionary tales: "Have you ever been on-line and received an instant message that says, 'Wanna talk dirty?' from some guy named 'HotPimp' or 'JoBlo?' Well, I have, and it makes me sick."[12] Another writer challenged Marlborough's new list of rules for Internet use, some of which are: "Attention to grammar, spelling, and arid content in an E-mail message is important, as you want individuals who receive your message to see your best work and respond intelligently," "Answer E-mail in a timely manner," "NEVER impersonate someone else on-line. Further, allowing others to believe you are an adult when you are not is wrong and potentially dangerous," and "Marlborough School does not sanction the use of the Internet to explore resources that are pornographic, violent, or abusive. Use of the system for these purposes, at school or at home, will result in revocation of ALL privileges and possible disciplinary action." Like Sharon in our interview, the author of the Ultra Violet article found these rules condescending and inappropriate, "As if Marlborough girls were a group of immature children who were computer illiterate."[13] The issue of what a "Marlborough girl" is or is not lies at the root of both arguments. The administrators' rules express their anxiety that the prized internal order of the school might be disturbed, especially when exposed to the public realm of the Internet. The students' responses imply that because the girls are part of this internal order, administrators need not restrict them; they know better than to behave in a manner that would discredit the school. Clearly, the concern for upper-class status evidenced by the discourses around computers at Marlborough is quite different from the more pragmatic approach taken at Pilgrim and Sinai Akiba.

While it was irrelevant to consider gender differences in the recreational use of computers at a girls school like Marlborough, this issue did arise at the other two institutions. For example, the computer teacher at Sinai Akiba expressed concern that her attention was unfairly distributed, since boys ask for help during free time while playing games or exploring the Internet, whereas girls do not make as many similar demands. She felt this situation represents a closed loop in which boys who ask for her time learn more, grow more interested, and ask for still more attention. This description brings Henderson's observations to mind; although referring to the 1910 study, the following statement speaks directly to Marilyn's fear: "A 'chicken-and-egg' situation seemed to create these acknowledged constraints on females' play behavior. Because females made fewer demands, they received less assistance. A lack of supervision and instruction resulted in a lack of involvement and thus, fewer demands."[14]

Indeed, most of the boys who responded to my survey said that they play computer games daily or every other day from a half hour to an hour on average; most girls play much less—about once a week for fifteen minutes. This behavior is, of course, overdetermined by such factors as gender coding, lack of appealing software for girls, and lack of marketing channels. Yet, beyond these issues, many of the girls I surveyed responded in ways such as "I have too many things to do" or "I'm too busy" when asked how often they play games. One twelve-year-old girl suggested that I improve my survey by choosing the word "use" instead of "play." She said that as the oldest child in her household, she is expected to help supervise her three younger sisters and assist with housework. This leaves her little time to play, she said, although she does use the computer for homework. Part of the reason for these responses may be that girls and boys also have different perceptions of how much free time they have and how they are supposed to spend it. Clearly, answers about how many hours per week they play games are as heavily influenced by what kids believe is an acceptable answer as by what the empirical number actually is.

Computers in the Domestic Sphere. The home can be seen as a place where the use of computers for leisure and education intersect. In my survey, most boys and girls used their home computer for both entertainment and homework. Lily Shashaani reports that in her study of 1,700 secondary school children, 68 percent of boys and 56 percent of girls have access to a computer at home. The percentage of male students as primary users of the computer, however, was twice that of female students, and a higher percentage of boys said that they had first learned about computers at home.[15] In my research, the percentage of home computer owners is much higher—all but one of the kids at the Sinai Akiba Academy had a computer at home, as did the majority of Pilgrim School children. These are private schools, which are typically attended by children of a higher economic bracket, whereas Shashaani's study was of public schools. Nevertheless, in my study, when a home computer was available, boys were the more frequent users, particularly for leisure and Internet activities (see appendix for specific results).

According to Shashaani, substantial stereotyping of computers as the purview of boys and men occurs at home. "Studies have shown that parents, especially fathers, encourage their sons more than their daughters to learn about computers. Parents most often purchase computers and computer games for their sons, and not for their daughters. . . . [A] lack of female-user role models at home may influence girls' self-confidence that learning and working with computers are difficult tasks, and that computers are in 'the masculine domain.' "[16] Likewise, Ann Colley cites a recent meta-analysis of 172 studies of the different socialization of boys and girls by parents that "found that the only area which showed a significant effect for both mothers and fathers was encouragement of sex-typed activities and perceptions of sex-stereotyped characteristics, where parents emphasize gender stereotypes in play and in household tasks."[17] Indeed, none of the girls I surveyed said that they had been bought a computer or cartridge entertainment system, while for many of the boys, this was the case. Moreover, many of my respondents said that their father or brother was their entrée into computer and software use. Fathers and brothers were also mentioned as an important way in which kids keep up with new software developments. Only two of my respondents listed women as their initial link to computing or software. As David Morely has observed, the use of media within the home must be considered with respect to established patterns of gender behavior within the family.[18] These patterns could have implications for girls' relationships to computers and software outside the home as well.

Computers in the Classroom. Computers, then, represent a significant element of boys' leisure, while for girls, they are a less important part of any free time. Extracurricular relationships to computers and software extend into the classroom. Computers in educational uses perform, broadly, in two fashions. At times, they are used to run educational software that is integrated into wider class syllabi. Other computer classes, such as those in programming, are exercises in learning computer logic and critical thinking. The different uses to which computers may be put in schools complicates attempts to generalize or even theorize about gender in educational computing. According to Colley,

> Computing is often associated with math or science, academic areas which are male-dominated. Indeed, children's attitudes to computing have been found to be similar to their attitudes to science and to be associated with attitudes to math. Although more enrollments in computer courses have been recorded for males, it has been pointed out that further scrutiny of the statistics shows that males outnumber females in programming courses, and that males spend more time programming than females, while similar numbers of males and females or even a majority of females is found when enrollments for other computing applications, especially word processing, are considered. Word processing can be regarded either as a computer application, or as an extension of typing, which is a female-dominated vocational skill and which has been stereotyped for females in studies of perceptions of school subjects.[19]

Colley's finding was partially upheld in my research. The association of computers with math and science was noted frequently. At the Pilgrim School, there were many more boys than girls in programming classes. One girl I spoke with said that boys are better at using computers because "men can relate better to machinery. They find machinery more interesting starting from bulldozers at age three up to hedge clippers at age thirty-five." One boy surveyed wrote that boys were better at computers "because boys are more nerds than girls." On the other hand, many boys and girls responded that there is no correlation between gender and computer ability, and several thought it was sexist of me to even pose the question.

While teachers and students sometimes argue that there is no difference between boys and girls' use of computers at school, it seems that some differences do exist. Educational software can exacerbate existing differences. Some educational software still employs the metaphors of traditional shoot-'em-up video games. In *Math Blaster*, one of the reward games is a classic arcade-style activity in which the player shoots space trash. In *Pilgrim Quest*, there are leisure areas where users can hunt or fish—after the fashion of traditional computer dexterity games. Research has shown that this type of activity is generally more appealing to boys than girls, presumably because of its similarity to games in which boys have previous expertise.[20] Also, in the popular educational games *Pilgrim Quest* and *Oregon Trail*, the few characters represented on-screen are male. As is often the case with entertainment software, even seemingly "genderless" characters in educational software are conventionally male—for example, in Word Attack III, Mostly Chrome, a shiny sphere, is male. This bias, however subtle, only exacerbates an already existing inequity of experience and comfort with computers and computer software between girls and boys.

Social pressure forms another possible influence on girls' use of computers at school. As Colley notes, "according to social learning theory, it is assumed that one major concern of females who participate in male-stereotyped areas of interest or achievement, in addition to beliefs concerning their lack of competence, is that they may be negatively rewarded because they are behaving in an unfeminine way."[21] Indeed, the one real "tomboy" I encountered in my research seemed rather an outsider from the girls' circle. This particular girl is extraordinarily competent with computers, uses several on-line services, e-mails, faxes, and plays a variety of flight simulation games. Her younger sister, however, was quick to define herself as "exactly the opposite of my sister. I am not a tomboy." This response may have as much to do with sibling rivalry as it does with perceptions of gender constraints, but it did point out that among many girls (and boys), it is often preferable to associate oneself with others who follow fairly traditional patterns of gender.

Given the stringent strictures of gender, particularly during youth, it is not surprising that many boys felt they were better at computers and computer games than girls—in a sense, they have to be. Considering the stakes in upholding masculinity, being a "tomboy" is one matter; being a "sissy" is a much more serious transgression. On the other hand, a number of boys surveyed answered that boys and girls are equal in terms of their ability—many of them wrote: "We are all equal" or "Boys and girls do equally well on the computer." What was more surprising was that some girls believed that they were not only equal to, but better than boys at using computers and games. While kids' attitudes toward computers frequently reflect traditional notions of gender, they sometimes challenge convention. These various responses must be located within larger cultural tensions. For numerous reasons, most boys have a relationship with computers and computing that most girls do not. At the same time, the responses from teachers and students indicate that there is an impulse toward gender equality. The traditional and the progressive, then, are simultaneously at play in behaviors and attitudes around computers.

Approaching Gender and Computing

My study revealed that the interplay between gender and the use of computers involves a negotiation between established orders and liberatory beliefs and behaviors that challenge convention. Before spending much time with kids, I had more utopian ideas about the ease with which gender might be transgressed. Yet despite cultural restraints, girls still express their belief in gender equality and have a wide range of preferences in software. Thus, what is definitive is that there is much more variety among girls than is typically assumed.

Precisely because of its institutional supports, Judith Butler challenges the category *woman* as grounds for theoretical pronouncements:

> If one "is" a woman, surely that is not all one is; the term fails to be exhaustive, not because a pregendered "person" transcends the specific paraphernalia of its gender, but because gender is not always constituted coherently or consistently in different historical contexts, and because gender intersects with racial, class, ethnic, sexual, and regional modalities of discursively constituted entities. As a result, it becomes impossible to separate out "gender" from the political and cultural intersections in which it is invariably produced and maintained.[22]

The same argument applies to "girls." My study shows that girls at Pilgrim School (which privileges fairly conventional approaches to computing) have a different experience with computers than girls at Marlborough School (where computer use intersects with upper-class ideologies and class anxieties). The experience of girls at Sinai Akiba (where computer use is often meshed with Judaism, as when students use software to make greeting cards for Jewish holidays) is an example of yet another social context that inflects computer use. Girls' use of computers must therefore be situated within heterogeneous cultural factors.

Given the social strictures placed on gender, particularly in relationship to computing, it is simplistic to say that girls can just transcend gender. In this sense, the question becomes not one of dispensing with the notion of gender entirely, but rather of how to mutate its directives. Shaw claims that involvement in nontraditional activities especially benefits girls:

> For adolescent girls, the need for activities which encourage independence and autonomy may be particularly great. . . . Since girls live in a male-dominated world, it may be important for them to challenge traditional "feminine" roles through participation in nontraditional activities. Indeed, this would seem to be consistent with the notion of identity development being enhanced through challenging activities and through the exploration of alternative ideas and alternative identities.[23]

According to Henderson, leisure activities provide the space for such resistance:

> If leisure experiences represent situations of choice and self-determination, they also provide opportunities for individuals to exercise personal

power, and such power can be used as a form of resistance to imposed gender constraints or restrictions."[24]

Yet the problem remains: given the available software, girls have little choice but to learn to negotiate texts that are constructed along highly traditional lines of gender. Even the newest software designed by women for girls hails them as future subjects within this essentialist system.

Girls may be inscribed within powerful circles of the social, but within those circles they maintain their heterogeneity. The only way to approach gender and computing, practically or theoretically, then, is to resist that which works to restrict feminine behavior, pleasure, and self-definition, and to encourage that which presses beyond conventional notions of the feminine as a monolithic category. Donna Haraway formulates a utopian cyborg world in which science and technology can provide fresh sources of power as old dichotomies are called into question.[25] Only when it dispenses with traditional relations of power can computer software begin to fulfill Haraway's vision. Producing products that girls would enjoy becomes, from this standpoint, a pleasure, not a problem.

Appendix

INTERVIEWS

Instead of transcribing the entire content of the interviews, I have edited together pieces of the interviewee's answers, verbatim. Their words are between quotation marks. Places where I have summarized their responses are not.

Teachers

1. What are your school's goals in computer education?

Marilyn: "Sinai Akiba has a 'technology plan' which hopes to develop more integration between traditional classes and my computer classes. We regard computers as a tool—we do not think it as important for all kids to learn computer languages as it is for us to meet the needs of individual kids and follow their interests."

Rick: "Pilgrim is attempting to use computers in conjunction with academic classes as well as to teach interested kids programming skills."

2. What are the main differences you notice between boys and girls' use of computers and software?

Both: There is no difference.

3. Would you say that girls have more, less, or equal confidence with computers than boys? What behaviors do you observe that makes you think this?

Both: (Initially said) there is no difference between boys and girls in terms of computer confidence.

4. What differences between boys and girls do you notice in terms of software preference?

Marilyn: "I use a lot of educational software at school, which isn't as biased along gender lines as typical computer games, so I don't see much difference between girls and boys."

Rick: "In most of my classes, I see none. We use a lot of applications which don't stress gender differences. However, more boys sign up for optional programming classes."

5. What differences do you notice in style of play or software use between girls and boys?

Both: None.

6. Would you say that either boys or girls tend to prefer to work in pairs?

Marilyn: "No, both work in pairs and work alone."

Rick: "I don't give my kids the choice. If I want them to pair up, I create the pairs."

7. Do you notice that boys or girls tend to use the computer more during free time?

Both: Boys spend more free time with computers to play games. (Also, both teachers have certain groups of "hacker" boys, and very few "hacker" girls, who use the computers during free time.)

8. What do you think can be done about any gender differences in terms of computer attitudes (by schools? parents? both?)?

Marilyn: "It's difficult for me to make a substantial change because I'm not the kids' main teacher; I'm not with them all day—only for about forty minutes at a time. Also, I think that people expect teachers to fix everything when there is so much pressure from the family and from society for girls and boys to act in specific ways."

Rick: "Boys tend to play computer and video games more than girls, which gives them an edge when they have to use computers at school. I think computer games are valuable tools for cognitive development, especially in terms of logic and critical thinking. Girls miss out on this experience."

My interviews with the teachers went quite differently than I had expected. I had assumed that both teachers would have much more to say about the differences between boys and girls in their classrooms, but both teachers initially said that there was no difference. Yet, toward the end of their interviews, Marilyn and Rick did discuss some differences in gender, and in Marilyn's case, prior to the interview, she once said that girls were less aggressive and confident than boys with computers.

Interview with Sharon (pseud.), the Marlborough Student, and Her Mother

Mother:

1. How important do you think computer education at school is for your daughter?

Mother: "I don't think it's as important as her other academic classes, especially because she uses the computer so much at home, so she's very familiar with it. She already knows many applications including graphics processing ones."

2. Why did you choose Marlborough for your daughter?

"Because it's the best school around, except for Harvard Westlake. My daughter used to go to Westlake, but she left because we both decided that a single-sex school would be better for her."

3. What advantages/disadvantages do you see to the school and specifically to single-sex education?

"My daughter doesn't get railroaded by the boys. In computer classes, the girls aren't competing with aggressive boys and computer nerds. On the other hand, I'm not sure she'll know how to deal with men, personally and professionally, later in life."

4. What skills do you hope your daughter will pick up by being involved with computers?

"I think she has most of the skills she needs already—she wants to be an artist, and she already knows Photo Shop. The rest of what she'll need will probably be a matter of on-the-job training."

5. Do you think that using computers for leisure, that is, games, Internet, etc., is worthwhile or a waste of time for your daughter?

"She doesn't have time for games. She almost always uses the computer for her homework. Sometimes she gets on the Internet, but it's mostly for research. Sometimes she uses the computer for her artwork, scanning and manipulating images."

Marlborough Student Sharon

1. Age/grade?
Sharon: Sixteen; eleventh.

2. What, for you, are the advantages and disadvantages of the Marlborough School, specifically of single-sex education?
"I went to a mixed school before, and I was relieved to get to Marlborough because I'm not dominated by boys and I get more attention, particularly in classes like computer classes and math. I'm able to compete and participate more in a single-sex environment. At Westlake, the math and computer teachers paid more attention to the boys, who asked more questions."

3. How much do you learn about computers at school?
"Not much; I have learned about computers at home."

4. How important is it for you to learn about computers? Software? And why?
"It's somewhat important, but I'm not sure how important. For example, I don't think I need to learn how to word process [although she already knows how] because I'm not going to be the secretary, typing things up; I'm going to be the one at the top."

5. When you're not in school, what do you do with computers?
"Mostly homework. Sometimes I work on my art."

6. Do you use computer games, video games, or the Internet for leisure?
"No, I never play games. I have a lot of homework and I'm also involved in a lot of school activities. I use the Internet for school research."

7. Do you think girls or boys are inherently better at computers/computer games? Why?
"Neither is inherently better; boys and girls have the same capabilities, it's a matter of their experience."

SURVEYS

I compiled forty-five surveys each from boys and girls at both Sinai Akiba and Pilgrim. Not every student answered every question, and some gave multiple responses to the same question.

1. What is your age?
Pilgrim girls and boys: Ten to sixteen.
Sinai Akiba girls and boys: Ten to Thirteen.

2. What is your grade?

   Pilgrim, Sixth to eleventh.

   Sinai Akiba: Fifth to eighth.

3. What is your ethnic background?

   Pilgrim: Examples, verbatim, included: Filipino, Japanese, African-American, African-American-Caucasian; Africa-American-European-American; Japanese-Chinese; Korean, Persian-Japanese; Black (Jamaican, mixed, lot of other stuff); Chinese-Korean; African-American; Irish and Swedish; and Japanese-Russian.

   Sinai Akiba: Primarily Russian, Persian, and Jewish.

4. What are your parents' jobs? Mom? Dad?

   Both: Respondents listed a wide variety of occupations. More Pilgrim students than Sinai students reported "not having" a dad. This did not seem to affect other responses, however. Pilgrim and Sinai students, for instance, responded similarly to questions about how they started playing games and with whom they play. Occupation examples from each school includes:

   Pilgrim: (Mothers) Administrator, manager of store, teacher, media manager, secretary (two), counselor, nurse, works in medical center. (Fathers) President of gallery, telephone repair, mail carrier, teacher, boss, manager of company, engineer, dentist.

   Sinai: (Mothers) property managers (three), bookkeeper, florist, gift baskets, sells medical equipment, doctors (four), artist and cooking teacher, works with dad, *Los Angeles Times.* (Fathers) lawyers (three), doctors (five), certified public accountant, teacher, carpet business, construction manager, music producer, writes for television, owns warehouse.

5. Do you take computer classes at school?

   Both: All respondents said yes, if not presently, then in the past.

6. If so, which computer classes do you take?

   Both: Most responded in terms such as "general" or "sixth grade computers." This question did not lead to as many specific answers as I would have liked—most kids who were taking programming classes, for example, did not mention it. This lack of specificity was a problem throughout, presumably caused by kids' tendency to rush through their answers, particularly in a survey of this length. Interviews would probably have led to more specific answers.

7. Do you use the school's computers during nonclass periods, free time, or after school? If so, what for?

   Pilgrim girls: Yes, for work: eight

                      Yes, for play: one

Yes, for play and work: ten

No: nineteen

Pilgrim boys: Yes, for work: four

Yes, for play: ten

Yes, for play and work: twelve

No: fifteen

Sinai girls: Yes, for work: ten

Yes, for play: three

Yes, for play and work: five

No: twenty-six

Sinai boys: Yes, for work: five

Yes, for play: eight

Yes, for play and work: nine

No: twenty

8. On a scale of 1 to 10, with 1 being "something boys do," 10 being "something girls do," and 5 being "neutral," how would you rate computers? What reasons would you give for this?

Please circle your answer:

1	2	3	4	5	6	7	8	9	10
boys				neutral					girls

Pilgrim girls (point on scale/number of responses):

4: two

5: thirty-five

8: three

Pilgrim boys (point on scale/number of responses):

4: six

5: twenty-four

7: one

Sinai girls (point on scale/number of responses):

2: two

4: one

5: forty

Sinai boys (point on scale/number of responses):

1: two

3: eight

5: thirty-two

Questions 9 and 10 generated many more comments than the others. I also saw a number of erasures on the surveys, indicating that the students had deliberated over their responses.

9. On a scale of 1 to 10, with 1 being "boys are much better," 10 being "girls are much better," and 5 being "neutral," who would you say is better at using computers, boys, girls, or neither? What reasons would you give for this?

1	2	3	4	5	6	7	8	9	10
boys				neutral					girls

Pilgrim girls (point on scale/number of responses):

4: five

5: thirty

6: six

8: four

Most of the girls whose answers skewed toward the "girl" end of the scale suggested that this was because girls type faster. One girl circled both 4 and 6 "Because girls type faster than boys and boys use the computer during recess." Most girls who felt that boys were better at using computers noted that boys spend more time on the computer than girls. Girls do not seem to believe that boys are necessarily inherently better than girls, even if they have adopted the popular notion that girls are better typists.

Typical comments accompanying neutral answers were "All people are equal," and "It's not a thing based by gender, it's a specific person, not boy or girl." Many students from both schools stressed the equality of boys and girls in questions 9 and 10, although more girls selected the neutral response than boys.

Pilgrim boys (point on scale/number of responses):

1: two

2: two

3: three

4: four

5: twenty

7: one

As has been widely observed, boys tend to rate boys more highly in terms of computer expertise than girls rate them. Some boys felt that there is something inherently different about boys: "Boys are more interested [in computers] than girls," "Boys are more nerds than girls." Others felt that boys are better at the computer because "There are more boys using the computer than girls," and "It depends how much you work with a computer." As did the girls, the boys who selected the neutral response added comments like "We are all equal."

Sinai girls (point on scale/number of responses):

1: two

3: three

4: three

5: thirty-two
6: one
7: one
10: two

The Sinai girls who felt that boys are better wrote comments such as "It just seems to interest them more," and "Some boys are faster and more into electronics." The girls who chose the neutral response wrote things such as "Why should for example girls be better than boys? Some boys are better than girls and some girls are better than boys!" "Stupid to be sexist!" and "We are all the same." The girls who felt that girls are better than boys thought this was so because girls are better typists—"We type much faster."

Sinai boys (point on scale/number of responses):

1: five
2: three
4: eight
5: twenty-eight

No Sinai boys responded that girls are better than boys at the computer. Boys who believed that boys are better gave reasons such as "Because boys use it more," and "I think boys spend more time on the computer." As usual, the explanations for a neutral answer were typically "Because boys and girls can do the same," and "It depends how much time a person will give to learn the computer."

10. On a scale of 1 to 10, with 1 being "boys are much better," 10 being "girls are much better," and 5 being "neutral," who would you say is better at using computer games and interactive software, boys, girls, or neither? What reasons would you give for this?

1	2	3	4	5	6	7	8	9	10
boys				neutral					girls

Pilgrim girls (point on scale/number of responses):

1: one
4: twelve
5: twenty-four
6: one

Boys were thought better "Because girls like to talk or shop more than using computers," and "I think boys are only capable for computer games because they usually know a lot about video games and stuff like that." The girl who believed that girls are better wrote, "Girls understand technology more. They don't just rush in putting things together."

Pilgrim boys (point on scale/number of responses):

1: sixteen

3: four

4: six

5: ten

The boys believed that boys are better because "Boys seem more interested in computer games and interactive software," "Boys because we play a lot more games than girls," "Girls are more mature and don't want to play computer games. They like to shop," and "Boys are very violent. Most games are very violent. Therefore, boys excel at games." Again, boys saw essential differences as well as differences in interests between boys and girls as explanations for the perceived superiority of boys.

Sinai girls (point on scale/number of responses):

1: one

3: one

4: five

5: thirty

6: one

7: one

8: one

10: two

Girls who skewed their answers toward the boy end of the scale gave such reasons as "Because girls mature faster, so boys would be more into games," and "Boys play computer games and Nintendo and stuff more often." Two girls divided their answer and circled numbers on both sides of the scale, arguing: "Boys like to play power games and girls like drawing and painting better," and "Some games are for girls and some are for boys."

The neutral answers included "Stupid to be sexist," and "Just the same."

Sinai boys (point on scale/number of responses):

1: ten

2: six

3: four

4: five

5: twenty

Again, no boys felt that girls were better. Reasons for the superiority of boys included "Because boys use it more," "Girls do other things," "Because there are more games for boys. Boys are more interested," and "Boys are more violent and most games are violent." These answers focused both on the behavior of girls and boys vis-à-vis computer games, and on essential differences between girls and boys. The neutral answers stressed the equality of all children.

11. Do you have a computer at home? If so, what do you use it for?

Sinai: All children except one had a computer at home, and most answered that they used it for homework and entertainment.

Pilgrim: twelve out of the ninety students did not have a computer at home. Those who did used it for work and entertainment.

12. Which are your three most favorite games or interactive titles, and what do you like most about these games (include computer games, CD-ROMs, Nintendo games, Sega games, etc.)?

Pilgrim girls: For some reason, the Pilgrim girls had a wider variety of stated preferences than did the Sinai girls. This may be because they are somewhat older, or the very religious families of the Sinai Akiba girls discourage them from playing violent games. The most frequently stated preferences of the Pilgrim girls were *Super Mario, Sonic the Hedgehog, Donkey Kong, Street Fighter, Mortal Kombat,* and *Tetris.* Reasons for preference usually stressed good graphics or challenge: "I like them because they have 'great!!!' graphics," or "They are challenging and because of the graphics."

Pilgrim boys: The Pilgrim boys' answers were much like those of the Sinai boys. This may be because boys are an established market base for computer games and hear more about games. Also, boys are often part of imagined communities of players that share information about good games. The most popular games were *John Madden, Mortal Kombat, Doom,* and *Street Fighter.* The reasons for these choices were "Guns and violence, fun game play," "challenge," and "I love sports games."

Sinai girls: Where in the World Is Carmen Sandiego and *Oregon Trail* were the most frequent answers, probably because the girls play these in school. There was a surprisingly wide variety of other responses, however, perhaps because girls have not been established as a target market by interactive software companies and tend to play whatever is available. Some answers included typical "boy" games, such as *Dark Forces, Doom II,* and *Minesweeper,* for reasons including "Strategic and mazelike," and "Challenge," although few girls gave reasons for their choices. Answers also included nonviolent games such as *7th Guest, Solitaire, Lion King, The Animals,* and *Myst.* The few reasons stated for these preferences emphasized that these games "make you think."

Sinai Boys: These answers were more predictable. Of course, it is possible that boys (and girls) felt some social pressure to answer in a certain way and avoided mentioning less boy-coded games that they might enjoy. Boys in both schools often listed sports games, which no girls did. The most frequently mentioned favorite games were *John Madden Football*, *Virtual Fighter*, *Doom*, *Descent*, *Carnage*, and *Mortal Kombat*. Less typical preferences included *Myst* and *Sim City*. Boys' reasons for their preferences were most typically "I like action," "I like sports games," "It's violent," and "It's the hardest game I've ever played."

13. Please number the following games according to which is your favorite game, with 1 being your most favorite, 2 being your second favorite, and so on.

———— *Myst*

———— *Where in the World Is Carmen Sandiego?*

———— *Oregon Trail*

———— *Tetris*

———— *Super Mario Brothers*

———— *Mortal Kombat*

———— *Street Fighter*

———— *Barbie*

———— *Minesweeper*

There was a remarkably wide range of response to this question among both boys and girls, except for *Barbie*, which generally received 9s. It is important to note, however, that some kids who responded may not have actually played all the games they numbered—I should have written something like, "If you have not played a game, please write a question mark next to it."

Pilgrim girls (game/average point on scale):

Myst: 5

Carmen: 5

Oregon Trail: 5

Tetris: 4

Super Mario Brothers: 4

Mortal Kombat: 3

Street Fighter: 4

Barbie: 9

Minesweeper: 4

Despite the fact that most girls list violence as what they dislike most about interactive games, they placed *Mortal Kombat* toward the high end of the scale of preference. Perhaps, although the violence bothers them, the speed, challenge, and option of choosing female characters hold some appeal.

Pilgrim boys (game/average point on scale):

Myst: 4

Carmen: 7

Oregon Trail: 6

Tetris: 4

Super Mario Brothers: 5

Mortal Kombat: 1

Street Fighter: 2

Barbie: 9

Minesweeper: 6

Although most of their responses were quite variable, the boys almost unanimously chose *Mortal Kombat* as their favorite with *Street Fighter* in second place.

Sinai girls (game/average point on scale):

Myst: 6

Carmen: 4

Oregon Trail: 4

Tetris: 5

Super Mario Brothers: 3

Mortal Kombat: 4

Street Fighter: 5

Barbie: 9

Minesweeper: 6

Again, the Sinai girls did not prefer fighting games such as *Street Fighter* and *Mortal Kombat* as much as the Pilgrim girls did.

Sinai boys (game/average point on scale):

Myst: 6

Carmen: 5

Oregon Trail: 5

Tetris: 4

Super Mario Brothers: 5

Mortal Kombat: 2

Street Fighter: 3

Barbie: 9

Minesweeper: 8

Like the Pilgrim boys, the Sinai boys preferred *Mortal Kombat* and *Street Fighter* to the other options, although their preference was not as strong. Again, this could be due to their home environments and/or their younger ages.

14. How did you get started playing games or using interactive software?

Pilgrim girls:

Male relative: six

Friends: ten

School: six

Television: one

Female relative: one
Magazines: one
Pilgrim boys:
Male relative: eight
Friends: sixteen
School: two
Television: two
Female relative: zero
Magazines: eight
Sinai girls:
Male relative: eight
Friends: three
School: six
Television: zero
Female relative: two
Magazines: zero
Sinai boys:
Male relative: four
Friends: fourteen
School: two
Television: zero
Female relative: one
Magazines: five

Male relatives seem to be a much more important entrée into computer games than female relatives. Also, boys are more likely to learn about games from magazines and friends than are girls.

15. How often do you play, and for how long at a time?

This question was unsuccessful because most kids did not know, or wrote only how often or how long. Further, it is important to note that these answers (like most of the others) may have much more to do with what kids think is an appropriate response than with empirical fact. From reading over the answers, however, it is apparent that boys play much more frequently than girls: in general, about once a day or every other day for roughly thirty minutes to an hour. Many boys answered that they played for hours on weekends. Girls responses were generally about once a week from fifteen to thirty minutes.

16. With whom do you play? Is it a mixed group, mostly boys, mostly girls, or alone?

Although it is usually assumed that girls prefer to play together, many girls play alone. This is, in part, because girls do not have communities of other players as do boys. Boys also play alone, or in groups and arcades. Both girls and boys said that when they play computer games with others, it is usually in same-sex groups.

Pilgrim girls:
Alone: twenty-two
Mixed group: seven
Girls: fifteen
Pilgrim boys:
Alone: fifteen
Mixed group: two
Boys: sixteen
Sinai girls:
Alone: seventeen
Mixed group: four
Girls: eight
Boys: two
Sinai boys:
Alone: twenty
Mixed group: two
Boys: ten

17. What do you think is most fun or what do you like best in interactive games?
Many more boys than girls had definitive answers, probably because of their broader experience with interactive games. The most frequent responses were:
Pilgrim girls: graphics, music, challenge, winning
Pilgrim boys: action, violence, graphics, speed, winning
Sinai girls: thinking, graphics, challenge, mystery, strategy
Sinai boys: violence, action, difficulty, challenge
While many boys listed violence (or blood, murder, and so on) among their preferences, no girls did. Both boys and girls often listed graphics and challenge as their preferences.

18. What do you dislike about some games?
Many more girls responded to this question than to question 17, and many responded in the same way. The most frequent responses were:
Pilgrim girls: boring, violence, too slow, bad graphics, too hard to learn to play
Pilgrim boys: boring, too slow, bad graphics, hard to learn to play
Sinai girls: boring, violence, too hard to learn to play, too slow
Sinai boys: boring, too slow, bad graphics

19. Do you use the Internet?

Pilgrim girls: yes: twenty-one; no: fourteen

Pilgrim boys: yes: nineteen; no: twelve

Sinai girls: yes: fourteen; no: thirty

Sinai boys: yes: twenty-two; no: fourteen

There were several problems with this question. Many of the kids did not get this far on the survey. Moreover, the Pilgrim School offers an Internet class, whereas Sinai Akiba does not have this option. Finally, the Pilgrim respondents were slightly older, thus it is more likely that their parents allow them Internet access.

20. If so, where, how often, with others or alone?

Again, this type of question does not elicit adequate responses because it comprises more than one question and kids often answer only one of the series. To generalize, however, I noted that most boys spend a considerable amount of time on the Internet—more than once a week, often daily—while girls spend much less time—about once a week. Almost all the kids said that they used the net alone.

21. What do you do on the Internet? Research for school, chat groups, surf the Web, other?

Almost all the responses said "everything."

22. Is there anything else you'd like to add?

Few kids answered this, but of those who did, more girls than boys were irritated by questions 8 to 10. Boys' responses usually referred to their computer or gaming prowess.

Pilgrim girl: "I don't think that boy-girl computer questions are necessary. It's the individual people."

Pilgrim boys: "I learn everything I can! 'I am invincible'—007 Goldeneye." "Yes! I am a Video Game Maniac!"

Sinai girl: "I think this survey had sexist questions referring to girls or boys being better. It depends on the child, not his/her sex."

Sinai boy: "Yes, I am smart with computers and video games."

Notes

1   Russel DeMaria, "Battle of the Sexes," Electronic Entertainment, September 1994, 34.

2   Maria Klawa and Catherine Wambach, quoted in Dana Blankenhorn, "Research on Kids' Software Use Complete," Clarinet Electronic News Service, 5 May 1994.

3   Gini Graham Scott, quoted in Janice Crotty, "Boys' Club," *PlayRight* 1, no. 2 (January 1994), 20–24.

4   Patricia Marks Greenfield, *Mind and Media: The Effects of Television, Video Games, and Computers* (Cambridge, Mass.: Harvard University Press, 1984), 105.

5   Yasmin Kafai, "Gender Differences in Children's Constructions of Video Games," in *Advances in Applied Developmental Psychology*, vol. 11, ed. Patricia M. Greenfield and Rodney R. Cocking (Norwood, N.J.: Ablex Publishing, 1996).

6   Karla A. Henderson, "A Feminist Analysis of Selected Professional Recreation Literature about Girls/Women from 1907–1990," *Journal of Leisure Research* 25, no. 2 (1993): 165–81.

7   Ibid., 166.

8   Ibid., 170.

9   Susan Shaw, "Leisure and Identity Formation in Male and Female Adolescents: A Preliminary Examination," *Journal of Leisure Research* 27, no. 3 (1995): 245.

10 Henderson, "Recreation Literature," 171.

11 Marsha Kinder, *Playing with Power in Movies, Television, and Video Games: From Muppet Babies to Teenage Mutant Ninja Turtles* (Berkeley: University of California Press, 1991); Angela McRobbie, "Dance and Social Fantasy," in Mica Nava and Angela McRobbie, eds., *Gender and Generation* (New York: Macmillan, 1984); Janice Radway, *Reading the Romance: Women, Patriarchy, and Popular Literature* (Chapel Hill: University of North Carolina Press, 1984); Jackie Stacey, *Star-Gazing: Hollywood Cinema and Female Spectatorship* (London: Routledge, 1994).

12 Christina Gregory, "Talkin' Dirty On-line," *Ultra Violet*, vol. 26, no. 3, 1 December 1995, 8.

13 Moye Ishimoto, "Disagreeing with the Computer Agreement," *Ultra Violet*, vol. 26, no. 3, 1 December 1995, 8.

14 Henderson, "Recreation Literature," 171.

15 Lily Shashaani, "Gender Differences in Computer Experience and Its Influence on Computer Attitudes," *Journal of Educational Computing Research* 11, no. 4 (1994): 349.

16 Ibid., 362.

17 Ann Colley, "Gender Effects in the Stereotyping of Those with Different Kinds of Computing Experience," *Journal of Educational Computing Research* 12, no. 1 (1995): 20.

18 David Morely, *Family Television: Cultural Power and Domestic Leisure* (London: Routledge, 1986).

19 Colley, "Gender Effects," 20.

20 See Rosemary E. Sutton, "Equity and Computers in the Schools: A Decade of Research," *Review of Educational Research* 61, no. 4 (winter 1991): 475.

21 Colley, "Gender Effects," 20.

22 Judith Butler, *Gender Trouble: Feminism and the Subversion of Identity* (London: Routledge, 1990), 3.

23 Shaw, "Leisure and Identity Formation," 247.

24 Karla A. Henderson, "Perspectives on Analyzing Gender, Women, and Leisure," *Journal of Leisure Research* 26, no. 2 (1994): 15.

25 Donna Haraway, *Simians, Cyborgs, and Women: The Reinvention of Nature* (New York: Routledge, 1991), 61.

Video Game Designs by Girls and Boys: Variability and Consistency of Gender Differences   *Yasmin B. Kafai*

Over the past ten years, interactive technologies have become a significant part of children's culture. Video games such as *Super Mario Brothers* or *Sonic* have found a stable place in children's playrooms, in particular games catering to boys' interests in sports, adventure, and combat.[1] Only recently has so-called "pink software" established a playground for girls, promoting games and software such as *Barbie's Fashion Designer* or the *Babysitter Club* that draw on characters and activities popular among girls. In many ways, the production of interactive toys and games seems to replicate gender differences found in traditional toys and games, and the interests these generate in children.[2]

There is ample evidence in the research literature for the existence of gender differences in children's video game interest, use, and performance.[3] These gender differences also appear when children are asked to make their own video games.[4] But there are some indicators that these differences are not as universal as they may appear at first: some software, such as *Where in the World Is Carmen Sandiego?* seem to have equal appeal for boys and girls, and some girls like to play video games albeit with different interpretations.[5] Furthermore, gender differences in play performance disappear after extended exposure, a claim that is also supported by research on girls' general use of and interest in technology.[6] While these are isolated indicators, they point out that gender differences are not as consistent as one might believe. It is possible that children display more versatility and range in their play interests, and that particular factors such as game structures or context settings might have an impact. Research on children's toy and play preferences has provided evidence that structures of toys and play settings can elicit certain behaviors from play participants.[7]

The current analysis of video games designed by boys and girls intends to shed some light on the discussion around gender differences by comparing and contrasting two different game design contexts. In one, I asked students between the ages of nine and ten to design and implement educational video games to teach fractions to younger students. In the other, I asked children to design and implement educational video games to teach younger students about the solar system. The context differences examined in this essay refer to those between subject matters: mathematics and science. In the following sections, I first review pertinent research and describe the context in which the students produced the video games. Next, I compare and contrast the games designed by boys and girls in the two different contexts, taking into consideration features such as genres, worlds, character design, interactions, and narrative. Finally, I address the context dependency of gender differences, and what insights these results provide for developing video game design and play environments.

Review of Research

The context dependency of gender differences in interactive technologies is not a well-researched area. As Catherine Garvey notes, most research on gender differences in children's toy preferences and play styles

> has focused on profiling behavior of boys as a group and girls as a group. It has as yet failed to pursue any of the interesting questions about the range and versatility of children's play behavior or the conditions under which children might demonstrate flexibility in the cognitive and communicative aspects of make-believe or other types of play.[8]

Most research has centered on documenting gender differences in relation to computer interest, use, and performance. Studies have pointed out gender differences in game-playing interests as well as use.[9] Other research has looked at gender differences in children's spatial and attentional skills while or as a consequence of playing video games.[10] These theories of gender differences have been further elaborated by studies that examined children's preferences based on their real and imaginary designs of video games and electronic machines. For example, I asked girls and boys to design and implement their own video games, and found that the games designed by girls differed significantly from those designed by boys according to the use of violent feedback, characters, and game genre.[11] In a related research approach, Cornelia Brunner et al.

asked girls and boys to design fantasy machines, and discovered that girls designed machines with humanlike qualities whereas boys focused on fantasy machines with numerous technical details.[12]

When researchers analyze how children perceive gender stereotypes in video games, interpretations vary. Researchers such as Marsha Kinder argue that the values embedded in movies, toys, television, and video games provide powerful stereotypes for children's thinking.[13] By contrast, Christine Gailey questions to what extent these messages are received as transmitted.[14] She investigates what values video games convey, how children as players interpret the play process, and what children get out of games. Her research has demonstrated that children do not accept the universals provided in video games; they make up their own descriptions. Irrespective of the considerable gender stereotyping found in many video games (for example, in portraying women as victims or prizes), girls seem to resolve the dilemma by redefining their positions by casting themselves in managerial roles.

While gender differences are pervasive, there are also several documented instances where they appear less prominent. Recent research interrogating the video game–playing performance of girls and boys found that repeated play exposure attenuated preexisting gender differences.[15] In analyzing computer programming performance, Marcia Linn noted that girls could be as effective as boys when given the same opportunities.[16] These results were supported by Idit Harel as well as my own research; in examining long-term software design activities, we both found no significant differences between boys and girls' programming performance and interest.[17]

Gender differences also seem less prominent in the formation of the motivational appeal of games. Thomas W. Malone and Mark R. Lepper created a taxonomy of intrinsic motivations based on their research of different educational games.[18] They found that the presence of game features such as challenge, curiosity, control, and fantasy—as well as cooperation, competition, and recognition—increased motivational value for all players. They only uncovered one instance where there were significant differences between boys and girls in what they liked about the games:

> The boys seemed to like the fantasy of popping balloons and the girls seemed to dislike this fantasy. The addition of musical rewards, on the other hand, appeared to increase for girls, but to decrease for boys, the intrinsic interest of the activity.[19]

These results convincingly suggest that boys and girls find many (but not all) of the same game features appealing. Research that analyzes players and programmers' self-explanations notes the particular personal resonances that these activities hold for people.[20] In my study of children's making of video games, I found significant gender differences in their choices of creating characters, their feedback, and their narrative development.[21] But I also observed that in other game features, such as game interaction, game worlds, and genres, there were trends rather than significant differences between girls and boys' game designs. In other words, while gender differences are prevalent, there is a much richer picture behind what motivates and interests children in the playing with and making of interactive technologies. What this research pointed out is that girls are interested in making video games, but their creations look different from those designed by boys. The students drew from models of commercially available software in many ways: boys emulated video game design in the beginning, including characters and prizes found in popular video games; girls took existing educational software as a model. Many of the designed game contexts had little to do with the learning content: fractions. For that reason, the second study chose a science topic, the solar system, as the learning content because it would provide a natural context: outer space. While certain topics in science, such as biology and environmental studies, have been known to attract larger numbers of women, it has been clear from the outset that both domains, mathematics and science, are not traditionally favored by girls.[22]

Research Context and Methodology

To examine the context dependency of gender differences in students' game designs, data sets from two different game design projects were analyzed. In each game design project, a class of sixteen fourth grade students was asked to program educational games to teach either fractions (hereafter the Mathematics Game Design Project or MGDP) or the solar system (hereafter the Science Game Design Project or SGDP) to third graders. The two classes were divided between girls and boys in the following way: the MGDP had eight girls and eight boys, and the SGDP had nine girls and seven boys with students coming from various ethnic backgrounds and ranging in age between nine and ten years. The students met every day and transformed their classroom into a game design studio for six months, learning programming, writing stories and dialogues, representing fractions or the solar system, creating package designs and advertisements, considering interface design issues, and devising teaching strategies.[23] The collaborative structure of the project provided opportunities for the game designers to discuss their work with their classmates, and to show it to their potential users as well as a wider public. Several "focus sessions" allowed the teacher and researcher to initiate dialogues around issues and ideas relevant to all game designers. Games, students' experiences playing games, what they learned, and programming ideas were among the topics reviewed at these occasions.

The research for both game design projects, MGDP and SGDP, took place at an inner-city public elementary school in Boston. One part of the school is an experimental site for the MIT Media Laboratory, which was established over twelve years ago, having since investigated, on a large scale, the implementation and rituals of a computer culture. The school houses fifteen classrooms with approximately 250 students and has 110 networked computers. The computers are arranged in four circles in open areas surrounded by classrooms with additional computers. While this feature distinguishes this site from more conventional classrooms, the student population is nevertheless characteristic of an inner-city school, with proportionately more Hispanic and African American students.

The most distinctive aspects of the regular classroom activities are that all the students have daily access to computers and use mostly the programming language Logo to create their own software, as opposed to using predesigned program packages. The implications of students' programming experience are important for understanding the results of this study. All of the students who participated in either MGDP or SGDP probably had more technical experience than most students in other schools. While programming the games was still a difficult enterprise, it was also feasible because the students had sufficient knowledge of programming to begin the task. Both girls and boys had the opportunity to build this technical knowledge over time, as there were enough computers for each student. Consequently, girls would spend as much time on the computer as boys did. Both studies were conducted at a time when most students did not have computers at home; for that reason, outside experiences were negligible.

While both game design projects took place in the same school context, the two studies did not happen at the same time nor were they working with the same students: the MGDP took place two years before the SGDP. But the two game design projects shared enough features to be comparable: the same teacher and researcher conducted both projects, and students for each entered with similar programming background and video game experience. Hence, it seems unlikely that the time difference of two years created a different cultural environment or impacted significantly the games designed by the students.

A combination of qualitative methods was used to document the students' ideas, thoughts, and progress in game development. Interviews were conducted to gather information about students' interest, knowledge, and evaluation of video games. In the interviews that I conducted individually with each

student before the two projects began, I found that all of them had an awareness of and hands-on experience with video games. The extent of the video
game play experience, however, varied considerably. The major difference was
between girls and boys: most boys played video games actively and consistently, whereas only two girls acknowledged having done so. To summarize,
the girls and boys' knowledge of video games were not comparable. Perhaps
this result is not surprising considering that the majority of commercial video
games are played by boys.[24]

Results

In all, thirty-two final video games were analyzed according to the following
video game features: the game genre; the game worlds and places created; the
game characters and supporting cast of actors developed by students; the
interaction modes and feedback provided for the player; and the narrative
development as part of the game structure. To facilitate comparisons, all the
results have been transformed into percentages, and game designs of the two
different contexts are compared for each gender (see table 1).

Game Genres. There are various kinds of video games and many different ways to
group them. In the game industry, five major types are distinguished: sports,
role-playing, action, strategy, and simulation. For this study, I divided the
students' games into the following categories: adventure, sports/skills, and
teaching. These categories, especially "adventure" and "sport," were based on
existing commercial game formats, whereas "teaching" is usually not found in
commercial video games. Moreover, this categorization is by no means exhaus-
tive or exclusive, since many games actually fall in several categories at the
same time. For example, an adventure game may also be a skill game as the
player has to overcome many obstacles demonstrating considerable athletic
skills. Or, a simulation game of city building may have educational purposes as
the player deals with the complexity of dynamic networked systems. Nevertheless, this general categorization may serve as a starting point. For the analysis
of the designed games, the category "adventure" has been used when the
player experienced extraordinary events or was sent to unknown places to be
explored. The category "skill" has been used for games of an athletic nature,
such as basketball or skiing. A third category was games that used the "teaching" context in an explicit fashion.

The "adventure" genre was a popular one in both contexts, this more so for
boys than girls. A central feature of many adventure games was the incorporation of the moral dilemma: the contest between good and evil. The player is on

Table 1. Overview of Game Design Features by Gender
in MGDP and SGDP Context

Games	Girls		Boys	
	MGDP	SGDP	MGDP	SGDP
Genre				
Adventure	38%	33%	88%	54%
Sport/skill	38%	0%	13%	14%
Teaching	24%	67%	0%	29%
Worlds				
Fantasy	25%	0%	75%	0%
Realistic	75%	100%	25%	100%
Player				
Generic "you"	63%	77%	13%	58%
Animal/fantasy	25%	0%	25%	0%
Gender specific	12%	23%	62%	42%
Cast				
Zero and two	88%	100%	25%	100%
Two and more	12%	0%	75%	0%
Feedback				
Violent with wrong answer	13%	0%	88%	0%
Narrative				
Presence	38%	22%	87%	28%

the good side fighting off the bad guys in order to achieve the goal. This morality issue was present in all the boys' games in the MGDP where the player either had to recover "a stolen fraction wand" or "a stolen jewel," or "defeat demons, evil fraction aliens, globe ghosts or mash Martians" in order "to receive a bucket full of gold, a trip to Orlandoville, a wedding to a princess," or "a ticket to the summer park." In the science-oriented games, few boys opted to include this feature in their designs, such as "supporting someone who has been captured by aliens." Often, the player engages the aliens in a game of tag in order to "recover information" and return to earth or land on a particular planet for exploration purposes. Most girls, on the other hand, did not include in either context the morality issue, with the exception of one girl whose game focused on saving Mars (SGDP); here, the player had to defeat aliens in order to continue the game.

The "sports" genre was selected by only a few students in either context: they used basketball on the moon (SGDP, boy) or dunking basketball for learning fractions (MGDP, boy), skiing down a hill (MGDP, girl), or navigating a maze (MGDP, boy) or spiderweb (MGDP, girl) (see figures 1a and 1b). These choices were mostly triggered by personal preferences. One could also argue that the "sports" genre, despite its prominent presence among commercial video games, did not lend itself easily to the design of educational games.

"Teaching" was the second most popular theme in both contexts. In the MGDP, the two "teaching" games were both located in the classroom and involved a teacher, whereas in the SGDP, the game designer engaged the player in word searches, a variant not observed in the MGDP context. These word searches were programmed by four students. The program displayed a grid of ten by ten letters, and the player was asked to "recognize" pertinent words related to the solar system (such as the names of planets or key concepts) by stamping over the appropriate letters (see figure 2a). This particular teaching technique might replicate students' science learning experience, which is more than often simply the memorization of the right words printed in boldface or colored type in science textbooks. Other "teaching" games asked the player to rearrange or recognize the correct order of the planets (see figure 2b).

One can speculate on why so many girls favored this particular game genre. One interpretation is that girls implicitly embedded a gender bias found among professional software designers when they develop products for boys or girls.[25] They found that expectations held by many software game designers are central in determining the way that the design interacts with the user. Software that is explicitly designed for girls is often classified as a "learning tool," while programs designed for boys are frequently classified as "games." Girls' preferences for this software format might have been based on their choice of designing for other girls, whereas the boys were designing for other boys as designated software users. Another explanation is that girls might have simply followed the directions of designing an educational video game down to the letter. While either interpretation offers some insights into possible motives for the choice of this genre, they do not provide an answer for why this genre became more prevalent with girls and boys in the SGDP compared to the MGDP context.

Game Worlds. The influence of context became even more evident in the choice of game worlds. All the game designs centered around a location (or the exploration of different locations). While the MGDP context generated the greatest variety of places—such as spiderwebs, coin grids, street scenes, and

Ideas .... Plans ... Ideas ... Plans ... Ideas   Name:

Date:

MY PLANS FOR TODAY:

Finish web. Decorate my screen

HOW MY SCREEN WILL LOOK LIKE:

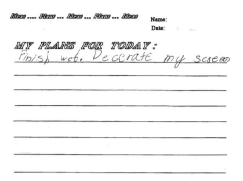

Ideas .... Plans ... Ideas ... Plans ... Ideas   Name:

Date:

MY PLANS FOR TODAY:

I'll make is so a fraction come out of a coin

HOW MY SCREEN WILL LOOK LIKE:

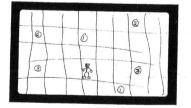

Figures 1a and b.
Designer notebook entries for Gaby and Trevor's game designs. Gaby's game describes a spider-web in which the player moves around as a fly (going away from the spider) and turns on fraction blocks where questions are posed. Trevor's map shows the different stations or levels of the world that the player has to pass.

PLANS ... IDEAS ... PLANS ... IDEAS ... PLANS ... IDEAS ....   NAME:

DATE:

MY PLANS FOR TODAY:

Today I will ~~start~~ make another word search.
It will be a second level. It will have these
words in it: solar system, rotate, tilt, equator,
stars, craters, moon and comet.

WHAT MY SCREEN WILL LOOK LIKE:

MY SHAPES:

craters
moon
comet
stars
rotate
SOLAR SYSTEM
EQUATOR
Tilt

PLANS ... IDEAS ... PLANS ... IDEAS ... PLANS ... IDEAS ....   NAME:

DATE:

MY PLANS FOR TODAY:

My plans are to have the planets mixed up but
the names on them. Then you have to get them
in the right order.

HOW MY SCREEN WILL LOOK LIKE:

MY SHAPES:

MIXED UP
PLANETS

Pluto   Venus Earth

Figures 2a and b.
Designer notebook entries for Cheryl and Rachel's game designs. Cheryl's design describes the word search and arrangement of words. Rachel's design shows the planets to be arranged in the right order.

map games—the worlds in the SGDP context were mostly located in space, either in the solar system or on an individual planet such as Mars. A major distinction could be drawn in the reality aspect of the game worlds. In many instances, game worlds could be described as either realistic because they featured well-known places such as classrooms, ski slopes, and airports, or as fantasy places because they were imaginary worlds in which the player would learn about the content.

All the game worlds in the SGDP context had a space setting, which given the nature of the games, would be considered "realistic." One distinction was whether the setting was centered around one planet or encompassed the whole solar system. Some games used the introduction sequence as an entrance to the solar system, whereas others situated travel through space and visited different planets (see figures 3a and 3b).

In contrast, the MGDP created greater variation between fantasy and realistic contexts. Many boys had invented fantasy places like "Orlandoville" or the "Island of the Goon." This choice might reflect boys' need for extended play space. Henry Jenkins observes that over the last fifty years, the play spaces of children—and in particular, those of boys—have moved from streets and play-grounds to the safety of children's homes.[26] Video games have provided the opportunity for boys to extend their play space into the virtual world. By contrast, most girls have been confined to the space of the home. This might explain their choice of more realistic settings, such as classrooms, ski slopes, and spiderwebs.

In their design of game worlds, the children made reference to features found in commercially available video and computer games. For example, a fraction game using warp zones was reminiscent of the *Super Mario Brothers'* tunnel system (see figure 4a). One science game followed the blueprint of an existing educational game that the girl designer had played when she was younger (see figure 4b). Many of the science games used the exploration of the solar system as the focal point, a feature found in popular educational games such as *Where in Space Is Carmen Sandiego* and *The Magic School Bus in Space*.

Development of Game Characters. The places or worlds in which the games were situated were populated with an interesting cast of characters. One group concerns the game character assigned to the player; the other describes the supporting cast of game actors. In the majority of games, the player became a generic "you," leaving the possibility open for the younger student to be a girl or boy. Take the following game introduction written by a girl in the MGDP context to situate a player of either gender:

PLANS ... IDEAS ... PLANS ... IDEAS ... PLANS ... IDEAS ....   NAME:

DATE:

MY PLANS FOR TODAY:

I will finish my startup page.
I will type all my programs on the
flipside and try to start on Mars.

HOW MY SCREEN WILL LOOK LIKE: **MY SHAPES:**

THINGS I DID AND PROBLEMS I HAD TODAY: NAME: DATE:

CHECK AS MANY AS NECESSARY
IN OVERALL : THE PROBLEMS I HAD TODAY WERE MOSTLY RELATED TO
_LOGO, _DESIGN, _TEACHING, √EXPLAINING, _GAME IDEAS, _SCIENCE

I got the title done and the color
and was really easy to do.

MY PLANS FOR TOMORROW:

Nothing much but sit around and
talk and play

HOW MY SCREEN WILL LOOK LIKE:

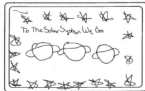

Figures 3a and b.
Designer notebook entries for Deanna's title screen design for her game, "The Solar System We Go," and Carleton's screen design for his "Cam Capsule" game.

> You want to go to the home of Zeus but the map was ripped up by the Greek God Hades. All of the Greek Gods and Godesses [sic] have a fraction of the map. You are to go to the Gods and Godesses [sic] one at a time and they will ask you a fraction problem. If you get it right you will get a fraction of the map. When you get the whole map you will be at the gate of Zeus' home. The bull at the gate will ask you three hard fraction problems. If you get them right you will go inside Zeus' home and get to become the God or Godess [sic] of fractions and meet Zeus!

In one solar system game, the girl designer provided the player with a choice to pick either "player 1" or "player 2," but made no reference to the gender of the player. The majority of games designed in the SGDP context used a generic character design.

The gender-specific character was chosen most often in the MGDP context. Most of the boys chose a fantasy figure, such as "Gemini" or "Swartz," and assumed that the player, too, would be male by choosing names like "Mike" or "Tommy." One might interpret this choice of gender-specific character design as also involving a more personal identification: the player and character are one and the same. Further, this form of player positioning chosen by the boys might reflect conventions in the commercial market. But these appeared, although to a lesser extent, in the SGDP context as well. The following game designed by a boy in the SGDP context provides a good example:

> It was a dark day for Commander Keen's fans everywhere. Their favorite hero had been seriously hurt while trying to start the enormous "Dope fish." After that he decided to take a little vacation. Little did he know that he was going to be captured by the Potato King, Hoopus Snoopus. Oh sure. I know what you are thinking. You're thinking that Hoopus Snoopus got turned into a hash brown in "Keen Dreams" but he has come back and he wants revenge. Who can save Keen? If you haven't guessed yet you must be really stupid, yes, it's his little brother Deen. That's why this game is called "Deens World."

Some of the player characters had fantasy names, as already noted above, making the relevance of gender more difficult to hypothesize. While there were some animal characters in the MGDP context, this feature was virtually absent within the SGDP.

In terms of additional cast members, we could observe further differences between the two game design contexts. There are a small number of additional characters designed in the SGDP context, always involving fictive aliens and, in one instance, fictional characters such as a commander and figure named

Name:

Plans .. Ideas .. Plans .. Ideas .. Plans .. Date:

PLANS AND IDEAS FOR TOMORROW :

do my map

Plans .. Ideas .. Plans .. Ideas .. Plans ..

PLANS ... IDEAS ... PLANS ... IDEAS ... PLANS ... IDEAS .... **NAME:**

DATE:

MY PLANS FOR TODAY:

My plans for today are that I make 18 cards and have the top ones match with the bottom in different orders. The game would be like Concentration

HOW MY SCREEN WILL LOOK LIKE:

MY SHAPES:

Figures 4a and b.
Designer notebook entries for Jero and Kim's game designs. Jero's map shows the different stations or levels of the world that the player has to pass. Kim's screen design shows the arrangement of cards and planets.

"Keen" (SGDP, boy). By contrast, the MGDP context generated greater variety in number and kind of characters. Most boys created several characters (for example, demons, aliens from planet Zork, magicians, dragons, soldiers from Loft, and goons) with fantasy names (such as Zork, Zarcon, Garvin, Sparzi, and Marley) for the game world in which the player had to interact and learn about fractions. In contradistinction, the girls created fewer additional characters in the MGDP context. It is apparent in this comparison that the girls had a significantly different take on the role that the players and actors have in the game.

These results run counter to some of the existing interpretations. It has been argued that commercial video game figures provided the inspiration for the game figures designed by the boys in the MGDP context. This contention gains support if one considers the abundance of available video games and their focus on a male audience.[27] For the girls, on the other hand, there are fewer examples to draw from because of the paucity of gender-appropriate video games. The choice of familiar and personal figures provides room for the interpretation that girls grounded their designs in what they knew and liked: Rosy liked cats, hence a cat plays a major role in her game; Miriam used a skier because she liked skiing; Gloria and Sina cast a teacher in their games. Another possibility is that the small number of supporting characters reflected preferred social groupings: girls have been known to play in smaller groups than boys.[28]

Still, we find in the SGDP context that the boys designed as few characters as the girls did. There are several possible explanations here. One could be that students only drew a small cast of characters because space missions are not known to involve many people, due to the restricted living space on spaceships. Then again, many commercial films and popular television programs usually feature a large cast of characters. It is unclear what generated the differences between the science and mathematics contexts.

Design of Game Feedback. The design of feedback to the player was a central feature in the games and linked to the quality of answers given by the player. The feedback modalities were either violent or nonviolent. "Game Over," by itself, would not constitute a violent feedback if it were not in connection with losing one's life or suffering harm by insulting the player's intelligence. Game actors either lose their lives before the game is over or as a result of it. In the SGDP context, no designer included violent feedback in cases where the player did not answer correctly; only one boy did not use violent feedback in the MGDP. The nonviolent feedback options were "sending the player back to another planet" (SGDP, girl), "not receiving a piece of the map" (MGDP, girl), or "having to start again from the top of the ski slope" (MGDP, girl).

In the MGDP context, the designers (and all of them were boys) developed a variety of violent feedback modalities. For example, game actors on the screen were "kicked to the moon," "turned into an ice cube," "sent frying to the underworld," or "mentally transformed." One boy made his surfer character insult the players' intelligence when they gave the wrong answer: "Let me see how smart you are, Dude or Dudette," and "So you are telling me you're dumb." The harm here is psychological rather than physical; but it is still harmful. Only one girl ended her game with a helicopter crash when the player did not give the right answer.

The issue of violent feedback is probably one of the most discussed features in video game play literature.[29] Many commercial video games, such as Mortal Kombat or Street Fighter, indulge in explicit images of violence and combat activities as so many markers of progress through the game. It is difficult to explain the absence of violent feedback in the SGDP context, especially among the boys, and particularly because it was such a prominent feature in the MGDP context. One of my explanations is that the space theme provided a context that focused on overcoming physical limitations, such as space travel, rather than people. As noted before, only three students included aliens that could have served the role of an adversary.

Design of Game Narrative. As students continued developing their games, defined characters, and outlined scenes, they often created a story that situated the actors in an imaginary yet meaningful context. In many instances, they were located in the introduction. One MGDP boy's game starts with the story of Jose, who gets lost and experiences a series of adventures over several days and nights:

> You are Jose, a third grade kid who gets lost and must find his way home. You will go on many different adventures. Along the way, people (or beasts, creatures, etc.) will ask you questions about fractions (you will type A, B or C, remember to press enter). If you get the question right, you will go on safely, but beware! Danger lurks if you get the question wrong. Have fun if you dare! Type play and press enter. "Where am I?" "I have to get home!" A mysterious man approaches you. "Hey kid, I'm Marley the Magician and I'm going to make you disappear if you don't tell me how much of this square is colored" says the man.

Another example is from a girl in the SGDP context. Her science game involves a player who gets kidnapped into space:

> One morning you wake up to find you are in a strange room like nothing you've ever seen. Suddenly three weird creatures come into your room.

You ask where you are and why it's so hot. They reply in a strange accent, "Sunspin or your Sun." Then you yell out: "The Sun! How can I be on the Sun?" One of the creatures answers, "Technolegy [*sic*]. We are intelligent creatures. We originally come from Gokk but you don't know about this planet yet. You will some . . . " "But why am I here?" you interrupt. The creatures just look at you and then walk out of the room closing the door and locking it behind them. Then a terrifying thought strikes you—you have been kidnapped into space.

While inclusion of narratives was not always practiced in the beginning of the design process, many students opted to include stories later on. There was a substantial difference between the two game design contexts, however: whereas many students chose to have some form of narrative in their fraction games, any explicit narrative is mostly absent in the SGDP, with the exception of a few games that used a story context to introduce the player to the game.

A possible reason for the popularity of the narrative in the MGDP context was that it could be considered a form of problem solving. It reconciled two seemingly adverse domains in a more coherent framework. In the fraction games, the narrative provided the glue that connected the different scenes or places *and* the instructional content. Furthermore, it allowed students to incorporate fantasy and decorate their worlds in a more appealing way. This was also one of the features that the children in Thomas Malone and Mark Lepper's study identified as appealing in playing games.[30]

While this is not a sufficient explanation for the infrequent use of narrative in the SGDP context, it is possible that the science context itself provided a narrative. In all the science games, the solar system or planets served as the starting point for the game designs, and the players' explorations and adventures. One could argue that in the science games, the content was intrinsically integrated with the game ideas—something that could not be stated for most fraction games. Nearly all the fraction games, with the exception of one game—in which the player was assembling fraction pieces of a map that had been ripped apart—had an extrinsic integration of content and game idea. Consequently, the designer had to work in the narrative to provide some connection between the game and content to be learned.

What Have We Learned about Gender Differences?

The comparative analyses of these two game design contexts presented a complex picture of the ways in which gender differences are simultaneously consistent *and* variable. The comparison of the different contexts, MGDP and SGDP, foregrounded observable shifts in preference for game format, realism of designed game worlds, gender and number of characters, quality of feedback, and presence of narrative. From the analysis of context differences by gender, it became clear that these shifts were mostly due to the boys' change of game design features. Looking over the girls' games, we discovered a remarkable consistency in design features across contexts. These results offer a first indicator of variations of game preferences within one gender.

This result may be a consequence of the research methodology used for assessing gender differences. Traditionally, researchers have observed children's game-playing performance in natural or experimental settings, or have asked children about their play interests in relation to choices from among already existing commercial toys and games. Asking children to create their own video games allowed some game features to emerge that were clearly found in commercial games. The influence of commercially available games was especially strong in the case of boys' games in the MGDP context. Many game designers took as their starting point ideas borrowed from popular video games, such as *Super Mario Brothers* or *Pacman*. Or, students referred to existing commercial games in their interpretations of their own games, as did this MGDP boy:

> Because you are playing the role of the character and you want to type in your things. Everything is you. And if you are, say, role playing for—I mean, in arcades it is someone else and in arcade games, you don't—role playing isn't like, you don't play the role, you just like someone, like the spaceship or the gun plays the role. . . . Role playing is when . . . actually *Dungeons and Dragons* is kind of role playing for, that is kind of, a play on words because you roll with dice to see if you shoot something, and you're also playing the role of the character. You see, in role playing in *Dungeons and Dragons* you have the character sheet. You write down your name, what you want your character to be, write down all his abilities and all his strengths. See you are playing his role, you try to kill monsters and get treasures. You are playing his role.

Many of the boys' game implementations include violent aspects, documented in the design of their feedback to player interactions. Violence is one of the most prominent features in commercial video games.[31] Hence, popular media offers paradigms for the organization of the game design (at least for boys).

Yet popular media do not provide similar models for girls. Rarely are female game figures cast in the main role. The thematic embedding of video games in hunts and adventures are not necessarily suited to girls' tastes. In the interviews, many girls also stated that they had no particular interest in pursuing video game playing because they did not like the games, their content, and their violent aspects. Due to this lack of popular models, girls choose as the starting point of their narrative a familiar and likable figure (such as Rosy's cat) or a familiar place (like Sina's classroom or Miriam's ski slope). In many ways, girls created their own worlds and characters while making their games, compensating for the sexism and violence found in many video games.[32]

This research approach allowed for the articulation of gender differences in alternative forms from those readily available through the commercial market at the time these studies were conducted. Moreover, it allowed for variability across contexts, and this was particularly true for boys. Some researchers have argued that

> girls are moving closer to boys in their identification with heroic figures, adventurous achievement, and pretend aggression than previous data claimed. This appears to reflect changes in television action programs, where more female heroines now appear, as well as the increased willingness of parents to tolerate adventure themes in girls' play. . . . We do not see a comparable trend among boys—that is, a move toward playing female games and using traditionally female toys.[33]

The convergence of game preferences observed in this study seems to suggest otherwise: here, one could say, it was the boys who adopted more "female" design features in their games. But these conclusions have to be drawn with care. Jerome Singer and Dorothy Singer noted the increasing presence of female role models in television programs as one reason for the observable transformations in girls' play.[34] The appearance of pink software on the market is too recent and probably not pervasive enough to argue for a similar situation in the programming of interactive software. Furthermore, the current titles seem to affiliate content more closely with traditional play arenas of girls. *Barbie's Fashion Designer*, which allows users to dress Barbie in different clothes, integrates smoothly within the existing play activities of girls. *The Babysitter Club* takes its inspiration from a popular book series, and provides a diary and schedules, in addition to letter paper printing designs. More recently, video game productions have placed girls and women in the role of protagonists.[35] It remains to be seen what impact these developments will have on girls' interest in video games and software, and whether similar trends can be observed in the interactive domain.

There is still an explanation required for why girls, in contrast to boys, were so consistent in their design choices. The choice of the two comparative contexts, mathematics and science, could be one reason. Girls' lesser interest in these subject areas is well documented in education research literature.[36] One could speculate on the variations one would see if the chosen contexts resonated better with girls' choices and interests, such as history and the social sciences. Future studies would need to investigate this issue more closely.

Last Words

The results of this research made visible the variability in gender differences. In particular, these results suggest that boys have more variability in their game design preferences than formerly understood. These results also point out the consistency in gender differences. Girls are not disinterested in video games or interactive technologies, they are simply interested in other features. The presence and success of pink software are testaments to this potential. Taken together, these results open the possibility to consider other video game designs for fun and learning than are currently available on the market.

But if the trends of casting more women in protagonist roles in television programming are an indicator of what might happen in interactive programming, then games with other features will also appeal to girls. The potential confluence of girls and boys' game interests might create contexts in which both of them could play and interact together. Preliminary results from networked, multiuser environments are a first indicator of this trend.[37] One such example is MOOSE (Multi Object Oriented Scripting Environment), developed for children.[38] In this multiuser environment, girls and boys create their own worlds with different places, objects, features, and activities. Ultimately, we need play environments that support children's versatility in expressing themselves that are not confined by boundaries of gender stereotypes, but defined by the unbounded limits of their imagination.

Acknowledgments

The research reported here was conducted during my time at the MIT Media Laboratory and at Project Headlight's Model School of the Future, and was supported by the IBM Corporation (Grant #OSP95952), the National Science Foundation (Grant #851031–0195), the McArthur Foundation (Grant #874304), the LEGO Company, Fukatake, and Apple Computer, Inc. The analyses of the data were supported in part by a grant from the University of California at Los Angeles Academic Senate. The ideas expressed here do not necessarily reflect the positions of the supporting agencies. Many thanks to V. Maithili, who helped with the analysis of the solar system games. I also wish to thank Joanne Ronkin and her students for their collaboration in both studies. Without them, this research would not have been possible.

Notes

1 See Eugene F. Provenzo Jr., *Video Kids: Making Sense of Nintendo* (Cambridge, Mass.: Harvard University Press, 1991).

2 Christine Garvey, *Play* (Cambridge, Mass.: Harvard University Press, 1990); Marsha Kinder, *Playing with Power in Movies, Television, and Video Games* (Berkeley: University of California Press, 1991); Dorothy G. Singer and Jerome L. Singer, *The House of Make-Believe: Play and the Developing Imagination* (Cambridge, Mass.: Harvard University Press, 1990); and Brian Sutton-Smith, *Toys as Culture* (New York: Gardner Press, 1986), 198.

3 See Jeffrey Goldstein, "Sex Differences in Toy Use and Video Game Play," in *Toys, Play, and Child Development*, ed. Jeffrey H. Goldstein (New York: Cambridge University Press, 1994), 110–29; and Provenzo, *Video Kids*.

4 See Yasmin B. Kafai, "Gender Differences in Children's Constructions of Video Games," in *Interacting with Video*, ed. Patricia M. Greenfield and Rodney R. Cocking (Norwood, N.J.: Ablex Publishing, 1996).

5 See Christine Ward Gailey, "Mediated Messages: Gender, Class, and Cosmos in Home Video Games," *Journal of Popular Culture* 2, no. 1 (1993): 81–97.

6 On "extended exposure," see Patricia M. Greenfield and Rodney R. Cocking, "Effects of Interactive Entertainment Technology on Development," *Journal of Applied Developmental Psychology* 15, no. 1 (1994): 1–2. On girls and technology, see Marcia C. Linn, "Fostering Equitable Consequences from Computer Learning Environments," *Sex Roles* 13, nos. 3–4 (1985): 229–40.

7 See Ken Karpoe and Robert Olney, "The Effect of Boys' or Girls' Toys on Sex-Typed Play in Preadolescents," *Sex Roles* 9 (1983): 507–18; and Hanna Ross and Herbert Taylor, "Do Boys Prefer Daddy or His Physical Style of Play?" *Sex Roles* 20 (1989): 23–33.

8 Gravey, *Play*, 154.

9 On interest, see Kori Inkpen, Rena Upitis, Maria Klawe, Ann Anderson, Mutundi Ndunda, Kamran Sedighian, Steve Leroux, and David Hsu, " 'We Have Never-Forgetful Flowers in Our Garden': Girls' Responses to Electronic Games," Technical Report 93–47, Department of Computer Science, University of British Columbia, December 1993; and Provenzo, *Video Kids*. On use, see Ron Kubey and Robert Larson, "The Use and Experience of the New Media among Children and Young Adolescents," *Communication Research* 17 (1990): 17–130.

10 See Patricia M. Greenfield, C. Craig Brannon, and David Lohr, "Two-Dimensional Representation of Movement through Three-Dimensional Space: The Role of Video Game Expertise," *Journal of Applied Developmental Psychology* 15, no. 1 (1994): 87–104; Patricia M. Greenfield, Patricia deWinstanley, Heidi Kilpatrick, and Daniel Kaye, "Action Video Games and Informal Education: Effects on Strategies for Dividing Visual Attention," *Journal of Applied Developmental Psychology* 15, no. 1, 105–24; Lynn Okagaki and Peter French, "Effects of Video Game Playing on Measures of Spatial Performance: Gender Effects in Late Adolescence," *Journal of Applied Developmental Psychology* 15, no. 1, 33–58; and Kaveri Subrahmanyam and Patricia M. Greenfield, "Effects of Video Game Practice on Spatial Skills in Girls and Boys," *Journal of Applied Developmental Psychology* 15, no. 1, 13–32.

11 Kafai, "Gender Differences."

12 Cornelia Brunner, Dorothy Bennet, Maria Clements, Jan Hawkins, Margaret Honey, and

Babette Moeller, "Gender and Technological Imagination" (paper presented at the annual meeting of the American Educational Research Association, Boston, Mass., 1990.

13   Kinder, *Playing with Power*.

14   Gailey, "Mediated Messages."

15   Greenfield and Cocking, "Interactive Entertainment Technology."

16   Linn, "Fostering Equitable Consequences."

17   Idit Harel, *Children Designers* (Norwood, N.J.: Ablex Publishing, 1991); and Yasmin B. Kafai, *Minds in Play: Computer Game Design as a Context for Children's Learning* (Hillsdale, N.J.: Lawrence Erlbaum, 1995).

18   Thomas W. Malone and Mark R. Lepper, "Making Learning Fun: A Taxonomy of Intrinsic Motivations for Learning," in *Conative and Affective Process Analyses*, vol. 3 of *Aptitude, Learning, and Instruction*, ed. Richard E. Snow and Michael J. Farr (Hillsdale, N.J.: Lawrence Erlbaum, 1987), 223–53.

19   Ibid., 226.

20   Sherry Turkle, *The Second Self: Computers and the Human Spirit* (New York: Simon and Schuster, 1984).

21   Kafai, "Gender Differences."

22   See Myra Sadker and David Sadker, *Failing at Fairness: How America's Schools Cheat Girls* (New York: Scribner's, 1994).

23   One of the primary intentions of these projects was to investigate game making as a context for learning Logo programming and fractions, among other things (see also Harel, *Children Designers*). For that reason, the games designed by the students are a special breed called educational games. Yet, as my analyses will indicate, it was this particular constellation that emphasized game aspects, since students had to think about how to create games that were educational and entertaining at the same time. In the following analysis, I focus more on the game aspects than the learning aspects, which are discussed more extensively in other publications (see, for example, Kafai, *Minds in Play*).

24   Greenfield, Brannon, and Lohr, "Two-Dimensional Representation"; and Provenzo, *Video Kids*.

25   Charles Huff and Joel Cooper, "Sex Bias in Educational Software: The Effects of Designers' Stereotypes on the Software They Design," *Journal of Applied Social Psychology* 17 (1987): 519–32.

26   Justine Cassell and Henry Jenkins, eds., *From Barbie to Mortal Kombat: Gender and Computer Games* (Cambridge, Mass.: MIT Press, 1998). See chapter 12 by Henry Jenkins, " 'Complete Freedom of Movement': Video Games as Gendered Play Spaces," 262–98.

27   Provenzo, *Video Kids*; and Kinder, *Playing with Power*.

28   See Lynn C. Moller, Sharon Hymel, and Karla H. Rubin, "Sex Typing in Play and Popularity in Middle Childhood," *Sex Roles* 26 (1992): 331–53.

29   Provenzo, *Video Kids*; and Shawn B. Silvern and Peter A. Williamson, "The Effects of Video Game Play on Young Children's Aggression, Fantasy, and Prosocial Behavior," *Journal of Applied Developmental Psychology* 8 (1987): 453–62.

30   Malone and Lepper, "Making Learning Fun."

31   Provenzo, *Video Kids*.

32   Gailey, "Mediated Messages."

33   Singer and Singer, *House of Make-Believe*, 80.

34   Ibid.

35   See Kris Goodfellow, "Beyond Barbie: Games by Women," *New York Times*, 11 November 1996.

36   Sadker and Sadker, *Failing at Fairness*.

37   See Sherry Turkle, *Life on the Screen* (New York: Simon and Schuster, 1996).

38   Amy Bruckman, "MOOSE for Children" (Ph.D. diss., Media Laboratory, Massachusetts Institute of Technology, 1997).

Selective Bibliography on Children's Media
Culture   *Karen Orr Vered*

The following references constitute a "suggested reading list" for further study of relevant issues around the general topic of children's visual media culture. Restricted mainly to works published in the last ten years, this list represents historical, critical, and qualitative approaches to different mass media and their audiences, especially those that present children as cognizant, selective, and active consumers of popular culture. Although this bibliography omits the wealth of quantitative studies that dominated the study of children's media in past decades, it does include several works that take a cognitive approach, particularly with reference to digital media and computer and video games, since they frequently combine subject observation, skills measurements, and qualitative interviews. Since the emphasis here is on visual media and culture, works on children's literature have been kept to a minimum, even though they constitute an important related area of study. The few selections on children's literature are included either because their subject matter has had cross-media significance, as in the case of *Little Orphan Annie*, or the work itself has the potential to significantly influence the study of visual media culture and the investigation of children's popular culture. With few exceptions, the majority of references stress children rather than adolescents or "youths," who are increasingly treated in Western culture as a distinct age grade that is neither adult nor child. Thus, the main goal of this selective bibliography is to highlight a growing body of work that identifies children, in all their particularities, as a distinct group of participants in, consumers of, and in some cases, producers of mass media culture—a group with its own distinctive practices, tastes, and histories.

Anderson, James. "Research on Children and Television: A Criticism." *Journal of Broadcasting* 25 (1981): 395–400.

Bazalgette, Cary, and David Buckingham, eds. *In Front of the Children: Screen Entertainment and Young Audiences.* London: British Film Institute, 1995.

Bryant, Jennings, and Daniel R. Anderson, eds. *Children's Understanding of TV.* New York: Academic Press, 1982.

Buckingham, David. *Children and Television: An Overview of Research*. London: British Film Institute, 1987.

——. *Children Talking Television: The Making of Television Literacy*. London: Falmer Press, 1993.

——. *Moving Images: Understanding Children's Emotional Responses to Television*. Manchester, U.K.: Manchester University Press, 1996.

——. *Reading Audiences: Young People and the Media*. Manchester, U.K.: Manchester University Press, 1993.

——, ed. *Watching Media Learning: Making Sense of Media Education*. London: Falmer Press, 1990.

Buckingham, David, and Julian Sefton-Green, eds. *Cultural Studies Goes to School: Reading and Teaching Popular Media*. London: Taylor and Francis, 1994.

Burbank, Lucille. "Children's Television: An Historical Inquiry on Three Selected Prominent, Long-Running, Early Childhood TV Programs." Ph.D. diss., Temple University, 1992.

Cassell, Justine, and Henry Jenkins, eds. *From Barbie to Mortal Kombat: Gender and Computer Games*. Cambridge, Mass.: MIT Press, 1998.

Cherland, Meredith Rogers. *Private Practices: Girls Reading Fiction and Constructing Identity*. London: Taylor and Francis, 1994.

Christian-Smith, Linda K., ed. *Texts of Desire: Essays on Fiction, Femininity, and Schooling*. London: Falmer Press, 1993.

Clifford, Brian R., Barrie Gunter, and Jill McAleer. *Television and Children: Program Evaluation, Comprehension, and Impact*. Hillsdale, N.J.: Lawrence Erlbaum, 1995.

Cole, Jeffrey. *The UCLA Television Violence Monitoring Report*. Los Angeles: University of California, Los Angeles, Center for Communication Policy, 1995.

Cullingford, Cedric. *Children and Television*. Hampshire, U.K.: Gower, 1984.

Davies, Maire Messenger. *Television is Good for Your Kids*. London: Hilary Shipman, Ltd., 1989.

——. *Fake, Fact, and Fantasy: Children's Interpretations of Television Reality*. Hillsdale, N.J.: Lawrence Erlbaum, 1997.

Deane, Paul. *Mirrors of American Culture: Children's Fiction Series in the Twentieth Century*. Metuchen, N.J.: Scarecrow Press, 1991.

deCordova, Richard. "Ethnography and Exhibition: The Child Audience, the Hays Office, and Saturday Matinees." *Camera Obscura* 23 (May 1990): 90–107.

——. "The Mickey in Macy's Window: Childhood, Consumerism, and Disney Animation." In *Disney Discourse: Producing the Magic Kingdom*, edited by Eric Smoodin, 203–13. New York: Routledge, 1994.

——. "Child-Rearing Advice and the Moral Regulation of Children's Movie-Going." *Quarterly Review of Film and Video* 15, no. 4 (1995): 99–109.

Dorfman, Ariel, and Armand Mattelart. *How to Read Donald Duck: Imperialist Ideology in the Disney Comic*, translated by David Kunzle. New York: International General, 1971.

Durndell, Alan, Peter Glissov, and Gerda Siann. "Gender and Computing: Persisting Differences." *Educational Research* 37, no. 3 (1995): 219–27.

Eiss, Harry, ed. *Images of the Child*. Bowling Green, Ohio: Bowling Green State University Popular Press, 1994.

Engelhardt, Tom. "Children's Television: The Shortcake Strategy." In *Watching Television*, edited by Todd Gitlin, 68–110. New York: Pantheon, 1986.

Escobedo, Theresa H. "Play in a New Medium: Children's Talk and Graphics at Computers." *Play and Culture* 5, no. 2 (1992): 120–40.

Federman, Joel, et al. *The Social Effects of Electronic Interactive Games: An Annotated Bibliography*. Studio City, Calif.: Mediascope, 1996.

Field, Mary. *Good Company: The Story of the Children's Entertainment Film Movement in Great Britain, 1943–1950*. London: Longmans, Green, [1952].

Friedman, Ted. "Making Sense of Software: Computer Games and Interactive Textuality." In *Cybersociety: Computer-Mediated Communication and Community*, edited by Steven G. Jones, 73–89. Thousand Oaks, Calif.: Sage Publications, 1995.

Fuller, Mary, and Henry Jenkins. "Nintendo and New World Travel Writing: A Dialogue." In *Cybersociety: Computer-Mediated Communication and Community*, edited by Steven G. Jones, 57–72. Thousand Oaks, Calif.: Sage Publications, 1995.

Gailey, Christine Ward. "Mediated Messages: Gender, Class, and Cosmos in Home Video Games." *Journal of Popular Culture* 27, no. 1 (1993): 81–94.

Giacquinta, Joseph B., Jo Anne Bauer, and Jane E. Levin. *Beyond Technology's Promise: An Examination of Children's Educational Computing at Home*. New York: Cambridge University Press, 1993.

Goldstein, Ruth M., and Edith Zornow. *The Screen Image of Youth: Movies about Children and Adolescents*. Metuchen, N.J.: Scarecrow Press, 1980.

Greenfield, Patricia Marks. *Mind and Media: The Effects of Television, Video Games, and Computers*. Cambridge, Mass.: Harvard University Press, 1984.

——. "Video Games as Cultural Artifacts." *Journal of Applied Developmental Psychology*, 15, no. 10 (1994): 3–12.

——, et al. "The Program-Length Commercial: A Study of the Effects of Television/Toy Tie-Ins on Imaginative Play." *Psychology and Marketing* 7, no. 4 (winter 1990); 237–55.

——, et al. "Cognitive Socialization by Computer Games in Two Cultures: Inductive Discovery or Mastery of an Iconic Code?" *Journal of Applied Developmental Psychology* 15, no. 1 (1994): 59–86.

Greenfield, Patricia Marks, Dorathea Farrar, and Jessica Beagles-Roos. "Is the Medium the Message? An Experimental Comparison of the Effects of Radio and Television on Imagination." *Journal of Applied Developmental Psychology* 7 (1986): 201–18.

Greenfield, Patricia Marks, and Jessica Beagles-Roos. "Radio vs. Television: Their Cognitive Impact on Children of Different Socioeconomic and Ethnic Groups." *Journal of Communication* 38, no. 2 (spring 1988): 71–92.

Greenfield, Patricia Marks, and Rodney R. Cocking, eds. *Interacting with Video*. Norwood, N.J.: Ablex Publishing, 1996.

Gunter, Barrie, and Jill McAleer. *Children and Television*. 2d ed. London: Routledge, 1997.

Hendershot, Heather. "The Strawberry Shortcake Doll: Odor, Disgust, Femininity, and Toy Design." In *Gendered Design/The Gendering of Design*, edited by Pat Kirkham. Manchester, U.K.: Manchester University Press, 1995.

——. *Saturday Morning Censors: Television Regulation before the V-Chip*. Durham, N.C.: Duke University Press, 1998.

Henderson, Karla A. "A Feminist Analysis of Selected Professional Recreation Literature about Girls/Women from 1907–1990." *Journal of Leisure Research* 25, no. 2 (1993): 165–81.

Hilton, Mary, ed. *Potent Fictions: Children's Literacy and the Challenge of Popular Culture*. London: Routledge, 1996.

Himmelweit, Hilde T., A. N. Oppenheim, and Pamela Vince. *Television and the Child*. Oxford: Oxford University Press, 1958.

Hodge, Robert, and David Tripp. *Children and Television: A Semiotic Approach*. Stanford, Calif.: Stanford University Press, 1986.

Home, Anna. *Into the Box of Delights: A History of Children's Television*. London: BBC Books, 1993.

Inkpen, Kori, et al. " 'We Have Never-Forgetful Flowers in Our Garden': Girls' Responses to Electronic Games." *Journal of Computing in Childhood Education* 5, no. 2 (1994): 383–403.

Innes, Sherrie A., ed. *Nancy Drew and Company: Culture, Gender, and Girls' Series*. Bowling Green, Ohio: Bowling Green State University Press, 1997.

Jackson, Kathy Merlock. *Images of Children in American Film: A Sociocultural Analysis*. Metuchen, N.J.: Scarecrow Press, 1986.

Jenkins, Henry. " 'Going Bonkers!': Children, Play and Pee-wee." *Camera Obscura* 17 (May 1988): 169–93.

Kafai, Jasmin B. *Minds in Play: Computer Game Design as a Context for Children's Learning*. Hillsdale, N.J.: Lawrence Erlbaum, 1995.

———. "Gender Differences in Children's Constructions of Video Games." In *Advances in Applied Developmental Psychology*, vol. 11, edited by Patricia M. Greenfield and Rodney R. Cocking. Norwood, N.J.: Ablex Publishing, 1996.

Kensinger, Faye Riter. *Children of the Series and How They Grew*. Bowling Green, Ohio: Bowling Green State University Popular Press, 1987.

Kinder, Marsha. *Playing with Power in Movies, Television, and Video Games: From Muppet Babies to Teenage Mutant Ninja Turtles*. Berkeley: University of California Press, 1991.

Kline, Stephen. "Limits to the Imagination: Marketing and Children's Culture." In *Cultural Politics in Contemporary America*, edited by Ian Angus and Sut Jhally, 299–316. New York: Routledge, 1989.

———. *Out of the Garden: Toys, TV, and Children's Culture in the Age of Marketing*. London: Verso, 1993.

Lesser, Gerald. *Children and Television: Lessons from "Sesame Street."* New York: Random House, 1972.

Long, Loretta Moore. "*Sesame Street*: A Space Age Approach to Education for Space Age Children." Ph.D. diss., University of Massachusetts, 1973.

Luke, Carmen. *Constructing the Child Viewer: A History of the American Discourse on Television and Children, 1950–1980*. New York: Praeger, 1990.

Lull, James. *World Families Watch Television*. Newbury Park, N.J.: Sage, 1988.

———. *Inside Family Viewing: Ethnographic Research on Television's Audiences*. London: Routledge, 1990.

McDonnell, Kathleen. *Kid Culture: Children, Adults and Popular Culture*. Toronto: Second Story Press, 1994.

McRobbie, Angela. *Feminism and Youth Culture: From Jackie to Just Seventeen*. Boston, Mass.: Unwin Hyman, 1991.

Melody, William. *Children's Television: The Economy of Exploitation*. New Haven, Conn.: Yale University Press, 1973.

Meyers, David. "Computer Game Genres." *Play and Culture* 3, no. 4 (November 1990): 286–301.

Montgomery, Kathryn. *Target: Prime Time*. New York: Oxford University Press, 1989.

Morley, David. *Family Television: Cultural Power and Domestic Leisure*. London: Comedia Publishing, 1986.

Noble, Grant. *Children in Front of the Small Screen*. London: Constable, 1975.

Palmer, Edward L. *Children in the Cradle of Television*. Lexington, Ky.: Lexington Books, 1987.

———. *Television and America's Children: A Case of Neglect*. New York: Oxford University Press, 1988.

———. *Toward a Literate World: Television in Literacy Education—Lessons from the Arab Region*. Boulder, Colo.: Westview Press, 1993.

Palmer, Edward L., Milton Chen, and Gerald S. Lesser. "*Sesame Street*: Patterns of International Adaptation." *Journal of Communication* 26, no. 2 (spring 1976): 109–23.

Palmer, Edward L., and Aimee Dorre, eds. *Children and the Faces of TV: Teaching, Violence, Selling.* New York: Academic Press, 1980.

Palmer, Patricia. *The Lively Audience: A Study of Children around the TV Set.* Sydney, Australia: Allen and Unwin, 1986.

Pappert, Seymour. *Mindstorms.* New York: Basic Books, 1980.

———. *The Children's Machine.* New York: Basic Books, 1993.

———. *The Connected Family: Bridging the Digital Generation Gap.* Atlanta, Ga.: Longstreet Press, 1996.

Polsky, Richard M. *Getting to Sesame Street: Origins of the Children's Television Workshop.* New York: Praeger, 1974.

Postman, Neil. *The Disappearance of Childhood.* London: W. H. Allen, 1982.

Provenzo, Eugene F., Jr. *Video Kids: Making Sense of Nintendo.* Cambridge, Mass.: Harvard University Press, 1991.

Rainsberry, F. B. *A History of Children's Television in English Canada, 1952–1986.* Metuchen, N.J.: Scarecrow Press, 1988.

Rose, Jacqueline. *The Case of Peter Pan: Or the Impossibility of Children's Fiction.* London: Macmillan Publishers Ltd., 1984.

Schneider, Cy. *Children's Television: The Art, the Business, and How It Works.* Chicago: NTC Business Books, 1988.

Sefton-Green, Julian, ed. *Digital Diversions: Youth Culture in the Age of Multimedia.* London: University College London, 1998.

Sefton-Green, Julian, and David Buckingham. "Digital Visions: Children's 'Creative' Uses of Multimedia Technologies." *Convergence* 2, no. 2 (fall 1996): 47–79.

Seiter, Ellen. *Sold Separately: Parents and Children in Consumer Culture.* New Brunswick, N.J.: Rutgers University Press, 1995.

Shashaani, Lily. "Gender Differences in Computer Experience and Its Influence on Computer Attitudes." *Journal of Educational Computing Research* 11, no. 4 (1994): 347–67.

Sherr, Susan. "Our Children, Our Enemies: Media Framing of Children-at-Risk." In *Pictures of a Generation on Hold: Selected Papers*, edited by Murray Pomerance and John Sakeris, 167–76. Toronto: Media Studies Working Group, 1996.

Simpson, Amelia S. *Xuxa: The Mega-Marketing of Gender, Race, and Modernity.* Philadelphia: Temple University Press, 1993.

Smith, Bruce. *The History of Little Orphan Annie.* New York: Ballantine, 1982.

Spigel, Lynn. *Make Room For TV.* Chicago: University of Chicago Press, 1992.

———. "Seducing the Innocent: Childhood and Television in Postwar America." In *Ruthless Criticism: New Perspectives in U.S. Communication History*, edited by Williams S. Solomon and Robert W. McChesney, 259–90. Minneapolis: University of Minnesota Press, 1993.

Steinberg, Shirley R., and Joe L. Kinchloe, eds. *Kinderculture: The Corporate Construction of Childhood.* Boulder, Colo.: Westview Press, 1997.

Sutton, Rosemary E. "Equity and Computers in the Schools: A Decade of Research." *Review of Educational Research* 61, no. 4 (winter 1991): 475–503.

Sutton-Smith, Brian. *Toys as Culture.* New York: Gardner Press, 1986.

Tichi, Cecelia. *Electronic Hearth: Creating an American Television Culture.* Oxford: Oxford University Press, 1991.

Tucker, Lauren R. "Calvin Klein Jeans Advertising: Kiddie Porn or Media Ado about Nothing?" In *Pictures of a Generation on Hold: Selected Papers*, edited by Murray Pomerance and John Sakeris, 195–204. Toronto: Media Studies Working Group, 1996.

Turkle, Sherry. *The Second Self: Computers and the Human Spirit*. New York: Simon and Schuster, 1984.

——. *Life on the Screen: Identity in the Age of the Internet*. New York: Simon and Schuster, 1995.

Turow, Joseph. *Entertainment, Education, and the Hard Sell*. New York: Praeger, 1981.

Walkerdine, Valerie. *Schoolgirl Fictions*. London: Verso, 1990.

——. *Daddy's Girl: Young Girls and Popular Culture*. Cambridge, Mass.: Harvard University Press, 1997.

Wartella, Ellen. "Producing Children's Television Programs." In *Audiencemaking: How the Media Create the Audience*, edited by James S. Ettema and D. Charles Whitney, 38–56. Thousand Oaks, Calif.: Sage Publications, 1994.

West, Elliot, and Paula Petrik, eds. *Small Worlds: Children and Adolescents in America, 1850–1950*. Lawrence: University of Kansas Press, 1992.

Willis, Paul. *Common Culture: Symbolic Work at Play in the Everyday Cultures of the Young*. Boulder, Colo.: Westview Press, 1990.

Willis, Susan. *A Primer for Daily Life*. London: Routledge, 1991.

Woolery, George W. *Children's Television: The First Thirty-Five Years, 1946–1981*. Vol. 2. Metuchen, N.J.: Scarecrow Press, 1983.

Zelizer, Viviana A. *Pricing the Priceless Child: The Changing Social Value of Children*. Princeton, N.J.: Princeton University Press, 1994.

Contributors

HEATHER GILMOUR is a senior producer at an Internet company in Los Angeles. She holds an M.A. in film production from the University of Texas at Austin, where she made a documentary on ranch women, *Not a Clinging Vine*, that was broadcast nationally on PBS. She also holds an M.A. in Critical Studies from the University of Southern California. She has recently been published in the *Journal of Film and Video*.

SEAN GRIFFIN, currently teaching in the Bay Area, received his Ph.D. in Critical Studies from the School of Cinema-Television at the University of Southern California. His book, *Tinker Belles and Evil Queens: The Walt Disney Company from the Inside Out*, is forthcoming. Griffin has also published articles in *Animation Journal* and the *Spectator*.

HEATHER HENDERSHOT is assistant professor of Media Studies at Queens College. She is the author of *Saturday Morning Censors: Television Regulation before the V-Chip*, also published by Duke University Press. She is writing a book on Christian fundamentalist culture.

HENRY JENKINS, Director of Comparative and Media Studies at MIT, is the author or editor of seven books, including *Textual Poachers: Television Fans and Participatory Culture*; *Hop on Pop: The Politics and Pleasure of Popular Culture*; and *The Children's Culture Reader*. He is currently working on a study of Doctor Seuss and his impact on American popular culture.

YASMIN B. KAFAI teaches at the University of California, Los Angeles, Graduate School of Education and Information Studies, where she also heads KIDS (Kids' Interactive Design Studios), a research group dedicated to exploring interactive multimedia design environments for young children. Her current research focuses on young children as designers of simulations and games and as builders of digital archives for science learning. Both projects are funded by the National Science Foundation. Further projects include the study of video games as learning environments in children's homes and schools via the World Wide Web. She recently published and edited two books, *Minds in Play: Computer Game Design as a Context for Children's Learning* and *Constructionism in Practice: Designing, Thinking and Learning in a Digital World* (with Mitchel Resnick), and has written various articles in the fields of education, developmental psychology, and computer and information science. Before coming to UCLA, she was at the MIT Media Laboratory for five years. Kafai holds an Ed.D. in education from Harvard University and an M.A. from the Technical University in Berlin.

JYOTSNA KAPUR teaches in the Department of Cinema and Photography at Southern Illinois University. She is writing a study called "Out of Control: The Transformation of Childhood in Late Capitalism," which examines the representations of childhood in Hollywood films produced for children in the 1990s and in marketing literature for children.

MARSHA KINDER is Professor of Critical Studies at the School of Cinema-Television at the University of Southern California. She is the author of over 100 published essays and 10 books on film and popular culture, including *Playing with Power in Movies, Television, and Video Games*. Kinder is currently Director of The Labyrinth Project, a research initiative at the USC Annenberg Center for Communication for expanding the language of interactive narrative in multimedia design. She is also coauthor and coproducer (with documentary filmmaker Mark Jonathan Harris) of an experimental CD-ROM game for teens called *Runaways*, which deals with issues of gender, race, and ethnicity.

SUSAN MURRAY is an assistant professor of Television and Radio at Brooklyn College, City University of New York. She is writing a book on the development of broadcast stardom in early television.

ELISSA RASHKIN received her Ph.D. in Communication Studies from the University of Iowa in 1997. She is working on a book on women filmmakers of Mexico.

ELLEN SEITER is Professor of Communication at the University of California at San Diego, where she teaches media studies and women's studies. She specializes in the study of children and the media and is the author of *Television and New Media Audiences* (1999) and *Sold Separately: Children and Parents in Consumer Culture* (1993). Her articles have appeared in *Cultural Studies, Feminist Review, Screen*, and *Frauen und Film*. Seiter received her M.F.A. and Ph.D. degrees from Northwestern University.

LYNN SPIGEL currently teaches in the Division of Critical Studies at the School of Cinema-Television at the University of Southern California. She is the author of several books on television and popular culture, including *Make Room for TV* and *The Revolution Wasn't Televised*. Spigel is a founding board member of Console-ing Passions, an international conference on television studies, and the general editor of the Console-ing Passions Book Series, which is published by Duke University Press.

KAREN ORR VERED is Lecturer in Screen Studies at Flinders University, South Australia, where she teaches digital media theory, television, and children's media courses. In June 1998 she programmed the White House Internet Summit on Digital Media Content for Children and Teens. Her work appears in the anthologies *Digital Diversions* and *Millennium Girls* and in the journals *The Velvet Light Trap, Spectator*, and *Visual Anthropology Review*. She received her Ph.D. in Critical Studies from the School of Cinema-Television at the University of Southern California. Her dissertation, "Schooling in the Digital Domain: Gendered Work and Play in a Computer Integrated Elementary Classroom," is an ethnography of children's leisure-time computer use in a mixed-gender classroom.

Index

Nikki, *Wild Dog of the North* (movie), 90

Ninja Turtles. *See* Teenage Mutant Ninja Turtles

Nintendo, 123, 264, 286. *See also* Electronic games: video games

Nixon, Richard (President), 142, 148

Nostalgia, 3, 7, 61, 69, 71, 75, 80, 95–98, 113, 117

Oakley, Annie, 115, 121 n.64

Odyssey, The (epic), 3

O. Henry, 189

Old Yeller (movie), 90

Oliver Twist (book), 186, 195. *See also* Children's literature: children's classics

101 Dalmations (movie), 90. *See also* Disney Productions

Oprah! (TV talk show), 248

Oregon Trail (electronic game), 274–75, 286–88

Our Gang (movie series), 63 n.25

Outcault, Richard, 32

Ozzie and Harriet (TV series), 248

Pacman (electronic game), 310

Palmer, Edward L. (Dr.), 154–55, 167

Palmer, Patricia, 158

Papert, Seymour, 9, 11. *See also* MIT Media Lab

Parents (magazine), 57, 132–33

Parents' Guide to Children's Reading, A, 92

Paris Is Burning (movie), 183–84

Parker, Fess, 102, 109, 111, 113–15. *See also* Davy Crockett: television series

Pascual-Leone, Juan, 144–45

Pasknik, Shelley, 8

Paulsen, Pat, 148

PBS. *See* Public Broadcast Service

Peanuts (kid strip), 32–34, 38–49, 52–61, 66–67, 76; "A Charlie Brown Christmas" (TV special), 33, 62 n.8; *The Gospel According to Peanuts* (book), 46; *Happiness Is a Warm Puppy* (novelty book), 55; Red Baron theme, 34, 49, 61; Snoopy, 34; space race theme, 34

Pedagogy, 24–26. *See also* Child care centers; Childhood: child raising practices; Cog-

nitive development; Montessori schools; Piaget, Jean

Pee-wee Herman, 5, 104; and *Pee-wee's Playhouse* (TV show), 188, 192

Pelé (soccer player), 205

Perón, Juan (President of Argentina), 215

Peter Pan (book), 56, 92, 113, 125, 128. *See also* Barrie, J. M.; Rose, Jacqueline

Phizacklea, Annie, 133

Phoenix, River, 224

Photoshop (computer software), 279

Piaget, Jean, 141, 144, 250. *See also* Cognitive development

Picasso, Pablo, 45, 55. *See also Guernica*

Pilgrim Quest (electronic game), 274–75

Pilgrim School, 268–74, 276–79, 280–91

Plante, Bill, 182

Plato, 3

Playing with Power in Movies, Television and Video Games (book), 184, 267

Plug-in Drug, The (book), 131. *See also* Winn, Marie

Plumb, John H., 124

Pocahontas (movie), 127. *See also* Disney Productions

Pokémons (toys), 7

Pornography, 3, 9, 10, 20; and the right to porn, 11. *See also* Internet: pornography

Postman, Neil, 122, 124, 129–30

Power Rangers. *See Mighty Morphin Power Rangers*

Prince Valiant (comic strip), 48

Project Head Start, 142–43

Provost, Jon, 81

Public Broadcast Service (PBS), 13, 139–40, 143, 145, 147, 172, 176 n.90, 179, 242

Purple Moon (software company), 9. *See also* Interval Research Group; Laurel, Brenda

Quayle, Dan (Vice President), 13

Queer theory, 5. *See also* Active readership

Race and ethnicity issues, 52–53, 143–45, 147, 150–51, 193, 205, 208, 212, 216, 218–19, 242, 251, 256, 281, 297. *See also* National identity: multiculturalism; Stereotypes

Library of Congress Cataloging-in-Publication Data

Kids' media culture / edited by Marsha Kinder.
p.   cm. — (Console-ing passions)
Includes bibliographical references and index.
ISBN 0-8223-2350-8 (cloth : alk. paper).
ISBN 0-8223-2371-0 (pbk. : alk. paper)
1. Mass media and children—United States.   2. Child
consumers—United States. I. Kinder, Marsha.   II. Series.
HQ784.M3 K54 1999   302.23'083—dc21   99-34384 CIP